VOICES OF VIOLENCE

"We must call a spade a spade . . . murder is the prinicpal agent of historical progress."—Karl Heinzen

"At the head of the country was the all-powerful government . . . against whom all open revolutionary attempts were hopeless. . . . Against this large organization . . . a handful of people, strong and terrible in their energy and elusiveness . . ."—Nikolai Morozov

"The idea that London could be laid in ashes in twenty-four hours was self-evident."—O'Donovan Rossa

"The urban guerilla's reason for existence, the basic condition in which he acts and survives, is to shoot."—Carlos Marighella

"We have risen to liberate our country, to drive the imperialists and the invaders out of it and to determine our fate by our own hands. . . . We have no alternatives to confrontation."—Open Letter by Hizballah

WALTER LAQUEUR is Chairman of the International Research Council of the Center for Strategic and International Studies in Washington, D.C.

YONAH ALEXANDER is the editor-in-chief of *Terrorism*, the leading journal in the field, and is Director of the Institute for Studies in International Terrorism at the State University of New York, Oneonta, New York.

Both are renowned experts on terrorism and have edited and written many books on history and politics.

THE TERRORISM READER

A HISTORICAL ANTHOLOGY

Revised Edition

EDITED BY
WALTER LAQUEUR AND YONAH ALEXANDER

A MERIDIAN BOOK

BOOKS ARE AVAILABLE AT QUANTITY DISCOUNTS WHEN USED TO PROMOTE PRODUCTS OR SERVICES. FOR INFORMATION PLEASE WRITE TO PREMIUM MARKETING DIVISION, PENGUIN BOOKS USA INC., 375 HUDSON STREET, NEW YORK, NEW YORK 10014.

Library of Congress Cataloging-in-Publication Data

The Terrorism reader.

1. Terrorism—History. 2. Violence—History.
I. Laqueur, Walter, 1921– . II. Alexander, Yonah.
HV6431.T49 1987 904′.7 86-31089
ISBN 0-452-00843-3

REGISTERED TRADEMARK—MARCA REGISTRADA

First Printing (New Revised Edition), June, 1987
Firist Printing, March, 1978

4 5 6 7 8 9 10 11

PRINTED IN THE UNITED STATES OF AMERICA

Contents

Part IV: Interpretations of Terrorism

Part V: The Last Decade

THE TERRORISM READER

Preface

Terrorism is one of the most widely publicized but least understood phenomena of our time. It is generally believed that political terrorism (including international terrorism and the use of "proxies") is of recent origin, that it is both a very dreadful and a very effective weapon, and that society has become so vulnerable to it that governments can no longer resist a handful of determined people. Frequently, terrorism is used as a synonym for every conceivable form of violence, thus negating its specific character and making its understanding even more difficult. But although terrorism has been used by various groups and movements, it still has a specific character of its own. It is not a civil war, a military insurgency, a *coup d'etat*, or guerrilla warfare. Terrorism is not a novel phenomenon; even in its modern form it can be traced back for at least a century and a half. At the same time, it is true that important changes have taken place concerning the motives, character, and aims of terrorism.

This new and revised edition of a book first published a decade ago reflects some of these changes. Although some of the groups whose manifestos were published in the first edition no longer exist (such as the Weathermen), others, such as the Tupamaros in Uruguay, have transformed themselves into political parties. On the other hand, international terrorism occurs more frequently now than a decade or two ago, and narco-terrorism, which virtually did not exist at the time, is now a phenomenon of some importance. A good case can be made in favor of the proposition that there is no terrorism per se (except perhaps on the level of abstraction) but only various terrorisms. For this reason, generalizations about terrorism are often difficult and sometimes impossible. In other words, what is true with regard to one terrorist group does not necessarily apply to another. Most of today's terrorists are certainly of a different mold—morally, politically, and in most other respects—than the Russian and Anarchist terrorists of the late nineteenth century.

The question as to whether it is justifiable to kill a political opponent has been discussed by philosophers and theologians for many centuries; in some civilizations the answer was so self-evident as to account for the absence of lengthy ideological disputations. How then, does one explain the widespread shock and confusion caused by the most recent wave of terrorism? Human memory is notoriously frail. When small terrorist groups appeared in various parts of the globe in the 1960s, two decades of relative calm had prevailed. Although there had been local wars, they had occurred in distant places. Before that, there had been a world war in which individual terrorism did not attract much attention, because hundreds of thousands of soldiers and civilians were being killed or, at the very least, were living in constant danger of losing their lives. All this may help to explain why a citizen of Paris, Moscow, or London living around 1900 would have been much less surprised and shocked by acts of terror than are his grandchildren.

Terrorism can be understood only in its historical context with regard to both its doctrine (the philosophy of the dagger and later of the bomb) and its practice. The present selection of historical documents traces the development of political terrorism through the ages, from early Greek and Roman tyrannicides to contemporary terrorist groups. Many sixteenth- and seventeenth-century thinkers were preoccupied with the question of whether killing was always murder, whereas the secret societies of the early nineteenth century were more intrigued by the question of whether it was politically effective. With the emergence of a doctrine of systematic terrorism fifty years later among the Russian populists, as well as among the anarchists, the Irish, the Armenians, and others, we reach the most recent period, for most aspects of contemporary terrorist theory and practice were discussed as long ago as the 1880s and 1890s.

Terrorism has been directed against dictatorships as well as democratic societies and has been practiced by the extreme left, the radical right, and also quite frequently by the nationalist-religious separatist movements. Illustrations of the various species of terrorism are included in this volume. In Part IV, a variety of interpretations of terrorism is given.

A reader of this kind, dealing with the phenomenon that has occurred on and off in the history of many countries, must be highly selective. Although the most recent manifestations of terrorism have been amply documented, sources on its antecedents have frequently been out of print for a long time, and some—Heinzen's "Murder,"

Most's essays, or Romanenko's (Tarnovski) brochure—have never before appeared in English.

We would like to express our gratitude to Professors Michel Confino, Bipan Chandra, Zvi Yavetz, and Dr. Zeev Ivianski for their advice on questions of detail, to Mr. Kimbriel Mitchell, who assisted me in my research, to the directors and staff of the Library of Congress, and British Museum, the London Library, the New York Public Library, the Swiss Federal Library in Bern, the Library of Trinity College in Dublin, the Tel Aviv University Library, the Wiener Library, the Widener Library at Harvard University, as well as to private collections in Paris, Biel, Berlin, and Vienna.

Finally, we would like to thank the following for providing translations: Janet Langmaid (French and German), Anthony Wells (German), Marion Rawson (Italian), and Hana Schlesinger (Russian). In the preparation of this new edition of *The Terrorism Reader*, much valuable help was extended by Janusz Bugajski, Michael Evans, and David G. Janssen.

The present volume was the fourth and last part of a study on guerrilla warfare and terrorism, written by Walter Laqueur. This new and enlarged edition is the product of collaboration between the author of the original study and Professor Yonah Alexander. A great deal has been written on these topics, but serious study of the subject is still in its infancy. It has been our intention to contribute to a better understanding and to the systematic study of the phenomenon by documenting its antecedents and making various interpretations of its contemporary manifestations more accessible.

Washington, D.C. W.L.
September 1986 Y.A.

PART I

Tyrannicide

Introductory Note

Terrorism "from below" has appeared since time immemorial, sometimes as a manifestation of religious protest, at others in the wake of political revolt and social uprisings. One of the earliest recorded examples is the *sicarii*, a highly organized religious sect consisting of "men of lower orders" in the Zealot struggle in Palestine (A.D. 66–73). Messianic hope and political terrorism were prominent features too of a much better known sect, the Assassins, who appeared in Persia and Syria in the eleventh century and were suppressed only by the Mongols in the thirteenth century. Contemporaneous observers described the Assassins as an order of almost ascetic discipline, who courted death and martyrdom and believed in a new millennium. However, the origins of the doctrine of terrorism can be traced much further back: resistance to despotism was frequently justified in the writings of ancient Greek and Roman authors. Plato and Aristotle regarded tyranny as a perversion, the worst form of government. The acts of the tyrannicides, from Harmodios and Aristogeiton onward, were glorified in the works of poets, playwrights, sculptors, and bards, and it was quite immaterial to them that some of these liberators were motivated mainly by personal reasons. Cicero noted in *De officiis* that tyrants had always come to a violent end and that the Romans usually acclaimed those who killed them. The civil virtues of Brutus and Cassius were praised by their fellow Romans—though not by all of them. Seneca was reputed to have said that no offering was more agreeable to god than the blood of a tyrant.

Medieval writers on tyrannicide generally chose well-known examples from the Bible as well as episodes from Greek and Roman history to demonstrate that usurpers should not be obeyed. The power of the king, as these writers saw it, was based on a contract with the people; if the king did not keep his part of the bargain, he could, and should, be removed. This, then, was the beginning of the concept of popular sovereignty, a concept discussed by both Protestant and Catholic authors.

In his *Republic* (Book IX), Plato (c. 429–347 B.C.) dealt with the character of a tyrant whose supreme misery was that "he has to be master of others when he is not master of himself." But the question of tyrannicide was more fully discussed in Aristotle's (384–322 B.C.) *Politics*. (It should be mentioned, however, that although the ancient Greeks regarded tyranny as the worst form of government, they thought little better of democracy.) The motif of tyrannicide also appears in the writings of ancient poets and playwrights. *The True History* of Lucian of Samosata (A.D. 120) relates how a man forced his way into the stronghold of a tyrant with the intention of killing him. Unable to find the tyrant, he kills his son, leaving the sword in his body. The tyrant finds his son dead and slays himself with the same sword. The assailant now claims that the killing of the son entitles him to the reward of tyrannicide.

The story of Marcus Junius Brutus (like those of Wilhelm Tell and Charlotte Corday, the slayer of Marat) has frequently been treated in world literature. Although Dante relegated the murderers of Caesar to the depths of hell, the Renaissance rescued them, and, in the eighteenth century, Brutus became something of a cult figure. The story of Brutus was told by Appian and Dio Cassius, but the classic account is that by Plutarch; it served as the inspiration for would-be tyrannicides until the early nineteenth century. Plutarch's *Lives* appeared in A.D. 105–115, a century and a half after Caesar's slaying. Marcus Tullius Cicero, on the other hand, was a contemporary of Brutus (his son served in the Roman army under him). Although he justified tyrannicide in his *De officiis*, Cicero was not personally involved in the plot leading to Caesar's murder.

A commentary on Thomas Aquinas (ca. 1225–1274) has been included in the present selection of texts in view of the enormous influence exerted by the writings of the Doctor Angelicus on Catholic writers of subsequent generations. It deals not with Aquinas's main work, the *Summa Theologica*, but with his *Scriptum in secundum Sententiarum librum*. Max Lossen's *Die Lehre vom Tyrannenmord in der Christlichen Zeit*, from which the commentary on Aquinas is excerpted, was published in Munich in 1894.

Even earlier, tyrannicide was discussed by John of Salisbury (ca. 1120–1180), Thomas à Becket's secretary who was exiled to France where he served as Bishop of Chartres. In *Policraticus*, his main work, tyranny per se is by no means condemned. Yet he contends that it is not only lawful but glorious to slay a tyrant if he sins against divine law, provided only that the killer is neither bound to the tyrant nor sacrifices honor and justice. *Policraticus* retained its influence until the sixteenth century when the question of tyrannicide became a central issue in the writings of the Monarchomachs, a school of mainly French Protestant writers. Perhaps the most influential of their pamphlets was *Vindiciae contra Tyrannos*, published in 1579 under the pen name Junius Brutus; the authorship is in dispute, but most historians believe that it was written by Duplessis Mornay (1549–1623), who was political adviser to the king of Navarre. He asks whether it is lawful to resist a prince who infringes the law of God, but he also raises other questions such as whether one should resist a prince who merely ruins the temporal state and into whose hands the organization of resistance should be entrusted. Among Catholic writers dealing with the topic, Juan de Mariana (1536–1624) is the most outstanding; he was a Jesuit professor who taught in Paris, Rome, and also Toledo, where his main work, *De rege et regis institutione*, was published. Mariana, like his contemporaries, got sidetracked by questions such as the use of poison which were hardly of paramount importance once the principle of tyrannicide had been accepted.

The most famous British works on tyrannicide are George Buchanan's *De Jure Regni apud Scotos*, published in London in 1579, and Saxby's *Killing No Murder* which appeared in 1657. Buchanan (1506–1582) was a great Scottish humanist whose book created a scandal and was burned by an act of Parliament. *Killing No Murder* appeared in Holland under a pen name, William Allen. The author was Colonel Edward Saxby, a Leveler and enemy of Cromwell; he was executed after his return to England in 1658. His pamphlet was frequently reprinted and was given a new lease on life between 1793 and 1804 in French translation. Vittorio Alfieri's *Della Tirannide* influenced a whole generation of militants of the Risorgimento, including Mazzini, because it lent strength to their belief that it was their sacred duty to remove those princes and princelings who stood in the way of Italy's unification. Alfieri (1749–1803) is better known as the greatest Italian writer of this period; *Della Tirannide*, written in the early 1780s, was first published only after the French Revolution.

Aristotle

The Origin of Tyranny

That tyranny has all the vices both of democracy and oligarchy is evident. As of oligarchy so of tyranny, the end is wealth (for by wealth only can the tyrant maintain either his guard or his luxury). Both mistrust the people, and therefore deprive them of their arms. Both agree too in injuring the people and driving them out of the city and dispersing them. From democracy tyrants have borrowed the art of making war upon the notables and destroying them secretly or openly, or of exiling them because they are rivals and stand in the way of their power; and also because plots against them are contrived by men of this class, who either want to rule or escape subjection. Hence Periander advised Thrasybulus to cut off the tops of the tallest ears of corn, meaning that he must always put out of the way the citizens who overtop the rest. And so, as I have already intimated, the beginnings of change are the same in monarchies as in other forms of government; subjects attack their sovereigns out of fear or contempt, or because they have been unjustly treated by them. And of injustice, the most common form is insult, another is confiscation of property.

The ends sought by conspiracies against monarchies, whether tyrannies or royalties, are the same as the ends sought by conspiracies against other forms of government. Monarchs have great wealth and honor which are objects of desire to all mankind. The attacks are made sometimes against their lives, sometimes against the office; where the sense of insult is the motive, against their lives. Any sort of insult (and there are many) may stir up anger, and when men are angry, they commonly act out of revenge, and not from ambition. For example, the attempt made upon the Peisistratidae arose out of the public dishonor offered to the sister of Harmodios and the insult to himself. He attacked the tyrant for his sister's sake, and Aristogeiton joined in the attack for the sake of Harmodios. A conspiracy was also

Aristotle, *Politics* Book V.

formed against Periander, the tyrant of Ambracia, because, when drinking with a favorite youth, he asked him whether by this time he was not with child by him. Philip, too, was attacked by Pausanias because he permitted him to be insulted by Attalus and his friends, and Amyntas the little, by Derdas, because he boasted of having enjoyed his youth. Evagoras of Cyprus, again, was slain by the eunuch to revenge an insult; for his wife had been carried off by Evagoras' son. Many conspiracies have originated in shameful attempts made by sovereigns on the persons of their subjects. Such was the attack of Crataeus upon Archelaus; he had always hated the connection with him, and so, when Archelaus, having promised him one of his two daughters in marriage, did not give him either of them, but broke his word and married the elder to the king of Elymaea, when he was hard-pressed in a war against Sirrhas and Arrhibaeus, and the younger to his own son Amyntas, under the idea that he would then be less likely to quarrel with the son of Cleopatra—Crataeus made this slight a pretext for attacking Archelaus, though even a less reason would have sufficed, for the real cause of the estrangement was the disgust which he felt at his connection with the king. And from a like motive Hellanocrates of Larissa conspired with him; for when Archelaus, who was his lover, did not fulfill his promise of restoring him to his country, he thought that the connection between them had originated, not in affection, but in the wantonness of power. Parrhon, too, and Heracleides of Aenos, slew Cotys in order to avenge their father, and Adamas revolted from Cotys in revenge for the wanton outrage which he had committed in mutilating him when a child.

Many, too, irritated at blows inflicted on the person which they deemed an insult, have either killed or attempted to kill officers of state and royal princes by whom they have been injured. Thus, at Mitylene, Megacles and his friends attacked and slew the Penthalidae, as they were going about and striking people with clubs. At a later date Smerdis, who had been beaten and torn away from his wife by Penthilus, slew him. In the conspiracy against Archelaus, Decamnichus stimulated the fury of the assassins and led the attack; he was enraged because Archelaus had delivered him to Euripides to be scourged; for the poet had been irritated at some remark made by Decamnichus on the foulness of his breath. Many other examples might be cited of murders and conspiracies which have arisen from similar causes.

Fear is another motive which has caused conspiracies as well in monarchies as in more popular forms of government. Thus Artapanes conspired against Xerxes and slew him, fearing that he would be accused of hanging Darius against his orders—he being under the impression that Xerxes would forget what he had said in the middle of a meal, and that the offense would be forgiven.

Another motive is contempt, as in the case of Sardanapulus, whom someone saw carding wool with his women, if the storytellers say truly; and the tale may be true, if not of him, of someone else. Dion attacked the younger Dionysius because he despised him, and saw that he was equally despised by his own subjects, and that he was always drunk. Even the friends of a tyrant will sometimes attack him out of contempt; for the confidence which he reposes in them breeds contempt, and they think that they will not be found out. The expectation of success is likewise a sort of contempt; the assailants are ready to strike, and think nothing of the danger, because they seem to have the power in their hands. Thus generals of armies attack monarchs; as, for example, Cyrus attacked Astyages, despising the effeminacy of his life, and believing that his power was worn out. Thus, again, Seuthes the Thracian conspired against Amadocus, whose general he was.

And sometimes men are actuated by more than one motive, like Mithridates, who conspired against Ariobarzanes, partly out of contempt and partly from the love of gain.

Bold natures, placed by their sovereigns in a high military position, are most likely to make the attempt in the expectation of success; for courage is emboldened by power, and the union of the two inspires them with the hope of an easy victory.

Attempts of which the motive is ambition arise from other causes. There are men who will not risk their lives in the hope of gains and rewards however great, but who nevertheless regard the killing of a tyrant simply as an extraordinary action which will make them famous and honorable in the world; they wish to acquire, not a kingdom, but a name. It is rare, however, to find such men; he who would kill a tyrant must be prepared to lose his life if he fail. He must have the resolution of Dion, who, when he made war upon Dionysius, took with him very few troops, saying, "that whatever measure of success he might attain would be enough for him, even if he were to die the moment he landed; such a death would be welcome to him." But this is a temper to which few can attain. . . .

There are two chief motives which induce men to attack tyrannies

—hatred and contempt. Hatred of tyrants is inevitable, and contempt is also a frequent cause of their destruction. Thus we see that most of those who have acquired, have retained their power, but those who have inherited, have lost it, almost at once; for living in luxurious ease, they have become contemptible, and offer many opportunities to their assailants. Anger, too, must be included under hatred, and produces the same effects. It is oftentimes even more ready to strike —the angry are more impetuous in making an attack, for they do not listen to reason. And men are very apt to give way to their passions when they are insulted. To this cause is to be attributed the fall of the Peisistratidae and of many others. Hatred is more reasonable, but anger is accompanied by pain, which is an impediment to reason, whereas hatred is painless.

In a word, all the causes which I have mentioned as destroying the last and most unmixed form of oligarchy, and the extreme form of democracy, may be assumed to affect tyranny; indeed the extreme forms of both are only tyrannies distributed among several persons.

Lucian of Samosata

The Tyrannicide

Two tyrants—a father advanced in years, a son in the prime of life, waiting only to step into his nefarious heritage—have fallen by my hand on a single day: I come before this court, claiming but one reward for my twofold service. My case is unique. With one blow I have rid you of two monsters: with my sword I slew the son; grief for the son slew the father. The misdeeds of the tyrant are sufficiently punished: he has lived to see his son perish untimely; and—wondrous sequel!—the tyrant's own hand has freed us from tyranny. I slew the son and used his death to slay another: in his life he shared the iniquities of his father; in his death, so far as in him lay, he was a parricide. Mine is the hand that freed you, mine the sword that ac-

The Works of Lucian of Samosata Vol. 2.

complished all: as to the order and manner of procedure, there, indeed, I have deviated from the common practice of tyrannicides: I slew the son, who had strength to resist me, and left my sword to deal with the aged father. In acting thus, I had thought to increase your obligation to me; a twofold deliverance—I had supposed—would entitle me to a twofold reward; for I have freed you not from tyranny alone, but from the fear of tyranny, and by removing the heir of iniquity have made your salvation sure. And now it seems that my services are to go for nothing; I, the preserver of the constitution, am to forego the recompense prescribed by its laws. It is surely from no patriotic motive, as he asserts, that my adversary disputes my claim; rather it is from grief at the loss of the tyrants, and a desire to avenge their death.

Bear with me, gentlemen, for a little, while I dwell in some detail upon those evils of tyranny with which you are only too familiar; I shall thus enable you to realize the extent of my services, and to enjoy the contemplation of sufferings from which you have escaped. Ours was not the common experience: we had not *one* tyranny, *one* servitude to endure, we were not subjected to the caprice of a single master. Other cities have had their tyrant: it was reserved for us to have two tyrants at once, to groan beneath a double oppression. That of the old man was light by comparison, his anger mildness, his resentment long-suffering; age had blunted his passions, checked their headlong impetus, and curbed the lust of pleasure. His crimes, so it is said, were involuntary; resulting from no tyrannical disposition in himself, but from the instigations of his son. For in him paternal affection had too clearly become a mania; his son was all in all to him; he did his bidding, committed every crime at his pleasure, dealt out punishment at his command, was subservient to him in all things; the minister of a tyrant's caprice, and that tyrant his son. The young man left him in possession of the name and semblance of rule; so much he conceded to his years: but in all essentials *he* was the real tyrant. By him the power of the tyrant was upheld; by him and by him alone the fruits of tyranny were gathered. He it was who maintained the garrison, intimidated the victims of oppression, and butchered those who meditated resistance; who laid violent hands on boys and maidens, and trampled on the sanctity of marriage. Murder, banishment, confiscation, torture, brutality; all bespeak the wantonness of youth. The father followed his son's lead, and had no word of blame for the crimes in which he participated. Our situation became unbearable: for when the promptings of passion draw support from the authority of rule, then iniquity knows no further bounds.

We knew moreover (and here was the bitterest thought of all) that our servitude must endure—ay, endure for ever; that our city was doomed to pass in unending succession from master to master, to be the heritage of the oppressor. To others it is no small consolation that they may count the days, and say in their hearts: "The end will be soon; he will die, and we shall be free." We had no such hope: there stood the heir of tyranny before our eyes. There were others—men of spirit—who cherished like designs with myself; yet all lacked resolution to strike the blow; freedom was despaired of; to contend against a succession of tyrants seemed a hopeless task.

Yet I was not deterred. I had reckoned the difficulties of my undertaking, and shrank not back, but faced the danger. Alone, I issued forth to cope with tyranny in all its might. Alone, did I say? nay, not alone; I had my sword for company, my ally and partner in tyrannicide. I saw what the end was like to be: and, seeing it, resolved to purchase your freedom with my blood. I grappled with the outer watch, with difficulty routed the guards, slew all I met, broke down all resistance—and so to the fountainhead, the wellspring of tyranny, the source of all our calamities; within his stronghold I found him, and there slew him with many wounds, fighting valiantly for his life.

From that moment, my end was gained: tyranny was destroyed; we were free men. There remained the aged father, alone, unarmed, desolate; his guards scattered, his strong protector slain; no adversary this for a brave man. And now I debated within myself: "My work is done, my aim achieved, all is as I would have it. And how shall this remnant of tyranny be punished? He is unworthy of the hand that shed that other blood: the glory of a noble enterprise shall not be so defiled. No, let some other executioner be found. It were too much happiness for him to die and never know the worst; let him see all, for his punishment, and let the sword be ready to his hand; to that sword I leave the rest." In this design I withdrew; and the sword—as I had foreseen—did its office, slew the tyrant, and put the finishing touch to my work.

And now I come to you, bringing democracy with me, and call upon all men to take heart and hear the glad tidings of liberty. Enjoy the work of my hands! You see the citadel cleared of the oppressors; you are under no man's orders; the law holds its course; honors are awarded, judgments given, pleadings heard. And all springs from one bold stroke, from the slaying of that son whom his father might not survive. I claim from you the recompense that is my due; and that in no paltry, grasping spirit; it was not for a wage's sake that I sought to serve my country; but I would have my deed confirmed by your award; I would not be disparaged by slanderous tongues, as one who attempted and failed, and was deemed unworthy of honor. . . .

Cicero

No Fellowship with Tyrants

For in exceptional circumstances that which is commonly held to be wrong is found on reflection not to be wrong. I shall illustrate my meaning by a special case which, however, has a general bearing. There is no greater crime than to murder a fellowman, especially a friend. Still who would say that he commits a crime who assassinates a tyrant, however close a friend? The people of Rome, I tell you, think it no crime, but the noblest of all noble deeds. Did expediency here triumph over virtue? No, virtue followed in the train of expediency. . . .

There can be no such thing as fellowship with tyrants, nothing but bitter feud is possible: and it is not repugnant to nature to despoil, if you can, those whom it is a virtue to kill; nay, this pestilent and godless brood should be utterly banished from human society. For, as we amputate a limb in which the blood and the vital spirit have ceased to circulate, because it injures the rest of the body, so monsters, who, under human guise, conceal the cruelty and ferocity of a wild beast, should be severed from the common body of humanity.

Cicero, *De officiis.*

Plutarch

Brutus

XVI. And now word was brought that Caesar was coming, borne on a litter. For in consequence of the dejection caused by his omens, he had determined not to sanction any important business at that time, but to postpone it, under pretext of indisposition. As he descended from his litter, Popilius Laenas, who, a little while before, had wished Brutus success in his enterprise, hurried up to him and conversed with him for some time, and Caesar stood and listened to him. The conspirators (for so they shall be called) could not hear what he said, but judging from their suspicions that what he told Caesar was a revelation of their plot, they were disconcerted in their plans, and mutually agreed by looks which passed between them that they must not await arrest, but at once dispatch themselves. Cassius and some others, indeed, had already grasped the handles of the daggers beneath their robes and were about to draw them, when Brutus observed from the mien of Laenas that he was asking eagerly for something and not denouncing anyone. Brutus said nothing, because many were about him who were not in the plot, but by the cheerfulness of his countenance gave courage to Cassius and his friends. And after a little while Laenas kissed Caesar's hand and withdrew. He had made it clear that it was in his own behalf and on something which closely concerned himself that he had consulted Caesar.

XVII. When the senate had preceded Caesar into the session room, the rest of the conspirators stationed themselves about Caesar's chair, as if they intended to have some conference with him, and Cassius is said to have turned his face toward the statue of Pompey and to have invoked it, as if it had understanding; but Trebonius drew Antony into conversation at the door and kept him outside. As Caesar entered, the senate rose in his honor, but as soon as he was seated the

Plutarch, *Lives* VI. With kind permission of Loeb Classical Library (Harvard University Press: William Heinemann).

conspirators surrounded him in a body, putting forward Tullius Cimber of their number with a plea in behalf of his brother, who was in exile. The others all joined in his plea, and clasping Caesar's hands, kissed his breast and his head. At first, Caesar merely rejected their pleas, and then, when they would not desist, tried to free himself from them by force. At this, Tullius tore Caesar's robe from his shoulders with both hands, and Casca, who stood behind him, drew his dagger and gave him the first stab, not a deep one, near the shoulder. Caesar caught the handle of the dagger and cried out loudly in Latin: "Impious Casca, what doest thou?" Then Casca, addressing his brother in Greek, bade him come to his aid. And now Caesar had received many blows and was looking about and seeking to force his way through his assailants, when he saw Brutus setting upon him with drawn dagger. At this, he dropped the hand of Casca which he had seized, covered his head with his robe, and resigned himself to the dagger strokes. The conspirators, crowding eagerly about the body, and plying their many daggers, wounded one another, so that Brutus also got a wound in the hand as he sought to take part in the murder, and all were covered with blood.

XVIII. Caesar thus slain, Brutus went out into the middle of the session room and tried to speak, and would have detained the senators there with encouraging words; but they fled in terror and confusion, and there was a tumultuous crowding at the door, although no one pressed upon them in pursuit. For it had been firmly decided not to kill anyone else, but to summon all to the enjoyment of liberty. All the rest of the conspirators, indeed, when they were discussing their enterprise, had been minded to kill Antony as well as Caesar, since he was a lawless man and in favor of a monarchy, and had acquired strength by familiar association with the soldiery; and particularly because to his natural arrogance and ambition he had added the dignity of the consulship, and was at that time a colleague of Caesar. But Brutus opposed the plan, insisting in the first place on a just course, and besides, holding out a hope of a change of heart in Antony. For he would not give up the belief that Antony, who was a man of good parts, ambitious, and a lover of fame, if once Caesar were out of the way, would assist his country in attaining her liberty, when their example had induced him to follow emulously the nobler course. Thus Antony's life was saved by Brutus; but in the fear which then reigned, he put on a plebeian dress and took to flight.

And now Brutus and his associates went up to the Capitol, their hands smeared with blood, and displaying their naked daggers they exhorted the citizens to assert their liberty. At first, then, there were cries of terror, and the tumult was increased by wild hurryings to and fro which succeeded the disaster; but since there were no further murders and no plundering of property, the senators and many of the common people took heart and went up to the men on the Capitol. When the multitude was assembled there, Brutus made a speech calculated to win the people and befitting the occasion. The audience applauding his words and crying out to him to come down from the Capitol, the conspirators took heart and went down into the forum. The rest of them followed along in one another's company, but Brutus was surrounded by many eminent citizens, escorted with great honor down from the citadel, and placed on the rostra. At sight of him the multitude, although it was a mixed rabble and prepared to raise a disturbance, was struck with awe, and awaited the issue in decorous silence. Also when he came forward to speak, all paid quiet attention to his words; but that all were not pleased with what had been done was made manifest when Cinna began to speak and to denounce Caesar. The multitude broke into a rage and reviled Cinna so bitterly that the conspirators withdrew again to the Capitol. There Brutus, who feared that they would be besieged, sent away the most eminent of those who had come up with them, not deeming it right that they should incur the danger too, since they had no share in the guilt.

John of Salisbury

On Slaying Public Tyrants

The well-known narrative of the Books of Kings and Chronicles shows, according to the authority of Jerome, that Israel was oppressed by tyrants from the beginning and that Juda had none but

John Dickinson, translator. *The Statesman's Book of John of Salisbury*, © 1963, pp. 368–371. Reprinted by permission of Prentice-Hall, Inc., Englewood Cliffs, New Jersey.

wicked kings save only David, Josiah, and Ezechiah. Yet I can easily believe that Salomon and perhaps some of the others in Juda recovered when God recalled them to the true way. And I will be readily persuaded that tyrants instead of legitimate princes were rightly deserved by a stiffnecked and stubborn people who always resisted the Holy Spirit, and by their gentile abominations provoked to wrath not Moyses only, the servant of the law, but God Himself, the Lord of the law. For tyrants are demanded, introduced, and raised to power by sin, and are excluded, blotted out, and destroyed by repentance. And even before the time of their kings, as the Book of Judges relates, the children of Israel were time without number in bondage to tyrants, being visited with affliction on many different occasions in accordance with the dispensation of God, and then often, when they cried aloud to the Lord, they were delivered. And when the allotted time of their punishment was fulfilled, they were allowed to cast off the yoke from their necks by the slaughter of their tyrants; nor is blame attached to any of those by whose valor a penitent and humbled people was thus set free, but their memory is preserved in affection by posterity as servants of the Lord. This is clear from the subjoined examples.

"The people of Israel were in bondage to Eglon the king of Moab for eighteen years; and then they cried aloud to God, who raised up for them a saviour called Aoth, the famous son of Iera, the son of Gemini, who used both hands with the same skill as the right hand. And the children of Israel sent presents to Eglon, the king of Moab, by him, and he made for himself a two-edged sword having in the midst a haft of the length of the palm of the hand, and girded himself therewith beneath his cloak on his right thigh, and presented the gifts to Eglon, the king of Moab. Now Eglon was exceeding fat; and when he had made an end of presenting the gifts, he went away after his companions who had come with him. But he himself turned back from Gilgal where the idols were, and said to the king, 'I have a secret word for thy ear, O king.' And the king commanded silence. And all that were about him having gone forth, Aoth came unto him. And he was sitting alone in a cool upper room. And Aoth said, 'I have a word from God unto thee.' And the king forthwith rose up from his throne. And Aoth put forth his left hand and took the dagger from his right thigh, and thrust it into his belly with such force that the haft also went into the wound after the blade, and the fat closed over it. And he did not draw out the sword, but left it in the body where it had entered. And straightway by nature's secret passages, the excrements of his belly burst forth. But Aoth closed the doors carefully, and fastened them with the bolt and departed by a postern."

And elsewhere, "Sisara, fleeing, came to the tent of Jael the wife of Abner Cinei. For there was peace between Jabin the king of Asor and the house of Abner Cinei. Therefore, Jael went forth to meet Sisara and said to him, 'Come in to me, my lord, come in and fear not.' And he, having entered her tent and been covered by her with a cloak, said to her, 'Give me, I pray thee, a little water because I thirst greatly.' And she opened a skin of milk, and gave him to drink, and covered him. And Sisara said to her, 'Stand before the door of the tent and when any shall come inquiring of thee and shall say "Is there any man here?" thou shalt say, "No, there is none." ' Then Jael, the wife of Abner, took a nail of the tent, and took likewise a hammer. And entering softly and silently, she put the nail upon the temple of his head, and striking it with the hammer, drove it through his brain fast into the ground. And thus passing from sleep into death he fainted away, and died." Did she thereby win the praise or the censure of posterity? "Blessed among women shall be Jael the wife of Abner Cinei," says the Scripture, "and blessed shall she be in her tent. He asked for water, and she gave him milk and offered him butter in a princely dish. She put her left hand to the nail, and her right hand to the workmen's hammer, and she smote Sisara, seeking in his head a place for a wound, and piercing his temple forcefully."

Let me prove by another story that it is just for public tyrants to be killed and the people thus set free for the service of God. This story shows that even priests of God repute the killing of tyrants as a pious act, and if it appears to wear the semblance of treachery, they say that it is consecrated to the Lord by a holy mystery. Thus Holofernes fell a victim not to the valor of the enemy but to his own vices by means of a sword in the hands of a woman; and he who had been terrible to strong men was vanquished by luxury and drink, and slain by a woman. Nor would the woman have gained access to the tyrant had she not piously dissimulated her hostile intention. For that is not treachery which serves the cause of the faith and fights in behalf of charity. For verily it was due to the woman's faith that she upbraided the priests because they had set a time limit upon the divine mercy by agreeing with the enemy that they would surrender themselves and deliver up the city if the Lord should not come to their aid within five days. Likewise it was because of her charity that she shrank from no perils so long as she might deliver her brethren and the people of the Lord from the enemy. For this is shown by her words as she went forth to save them: "Bring to pass, Lord," she prayed, "that by his own sword his pride may be cut off, and that he may be caught in the net of his own eyes turned upon me, and do Thou destroy him, through the lips of my charity. Grant to me constancy of soul that I may despise him, and fortitude that I may destroy him. For it will be a glorious monument of Thy name when the hand of a woman shall strike him down."

"Then she called her maid, and, going down into her house, she took off her hair-cloth from her, and put away the garments of her widowhood, and bathed her body and anointed herself with the finest myrrh, and parted the hair of her head, and placed a mitre upon her head, and clothed herself with garments of gladness, binding sandals upon her feet, and donned her bracelets and lilies and earrings and finger-rings, and adorned herself with all her ornaments. And the Lord gave her more beauty because all this toilet was for the sake of virtue and not of lust. And therefore the Lord increased her beauty so that she appeared to the eyes of all men lovely beyond compare." And thus arriving at her destination, and captivating the public enemy, "Judith spake unto Holofernes, saying: 'Receive the words of thy handmaid, for if thou wilt follow them, God will do a perfected work with thee. For Nebugodonosor, the king of the earth, liveth, and thy virtue liveth, which is in thee for the correction of all erring souls, since not men alone, but also the beasts of the field serve him through thee, and obey him. For the strength and industry of thy mind is heralded abroad to all nations, and it has been told to the whole age that thou alone art mighty and good in all his kingdom, and thy discipline is preached to all nations.' " And in addition she said, "I will come and tell all things to thee, so that I may bring thee through the midst of Jerusalem, and thou shalt have all the people of Israel as sheep that have no shepherd; and not a single dog shall bark against thee, because these things are told to me by the providence of God." What more insidious scheme, I ask you, could have been devised, what could have been said that would have been more seductive than this bestowal of mystic counsel? And so Holofernes said: "There is not another such woman upon the earth in look, in beauty, or in the sense of her words." For his heart was sorely smitten and burned with desire of her. Then he said, "Drink now and lay thee down for jollity since thou hast found favor in my sight." But she who had not come to wanton, used a borrowed wantonness as the instrument of her devotion and courage. And his cruelty she first lulled asleep by her blandishments, and then with the weapons of affection she slew him to deliver her people. Therefore she struck Holofernes upon the neck, and cut off his head, and handed it to her maid that it might be placed in a wallet to be carried back into the city which had been saved by the hand of a woman.

The histories teach, however, that none should undertake the death of a tyrant who is bound to him by an oath or by the obligation of fealty. For we read that Sedechias, because he disregarded the sacred obligation of fealty, was led into captivity; and that in the case of another of the kings of Juda whose name escapes my memory, his eyes were plucked out because, falling into faithlessness, he did not keep before his sight God, to whom the oath is taken; since sureties for good behavior are justly given even to a tyrant.

But as for the use of poison, although I see it sometimes wrongfully adopted by infidels, I do not read that it is ever permitted by any law. Not that I do not believe that tyrants ought to be removed from our midst, but it should be done without loss of religion and honor. For David, the best of all kings that I have read of, and who, save in the incident of Urias Etheus, walked blamelessly in all things, although he had to endure the most grievous tyrant, and although he often had an opportunity of destroying him, yet preferred to spare him, trusting in the mercy of God, within whose power it was to set him free without sin. He therefore determined to abide in patience until the tyrant should either suffer a change of heart and be visited by God with return of charity, or else should fall in battle, or otherwise meet his end by the just judgment of God. How great was his patience can be discerned from the fact that when he had cut off the edge of Saul's robe in the cave, and again when, having entered the camp by night, he rebuked the negligence of the sentinels, in both cases he compelled the king to confess that David was acting the juster part. And surely the method of destroying tyrants which is the most useful and the safest, is for those who are oppressed to take refuge humbly in the protection of God's mercy, and lifting up undefiled hands to the Lord, to pray devoutly that the scourge wherewith they are afflicted may be turned aside from them. For the sins of transgressors are the strength of tyrants. Wherefore Achior, the captain of all the children of Amon, give this most wholesome counsel to Holofernes: "Inquire diligently, my lord," said he, "whether there be any iniquity of the people in the sight of their God, and then let us go up to them, because their God will abandon them and deliver them to thee, and they shall be subdued beneath the yoke of thy power. But if there be no offense of this people in the sight of their God, we shall not be able to withstand them, because their God will defend them, and we shall be exposed to the reproach and scorn of all the earth."

Thomas Aquinas and the Question of Tyrannicide

In his chief theological work, the *Summa Theologica*, Thomas touches on the question of tyrannicide only fleetingly, in the course of a discussion of other ethical problems. The question of whether rebellion is a separate mortal sin is here answered in the affirmative and the contention that—according to the philosopher's teaching—the liberation of a people from tyranny is to be considered a laudable act met by the assertion that the shaking off of the yoke of tyranny is only to be counted an act of rebellion if it has rebellion as a consequence. Otherwise, it is rather the tyrant than the people who is to be considered the rebel. The killing of tyrants is nowhere explicitly discussed in the work; however, we find an indication of St. Thomas's views in those passages of the *Summa* where he deals with the right of self-defense and its limits. Here, following St. Augustine, he restricts the right to kill another human being to those cases where it is done by public authority and in the best interests of the common weal. Self-defense on the part of an individual is permitted only insofar as it is an act of justifiable self-preservation—*cum moderamine inculpatae tutelae*—a proviso which has since provided welcome ground for sophistic interpretation, but which Thomas himself narrowed down even further by saying that the killing of an assailant was permitted only when it happened unintentionally and accidentally—*praeter intentionem et per accidens*.

A thorough treatment of the concept of the tyrant, and one which is very largely a continuation of the arguments in Aristotle's *Politics*

Max Lossen, *Die Lehre vom Tyrannenmord in der Christlichen Zeit* (Munich, 1894).

—can be found in the first book on "The Rule of Princes," a work which can without doubt be attributed to him and which he wrote during the last years of his life. For him, too, just as monarchy is the best form of government, so tyranny, the corruption of monarchy, is the worst. In exactly the same way as the Ancients, Thomas depicts the tyrant as a violent ruler, more comparable to a wild animal than a human being, who panders entirely to his own passions, sows discord among his subjects, drives them into poverty and degradation, and in short reduces them to the level of slaves. Thomas gives three means of either preventing or removing such tyrants: the first is to constitute the monarchy in such a way that the people (*multitudo*) retains the right of deposition—expressed in modern terminology, the establishment of popular sovereignty. The second means is appeal to a higher authority. Thomas does not state explicitly who this authority might be for his own age, but from what he says later we can unhesitatingly conclude that he is thinking in the first instance of the Roman Pope, for whom he arrogates the right to depose a tyrannical and, more especially, a stubbornly heretical prince and even to sentence him to death. For the Middle Ages, however, the responsibility for carrying out this sentence would hardly lie with the Church but, very probably, with the prince of a neighboring territory. The example of Aod adduced by John of Salisbury he rejects, firstly on the grounds that the murdered Eglon was not a legitimate prince acting in a tyrannical way but an open enemy, and secondly and more emphatically by setting the teaching of the Apostles and the example of the Christian martyrs against the examples of the Old Testament.

Finally, as his third remedy against unbearable tyranny, Thomas recommends prayer to the King of Kings, to God, who can move the king's heart howsoever he pleases, and conversion from sinfulness; for tyrannical kings are a punishment sent by God, who allows a hypocrite to reign because of the sins of the people.

Thomas expounds very similar ideas in his commentary on Aristotle's *Politics*. By contrast, there is one passage in his writings in which he appears to be putting forward a different viewpoint and it is this passage which has often been used to justify the claim that the teachings of later scholars in general, and of the Jesuits in particular, in no way differed from those of the "Angel" of the school. The passage in question is the famous one from the commentary on the "Magister Sententiarum" where the question of in which cases a potentate is not from God is discussed scholastically. One of the reasons advanced for why no one need obey an unlawful usurper is that Tullius praises Caesar's murderers as tyrannicides. Thomas tries to qualify this argument by maintaining that Tullius is in this case speaking of a violent usurper against whom no appeal to a higher judge was possible—"in this case, he concludes, he who kills the tyrant in order to liberate his country is praised and rewarded."

St. Thomas's apologists have been right to point out that undue weight should not be placed on this single, ambiguous passage from a youthful work, at the expense of those others where he declares himself to be firmly opposed to tyrannicide; they have, however, been wrong to dispute that the passage does indeed contain a qualified justification of tyrannicide—the murdering of a *"tyrannus in titulo."* A less partisan observer would have to concede that in this case the great theologian allowed himself to be directed more by his heathen authorities than by the prescriptions of the Gospels.

"Junius Brutus"
(*Duplessis Mornay*)

In Defense of Liberty

It is then lawful for Israel to resist the king, who would overthrow the law of God and abolish His church; and not only so, but also they ought to know that in neglecting to perform this duty, they make themselves culpable of the same crime, and shall bear the like punishment with their king.

If their assaults be verbal, their defense must be likewise verbal; if the sword be drawn against them, they may also take arms and fight either with tongue or hand, as occasion is: yea, if they be assailed by surprisals, they may make use both of ambuscades and countermines, there being no rule in lawful war that directs them for the manner, whether it be by open assailing their enemy, or by close surprising; provided always that they carefully distinguish between advantageous stratagems and perfidious treason, which is always unlawful.

"Junius Brutus," *Vindiciae contra Tyrannos* (n.p., 1579).

But I see well, here will be an objection made. What will you say? That a whole people, that beast of many heads, must they run in a mutinous disorder, to order the business of the commonwealth? What address or direction is there in an unruly and unbridled multitude? What counsel or wisdom to manage the affairs of state?

When we speak of all the people, we understand by that, only those who hold their authority from the people, to wit, the magistrates, who are inferior to the king, and whom the people have substituted, or established, as it were, consorts in the empire, and with a kind of tribunitial authority, to restrain the encroachments of sovereignty, and to represent the whole body of the people. We understand also the assembly of the estates, which is nothing else but an epitome, or brief collection of the kingdom, to whom all public affairs have special and absolute reference; such were the seventy ancients in the kingdom of Israel, amongst whom the high priest was, as it were, president, and they judged all matters of greatest importance, those seventy being first chosen by six out of each tribe, which came out of the land of Egypt, then the heads or governors of provinces. In like manner the judges and provosts of towns, the captains of thousands, the centurions and others who commanded over families, the most valiant, noble, and otherwise notable personages, of whom was composed the body of the states, assembled divers times as it plainly appears by the word of the holy scripture. At the election of the first king, who was Saul, all the ancients of Israel assembled together at Kama. In like manner all Israel was assembled, or all Judah and Benjamin, etc. Now, it is no way probable that all the people, one by one, met together there. Of this rank there are in every well-governed kingdom the princes, the officers of the crown, the peers, the greatest and most notable lords, the deputies of provinces, of whom the ordinary body of the estate is composed, or the parliament or the diet, or other assembly, according to the different names used in divers countries of the world; in which assemblies, the principal care is had both for the preventing and reforming either of disorder or detriment in church or commonwealth.

For as the councils of Basil and Constance have decreed (and well decreed) that the universal council is in authority above the bishop of Rome, so in like manner, the whole chapter may overrule the bishop, the university the rector, the court the president. Briefly, he, whosoever he is, who has received authority from a company, is inferior to that whole company, although he be superior to any of the particular members of it. Also is it without any scruple or doubt that Israel, who demanded and established a king as governor of the public, must needs be above Saul, established at their request and for Israel's sake, as it shall be more fully proved hereafter. And for so much as an orderly proceeding is necessarily required in all affairs discreetly addressed, and that it is not so probably hopeful that order shall be observed amongst so great a number of people; yea, and that there oftentimes occur occasions which may not be communicated to a multitude, without manifest danger of the commonwealth: we say, that all that which has been spoken of privileges granted, and right committed to the people, ought to be referred to the officers and deputies of the kingdom: and all that which has been said of Israel, is to be understood of the princes and elders of Israel, to whom these things were granted and committed as the practice also has verified.

The queen Athalia, after the death of her son Ahazia, king of Judah, put to death all those of the royal blood, except little Joas, who, being yet in the cradle, was preserved by the piety and wisdom of his aunt Jehoshabeah. Athalia possessed herself of the government and reigned six years over Judah. It may well be the people murmured between their teeth, and dare not by reason of danger express what they thought in their minds.

Finally, Jehoiada, the high priest, the husband of Jehoshabeah, having secretly made a league and combination with the chief men of the kingdom, did anoint and crown king his nephew Joas, being but seven years old. And he did not content himself to drive the Queen Mother from the royal throne, but he also put her to death, and presently overthrew the idolatry of Baal. This deed of Jehoiada is approved, and by good reason, for he took on him the defense of a good cause, for he assailed the tyranny, and not the kingdom. The tyranny (I say) which had no title, as our modern civilians speak. For by no law were women admitted to the government of the kingdom of Judah. Furthermore, that tyranny was in vigor and practice. For Athalia had with unbounded mischief and cruelty invaded the realm of her nephews, and in the administration of that government committed infinite wickedness, and what was the worst of all, had cast off the service of the living God to adore and compel others with her to worship the idol of Baal. Therefore then was she justly punished, and by him who had a lawful calling and authority to do it. For Jehoiada was not a private and particular person, but the high priest, to whom the knowledge of civil causes did then belong. And besides, he had for his associates the principal men of the kingdom, the Levites, and being himself the king's kinsman and ally. Now for so much as he assembled not the estates at Mizpah, according to the accustomed manner, he is not reproved for it, neither for that he consulted and contrived the matter secretly, for that if he had held any other manner of proceeding, the business must probably have failed in the execution and success.

A combination or conjuration is good or ill, according as the end whereunto it is addressed is good or ill; and perhaps also according as they are affected who are the managers of it. We say, then, that the princes of Judah have done well, and that in following any other course they had failed of the right way. For even as the guardian ought to take charge and care that the goods of his pupil fall not into loss and detriment, and if he omit his duty therein, he may be compelled to give an account thereof, in like manner, those to whose custody and tuition the people have committed themselves, and whom they have constituted their tutors and defenders ought to maintain them safe and entire in all their rights and privileges. To be short, as it is lawful for a whole people to resist and oppose tyranny, so likewise the principal persons of the kingdom may as heads, and for the good of the whole body, confederate and associate themselves together; and as in a public state, that which is done by the greatest part is esteemed and taken as the act of all, so in like manner must it be said to be done, which the better part of the most principal have acted, briefly, that all the people had their hand in it. . . .

Now, seeing that the people choose and establish their kings, it follows that the whole body of the people is above the king; for it is a thing most evident that he who is established by another is accounted under him who has established him, and he who receives his authority from another is less than he from whom he derives his power. Potiphar the Egyptian sets Joseph over all his house; Nebuchadnezar, Daniel over the province of Babylon; Darius the six-score governors over the kingdom. It is commonly said that masters establish their servants, kings their officers. In like manner, also, the people establish the king as administrator of the commonwealth. Good kings have not disdained this title; yea, the bad ones themselves have affected it; insomuch, as for the space of divers ages, no Roman emperor (if it were not some absolute tyrant, as Nero, Domitian, Caligula) would suffer himself to be called lord. Furthermore, it must necessarily be that kings were instituted for the people's sake, neither can it be that for the pleasure of some hundreds of men, and without doubt more foolish and worse than many of the other, all the rest were made, but much rather that these hundred were made for the use and service of all the other, and reason requires that he be preferred above the other, who was made only to and for his occasion: so it is that for the ship's sail the owner appoints a pilot over her, who sits at the helm and looks that she keep her course, nor run not upon any dangerous shelf; the pilot doing his duty is obeyed by the mariners; yea, and of himself who is owner of the vessel, notwithstanding, the pilot is a servant as well as the least in the ship, from whom he only differs in this, that he serves in a better place than they do.

In a commonwealth, commonly compared to a ship, the king holds the place of pilot, the people in general are owners of the vessel, obeying the pilot, whilst he is careful of the public good; as though this pilot neither is nor ought to be esteemed other than servant to the public; as a judge or general in war differs little from other officers, but that he is bound to bear greater burdens and expose himself to more dangers. By the same reason also which the king gains by acquist of arms, be it that he possesses himself of frontier places in warring on the enemy, or that which he gets by escheats or confiscations, he gets it to the kingdom and not to himself, to wit, to the people, of whom the kingdom is composed, no more nor less than the servant does for his master; neither may one contract or oblige themselves to him, but by and with reference to the authority derived from the people. Furthermore, there is an infinite sort of people who live without a king, but we cannot imagine a king without people.

Juan de Mariana

Whether It Is Right to Destroy a Tyrant

Besides, we reflect, in all history that whoever took the lead in killing tyrants was held in great honor. What indeed carried the name of

Juan de Mariana, *The King and the Education of the King.*

Thrasybulus in glory to the heavens unless it was the fact that he freed his country from the oppressive domination of the Thirty Tyrants? Why should I mention Harmodios Aristogeiton. Why the two Brutuses, whose praise is most gratefully enshrined in the memory of posterity and is born witness to with the peoples' approval? Many conspired against Domitius Nero with luckless result, and yet without censure, but rather with the praise of all ages. Thus Caius, a grievous and sinful monster, was killed by the conspiracy of Charea; Domitian fell by the sword of Stephen, Caracalla, by Martial's. The praetorians slew Elagabalus, a monstrosity and disgrace of the empire—his sin atoned for by his own blood.

Whoever criticized the boldness of these men, and not rather considered it worthy of the highest commendations? Also, common sense, like the voice of nature, has been put into our minds, a law sounding in our ears, by which we distinguish the honest from the base.

You may add that a tyrant is like a beast, wild and monstrous, that throws himself in every possible direction, lays everything waste, seizes, burns, and spreads carnage and grief with tooth, nail and horn.

Would you be of the opinion that anyone who delivered the state safely at the peril of his own life ought to be ignored, or rather would you not honor him? Would you determine that all must make an armed fight against something resembling a cruel monster that is burdening the earth? And that an end to butchery would not be reached so long as he lived? If you should see your most dear mother or your wife misused in your presence, and not aid if you were able, you would be cruel and you incur the opprobrium of worthlessness and impiety. Would you leave to the tyrant your native land, to which you owe more than to your parents, to be harassed and disturbed at his pleasure? Out with such iniquity and depravity! Even if life, safety, fortune are imperiled, we will save our country free from danger, we will save our country from destruction.

These are the arguments of both sides; and after we have considered them carefully it will not be difficult to set forth what must be decided about the main point under discussion. Indeed in this I see that both the philosophers and theologians agree, that the prince who seizes the state with force and arms, and with no legal right, no public, civic approval, may be killed by anyone and deprived of his life and position. Since he is a public enemy and afflicts his fatherland with every evil, since truly and in a proper sense he is clothed with the title and character of tyrant, he may be removed by any means and gotten rid of by as much violence as he used in seizing his power.

Thus meritoriously did Ehud, having worked himself by gifts into the favor of Eglon, king of the Moabites, stab him in the belly with a poniard and slay him; he snatched his own people from a hard slavery, by which they had been oppressed for then eighteen years.

It is true that if the prince holds the power with the consent of the people or by hereditary right, his vices and licentiousness must be tolerated up to the point when he goes beyond those laws of honor and decency by which he is bound. Rulers, really, should not be lightly changed, lest we run into greater evils, and serious disturbances arise, as was set forth at the beginning of this discussion.

But if he is destroying the state, considers public and private fortunes as his prey, is holding the laws of the land and our holy religion in contempt, if he makes a virtue out of haughtiness, audacity, and irreverence against heaven, one must not ignore it.

Nevertheless, careful consideration must be given to what measures should be adopted to get rid of the ruler, lest evil pile on evil, and crime is avenged with crime.

In this the procedure should be by the following steps: first the prince must be warned and invited to come to his senses. If he complies, if he satisfies the commonwealth, and corrects the error of his way, I think that it must stop there, and sharper remedies must not be attempted. If he refuses to mend his ways, and if no hope of a safe course remains, after the resolution has been announced, it will be permissible for the commonwealth to rescind his first grant of power. And since war will necessarily be stirred up, it will be in order to arrange the plans for driving him out, for providing arms, for imposing levies on the people for the expenses of the war. Also, if circumstances require, and the commonwealth is not able otherwise to protect itself, it is right, by the same law of defense and even by an authority more potent and explicit, to declare the prince a public enemy and put him to the sword.

Let the same means be available to any individual, who, having given up the hope of escaping punishment and with disregard for his personal safety, wishes to make the attempt to aid the commonwealth.

You would ask what must be done, if the practicability of public assembly is taken away, as can often happen. There will be, truly, in my opinion at least, no change in the decision, since, when the state is crushed by the tyranny of the ruler and facility for assembly is taken away from the citizens, there would be no lack of desire to destroy the tyrant, to avenge the crimes of the ruler, now plainly seen and intolerable, and to crush his destructive attempts. And so, if the sacred fatherland is falling in ruins and its fall is attracting the public enemies into the province, I think that he who bows to the public's prayers and tries to kill the tyrant will have acted in no wise unjustly. And this is strengthened enough by those arguments against the tyrant which are put at a later place in this discussion.

So the question of fact remains, who justly may be held to be a tyrant, for the question of law is plain that it is right to kill one.

Now there is no danger that many, because of this theory, will make mad attempts against the lives of the princes on the pretext that they are tyrants. For we do not leave this to the decision of any individual, or even to the judgment of many, unless the voice of the people publicly takes part, and learned and serious men are associated in the deliberation.

Human affairs would be very admirably carried on, if many men of brave heart were found in defense of the liberty of the fatherland, contemptuous of life and safety; but the desire for self-preservation, often not disposed to attempt big things, will hold back very many people.

Finally, we are of the opinion that upheavals in the commonwealth must be avoided. Precaution must be taken lest joy run wild briefly on account of the deposition of a tyrant and then turn out sterile. On the other hand, every remedy must be tried to bring the ruler to right views before that extreme and most serious course is reached. But if every hope is gone, if the public safety and the sanctity of religion are put in danger, who will be so unintelligent as not to admit that it is permissible to take arms and kill the tyrant, justly and according to the statutes? Would one, perhaps, be influenced unduly that the proposition was disapproved by the Fathers in the fifteenth session of the Council of Constance, that "a tyrant may and ought to be killed by any subject, not only openly with violence but also through conspiracy and plots"? But this decision I do not find approved by the Roman Pontiff, Martin V, nor by Eugenius or his successors, by whose consent the legality of the proceedings of ecclesiastical councils is confirmed; this council's decrees especially needed approval, since we know that it was held not without disturbance of the Church on account of the three-way disagreement of claimants struggling for the supreme pontificate.

So, it is generally known that it is legal to kill a tyrant openly by force of arms, either by breaking into his palace or by starting a civil disturbance.

But it has been undertaken also by guile and treachery. This Ehud did; by bringing gifts and feigning a message from above he got close enough, and when the witnesses had left he killed Eglon, king of the Moabites.

It is, indeed, more manly and spirited to show your hate openly, to rush upon the enemy of the state in public; but it is not less prudent to seize the opportunity for guileful stratagems, which may be carried out without commotion and surely with less public and individual danger.

So, I praise the custom of the Lacedaemonians in their sacrificing to Mars, the protector in battle (as deluded antiquity thought), with a white cock, that is, when the victory had been gained in battle. When, however, the enemy were overcome by ambushes and cunning, they sacrificed a fat bull; as if it is more outstanding to conquer the enemy and keep the army intact by prudence and reasoning power, which distinguish us as men, than by main strength and robustness, in which we are surpassed by the beasts. Besides, there is the point of great loss on one's side.

Yet there is a question whether there is equal virtue in killing a public enemy and tyrant (indeed, they are considered the same) by poison and lethal herbs. A certain prince asked me this years ago in Sicily, when I was teaching theology in that island. We know that it has often been done. We do not think that there will be anyone, bent on killing, who, because of the opinion of the theologians, will neglect and pass up the offered opportunity of inflicting this kind of death and prefer to make the assault with the sword; especially in view of the lesser danger and the greater hope of escape. By this method the public joy is not less, when the enemy is destroyed, but the author and architect of the public safety and liberty is saved.

However, we regard not what men are likely to do but what is permitted by natural law; and from a rational standpoint, what difference does it make whether you kill by steel or poison, especially since the means of acting by fraud and deceit are conceded? Now, there are many examples in ancient and modern history of enemies killed in this manner. It is, of course, hard to poison a prince, surrounded as he is by his ministers of the court; besides, he is in the habit of having his food tried by a taster. It is difficult to break through the massive citadel of the regal mode of life.

But if an opportune occasion would be offered, who will have such an acute intellect, be so keen in discrimination as to strive to distinguish between the two kinds of death? At least, I will not deny that great force inheres in these arguments; that there will be those that are led on by these reasons and will approve this type of death, as in consonance with justice and equity and in agreement with what has been said—namely, that a tyrant or public enemy is killed justly by using not only an assassin but also a poisoner.

Nevertheless we see that it is not in accordance with our customs to do what was done at Athens and Rome frequently in the olden time, in that those convicted of capital crimes were gotten rid of by poison. Truly we think it cruel, and also foreign to Christian principles to drive a man, though covered with infamy, to the point that he commit suicide by plunging a dagger into his abdomen, or by taking deadly poison which has been put into his food or drink. It is equally contrary to the laws of humanity and the natural law; since it is forbidden that anyone take his own life.

We deny therefore that the enemy, whom we admit it is lawful to kill by treachery, may be made away with by poison.

George Buchanan

War with the Enemy of All Mankind

B: Now if a King do those things which are directly for the dissolution of society, for the continuance whereof he was created, how do we call him? *M:* A Tyrant, I suppose. *B:* Now a Tyrant hath not only no just authority over a people but is also their enemy. *M:* He is indeed an enemy. *B:* Is there not a just and Lawful war with an

George Buchanan, *De Jure Regni apud Scotos* (London, 1680).

enemy for grievous and intolerable injuries? *M:* It is forsooth a just war. *B:* What war is that which is carried on with him who is the enemy of all mankind, that is, a Tyrant? *M:* A most just war. *B:* Now a Lawful war being once undertaken with an enemy, and for a just cause, it is Lawful not only for the whole people to kill that enemy, but for every one of them. *M:* I confess that. *B:* May not everyone out of the whole multitude of mankind assault, with all the calamities of war, a Tyrant who is a public enemy, with whom all good men have a perpetual warfare? *M:* I perceive all Nations almost to have been of that opinion. For Thebe is usually commended for killing her husband, Timoleon for killing his brother, and Cassius for killing his son: and Fulvius for killing his own son going to Catiline, and Brutus for killing his own sons and kinsmen, having understood they had conspired to introduce Tyranny again: and public rewards were appointed to be given, and honors appointed by several Cities of Greece to those that should kill Tyrants. So that (as is before said) they thought there was no bond of humanity to be kept with Tyrants. But why do I collect the assent of some single persons, since I can produce the testimony almost of the whole world? For who doth not sharply rebuke Domitius Corbulo for neglecting the safety of mankind, who did not thrust Nero out of his Empire, when he might very easily have done it? And not only was he by the Romans reprehended, but by Tyridates the Persian King, being not at all afraid, lest it should afterward befall an example unto himself. But the minds of most wicked men enraged with cruelty are not so void of this public hatred against Tyrants but that sometimes it breaketh out in them against their will and forceth them to stand amazed with terror at the sight of such a just and Lawful deed. When the Ministers of Caius Caligula, a most cruel Tyrant, were with the like cruelty tumultuating, for the slaughter of their Lord and Master, and required those that had killed him to be punished, now and then crying aloud, Who had killed the Emperor, one of the Senators standing in an eminent high place from whence he might be heard, cried out loud: I wish I had killed him. At which word these tumultuary persons void of all hu- anity stood as it were astonished, and so forebore anymore to cry tumultuously. For there is so great force in an honest deed that ery lightest show thereof, being presented to the minds of men, ost violent assaults are allayed, and fierce fury doth languish, dness nill it will it doth acknowledge the sovereignty of Neither are they of another judgment who with their loud cries mix heaven and earth together. Now this we do easily understand either from hence, that they do reprehend what now is done, but do commend and approve the same seemingly more atrocious, when they are recorded in an old history: and thereby do evidently demonstrate that they are more obsequious to their own particular affections than moved by any public damage. But why do we seek a more certain witness what Tyrants do deserve than their own conscience? Thence is that perpetual fear from all, and chiefly from good men: and they do constantly see hanging above their own necks the sword which they hold still drawn against others, and by their own hatred against others they measure other men's minds against them. But contrariwise good men, by fearing no man, do often procure their own hazard, whilst they weigh the goodwill of others toward them, not from the vicious nature of men, but from their own desert toward others. *B:* You do then judge that to be true, that Tyrants are to be reckoned in the number of the most cruel brute beasts; and that tyrannical violence is more unnatural than poverty, sickness, death, and other miseries which may befall men naturally. *M:* Indeed when I do ponder the weight of your reasons, I cannot deny but these things are true. But whilst hazards and inconveniences do occur, which follow on the back of this opinion, my mind, as it were tied up with a bridle, doth instantly, I know not how, fail me, and bendeth from that too stoical and severe right way toward utility, and almost falleth away. For if it shall be lawful for any man to kill a Tyrant, see how great a gape you do open for wicked men to commit any mischief, and how great hazard you create to good men: to wicked men you permit licentiousness, and lets out upon all the perturbation of all things. For he that shall kill a good King, or at least none of the worst, may he not pretend by his wicked deed some show of honest and Lawful duty? Or if any good subject shall in vain attempt to kill a prince worthy of all punishment, or accomplish what he intended to do, how great a confusion of all things do you suppose must needs follow thereupon? Whilst the wicked do tumultuat, raging that their head and leader is taken away from them, neither will all good men approve the deed, nor will all those who do approve the deed defend the doer and author of their liberty against a wicked crew . . .

Edward Saxby

Killing No Murder

To us particularly it belongs to bring this monster to justice, whom he hath made the instruments of his villany, and sharers in the curse and detestation that is due to himself from all good men. Others only have their liberty to vindicate, we our liberty and our honor. We engaged to the people with him, and to the people for him, and from our hands they may justly expect a satisfaction of punishment, being they cannot have that of performance. What the people at present endure, and posterity shall suffer, will be all laid at our doors: for only we under God have the power to pull down this Dragon which we have set up. And if we do it not, all mankind will repute us approvers of all the villanies he hath done, and authors of all to come. Shall we that would not endure a king attempting tyranny, shall we suffer a professed tyrant? We that resisted the lion assailing us, shall we submit to the wolf tearing us? If there be no remedy to be found we have great reason to exclaim: *"Utinam te potius (Carole) retinuissemus quam hunc habuissemus, non quod ulla sit optanda servitus, sed quod ex dignitate Domini minus turpis est conditio servi"*; we wish we had rather endured thee (O Charles) than have been condemned to this mean tyrant; not that we desire any kind of slavery, but that the quality of the master something graces the condition of the slave.

But if we consider it rightly what our duty, our engagements, and our honor exact from us, both our safety and our interest oblige us to, and it is as unanswerable in us to discretion, as it is to virtue, to let this viper live. For first, he knows very well it is only we that have the power to hurt him, and therefore of us he will take any course to secure himself: he is conscious to himself how falsely and perfidiously he hath dealt with us, and therefore he will always fear that from our revenge which he knows he hath so well deserved.

Lastly, he knows our principles, how directly contrary they are to that arbitrary power he must govern by, and therefore he may reason-

Killing No Murder (anonymous pamphlet).

ably suspect that we that have already ventured our lives against tyranny will always have the will, when we have the opportunity, to do the same again.

These considerations will easily persuade him to secure himself of us, if we prevent him not, and secure ourselves of him. He reads in his practice of piety, *"chid diviene patron,"* etc.: he that makes himself master of a city that hath been accustomed to liberty, if he destroys it not, he must expect to be destroyed by it. And we may read too in the same author, and believe him, that those that are the occasion that one becomes powerful he always ruins them if they want the wit and courage to secure themselves.

Now as to our interest, we must never expect that he will ever trust those that he hath provoked and feared; he will be sure to keep us down, lest we should pluck down him. It is the rule that tyrants observe when they are in power, never to make much use of those that helped them to it; and indeed it is their interest and security not to do it, for those that have been the authors of their greatness, being conscious of their own merit, they are bold with the tyrant, and less industrious to please him. They think all he can do for them is their due, and still they expect more; and when they fail in their expectations—as it is impossible to satisfy them—their disappointment makes them discontented, and their discontent is dangerous. Therefore all Tyrants follow the example of Dionysius, who was said to use his friends as he did his bottles: when he had use for them he kept them by him, and when he had none, that they should not trouble him and lie in his way, he hung them up.

But, to conclude this already over-long paper: let every man to whom God hath given the spirit of wisdom and courage be persuaded by his honor, his safety, his own good, and his country's, and indeed the duty he owes to his generation and to mankind, to endeavor by all rational means to free the world of this pest. Let not other nations have the occasion to think so meanly of us as if we resolved to sit still and have our ears bored, or that any discouragement or disappointments can ever make us desist from attempting our liberty, till we have purchased it, either by this monster's death or by our own. Our nation is not yet so barren of virtue that we want noble examples to follow amongst ourselves. The brave Sindercombe hath shown as great a mind as any old Rome could boast of; and had he lived there his name had been registered with Brutus and Cato, and he had had his statues as well as they.

But I will not have so sinister an opinion of ourselves, as little generosity as slavery hath left us, as to think so great a virtue can want its monuments even amongst us. Certainly in every virtuous mind there are statues reared to Sindercombe. Whenever we read the elegies of those that have died for their country; when we admire those great examples of magnanimity that have tried tyrants' cruelties; when we extol their constancies, whom neither bribes nor terrors could make betray their friends; it is then we erect Sindercombe's statues, and grave him monuments, where all that can be said of a great and noble mind we justly make an epitaph for him. And though the tyrant caused him to be smothered, lest the people should hinder an open murder, yet he will never be able either to smother his memory or his own villany. His poison was but a poor and common device to impose only on those that understood not tyrants' practices and are unacquainted, if any be, with his cruelties and falsehoods. He may therefore if he please take away the stake from Sindercombe's grave, and if he have a mind it should be known how he died, let him send thither the pillows and feather beds with which Barkstead and his hangman smothered him. But, to conclude: let not this monster think himself the more secure that he hath suppressed one great spirit; he may be confident that *"longus post illum sequitur ordo idem petentium decus."*

There is a great roll behind, even of those that are in his own muster rolls, that are ambitious of the name of the deliverers of their country; and they know what the action is that will purchase it. His bed, his table, is not secure; and he stands in need of other guards to defend him against his own. Death and destruction pursue him wheresoever he goes: they follow him everywhere, like his fellow-travelers, and at last they will come upon him like armed men. Darkness is hid in his secret places, a fire not blown shall consume him; it shall go ill with him that is left in his tabernacle. He shall flee from the iron weapon, and a bow of steel shall strike him through, because he hath oppressed and forsaken the poor, because he hath violently taken away a house which he builded not. We may be confident, and so may he, that ere long all this will be accomplished: for the triumphing of the wicked is but short, and the joy of the hypocrite but for a moment. Though his Excellency mount up to the heavens, and his head reacheth unto the clouds, yet he shall perish forever like his own dung. They that have seen him shall say, Where is he?

Vittorio Alfieri

On Tyranny

Tyrannical rule can only be maintained by the will of all, or of the majority of a people; and only the will of all, or of the majority, can really destroy it. But since, under our tyrannies, the mass of the people have no notion of any other government, how can this new idea of liberty be instilled into them? To my grief I have to reply that no one has any means of producing, in a short space of time, such an effect; and that in the countries where tyranny has been rooted for many generations it will take many more before public opinion slowly lays it bare.

Thus I perceive that owing to this fatal truth the European tyrants pardon me for all that until now I have argued against them. But in order somewhat to moderate this no less stupid than inhuman pleasure of theirs I must observe that although there are no prompt and efficacious remedies against tyrannical government, there are, however, many, and one above all, rapid in the extreme and infallible, against tyrants.

Remedies against a tyrant lie within the reach of any and all private individuals, however obscure; but the most sure, efficacious, and swift measures against tyrannic rule lie in the hands, strange as it may seem, of the tyrant himself: as I will explain. A man of fierce and freedom-loving spirit, when outraged as a private person or when deeply shocked by outrages against a whole people, can be certain of acting effectively against the tyrant by himself, and at once, with cold steel; and if many of such a bold spirit were to unite under tyrannies, very soon the mass of the people themselves would change its attitude of mind and at the same time bring about the end of despotic rule. But since men of such resolute character are rare, especially under these evil rulers, and since the elimination of the tyrant alone usually has no other effect than that of increasing the tyranny, I shudder to

Vittorio Alfieri, *Della Tirannide*, Vol. II, Chap. 7.

have to express here a very hard truth; which is, that cruelty itself, constant injustice, plundering, and atrocious corrupt practice on the part of the tyrant form the surest and most speedy remedy against tyrannic government. The more guilty and villainous the ruler is and the further he goes in open abuse of his unlimited wrongful authority, the more will he leave room for hope that the people will at last resent it, will listen and understand, and becoming inflamed with a passion for the truth will solemnly put an end forever to so violent and irrational a form of government. It must be borne in mind that the mass of the people very rarely is persuaded of the possibility of an evil that it has not itself experienced, and experienced at length; therefore the common herd does not regard despotism as a monstrous form of government until one or more successive monsters ruling over them have given grievous and undeniable proof of unheard-of monstrous excesses.

If it should ever happen that a good citizen were able to become the minister of a tyrant and were to have determined to carry out the sublime resolve to sacrifice his own life and even his own reputation in order effectively and speedily to rid the state of despotism, he would have no better nor more certain means to use than to let the tyrant continue his evil ways and to advise him in this sense, even instigating him to indulge his violent nature to the full, so that in abandoning him to the most atrocious excesses he renders his person and his authority hateful and intolerable to everyone. And I expressly use these particular words: "his person," "his authority," and "to everyone"; because every private outrage by the tyrant will only injure himself, but all public excesses, added to the private ones, will bring both tyrannic rule and the tyrant equally into disrepute and by enraging the people as a whole and individually will equally injure both tyrannic government and the tyrant; and could be able therefore to destroy both at the same time. These infamous and atrocious means employed by the minister (as I readily acknowledge them to be) are undoubtedly and always have been the only speedy and efficacious means of accomplishing so important and difficult an undertaking. It horrifies mc to say so, but it is yet more horrifying to think of what these governments are, in which if a good man were to wish to achieve with the greatest certainty and speed the supreme good of all, he would find himself forced first into wrongdoing and infamy, or else into giving up an undertaking otherwise impossible to carry out. Such a man therefore can never be found, and the rapid effect of the abuse of tyrannical rule can only be expected through a truly wicked minister. But the latter, not wishing to lose more than his reputation (of which he generally has had none) and determined to retain to the full his usurped authority, his booty and his life, will prefer to allow the tyrant to become cruel and evil only insofar as to render his subjects wretched, but never to such a pitch as to rouse them to fury and vengeance.

From this it comes about that in this much milder century the art of ruling despotically has become more subtle and (as I have shown in Book I) is based on not only well-concealed and varied but firm foundations that so long as the tyrant does not commit excesses, or very rarely, against the mass of the people and almost never against individuals except under the guise of some appearance of legality, tyranny seems assured of lasting for ever.

But now I hear voices about me exclaiming: "How is it, then, that if these tyrannies are moderate and possible to endure, you expose and persecute them with such heat and rancor?"—Because it is not always the cruelest of injuries that offend most cruelly: because injuries should be measured by their greatness and their effects rather than their force; because, in short, the man who takes from you a few ounces of blood every day kills you in the end no less inevitably than he whose sudden violence causes you at once to bleed to death; but makes you suffer much more. To feel all one's spiritual qualities numbed, all man's rights reduced or taken away, every magnanimous impulse curbed or distorted, and to have to suffer a thousand other offenses which, were I to enumerate them here one by one would make me appear too tedious and self-important an accuser: when a man's true life is in the spirit and the intellect, is not living in such fear a continual dying? Of what importance is it to a man, who feels himself born to act and think nobly, to preserve in trepidation the life in his body, his possessions and the rest of what he cares for (though without any security) when he must lose, without hope of ever regaining them, all, absolutely all, the truest and most noble gifts of the spirit?

PART II

The Origins of Modern Terrorism

Introductory Note

Conspiracy was in the air as secret societies multiplied in the first third of the nineteenth century. The most influential plotter was Philippe Buonarroti (who had assisted Baboeuf in 1795); his best-known heir was Auguste Blanqui (1805–1881). But neither preached terrorism: their central idea was one of a conspiracy leading to a sudden coup, barricades, and street fighting which would result in the overthrow of the old order. (Excerpts from Blanqui's "Instructions for an Insurrection" are reprinted in *The Guerrilla Reader* [New York: New American Library, 1977].) Terrorist practice was more frequent in the Italian secret societies (better known as Carbonari). A somewhat sensational but basically correct account was provided by Bartoldi, a Prussian diplomat in Italy in his *Memoirs of the Secret Societies of the South of Italy* (London, 1821). Little is known about Bartoldi, who in fact might have been Bartholdy (1779–1825), Prussian Consul General in Rome from 1815 and an uncle of Felix Mendelssohn.

The idea of mobilizing the criminal underworld in a revolutionary struggle appeared first in the writings of the early German socialist Wilhelm Weitling (1808–1871) who, in turn, influenced Bakunin. Weitling's ideas on the subject appear in his *Garantien der Harmonie und Freiheit* and more openly in letters to friends which were apparently intercepted and edited on behalf of the Swiss government by J. K. Bluntschli, *Die Kommunisten in der Schweiz* (Zürich, 1843). Bluntschli was one of the most important nineteenth-century theorists of international law. Karl Heinzen's *Der Mord* (Murder) is the most important ideological statement of early terrorism; published in early 1849, it was reprinted and quoted innumerable times among the advocates of "direct action." It first appeared in 1849 in a journal edited by German political refugees in Biel, Switzerland. The original title, *Die Revolution*, was unacceptable to the authorities, but after the editor decided to drop the "R," the paper was passed. Heinzen's extremist ideas were opposed and sometimes ridiculed by many of his radical contemporaries, including Marx and Engels, who singled him out for attack because, for all his radicalism, he was not a socialist. Like Weitling, Heinzen emigrated to America after the revolution of 1848–1849, where he edited various German language newspapers. He died in Boston ("the only civilized place in America") in 1880.

The concept of systematic terrorism and its use in revolutionary strategy first appeared between 1869 and 1881 in the writings of the Russian revolutionaries. Whether the famous "Catechism" was written by Nechaev or Bakunin has remained a bone of contention among historians, but most experts now believe that the former was its author. The background to the Nechaev affair, which preoccupied the Russian revolutionary movement for years, has been described in various books, most recently and most authoritatively in Michel Confino's *Révolution dans le Révolution* (Paris, 1973). Bakunin's influence was greatest on both the Russian revolutionary movement and on anarchism, especially in southern Europe.

The two most prominent advocates of terrorist action were Nikolai Morozov and G. Tarnovski (i.e., G. Romanenko), whose pamphlets appeared in Geneva in 1880. Both were members of the *Narodnaya Volya* which plotted and ultimately succeeded in killing the Czar in 1881. Morozov was arrested and sentenced to a long prison sentence. He studied physics, chemistry and astronomy and eventually became an honorary member of the Soviet Academy of Sciences. Though not a Marxist, he decided to stay in Russia after the Bolsheviks came to power and died at the ripe old age of ninety-two after the Second World War. While Morozov, after his release from prison, had sympathized with the liberal constitutionalists, Tarnovski—Romanenko moved to the extreme right and became one of the ideologists of the anti-Semitic Black Hundred. Serge Stepniak-Kravchinski's *Underground Russia* is a sympathetic and, on the whole, accurate account of the main figures of the Russian revolutionary movement of the 1870s. First published in Italian, it was translated into many languages and is widely read to this day. Kravchinski (1851–1895) was actively involved in terrorist operations; he escaped to London, where he died in a traffic accident.

The other main focus of terrorist thought was early anarchism. The role that a few courageous men, dissatisfied with words, might play was forcefully revealed in Prince Pyotr Kropotkin's (1842–1921) *The Spirit of Revolt*, first published in *Le Révolté* (Geneva, 1880). Instructions on how to play such a role were provided in many newspaper articles appearing in John Most's *Freiheit*, the leading German language newspaper advocating terrorist action. *Freiheit* was first published in London (1879–1881) and later in New York. Most had been a Social Democratic deputy to the Reichstag who, like many others, had to leave Germany following Bismarck's anti-socialist emergency laws. His writings also influenced the radical wing of the American labor movement, as can easily be ascertained from the speeches of the main defendants in the Haymarket Trial. In France the *ère des attentats* had tremendous repercussions as far as the press and public opinion were concerned, but their political impact was nil, for, unlike in Russia, these were actions of individuals rather than of organized groups.

Lastly there was Irish terrorism as advocated by O'Donovan Rossa (1831–1915) and others in the United States. A "Skirmishing Fund" was established in the 1870s to help the dynamiters. But the results were disappointing with only a few Irish patriots supporting O'Donovan Rossa. Moreover, the Irish underground was riddled with informers. As an Irish-American humorist remarked in the understatement of a decade: "Irish-American terrorists were always unlucky, maybe they were indiscreet. Perhaps they dropped a hint of their intentions." (Desmond Ryan, *The Phoenix Flame*, London, 1937, page 215.) William Mackey Lomasney (1841–1884) was one of the most remarkable Fenian dynamiters. He lost his life in an attempt to bomb London Bridge. His personality is described in Devoy's *Recollections of an Irish Rebel*, one of the most important accounts of the Irish nationalist movement. John Devoy (1842–1928) won fame as a Fenian organizer and was later one of the leaders of the "physical force" party among Irish-Americans, even though he had dissociated himself from Rossa's terrorist projects.

Bartoldi

Dagger and Poison

During the last winter and spring (1817) fires, which were reported to have succeeded each other rapidly, took place, accompanied with

Bartoldi, *Memoirs of the Secret Societies of the South of Italy* (London, 1821).

the escape of convicts and prisoners in various places, from Bologna to Spoleto, where the sectaries particularly abounded. These fires were discovered to be generally suppositious, although some were really accidental. The escape of prisoners could only have been effected by cooperation from without. This, with the support of other arguments, warranted the conclusion, that all was owing to the sectaries, whose object was to unsettle the people of those provinces, to promote brigandage, to call the attention of the government forces against robbers, and to divert them from their stations, by which means the intended revolt would have been easily and securely effected.

The sentiments . . . were echoed by the speeches of the members in language equally specific, and corresponding with the object of the revolt. Such too were the discourses held by the chief orators and sectaries in various meetings, both before and after the date of Papis's letter. In one of these meetings held at S. Elpidio, the sacred purple was strongly inveighed against, and it was announced that the day would come when it would be changed into a mantle of blood. In another, held subsequently in the same place, the necessity of destroying monarchy, and especially the holy authority of the Pope, was set forth; and the sectaries were exhorted to undertake any project, however difficult, for the purpose of regaining liberty. In another, held at S. Ginnesio, it was recommended to the members to provide themselves with arms and ammunition to serve as occasion offered; for, they were told, liberty and independence would soon be attained. In another, held at Macerata, in inculcating the necessity of rigid attention to secrecy with respect to the operations of the Society, a threat of death by the poignard was expressed against those who should attempt to violate their oath, and it was hinted that the same means would be necessary, ere the happy moment would arrive, when liberty would be regained, and the yoke of the present government thrown off. At Loreto, on the establishment of the Guelph Council, a discussion was held on the revolution which was shortly to take place, and on the satisfactory accounts of preparations for it, in consequence of which all the sectaries evinced a determination to follow it up. At Monte Lupone the same subject was discussed, and the members animated each other to action, declaring themselves eager for the crisis, and exulting in the prospect of establishing an independent republic.

Again, at Montolmo, in another assembly, the members were assured that liberty and independence would be soon regained. In another, at Monte Lupone, held on the 5th of June, one of the sectaries, grasping a dagger in his hand, caused his companions to renew their oath of secrecy, and declared that whoever betrayed it should perish by the weapon he held. After this preface he showed the advantages that would be obtained by taking the reins of power out of the hands of the actual government, and by erecting an independent republic. Another member recommended the imitation of Brutus, by dethroning tyrants and destroying monarchy, and by erecting upon their ruins an independent republic—and concluded that in a short time the yoke of the present government would be thrown off, exhorting his associates to provide themselves for this object, even with poisoned weapons (*arme anche avvelenate*) and with ammunition, in order to be ready on the first opportunity.

The plan for the execution of the revolt was the most terrible and sanguinary. An incendiary proclamation was to have been circulated in the Marches and other provinces of the state, immediately on the breaking out of the conspiracy in Macerata, to excite the people to join it. To that place the various Vendite of the Carbonari and Councils of the Guelphs, expressly informed of the event, were to have sent, in the same night, a number of armed rebels of their order. These were to have been admitted into the city, in which part of the sectaries were to have been ready to act. The watchword for the rebel bands in answer to the challenge, "*Chi evviva?*" was to have been, "*San Teobaldo*" (whom the Carbonari consider the protector of the order). The other secret word among the leaders was "*Vendetta al Popolo.*" Having insinuated themselves by stratagem into the places where the government troops are stationed, they would have overpowered them and deprived them of their arms, confining such as were unwilling to take a part in their operations. In the same manner, entering the public prisons, they would have confined the keepers, and released the prisoners, selecting from the latter those who are fit to bear arms.

Afterwards dividing the number of the rebels into patrols of twelve men, some were to have attacked the public treasuries, others the habitations of rich private individuals whose property was to have been plundered; and some, known to be hostile to the sect, were to have been seized and conducted to the deep subterraneous cells of the Monastery of Santa Chiara, which was fixed upon as a rebel station—there they were to be destroyed by fire or poison, their relations being made to believe that they were sent as hostages elsewhere. The plunder, under the faith and responsibility of the appointed heads of the patrols, was to have been deposited in the Convent "dei Bernabiti," where others would have registered it, to be afterwards employed in the necessary expenses. The principal civil and ecclesiastical authorities would not have been exempted from seizure and imprisonment. . . .

In the midst of these insidious proceedings, they did not omit to impose, by means of crime, on the sectaries themselves, as well as on the uninitiated, called by them Pagans, to remove every possible obstacle to the free prosecution of their labors; as well as to confirm the former in the obligations they had contracted, and to convince both of the formidable power of the Society. Several individuals, who were adverse to their maxims, were destined to the poignard, and were actually wounded in a sudden attack, one of them mortally. These victims were (in addition to their colleague Priola, of S. Elpidio, accused of perjury) Feliziani of Ascoli; the advocate Martini, judge in the tribunal at Fermo; the commissary of police, Ricci; the legal vicar of Petritoli, D. Ignazio Scarsini; Valeriani of Montelpare; and the brigadier of Carabiniers, Pastori, who, after repeated threats of death, conveyed in public notices, although he escaped a pistol shot, was afterwards poisoned, etc.; such aggressions and homicide (without reckoning that of Pastori) having been committed without any *immediate* cause, in the *night*, by persons *unknown*, and in *disguise*.

In fact, it is a system universally observed by the Carbonari, that every one of them should be armed with a poignard, as the hand grasping a dagger upon the seals of the order denotes; nor do they deny this.

When a new member is admitted to their Society, they brandish these weapons before the novice; intimating that they will be always ready in his defense, if he is faithful to the Society, and that they will shed his blood if he violates his oath.

It is on this account that all the accused, in whatever manner they have confessed, tremble lest they should fall beneath the stilettoes of their colleagues, which would infallibly happen if their confessions were made public. It is on this account they entreat secrecy. The expressions employed by Massone, president of the Supreme Vendita of the Carbonari, and of the Guelph Council at Ancona, on this subject, are very remarkable.

"Giacomo Papis," (this particular mention of his name seems to prove that he is fully informed on this subject), "Giacomo Papis fears the vengeance of the sect much more than the decision of justice in the present cause." This terror, unlike other circumstances of which this is not the place to treat, accounts of itself for the crimes above alluded to. Poison was at last called in to aid the poignard, as fitter to destroy in some circumstances, by placing the assassin in less danger. This atrocious system, notwithstanding the restriction of the chief sectaries, is at this moment followed up by the most abandoned of the order, who are not easily shaken in their resolutions. But their audacity went still farther, although the vigilance of government, toward the end of 1816, was enabled to check the course of these proceedings, by the arrest of some individuals at Ascoli. The sectaries did not desist from the practices above alluded to, but, more insolent than ever, dared to conspire against the sovereign and his throne.

Karl Heinzen

Murder

I

We must call a spade a spade. The truth must out, whether it seems amiable or terrible, whether it is dressed in the white of peace or the red of war. Let us then be frank and honest, let us tear away the veil and spell out in plain speech what the lesson is which is now being illustrated every day before our eyes in the form of actions and threats, blood and torture, cannons and gallows by both princes and freedom-fighters, Croats and democrats; to wit, that murder is the principal agent of historical progress.

The egoists begin the murdering, and the men of ideas reply in kind. Twist and turn as they may, neither party can escape either murdering or being murdered, and the "ultima ratio" of both is quite simply the obliteration of their enemies.

Die Evolution (Biel, February–March, 1849).

A wide variety of names have been coined for the art of obliterating one's enemy. In one country they have him put to death "legally" by an executioner and call it the death penalty; in another, they lie in wait with stiletto blades behind hedges and call it assassination; in another they organize obliteration on a grand scale and call it war. Examined in the clear light of day, these various appellations appear for what they are, entirely superfluous, being all expressions of what is fundamentally one and the same thing, and whether I am executed or assassinated or torn to pieces, the end effect is the same. I am dispatched to the other world and this dispatching to the other world was the purpose of my enemy. No clear-thinking, rational person can accept the hair-splitting distinctions by which certain methods of obliterating the enemy are justified and others condoned; such distinctions rest on theological and legal fictions and do not in any way alter the facts of the matter, which are that in each case it is purely and simply a question of obliterating one's enemy.

We maintain, in conformity with the fundamental principles of humanity and justice, that any voluntary killing of another human being is a crime against humanity, that no one under any pretext whatsoever has the right to destroy another's life and that anyone who does kill another or has him killed is quite simply a murderer. But against our enemies, with their executioners and soldiers, their laws of "high treason" and their inquisitions, their cannons and needle-guns, their shrapnel and Congreves, we are able to achieve precious little with our humanity and our ideas of justice, and merely to claim in some places that an inquisitor or a general is as much a murderer as any bandit or partisan would only serve to convince ourselves that we may quite "legitimately" be done away with.

Let us, then, be practical, let us call ourselves murderers as our enemies do, let us take the moral horror out of this great historical tool and just examine closely whether perchance our enemies may claim a special privilege in the matter of murder. If to kill is always a crime, then it is forbidden equally to all; if it is not crime, then it is permitted equally to all. Once one has overcome the objection that murder per se is a crime, all that remains is to believe one is in the right against one's enemy and to possess the power to obliterate him. Simple logic as much as the facts of history compels this conclusion. We do not desire *any* killing, *any* murder, but if our enemies are not of the same mind, if they can justify murder, even going so far as to claim a special privilege in the matter, then necessity compels us to challenge this privilege; and it is no great step from this necessity to becoming Robespierre and to the adoption of Robespierre's role, condemning hundreds of thousands to the scaffold in the interests of humanity.

We take as our fundamental principle, taught us by our enemies, that murder, both of individuals and masses, is still a necessity, an unavoidable instrument in the achievement of historical ends. Let us now consider various attitudes to the question, in order to illustrate when the use of this bloody instrument is justified and when not.

As schoolchildren, we were excited and thrilled by the story of those two youthful heroes Harmodios and Aristogeiton, who murdered the tyrant Hipparchos. Those who told us the story, who presented this murder to us as a glorious deed, were "the king's" teachers, men who oozed morality, loyalty, and the fear of God from every pore. We never heard them say that Harmodios and Aristogeiton were "heinous murderers," "anarchists," "agitators," etc., nor that the victim Hipparchos was a "legitimate ruler," a "sacred person," etc., nor that, instead of opting to murder him they should have attempted to remove him "by constitutional means." Now what conclusion are we to draw from this?

Pupils in every school in the land are made to recite a poem composed by the highly moral Schiller, who at the very beginning has an "assassin" "creep up on a tyrant" with a "dagger concealed in his cloak," and then subsequently makes the tyrant a friend of the murderer's. What are we to conclude from this?

Mucius Scaevola slipped into Porsenna's camp with the intention of murdering an enemy dangerous to his fatherland. By mistake he killed Porsenna's scribe. Later he told Porsenna that 300 other Romans besides himself had sworn to kill him. In all the history books and schools, Mucius Scaevola is praised to the skies as a hero, and it would never occur to anyone to be scandalized by the fact that there were 300 other Romans ready to take his place. What are we to conclude from this?

One of the chief enemies of the great Caesar, and one of his assassins, was Junius Brutus, the favorite Caesar loved so tenderly and who may even have been his own dear son. No one has yet been roused to indignation by the fact that this republican suppressed all human feeling and gratitude in order to become a murderer, perhaps even a parricide; on the contrary, royalists, moralists, republicans, and "anarchists" all still consider him to be one of the greatest men in history and "the last Roman." What are we to conclude from this?

In heathen antiquity, the murder of a tyrant was right, honorable, and one's duty, and no "king's" teacher or professor in our Christian era would ever dream of trying to correct them on this score. What are we to conclude from this?

Let us take a few examples from more recent history.

Sand murdered the traitor Kotzebue with a dagger instead of killing him with a stroke of the pen.

The reactionaries denounced him, while the liberals expressed regret that he had risked his life in killing a man whose position and person did not warrant such action. What are we to conclude from this?

A young man from Germany by the name of Statz tried to murder Napoleon but was caught and disarmed. This young man Statz was lauded for his attempt and his name would doubtless have become one of the most celebrated among the moral Germans if he had succeeded in carrying out his deed, if he had plunged a dagger into the body of the most powerful man in history. What are we to conclude from this?

In Frankfurt am Main two deputies, Lichnowski and Auerswald, were murdered. The entire reactionary and constitutional party boiled over with indignation and the central authorities mobilized half the continent to try and catch the murderers. In Vienna, another deputy, Robert Blum, was murdered by Windisch grätz's executioners and in his honor the central authorities made a few preliminary inquiries from which nothing followed. If R. Blum had been a German prince rather than a German deputy, the "National Parliament" would have instructed the central authorities to declare war on Austria. What are we to conclude from this?

In Frankfurt, it was Prince Lichnowski and Count Auerswald who were murdered. In Vienna, it was simply Robert Blum, man of the people, who was murdered. On the occasion of this first murder, the reactionary party raised an unending hue and cry against the "anarchists"; when, however, a collection was taken for Mr. Auerswald's descendants, the token of sympathy raised by this rich party proved to be a very paltry sum. The second murder caused such sorrow within the dead man's party that memorial services were held in hundreds of churches and his family very rapidly became rich. What are we to conclude from this?

Here are a few conclusions which follow irrefutably from these facts:

1. It seems that what is decisive in the way history judges a murder is the motive. History does not appear to condemn murder itself.

2. It seems that moral reactions to a murder are closely linked to the self-interest of those reacting, for that which is esteemed a virtue among the ancients would be considered a crime in our age of police rule. None of the teachers who so enthusiastically translate accounts of murderous deeds from the Greek tongue into the German would dare recommend a "translation" of the deeds themselves.

3. The courageous bearing of the murderer seems to be of equal weight in the scales of judgment as the success of the attempt.

4. It seems that murder is only justified when it selects a victim whose elimination also signifies the removal of a representative or upholder of a pernicious principle.

5. It seems that it is not just the "petty thieves" but also the petty murderers who are "hanged," while the "big" ones get off scot-free.

6. It seems that only the party of freedom has martyrs, the reactionary party having nothing but tools.

We are driven to similar conclusions when we consider mass murder, organized murder, or war, as it is called. In the past it is the most just who are in the right, in the present it is the most strong. In the past, motive is the determining factor, in the present, self-interest. In the past, justice is the judge, in the present, the party. In the past, it is the idea which is decisive, in the present, it is expediency. Organized murder, war, is accepted as a necessity per se; it is a tool, like a knife, and the only question of any relevance is whether it is used to this or that end and, further, whether it succeeds or fails in achieving it.

Thus we see that in practice, once killing has been accepted, the moral stance is seen to have no foundation, the legal is seen to be ineffectual, and the political is alone of any significance. Is the end achieved? This is the only question which you cultivators and organizers of murder permit us to ask ourselves, by forcing us to adopt your theory of murder.

It is possible that murder is not only an historical but also a physical necessity. It is possible that the atmosphere or the earth's crust requires a certain quantity of human blood to satisfy its chemical or other interests. However, even should such a requirement on nature's part exist, no one is ever going to manage to persuade us that the blood of aristocrats is less suitable than the blood of democrats. There is as yet no law of physics stating that it is only those who champion the rights of man who must give their quota to satisfy history's or nature's need for blood. We shall therefore have to ask ourselves whether the time has not yet come—or is not coming—and whether we will not very soon be sufficiently strong to make some claims on our enemies. It would appear that it is in the nature of the democratic party all at once to make huge demands in settlement of the debts which the other party has gradually accumulated with it. The French Revolution of the last century was an example of just such a settlement of an outstanding murder account, and, if we are to believe the signs, there will presently be a repeat of the French Revolution on a European scale. The reactionary party has never had any reservations about murdering others and has fewer than ever at the present time. "Have I the means to carry out the murder and will it achieve its purpose?" This is the only question the reaction has ever asked itself.

What answer do we get when we ask ourselves this question? Being the conscientious Germans we are, we first inquire of our teachers whether we would have been committing more of a crime than Harmodios, Mucius or Brutus were we to have done away with a Metternich, a Nicholas, a Windischgrätz or a Ferdinand of Naples—in other words, were we to have dispatched to the other world several individuals who have been responsible for torturing and murdering millions. If our teachers speak the language of the Greeks and Romans, they will have to answer: ask your own capacity for self-sacrifice and your courage. If, however, they speak German, they will call for the police. How are we to escape from this dilemma?

Our enemies will come to our aid. With homicidal violence, our enemies are at present urging upon us the lesson that murder is the chief instrument of historical progress and that the most valuable art to be versed in in our time is that of destroying human life. Ferdinand bombards Naples, Radetsky murders the Lombards, Windischgrätz mounts an attack on Vienna, Jellachich allows his Croats to roll about in the entrails of their victims, "Olim der Grosse" keeps all his murderers at their posts, and in the background stands the Czar with hundreds of thousands of bloodthirsty comrades. None of these men thinks twice about destroying whole towns, ruining whole countries, having the most honorable men shot, the most innocent murdered, women abused, children impaled, in short about reviving all the bestiality and barbarity of former times, in order to save a few crowns and keep the rights of man at bay. And we?

Invention tends to go hand in hand with developments in other spheres. Our enemies, with their means of mass destruction, will stimulate inventions which vie with the present armies as agents of destruction. The greatest benefactor of mankind will be he who makes it possible for a few men to wipe out thousands. So when we hear that train-loads of murderer's accomplices have been hurled from the track by a thimble full of fulminating silver placed under the rails; or that bombs, filled to the brim and complete with detonator, have been placed beneath paving stones in order to tear apart whole companies of invading barbarians as soon as they arrive; or that, perhaps, containers filled with poison, which burst in the air, can rain down ruin on entire regiments; or that underground rooms full of fulminating silver can blow whole towns into the air, complete with their 100,000 murderous slaves, then in such methods we shall perceive only to what desperate measures the party of freedom has been driven by the mass party of the barbarians. To have a conscience with regard to the murdering of reactionaries is to be totally unprincipled. They wreak destruction, in any way they can, thereby obliging us to respond in kind as defenders of justice and humanity. Kossuth was a man of great energy, but Kossuth did not show sufficient interest in inventions and Kossuth overlooked the possibilities of fulminating silver.

Even if we have to blow up half a continent or spill a sea of blood, in order to finish off the barbarian party, we should have no scruples about doing it. The man who would not joyfully give up his own life for the satisfaction of putting a million barbarians into their coffins carries no Republican heart within his breast.

II

In my last article, I said that "the greatest benefactor of mankind will be he who makes it possible for a few men to wipe out thousands."

The entire democratic party should make it its business to bring about this state of affairs. We are surely now agreed that murder, in both its passive and active forms, is something we cannot avoid; and if the only choice we have is either to be murdered for freedom's sake or to murder for it, it is difficult to imagine any democrat having such humane feelings toward the barbarians that he would obediently place his own head on the chopping block. So there can really be no doubt about which alternative to choose; and all that we have to concern ourselves with is gaining the upper hand in the mortal struggle which is about to erupt—or has already erupted—with the party of the barbarians. Hitherto, the barbarian party has been far superior to us in the matter of murder. Murder has for centuries been their chief of study; they have trained and organized hundreds of thousands of murderous lackeys; they have on their side such hoards of instruments of murder and means of destruction that one could without being an Archimedes—providing the "*da mihi punctum*" has been satisfied—deprive astronomy of several exquisite planets and stars. All that nature, science, art, industry, zeal, avarice, and bloodthirstiness have been able to produce or invent is at the disposal of the barbarians' party in its efforts to destroy, to murder the humane party, the party of freedom: blood is their alpha, blood their omega, blood their end, blood their means, blood their delight, blood their life, blood their dream, blood their endeavor, blood their first principle, and blood their last. So be it, then: blood for blood, murder for murder, destruction for destruction. The spirit of freedom must raise itself up to its full height, show its true vigor, and if it goes under, it must turn destroyer.

People have said so often that the freedom party has no need to concern itself with numbers, that its principle alone is sufficient assurance of victory, that ultimately it will overcome any enemy no matter how powerful, etc.; they cite the cases of the Greeks, the Swiss, the Dutch; for centuries now they have been regurgitating the same few examples to give us consolation and bolster our hopes. In my opinion, these few crumbs of comfort only feed our indecision and our superstition. Of course, it is as certain that progress will finally overcome reaction as it is certain that spring will finally overcome winter; but the general truth of this statement does not rule out the myriad variables of Where? How? and How Long?—variables which can be so important, so crucial, that for entire peoples and for entire centuries the law of progress may shrivel up into nothing, whereas with the aid of a few pistol shots, a few cannons or a few pounds of fulminating silver, the same law might be made reality for those same peoples and centuries.

Hence, this mere, vague belief in the moral force and ultimate victory of the party of freedom over that of the barbarians is merely a soporific, an instrument of self-destruction. Simple common sense refuses to accept a "law" which forbids one to defend oneself against certain attack until the murderer's knife is at one's throat; as it would refuse to accept a law instructing fathers to permit themselves to be killed in order that their sons might learn to defend themselves; as it would refuse to accept a law forbidding one to fire no more than one shot at the enemy for every ten he fires; as it would refuse to accept a law instructing one to use water sprinklers against an enemy who fights with poison and fire; as it would refuse to accept a law instructing one to trust in future reconciliation with an enemy whose very nature is rebarbative to peace-making and the very principle of whose being is that he will never get any better. Therefore, once again, I say we must answer blood with blood, murder with murder, destruction with destruction.

Those who point to the progressive minority's qualitative superiority over the reactionary majority have in most cases failed to perceive how the conditions and circumstances of the struggle have changed. One gun has more courage than a thousand freedom-fighters and it is a matter of the purest indifference to case-shot and shrapnel whether they are to decimate a troop of Spartans or Thebans, a corps of confederates, or a corps of Hungarians. In earlier times, before the present system of standing armies arose, before courage and physical strength were replaced by mere instruments of murder, before it became possible for cowards to wreak destruction from a great distance away, before the business of equipping an army began to cost the people as much as half their entire wealth, before the possession of and training in arms had reached the inequality we see today and when it was possible to fight man to man, "eyeball to eyeball"—then, admittedly, it was possible for a small band of men inspired by the spirit of freedom and by a courage born of desperation to defeat with ease a superior force of murderous lackeys, who were simply acting on some despot's orders. In modern times, however, circumstances have changed. Certainly, the spiritual force driving the combatants is still of importance, and, where there is equality of instruments of destruction, a corps of freedom-fighters will rout any troop of despot's mercenaries of the same size. But the barbarian party's superiority in

organization
training
numbers
means of destruction

has, as we see from almost all the battles of recent times, grown so great that it is simply ridiculous to claim this superiority can be counterbalanced by the freedom-fighter's spirit and his knowledge of the rightness of his cause.

We must become more practical than we are, we must become more resolved, we must become more energetic, we must become more reckless. The "Spirit of Freedom" will have to familiarize itself with daggers and poison, and "the good cause" will have to study the mysteries of power and fulminating silver.

The aim of our study must be to eliminate the superiority of the barbarian party through the invention of new methods of killing, so as to nullify the numerical advantage of the organized masses by means of instruments of destruction which

1. can be operated by a small number of people

2. do greater damage, the greater the mass of those against whom they are used.

The barbarian party has gun foundries in which to produce guns, powder mills in which to manufacture powder, and it has complete freedom to mount its guns and pour in the powder. We have none of these things. We have no money to buy guns with, and even had we the guns, we should never be able to bring them out into the open: a few policemen would immediately relieve us of them. The first question is thus whether it is not possible to invent instruments which can be made without being seen, be transported without attracting notice, be operated without any great effort, and which are, in sum, no less effective than big guns?

The barbarian party possesses shrapnel, Congreve missiles, etc. Such instruments are only of use, or practical, when one wishes to wipe out masses of people. A Congreve hurled into the middle of a group of a few hundred can scatter or kill a few hundred; thrown at one single man, it may fail to hit even this individual and even if it does achieve its object, it kills only this one individual, for all its destructive power. Would it not be possible, then, to devise some sort of missile which one man can throw into a group of a few hundred, killing them all? We need instruments of destruction which are of little use to the great masses of the barbarians when they are fighting a few lone individuals but which give a few lone individuals the terrifying power to threaten the safety of whole masses of barbarians. Our powers of invention will thus have to be directed toward the concentration, the homeopathic—as it were—preparation of those substances whose destructive powers physics and chemistry have brought to light, and toward solving the problem of how these substances can be used in a way which minimizes their cost, makes them easy to transport, and diminishes the effort required to propel them. For instance, were it possible with no more than a shotgun to fire into the massed ranks of an army a capsule equal in effect, on contact, to a shrapnel-shell or a case-shot, then a dozen democratic partisans would be able to do more damage than an entire battery of barbarian artillery and the large-scale organization and huge accumulation of instruments of death to which the barbarian party owes its superiority would in a short space be rendered useless.

Being myself neither a chemist, nor a sergeant-artificer, nor a gunner, I am in no position to judge whether the problems an invention along these lines would pose are, in fact, insuperable; however, from what man's powers of invention have achieved so far, I take it they are not. These revolutionaries who, like the Italians, Poles, and Hungarians, have no shortage of funds, should put up the prize money for an open competition—it would not be long before success was achieved.

As much, however, as new inventions, we desperately need firmness of purpose, that revolutionary firmness of purpose which is prepared to oppose the barbarians' system of murder and violence with any means which help to fulfill the aim of destroying them. When at the start of the Hungarian war, the Hungarians began using chain-shot and the humane Windischgrätz protested against this inhuman violation of the conventions of war, the Hungarians declared they would lay their inhuman chain-shots aside if Herr Windischgrätz would hand over to them a few humane batteries of Congreves. It is exceedingly naïve of professional barbarians who take their greatest delight and derive their greatest honor from murdering men in their thousands, to appeal in the name of humanity to the conventions of war when their weaker enemy attempts to reduce his superiority by newer, more effective weapons. It is not contrary to the dictates of "humanity" for Herr Windischgrätz as a myrmidon of despotism, to set Vienna in flames and order the Hungarians to be mown down. But it is contrary to the "conventions of war" for the Hungarians, defending what it is their right to defend, to use chain-shot in attempting to stop bands of Croatian murderers invading their territory. What a fuss did Herr Windischgrätz make when the Hungarians poisoned all the meat before they retreated from Raab! To be frank, the only regret I have about the whole affair is that a few thousand of those wild animals who call themselves Croats and saviors of Austrian despotism did not eat sufficiently large quantities of that poisoned meat to snuff it. In my view, it is "more shameful" and "more immoral" to poison a few thousand rats than a few thousand of those Croats. If the Croats and their masters do not wish to be poisoned and shot at with chain-shot in Hungary, there is one very simple way of ensuring they are not: to wit, to leave the Hungarian people in peace and their rights unchallenged. Once, however, they violate those rights, once they close in on the Hungarians as murderers, the Hungarians have the authority and the duty to use any means whatever to achieve their end, which is the destruction of an enemy superior to them in numbers, organization, or instruments of death. The Hungarians would now be a lot better off had they been a little more inhumane and more consistently violated the "conventions of war"; the same is true of the Italians. The revolutionaries must try to bring about a situation where the barbarians are afraid for their lives every hour of the day or night. They must think that every drink of water, every mouthful of food, every bed, every bush, every paving stone, every path and footpath, every hole in a wall, every slate, every bundle of straw, every pipe bowl, every stick, every pin may be a killer. For them, as for us, may fear be the herald and murder the executor. Murder is their motto, so let murder be their answer, murder is their need, so let murder be their payment, murder is their argument, so let murder be their refutation.

The European barbarian party has left us no other choice than to devote ourselves to the study of murder and refine the art of killing to the highest possible degree. Recently the Austrians have been rather overdoing a public boast that they have invented balloons of death which they intend to use to set fire to Venice. It has not occurred to anybody to appeal to Humanity and Morality about this. The entire "humane" and "moral" world will, in all likelihood, get convulsions when a revolutionary insists that the freedom party must meet the murdering of the barbarian party with murder themselves.

The path to Humanity will pass through the zenith of Barbarity. Our enemies have made this principle a law of politics and we shall either have to observe this "law," follow this "constitutional path," or be buried, and our freedom with us.

Mikhail Bakunin

Revolution, Terrorism, Banditry

Banditry is one of the most honorable ways of life within the Russian state. Since the establishment of the Muscovite state, it has represented a desperate protest by the people against the infamous social order, perfected on the Western pattern and still further consolidated by Peter's reforms and the benign Alexander's grants of freedom. The bandit is the people's hero, defender, savior. He is the implacable enemy of the state and the whole social and civil order set up by the state; he is a fighter to the death against the entire civilization of the aristocratic *Chinovniks* and governmental priesthood.

Without understanding the essential nature of the bandit, no man will ever understand the history of the Russian people. Without sympathy for that nature, he cannot sympathize with the life of the Russian people; he has no heart for the people's age-old immeasurable suffering; he has thrown in his lot with their enemies, the supporters of state supremacy.

The nature of Russian banditry is cruel and ruthless; yet no less cruel and ruthless is that governmental might which has brought this kind of bandit into being by its wanton acts. Governmental cruelty has engendered the cruelty of the people and made it into something necessary and natural. But between these two cruelties, there still remains a vast difference; the first strives for the complete annihilation of the people, the other endeavors to set them free.

Since the Muscovite state was founded, there has been no break in the Russian organization of banditry. In it the memory of the people's humiliation is preserved; in itself alone, it is proof of the passion, vitality, and strength of the people. Should banditry cease in Russia, that would mean that either final extinction or complete freedom had come to the people.

Mikhail Bakunin, *Neskolko slov k molodym bratyam v Rossii* (Geneva, 1869), reprinted in M. P. Dragomanov's edition of the exchange of letters between Bakunin and Herzen and Ogarev.

In Russia, the bandit is the only true revolutionary—a revolutionary without fine phrases, without book-learned rhetoric, an implacable, tireless, indomitable, practical revolutionary, a social revolutionary sprung from the people, though with no politics and no social status. . . . In the difficult intervals when the whole world of working peasants sleep what seems to be a sleep with no awakening, crushed by the whole burden of the state, the world of bandits in the forests carries on its desperate fight and battles on until at last the Russian villages awake. And should these two kinds of rebellion, that of the bandit and that of the peasant, ever unite, then the people's revolution will come about. The movements of Stenka Rasin and Pugachev were, in fact, just this.

And now the underground river of banditry flows unbroken from Petersburg to Moscow, from Moscow to Kasan, from Kasan to Tobolsk, to the mines of the Altai, to Irkutsk and Nerchinsk. The robbers, dispersed throughout Russia, in the forests, the towns and villages, and the captives in the innumerable prisons of the empire—they all make up one inseparable, tightly knit world, the world of the Russian revolution. Here and only here has there long been a genuine revolutionary conspiracy. And so, whoever truly wants to conspire in Russia, whoever desires the people's revolution should find his way into this world. . . . The time of general revolt approaches. . . . The villages are not asleep. . . . No! They are in rebellion. From all ends of the empire groans, plaints, and threats resound. In the north, in the east, in the Baltic provinces, significant popular risings have already occurred. Beneath the soldiers' bayonets, the blood of the people has begun to flow more strongly than ever before. Yet the measure of the people's patience is exhausted; death by starvation is no easier than death by bayonet or bullet. Now the people will no longer fall asleep and the number of isolated risings will grow ever greater. The tally of those who flee into the forest also grows ever greater; the world of banditry is awake and alert once more. . . . The anniversaries of Stenka Rasin and Pugachev draw near, when the memory of the people's champions must be honored. . . . All must arm themselves for that celebration. . . .

What, in truth, is now our task?

We must take the path at present shown to us by the government, which drives us out of academies, universities, and schools; let us then, brothers, as one man fling ourselves among the people, the popular movement, the bandit and peasant revolts, and, while maintaining our true, firm friendship, we will unite the isolated peasant outbursts into a well-planned yet relentless revolution. . . .

Even if we recognized no activity other than the cause of destruction, we should still be of the opinion that the forms which that activity might take could be multiplied to an extraordinary degree. Poison, dagger, noose, and the like! . . . Everything in this fight is equally sanctified by the revolution. So the field is open! . . . The victims are marked out by the unconcealed indignation of the people! And so may all honest and fresh minds, after centuries of degradation, pluck up courage for a renewal of life! Dismal be the last days of the leech upon the body politic! Lamentations of fear and remorse will re-echo throughout society. Beggarly writers will strike lyric notes. Shall we pay heed to them? . . . By no means! . . . We must remain impassive in the face of all this howling and not enter into any compromises with those destined to perish. They will call it terrorism! . . . They will give it some resounding nickname! All right, it's all the same to us. We don't care for their opinion. We know that in all Europe not a single person leads a quiet bourgeois life or can with honor reproach us without being forced into hypocrisy. From contemporary literature, made up of nothing but denunciation and flattery, from venal literature nothing but beastliness and tittle-tattle can be expected. The interests of applied science today are the interests of the Tsar and of capital, which it exclusively serves, exclusively—because up to now not a single discovery has been utilized for the good of the people: all discoveries are either exploited by fine gentlemen, dilettantes or moneymakers, or else used to increase military power. None of the inventive talent of academics is directed toward the needs of the people. Therefore, the interests of this applied science are not ours, either. Need we, then, even speak of social science? Who does not know the names of dozens of dear ones who have been exiled to Siberia or elsewhere because they wished to restore the rights of man with the sincere words of a warm conviction. Their ardent speeches, breathing faith and love were stifled by brute force. . . .

The present generation must in its turn produce an inexorable brute force and relentlessly tread the path of destruction. The healthy, uncorrupted mind of youth must grasp the fact that it is considerably more humane to stab and strangle dozens, nay hundreds, of hated beings than to join with them to share in systematic *legal* acts of murder, in the torture and martyrdom of millions of peasants. These are the acts that our *Chinovniks*, our scholars, priests, and traders share in, in a word by all the people of standing who, directly or indirectly, oppress those who have no standing! . . . So may all healthy young minds forthwith set themselves to the *sacred cause* of rooting out evil, purifying and clearing Russia's soil by fire and sword, and join fraternally with those who will do likewise throughout Europe.

Sergey Nechaev

Catechism of the Revolutionist (1869)

Principles by Which the Revolutionary Must Be Guided

1. The revolutionary is a doomed man. He has no interests of his own, no affairs, no feelings, no attachments, no belongings, not even a name. Everything in him is absorbed by a single exclusive interest, a single thought, a single passion—the revolution.

2. In the very depths of his being, not only in words but also in deeds, he has broken every tie with the civil order and the entire cultured world, with all its laws, proprieties, social conventions, and its ethical rules. He is an implacable enemy of this world, and if he continues to live in it, that is only to destroy it more effectively.

3. The revolutionary despises all doctrinairism and has rejected the mundane sciences, leaving them to future generations. He knows of only one science, the science of destruction. To this end, and this end alone, he will study mechanics, physics, chemistry, and perhaps medicine. To this end he will study day and night the living science: people, their characters and circumstances and all the features of the present social order at all possible levels. His sole and constant object is the immediate destruction of this vile order.

The "Catechism" has been translated many times. It is reprinted here from M. Confino, *Daughter of a Revolutionary* (Alcove Press, London, 1974), with the kind permission of author and publisher.

4. He despises public opinion. He despises and abhors the existing social ethic in all its manifestations and expressions. For him, everything is moral which assists the triumph of revolution. Immoral and criminal is everything which stands in its way.

5. The revolutionary is a dedicated man, merciless toward the state and toward the whole of educated and privileged society in general; and he must expect no mercy from them either. Between him and them there exists, declared or undeclared, an unceasing and irreconcilable war for life and death. He must discipline himself to endure torture.

6. Hard toward himself, he must be hard toward others also. All the tender and effeminate emotions of kinship, friendship, love, gratitude, and even honor must be stifled in him by a cold and single-minded passion for the revolutionary cause. There exists for him only one delight, one consolation, one reward and one gratification—the success of the revolution. Night and day he must have but one thought, one aim—merciless destruction. In cold-blooded and tireless pursuit of this aim, he must be prepared both to die himself and to destroy with his own hands everything that stands in the way of its achievement.

7. The nature of the true revolutionary has no place for any romanticism, any sentimentality, rapture, or enthusiasm. It has no place either for personal hatred or vengeance. The revolutionary passion, which in him becomes a habitual state of mind, must at every moment be combined with cold calculation. Always and everywhere he must be not what the promptings of his personal inclinations would have him be, but what the general interest of the revolution prescribes.

8. The revolutionary considers his friend and holds dear only a person who has shown himself in practice to be as much a revolutionary as he himself. The extent of his friendship, devotion, and other obligations towards his comrade is determined only by their degree of usefulness in the practical work of total revolutionary destruction.

9. The need for solidarity among revolutionaries is self-evident. In it lies the whole strength of revolutionary work. Revolutionary comrades who possess the same degree of revolutionary understanding and passion should, as far as possible, discuss all important matters together and come to unanimous decisions. But in implementing a plan decided upon in this manner, each man should as far as possible rely on himself. In performing a series of destructive actions each man must act for himself and have recourse to the advice and help of his comrades only if this is necessary for the success (of the plan).

10. Each comrade should have under him several revolutionaries of the second or third category, that is, comrades who are not completely initiated. He should regard them as portions of a common fund of revolutionary capital, placed at his disposal. He should expend his portion of the capital economically, always attempting to derive the utmost possible benefit from it. Himself he should regard as capital consecrated to the triumph of the revolutionary cause; but as capital which he may not dispose of independently without the consent of the entire company of the fully initiated comrades.

11. When a comrade gets into trouble, the revolutionary, in deciding whether he should be rescued or not, must think not in terms of his personal feelings but only of the good of the revolutionary cause. Therefore he must balance, on the one hand, the usefulness of the comrade, and on the other, the amount of revolutionary energy that would necessarily be expended on his deliverance, and must settle for whichever is the weightier consideration.

12. The admission of a new member, who has proved himself not by words but by deeds, may be decided upon only by unanimous agreement.

13. The revolutionary enters into the world of the state, of class, and of so-called culture, and lives in it only because he has faith in its speedy and total destruction. He is not a revolutionary if he feels pity for anything in this world. If he is able to, he must face the annihilation of a situation, of a relationship, or of any person who is a part of this world—everything and everyone must be equally odious to him. All the worse for him if he has family, friends, and loved ones in this world; he is no revolutionary if they can stay his hand.

14. Aiming at merciless destruction the revolutionary can and sometimes even must live within society while pretending to be quite other than what he is. The revolutionary must penetrate everywhere, among all the lowest and the middle classes, into the houses of commerce, the church, the mansions of the rich, the world of the bureaucracy, the military, and of literature, the Third Section [the Secret Police], and even the Winter Palace.

15. All of this foul society must be split up into several categories: the first category comprises those to be condemned immediately to death. The society should compile a list of these condemned persons in order of the relative harm they may do to the successful progress of the revolutionary cause, and thus in order of their removal.

16. In compiling these lists and deciding the order referred to above, the guiding principle must not be the individual acts of villainy committed by the person, nor even by the hatred he provokes among the society or the people. This villainy and hatred, however, may to a certain extent be useful, since they help to incite popular rebellion. The guiding principle must be the measure of service the person's death will necessarily render to the revolutionary cause. Therefore, in the first instance all those must be annihilated who are especially harmful to the revolutionary organization, and whose sudden and violent deaths will also inspire the greatest fear in the government and, by depriving it of its cleverest and most energetic figures, will shatter its strength.

17. The second category must consist of those who are granted temporary respite to live, solely in order that their bestial behavior shall drive the people to inevitable revolt.

18. To the third category belong a multitude of high-ranking cattle, or personages distinguished neither for any particular intelligence nor for energy, but who, because of their position, enjoy wealth, connections, influence and power. They must be exploited in every possible fashion and way; they must be enmeshed and confused, and, when we have found out as much as we can about their dirty secrets, we must make them our slaves. Their power, influence, connections, riches and energy thus become an inexhaustible treasure-house and an effective aid to our various enterprises.

19. The fourth category consists of politically ambitious persons and liberals of various hues. With them we can conspire according to their own programs, pretending that we are blindly following them, while in fact we are taking control of them, rooting out all their secrets and compromising them to the utmost, so that they are irreversibly implicated and can be employed to create disorder in the state.

20. The fifth category is composed of doctrinaires, conspirators, revolutionaries, all those who are given to idle peroration, whether before audiences or on paper. They must be continually incited and forced into making violent declarations of practical intent, as a result of which the majority of them will vanish without a trace and real revolutionary gain will accrue from a few.

21. The sixth, and an important category is that of women. They should be divided into three main types: first, those frivolous, thoughtless, and vapid women who we may use as we use the third and fourth categories of men; second, women who are ardent, gifted, and devoted, but do not belong to us because they have not yet achieved a real, passionless, and practical revolutionary understanding: these must be used like the men of the fifth category; and, finally there are the women who are with us completely, that is, who have been fully initiated and have accepted our program in its entirety. We should regard these women as the most valuable of our treasures, whose assistance we cannot do without.

Nikolai Morozov

The Terrorist Struggle

What is the likely fate of this new form of revolutionary struggle which could be called "terroristic revolution"?

In order to give a more or less positive answer to this question, it is important to review the meaning of the movement and its conditions.

Matters were as follows: at the head of the country was the all-powerful government with its spies, prisons, and guns, with its millions of soldiers and voluntary government servants who either knew or were ignorant of what they represented. It is the government against whom all the national uprisings and all the open revolutionary attempts of youth were helpless. It was a government that managed the country with an iron hand and was capable with one gesture of its leader to destroy tens of thousands of the obvious enemies. Against this large organization, the depressed, intelligent Russian youth brought forth a handful of people insignificant as to numbers but strong and terrible in their energy and elusiveness. The active, spontaneous revolutionary struggle was concentrated in this small group. To the pressure of the all-powerful enemy it opposed impenetrable secrecy.

Nikolai Morozov, *Terroristicheskaya Borba* (Geneva, 1880). This translation is reprinted from Feliks Gross, *Violence in Politics* (Mouton & Co., the Hague, 1972) with the kind permission of author and publisher.

This small group was not afraid of the enemy's numerous spies since it protected itself by the way it carried on the struggle; revolutionaries did not need to get close to a lot of strange, little-known people and were able to choose only those men for comrades in their small group who were already tested and trustworthy. The III section (of the secret police) knows how few members of this group fell into the hands of the government through the activity of the government's spies.

The revolutionary group is not afraid of bayonets and the government's army because it does not have to clash, in its struggle, with this blind and insensible force, which strikes down those whom it is ordered to strike. This force is only dreadful to the obvious enemy. Against the secret one it is completely useless.

The real danger lies in the carelessness among the revolutionaries since it may destroy individual members of the organization, but this destruction will be only temporary anyway. Elements from a better segment of society, which are hostile to government, will produce new members who will continue to work for the cause.

The revolutionary group is immortal because its way of struggle becomes a tradition and part of people's lives.

The secret assassination becomes a terrible weapon in the hands of such a group of people. "The 'Malicious Will' eternally bent to one viewpoint becomes extremely resourceful and there is no possibility of saving oneself from its assault." In such a way Russian newspapers described another attempt on the Tsar's life. It is true that human resourcefulness is unlimited.

No one would have believed before November 19 that in spite of all the police measures it would be possible to mine the railroad during the Tsar's return from Livadja. Before November 19 no one would have believed that the conspirators could penetrate to the Tsar's castle. But terroristic struggle has exactly this advantage that it can act unexpectedly and find means and ways which no one anticipates.

All that the terroristic struggle really needs is a small number of people and large material means.

This presents really a new form of struggle.

It replaces by a series of individual political assassinations, which always hit their target, the massive revolutionary movements, where people often rise against each other because of misunderstanding and where a nation kills off its own children, while the enemy of the people watches from a secure shelter and sees to it that the people of the organization are destroyed. The movement punishes only those who are really responsible for the evil deed. Because of this the terroristic revolution is the only just form of a revolution.

At the same time, it is also the most convenient form of a revolution.

Using insignificant forces it had an opportunity to restrain all the efforts of tyranny which seemed to be undefeated up to this time.

"Do not be afraid of the Tsar, do not be afraid of despotic rulers because all of them are weak and helpless against secret, sudden assassinations," it says to mankind.

This is the meaning of the movement which is now developing in Russia. Never before in history were there such convenient conditions for the existence of a revolutionary party and for such successful methods of struggle.

When a whole new row of independent terroristic societies will arise in Russia together with the already existing terroristic groups and when these groups will come to know each other during their struggle, they will all unite into one common organization. If this organization will start its activities against the government, and if the hard two-year struggles of Russian terrorists left any impressions on Russia's youth, then there can be no doubt that the last days of the monarchy and of brutal force will soon be over. A wide path will be open for socialist activities in Russia.

Terroristic movement in Russia has another distinctive feature, which we, its contemporaries, hardly notice, but which has an important meaning. This feature alone can bring about a turning point in the history of revolutionary struggle.

Hatred toward national oppressors was always powerful in mankind, and many times selfless people tried to destroy the life of the one who personified violence, at the price of their own lives. However, each time they tried, they perished. The act of human justice against tyranny had been accomplished but it was also followed by retribution.

In the deathly silence of the depressed witnesses the bloody executioner's block arose, human sacrifice was offered to the idol of monarchy, and national Nemesis lowered again its slightly raised head. The momentary satisfaction of higher justice was now dimmed by the destruction of a generous and selfless man. The very thought about the Tsar's assassination finally turned into something terrible and tragic. It soon evoked rather a notion of hopeless despair and magnanimous suicide than the idea of irreconcilable struggle with oppression . . . This thought told the people of terrible moral sufferings, of unbearable internal agony which the Tsar's killer had to live through, before he finished his account with life and accomplished his feat which appeared to be exceptional, unattainable and not normal. The Tsar knew that such magnanimous heroes were very few, and when he recovered from the first shock, he continued his reign of violence.

Contemporary terroristic struggle is not like this at all. Justice is done here, but those who carry it out remain alive. They disappear without a trace and thus they are able to fight again against the enemy, to live and to work for the cause. Sad feelings do not tarnish the realization of restored human dignity.

That was the struggle of despair and self-sacrifice; this is the struggle of force against force, of equal against equal; struggle of heroism against oppression, of knowledge and education against bayonets and gallows.

Now the struggle does not speak to people of hopelessness and self-sacrifice. No, now it tells them about the powerful love of freedom which is capable of making a hero out of a man, which can give people gigantic strength to accomplish almost superhuman deeds.

The tsars and despots who oppress the nation cannot live peacefully any longer in their palaces. The unseen revenger will let them know by a deafening explosion that their time has come and the despots will feel that the earth is collapsing under their feet among the sounds of music, the frightened screams of innumerable crowds, during the dessert at a refined dinner. . . .

. . . Terroristic struggle is equally possible under the absolute force or under the constitutional brutal force, in Russia as well as in Germany. Brutal force and despotism are always concentrated either in a few or more often in one ruling person (Bismarck, Napoleon) and stop with his failure or death. Such people should be destroyed in the very beginning of their career, be they chosen by an army or plebiscite. The wide and easy road opened in the country for ambitious people trying to strengthen their power on the remains of national freedom should be made hopeless and dangerous by anti-government terrorists. Thus, not too many volunteers will try to make use of it. In Russia, where rough force and despotism became traditional in the present dynasty, the course of terror became considerably complicated and perhaps a number of political assassinations and tsar killings are necessary. However, the contemporary terrorists who for two years fought the government, being supported only by the strength of their convictions, have shown that, even without clarifying the ideas of their struggle, it has many chances to succeed, even in this kingdom of despotism. Success of the terroristic movement will be inevitable if the future terroristic struggle will become a deed of not only one separate group, but of an idea, which cannot be destroyed by people. Then in place of those fighters who will perish, new ones and new revolutionaries will appear until the goal of the movement will be achieved.

The goal of the terroristic movement in our country should not become concentrated only on disarraying contemporary Russian despotism. The movement should make the struggle popular, historical, and grandiose. It should bring the way of struggle into the lives of people in such a manner that every new appearance of tyranny in the future will be met by new groups of people from the better elements of society, and these groups will destroy oppression by consecutive political assassinations. "Every man has a right to kill a tyrant and a nation cannot take away this right even from one of its citizens," said St. Just during the trial of Louis Capet. These words should become a slogan for the future struggle and violence.

There is no possibility to suppose that there won't be the necessary elements for this kind of struggle. Devotion to the idea, heroism and selflessness did not disappear from humanity during its darkest period of history, when it seems that oppression would crush the last gleam of life and consciousness of people. The gleam sparkled secretly in the heart of the country and broke free here and there as with a shot from Wilhelm Tell, or Babeuf's conspiracy or Decembrists' attempted struggle. The spontaneous, massive struggle against oppression throughout history was parallel to another struggle, which although unconscious and not systematic, nevertheless was continuous and irreconcilable. This other movement became evident because of a number of attempts at political assassinations. With every centennial this struggle became more energetic and active and never were the attempts on the Tsar's life so numerous as in the last thirty years. There were the following facts concerning the struggle of underground fighters from 1848, without taking into account numerous assassinations and attempts at assassination of public statesmen of Russia and America: attempt on the life of the Count of Modena, attempt to assassinate a Prussian prince, attempt on the life of Queen Victoria, seriously wounding Emperor Francis Joseph on the bastions of Vienna, attempt on the life of Victor Emmanuel, assassination of Ferdinand III of Parma, attempt on the life of the Spanish Queen, wounding of Ferdinand of Naples by bayonets, shooting of Queen of Greece, assassination of Prince Mikhail of Serbia, attempt on life of Humbert, two attempts on life of King Alfonso during his short reign, four attempts on life of Wilhelm, wounding him twice seriously, six attempts to assassinate Napoleon III in all possible ways, six attempts on life of Emperor Alexander II, of which only one was discovered while being carried out.

All these actions, which were carried out continuously and consequently at the time when the terroristic struggle had not yet been turned into a system, deprives of all foundation the assumption that these actions would cease in the future when terror acquires theoretical foundation.

But there is another reason which makes such assumption unlikely. We know that any historical struggle, any historical development, will move along the line of least resistance. All offsprings of movement turning to another direction bruise themselves against the obstacles they encounter on their way. Terroristic struggle which strikes at the weakest spot of the existing system will obviously be universally accepted in life. The time will come when the present, unsystematic attempts will merge into one wide stream and then no despotism or brutal force will be able to stand up against them. The task of the contemporary Russian terrorists is to summarize theoretically and to systematize practically this form of revolutionary struggle, which goes on for a long time. Political assassinations alone should become an expression of this rich, consistent system.

We know the importance of the influence of ideas on man. In distant antiquity these ideas brought about Christianity and from fires and crosses they foretold near freedom to the world. In the dark calm of medieval ages they were responsible for the Crusades and for many years they attracted people to the dry and unfertile plains of Palestine. In the last 100 years these ideas summoned revolutionary and socialist movements, and the fields of Europe and America were covered with the blood of new fighters for freedom and humanity.

When a small handful of people appears to represent the struggle of a whole nation and is triumphant over millions of enemies, then the idea of terroristic struggle will not die once it is clarified for the people and proven that it can be practical. Each act of violence and force will give birth to new revengers and each tyrant will create new Solovjevs and Nobilings. Thus, the very existence of despotism and monarchy will quickly become impossible.

Furthermore, it will not be difficult for the revolutionaries-terrorists, once they have succeeded, to direct their efforts to the preparation of social revolution of the whole nation. All the same, the ideas of the revolutionaries will live in the memories of the masses, and every manifestation of violence (on the part of government) will bring forth new terroristic groups. It will not be known where these groups will disappear to, or where they will come from.

Russian terrorists have two highly important tasks.

1. They should clarify theoretically the idea of terroristic struggle, which up to now is understood differently by different people. Along with the preaching of socialism, preaching on future struggle is essential among these classes of population where propaganda is still possible despite the unfavorable conditions. This can be accomplished because these classes, by their customs and traditions, are close to the revolutionary party. Only then will the struggle receive an influx of fresh forces from the population, and these forces are essential for a determined and long struggle.

2. The terroristic party should show in practice the usefulness of the means it employs. The party should bring about the final disorganization, demoralization, and weakening of government for its actions of violence against freedom. This should be achieved through a consistent, punishing system used by terrorists. This system should make the government weak and incapable of taking any measures for the oppression of freedom of thought and against actions carried out for the national welfare.

By accomplishing these two tasks the terroristic party will establish its way of struggle as a traditional one and will destroy the very possibility of despotism's recurrence in the future.

The future will show if the contemporary terrorists will live up to their standards. We are, however, deeply convinced that the terroristic movement will overcome all the obstacles in its way; the triumph of the cause will show all the antagonists that the terroristic movement fully satisfies the conditions of contemporary reality, which put this form of struggle in the forefront.

G. Tarnovski

Terrorism and Routine

The terrorist revolution is a pointed manifestation of the abnormalities of social relations in Russia. This is the "direct correlation"; in other words, these are the causes of terrorism.

As to its significance and consequence, even here our author [Dragomanov] does not betray himself; he does not acknowledge its social significance although he does not deny its political meaning.

Do you realize, Mr. Dragomanov, that in these matters it is now time to stop imparting a special importance to the titles of school textbooks and to stop looking at public life as if it was a set of categories with political types in one section and social life in quite a different one?

You ask, what significance can a few crowned heads have in the annihilation of social slavery? We do not know whether there can be any such question from the point of view of routine word games or appropriateness, but, as far as real progress is concerned, there can be no question at all. Where the full social liberation of mankind is concerned, political freedom, as we have defined it above, and the republic, are the first steps without which the rest is impossible. This is the real metaphysical point of view on this question; the existence of crowned vampires, kings, and czars is far from being a matter of indifference.

When you speak about self-defense and public defense (terrorism), you refer to the latter as "secret," wishing to imply something dirty by the use of this title. Kovalsky defended his fiat against evil-doers and robbers, gun in hand; as you so truly observe, amongst honorable people there can be no two opinions about this. But some people have made a generalization about this and have wished to strike one of the main perpetrators of death, not just Kovalsky. These people have decided to strike a blow at the very system of crime enmeshing Russia. In other words, they have moved from their own to a public point of view. "This," you say, "is dirty."

* G. Tarnovski (g. Romanenko): *Terrorizm i Rutina* (Geneva, 1880).

In your opinion the necessary defense of an isolated individual is praiseworthy. You say, however, that the public conscience denies the whole nation's right to necessary defense.

This is what we shall say to you this time, Mr. Dragomanov. Terrorists, the defenders of the people, have the right to ignore the public conscience which "always denies" the defense of the people. This is the conscience of the society whose representatives are the Alexander IIs, the Totlebens, the Tolstoys, persons with interests hostile to the people. If their "conscience" rises against terrorists, that is perfectly natural. And the fact that you were unable to renounce the views of this "society" and decided to look at terrorists through their moral glass is very, very sad.

With regard to the attacks on the moral aspect of terrorism, let us set down a few words. Let us suppose you, Mr. Dragomanov, to be "in the gray depths of eternity." Let us take any revolt aiming to save one's homeland, let us take the revolt led by Mucius Scaevola. Was that not a lofty, even heroic exploit, so morally beyond dispute that it is even glorified in children's school textbooks?

But we are now bounded by the prosaic present. Before us is a gang of worthless louts exploiting poor, hungry Russia, writhing in a wild frenzy on ground spattered with the blood of the finest people. At its head is the Czar, without heart or reason, who has made it his aim to stifle all those who show signs of life. The defense of public life has passed into the hands of people who have decided to rid Russia of the tyrant, whatever the cost. What will you say to that? "Immoral," replies your article. One case is lofty and the other, exactly the same, is disgusting. It is only disgusting because it is "not accepted," it is only immoral because it is taking place in front of your very eyes in circumstances to which you are used to applying the narrow criterion of the status quo.

No, Mr. Dragomanov: If the main aim of your work is to preserve "innocence" of this kind, you should not allow yourself into the sphere of politics and national liberation. Here, there are other aims and another criterion. For the good of the homeland we have to sacrifice this foreign way of life and not stand too much in awe of our own way of life. Here, he who takes upon himself the courage to judge such historical facts as revolution, whether of the masses or of terrorists, must be able to renounce conventional morality and raise himself to the natural laws of justice and morality. And from this point of view of the highest justice, all revolution as a means of liberating the people is moral, already moral because it gives the people the possibility of living a moral way of life.

Morals are inconceivable without freedom. Under the pressure of despotism there is subjection, hypocrisy, venality. There are not and cannot be morals because there is neither individual free choice nor self-determination. Thus are the development of society and the well-being of a nation the consequences of a successful revolution. And in the social sense only that is moral which furthers society's freedom, development, and material benefit. Everything hostile to this is immoral and is destined to destruction in the view of every thinking person. And that is not all.

Every member of society must, in the name of these same morals, be determined that the suffering borne by the people during the revolution should be reduced to the minimum and should not be in vain, that is to say, that the revolution should achieve its aim to the greatest extent possible. Furthermore, it should remove the very possibility of repeating in the future those actions which were the cause of the people's suffering. In this regard one must not forget that steps toward freedom were and are made in history only under the excesses of tyranny and in the face of historical movement. Consequently, it is only in such a movement that the people can find a safe measure against the encroachments of despotism. These are the bases on which to estimate the moral worth of revolution. And if we compare, for example, popular revolution (on which you comment further) as a means of attaining political freedom with terrorist revolution, with a system of political murders, then it is not hard to convince oneself which form to prefer.

During a popular revolution the greatest strength of the nation, its soldiers, perish, while those same perpetrators of evil calmly observe the conduct of the battle and at the critical moment bolt from the rear wing, as did Louis Philippe, or remain in their place, having temporarily put on sheep's clothing but ready at the first opportunity to cast it off and take up their former trade again. Sometimes this is the essence of tragi-comedy in reality: the blood of the innocent flows in rivers and the results are the more trivial as more blood is spilled and as the people grow more weary.

Terrorist revolution is not like this. Even when a few innocent people do suffer, as with the soldiers during the explosion at the Winter Palace, that is a straightforward "*casus belli.*" Terrorism directs its blows against the real perpetrators of evil. When the suffering of the people is ended, the meaning of the revolt will crystallize: it will become more intelligible to the public consciousness and will educate the people to despise despotism. The government itself helps in this; as is its usual custom, it intensifies its atrocities which are purposeless, even harmful to itself, but on which everything that is savage, uncontrollable, and mindless relies in such circumstances.

Like everything new and unprecedented, terrorist revolution at first brings a certain perturbation into society, but the greater part of society has understood what it stands for. This initial confusion changes to jeers and anger directed against the despot and it moves to sympathize with the revolution. Its outcome is practically assured; it now depends solely on the mind and energy of those who practice it.

Also, the position of the representatives of autocracy is completely changed by the presence of terrorism as a system.

From the point of view of a healthy social morality, the removal of those individuals who bring down a whole nation to the level of a herd in order to exploit and humiliate it is a duty prescribed by the laws of natural justice for everyone who still retains even a fraction of consciousness or humanity untainted by slavery.

The life of a tyrant changes from one of luxurious, sensuous ease to that of a tormented life full of tragedy of the kind paraded in front of our eyes by the Czar, trembling every moment for his criminal existence. And nowhere will he find a word of compassion; everyone, gazing at these Macbeth-like agonies will say maliciously, "Thieves never prosper." The true value of the Czar's position will become clear.

This is the wise way to national liberation. *"C'est une révolution vraiment scientifique,"* as a certain Frenchman said of Russian terrorism. Understand that well, gentlemen, and don't forget it! Remember that terrorist revolution is completely moral in its aims, more reasonable, humanitarian, and consequently more ethical in the methods which it uses than mass revolution.

Considering terrorism from the point of view of "purity of methods," we shall not bore ourselves and our readers by analyzing the models of deep thinking and consistency with which Mr. Dragomanov's essentially petty article is crammed. Let us move on directly to the finale and to Mr. Dragomanov's concluding suggestion.

Here is what the author of "Terrorism and Freedom" says on page 11 of his article. "We believe that political murders, even setting aside their moral inconvenience" (how he loves this word "convenience"), "have only a negative significance: they humiliate the government but do not subvert it." (But surely subversion is not a negative manifestation.) "In our view only an open attack on the political structure can lead Russia into a new path." (Here the same attack already appears to be positive; there is even a guide on the "new path.") "This attack by word and deed on the part of properly organized political societies is composed of citizens and soldiers in all Russia's territories and among all her peoples."

Mr. Dragomanov does not agree with the "authors of the Petersburg Proclamations"; he believes that terror cannot achieve freedom. Why? Because the results will only be negative. What a truly pedestrian argument!

At the beginning of this century, when railways were being constructed in France, the "eminent" Thiers disputed their value, arguing that such an undertaking was impracticable because "the wheels would not turn round." This advocate of conservatism was, of course, completely ignorant about engineering but had to think up some "sufficient basis" for argument against this innovation which no well-run state had ever tried before. That is why he stated that "the wheels will not turn round." Our author too, in trying to find similar "bases" for his argument, has come up with the phrase "negative results." How could you lose sight of the fact that the difference between negative and positive results is relative and has no objective meaning? We can express one and the same idea both positively and negatively. We can say that a man is full or not hungry, stupid or not clever. If you like, one can express the term "progress" negatively as the destruction of arbitrary rule and exploitation in all its forms.

If you do not find these examples of plain common sense quite clear or sufficiently convincing, remember Hegel's famous abstract, and yet entertaining, words "Life and non-life are identical" and hold on to his meaning.

And now tell me, is it possible to construct a negation of terrorism on such a negative basis? What will happen is that you will not deny its results but will only obscure them with a kind of mist with which you will adorn your final proposal "to lead Russia into a new path." What do you mean by this "open attack"? If you see here mass revolution, do you consider it possible and reasonable to arouse the Russian common man to fight for political freedom, bearing in mind his historical separation from the intelligentsia, his life of want and his hard struggle for a piece of bread? He will have to be truly imbued with the need for political freedom.

Is it so hard to understand that all your "citizens and soldiers," all your "peoples" belong essentially to the intelligentsia? This intelligentsia is thus obliged, yes obliged, to bear political freedom in Russia upon its shoulders, using terror as its means.

You, however, deny terrorism because of its "moral inconvenience." What will remain of your "program of action" after such denial and self-denial? "Pure means," "absolutely pure methods," "moral comfort," in other words, "Misery have a heart."

We draw this conclusion:

It is unsuitable to launch out onto the open sea of national liberation with a moral compass and ill-assorted luggage fit only for home life. You will not heed this until you find yourselves on a tow-boat with the Czar's henchmen.

Serge Stepniak-Kravchinski

Underground Russia

The government, however, seemed bent on exasperating not only the liberals but also the revolutionists. With a vile desire for vengeance, it redoubled its cruelty against the socialists, whom it had in its power. The Emperor Alexander II even went so far as to annul the sentence of his own senate, which, under the form of a petition for pardon, acquitted most of the accused in the trial of the 193.

What government therefore was this which acted so insolently against all the laws of the country, which was not supported, and did not wish to be supported, by the nation, or by any class, or by the laws which it had made itself? What did it represent except brute force?

Against such a government everything is permitted. It is no longer a guardian of the will of the people, or of the majority of the people. It is organized injustice. A citizen is no more bound to respect it than to respect a band of highwaymen who employ the force at their command in rifling travelers.

Serge Stepniak-Kravchinski: *Underground Russia* (London, 1883).

But how shake off this *camarilla* entrenched behind a forest of bayonets? How free the country from it?

It being absolutely impossible to overcome this obstacle by force, as in other countries more fortunate than ours, a flank movement was necessary, so as to fall upon this *camarilla* before it could avail itself of its forces, thus rendered useless in their impregnable positions.

Thus arose the terrorism.

Conceived in hatred, nurtured by patriotism and by hope, it grew up in the electrical atmosphere, impregnated with the enthusiasm awakened by an act of heroism.

On August 16, 1878, that is five months after the acquittal of Zassulic, the terrorism, by putting to death General Mesentzeff, the head of the police and of the entire *camarilla*, boldly threw down its glove in the face of autocracy. From that day forth it advanced with giant strides, acquiring strength and position, and culminating in the tremendous duel with the man who was the personification of despotism.

I will not relate its achievements, for they are written in letters of fire upon the records of history.

Three times the adversaries met face to face. Three times the terrorist by the will of fate was overthrown, but after each defeat he arose more threatening and powerful than before. To the attempt of Solovieff succeeded that of Hartman, which was followed by the frightful explosion at the Winter Palace, the infernal character of which seemed to surpass everything the imagination could conceive. But it was surpassed on March 13. Once more the adversaries grappled with each other, and this time the omnipotent Emperor fell half dead to the ground.

The terrorist had won the victory in his tremendous duel, which had cost so many sacrifices. With a whole nation prostrate he alone held high his head, which throughout so many tempests he had never bent.

He is noble, terrible, irresistibly fascinating, for he combines in himself the two sublimities of human grandeur: the martyr and the hero.

He is a martyr. From the day when he swears in the depths of his heart to free the people and the country, he knows he is consecrated to death. He faces it at every step of his stormy life. He goes forth to meet it fearlessly, when necessary, and can die without flinching, not like a Christian of old, but like a warrior accustomed to look death in the face.

He has no longer any religious feeling in his disposition. He is a wrestler, all bone and muscle, and has nothing in common with the dreamy idealist of the previous luster. He is a mature man, and the unreal dreams of his youth have disappeared with years. He is a socialist fatally convinced, but he understands that a social revolution requires long preparatory labor, which cannot be given until political liberty is acquired. Modest and resolute, therefore, he clings to the resolution to limit for the present his plans that he may extend them afterward. He has no other object than to overthrow this abhorred despotism, and to give to his country what all civilized nations possess, political liberty, to enable it to advance with a firm step toward its own redemption. The force of mind, the indomitable energy, and the spirit of sacrifice which his predecessor attained in the beauty of his dreams, he attains in the grandeur of his mission, in the strong passions which this marvelous, intoxicating, vertiginous struggle arouses in his heart.

What a spectacle! When had such a spectacle been seen before? Alone, obscure, poor, he undertook to be the defender of outraged humanity, of right trampled underfoot, and he challenged to the death the most powerful empire in the world, and for years and years confronted all its immense forces.

Proud as Satan rebelling against God, he opposed his own will to that of the man who alone, amid a nation of slaves, claimed the right of having a will. But how different is this terrestrial god from the old Jehovah of Moses! How he hides his trembling head under the daring blows of the terrorist! True, he still stands erect, and the thunderbolts launched by his trembling hand often fail; but when they strike, they kill. But the terrorist is immortal. His limbs may fail him, but, as if by magic, they regain their vigor, and he stands erect, ready for battle after battle until he has laid low his enemy and liberated the country. And already he sees that enemy falter, become confused, cling desperately to the wildest means, which can only hasten his end.

It is this absorbing struggle, it is this imposing mission, it is this certainty of approaching victory, which gives him that cool and calculating enthusiasm, that almost superhuman energy, which astounds the world. If he is by nature a man capable of generous impulses, he will become a hero; if he is of stronger fiber, it will harden into iron; if of iron, it will become adamant.

He has a powerful and distinctive individuality. He is no longer, like his predecessor, all abnegation. He no longer possesses, he no longer strives after, that abstract moral beauty which made the propagandist resemble a being of another world; for his look is no longer directed inwardly but is fixed upon the hated enemy. He is the type of individual force, intolerant of every yoke. He fights not only for the people, to render them the arbiters of their own destinies, not only for the whole nation stifling in this pestiferous atmosphere, but also for himself; for the dear ones whom he loves, whom he adores with all the enthusiasm which animates his soul; for his friends, who languish in the horrid cells of the central prisons, and who stretch forth to him their skinny hands imploring aid. He fights for himself. He has sworn to be free and he will be free, in defiance of everything. He bends his haughty head before no idol. He has devoted his sturdy arms to the cause of the people. But he no longer deifies them. And if the people, ill-counseled, say to him "Be a slave," he will exclaim "No"; and he will march onward, defying their imprecations and their fury, certain that justice will be rendered to him in his tomb.

Such is the terrorist. . . .

The isolation of the Russian government can only be compared with that of a hated foreigner in a conquered country. The best proof of this is, as I have already said, its inability to overcome the terrorists. To illustrate this, however, I will relate a few little incidents of revolutionary life.

It must be admitted, to begin with, that, as conspirators, the Russian revolutionists, with few exceptions, are not worth much. The Russian disposition, generous, listless, undisciplined; the love of openness; the habit of doing everything "in common," render it little adapted to conform to the vital principle of conspiracy; to tell what is to be told only to those to whom it is essential to tell it, and not to those to whom it may merely be told without danger. Examples such as Perovskaia or Stefanovic are very rare among the Russians. Thus, the revolutionary secrets are usually very badly kept, and no sooner have they passed out of the organization than they spread abroad with incredible rapidity throughout the nihilist world, and not unfrequently pass from city to city. Notwithstanding this, the government never knows anything.

Thus, before the publication of the newspaper *Zemlia i Volia*, conducted by "illegal" men, a secret revolutionary and socialist journal was issued in St. Petersburg,—Nacialo, which was not the organ of the organization, but of an isolated "circle," and its conductors were four or five "legal" men. All St. Petersburg knew them, and could name them. But the police, although they were run off their legs in search of traces of this newspaper, knew nothing, and never learnt anything about it; so that some of the conductors of the paper, who have not been compromised in other matters, remain safe and sound to this day.

The sale of the most terrible of the terrorist papers, the *Narodnaia Volia*, is carried on in St. Petersburg in the most simple manner imaginable; in every higher school, in every class of society, and in all the principal provincial towns, there are men, known to everybody, who undertake this commission; and receiving a certain number of the copies of the paper, sell it to everybody who wants it, at twenty-five kopecks the number in St. Petersburg, and thirty-five in the provinces.

Here is another fact, which will seem much more strange, but which, notwithstanding, is perfectly true.

The immense dynamite conspiracy, organized by the executive committee in 1879, for the Emperor's journey to and from St. Petersburg and the Crimea, perhaps the greatest undertaking ever organized by a secret society: this conspiracy was on too grand a scale to be carried out by the forces of the organization alone; outsiders had therefore to be taken from that vast world around it which is always ready to render it any kind of service. It is not to be wondered at that, with so many people, the secret of the attempts in preparation should leak out, and quickly spread throughout all Russia. The precise places were not known, certainly; but every student, every barrister, every writer not in the pay of the police, knew that "the Imperial train would be blown up during the journey from the Crimea to St. Petersburg." It was talked about "everywhere," as the phrase runs. In one city a subscription was even got up, almost publicly, for this purpose, and about 1,500 roubles were collected, all of which were paid into the coffers of the committee.

Yet the police knew nothing. Of the six attempts belonging to that period, one alone was discovered, that of Logovenco, by mere chance. The arrest of Goldenberg with a supply of dynamite, which also occurred by mere chance, at the Elisabetgrad Station, was the circumstance which aroused suspicion that something was in preparation, and caused precautions to be taken in the arrangements of the trains.

These facts, and others of the same kind which I could multiply indefinitely, give an idea, it appears to me, of the respective positions of the government and the revolutionists.

The terrorists have before them, not a government in the European sense of the word—for then, owing to the disproportion of strength, the struggle would be impossible—but a *camarilla*, a small and isolated faction, which represents only its own interests, and is not supported by any class of society.

Thus the struggle, although extremely difficult, becomes possible, and may last for years and years.

What will be the end?

That depends upon the line of conduct adopted by the government.

One thing is evident; it will never succeed in putting down the terrorism by retaliation. Precisely because they are few, the terrorists will remain invincible. A victory obtained over a revolution like that of Paris gives to the conqueror at least ten or fifteen years of peace; for with a hundred thousand victims, all that is noblest, most generous, and boldest in a nation is exterminated, and it languishes until a fresh generation arises to avenge its slaughtered fathers. But what avails in a country like Russia, the loss of a handful of men, which from time to time the government succeeds in snatching from the ranks of the organization?

The survivors will continue the struggle with an ardor increased by the desire of vengeance. The universal discontent will provide them with pecuniary means. The young men, animated as they are by the example of so many heroes, are near to supply an immense and inexhaustible source of new recruits; and the struggle will continue still more fiercely.

But if the terrorists cannot be overcome, how are they to overcome the government?

A victory, immediate, splendid, and decisive, such as that obtained by an insurrection, is utterly impossible by means of terrorism. But another victory is more probable, that of the weak against the strong, that of the "beggars" of Holland against the Spaniards. In a struggle against an invisible, impalpable, omnipresent enemy, the strong is vanquished, not by the arms of his adversary, but by the continuous tension of his own strength, which exhausts him, at last, more than he would be exhausted by defeats.

Such is precisely the position of the belligerent parties in Russia.

The terrorists cannot overthrow the government, cannot drive it from St. Petersburg and Russia; but having compelled it, for so many years running, to neglect everything and do nothing but struggle with them, by forcing it to do so still for years and years, they will render its position untenable. Already the prestige of the imperial government has received a wound which it will be very difficult to heal. An emperor who shuts himself up in a prison from fear of the terrorists, is certainly not a figure to inspire admiration.

On this point I could already cite many things which circulate in the army, and among the people. What will be said if he remains shut up another year or two? And how can he do otherwise than remain shut up if he continues his policy?

But it is not on the moral side alone that the government is the worse off.

In this struggle between liberty and despotism, the revolutionists, it must be confessed, have on their side an immense advantage, that of time. Every month, every week, of this hesitation, of this irresolution, of this enervating tension, renders the position of their adversary worse, and consequently strengthens their own.

Pyotr Kropotkin

The Spirit of Revolt

There are periods in the life of human society when revolution becomes an imperative necessity, when it proclaims itself as inevitable. New ideas germinate everywhere, seeking to force their way into the light, to find an application in life; everywhere they are opposed by the inertia of those whose interest it is to maintain the old order; they suffocate in the stifling atmosphere of prejudice and traditions. The accepted ideas of the constitution of the state, of the laws of social equilibrium, of the political and economic interrelations of citizens, can hold out no longer against the implacable criticism which is daily undermining them whenever occasion arises—in drawing room as in

First published in *Le Révolté* (Geneva, 1880), translated by Arnold Roller (i.e., Siegfried Nacht).

cabaret, in the writings of philosophers as in daily conversation. Political, economic, and social institutions are crumbling; the social structure, having become uninhabitable, is hindering, even preventing, the development of the seeds which are being propagated within its damaged walls and being brought forth around them.

The need for a new life becomes apparent. The code of established morality, that which governs the greater number of people in their daily life, no longer seems sufficient. What formerly seems just is now felt to be a crying injustice. The morality of yesterday is today recognized as revolting immorality. The conflict between new ideas and old traditions flames up in every class of society, in every possible environment, in the very bosom of the family. The son struggles against his father, he finds revolting what his father has all his life found natural; the daughter rebels against the principles which her mother has handed down to her as the result of long experience. Daily, the popular conscience rises up against the scandals which breed amidst the privileged and the leisured, against the crimes committed in the name of *the law of the stronger*, or in order to maintain these privileges. Those who long for the triumph of justice, those who would put new ideas into practice, are soon forced to recognize that the realization of their generous, humanitarian, and regenerating ideas cannot take place in a society thus constituted; they perceive the necessity of a revolutionary whirlwind which will sweep away all this rottenness, revive sluggish hearts with its breath, and bring to mankind that spirit of devotion, self-denial, and heroism, without which society sinks through degradation and vileness into complete disintegration.

In periods of frenzied haste toward wealth, of feverish speculation and of crisis, of the sudden downfall of great industries and the ephemeral expansion of other branches of production, of scandalous fortunes amassed in a few years and dissipated as quickly, it becomes evident that the economic institutions which control production and exchange are far from giving to society the prosperity which they are supposed to guarantee; they produce precisely the opposite result. Instead of order they bring forth chaos; instead of prosperity, poverty and insecurity; instead of reconciled interests, war; a perpetual war of the exploiter against the worker, of exploiters and of workers among themselves. Human society is seen to be splitting more and more into two hostile camps, and at the same time to be subdividing into thousands of small groups waging merciless war against each other. Weary of these wars, weary of the miseries which they cause, society rushes to seek a new organization; it clamors loudly for a complete remodeling of the system of property ownership, of production, of exchange and all economic relations which spring from it.

The machinery of government, entrusted with the maintenance of the existing order, continues to function, but at every turn of its deteriorated gears it slips and stops. Its working becomes more and more difficult, and the dissatisfaction caused by its defects grows continuously. Every day gives rise to a new demand. "Reform this," "Reform that," is heard from all sides. "War, finance, taxes, courts, police, everything must be remodeled, reorganized, established on a new basis," say the reformers. And yet all know that it is impossible to make things over, to remodel anything at all because everything is interrelated; everything would have to be remade at once; and how can society be remodeled when it is divided into two openly hostile camps? To satisfy the discontented would be only to create new malcontents.

Incapable of undertaking reforms, since this would mean paving the way for revolution, and at the same time too impotent to be frankly reactionary, the governing bodies apply themselves to half-measures which can satisfy nobody, and only cause new dissatisfaction. The mediocrities who, in such transition periods, undertake to steer the ship of state, think of but one thing: to enrich themselves against the coming debacle. Attacked from all sides they defend themselves awkwardly, they evade, they commit blunder upon blunder, and they soon succeed in cutting the last rope of salvation; they drown the prestige of the government in ridicule, caused by their own incapacity.

Such periods demand revolution. It becomes a social necessity; the situation itself is revolutionary.

When we study in the works of our greatest historians the genesis and development of vast revolutionary convulsions we generally find under the heading, "The Cause of the Revolution," a gripping picture of the situation on the eve of events. The misery of the people, the general insecurity, the vexatious measures of the government, the odious scandals laying bare the immense vices of society, the new ideas struggling to come to the surface and repulsed by the incapacity of the supporters of the former regime—nothing is omitted. Examining this picture, one arrives at the conviction that the revolution was indeed inevitable, and that there was no other way out than by the road of insurrection.

Take, for example, the situation before 1789 as the historians picture it. You can almost hear the peasant complaining of the salt tax, of the tithe, of the feudal payments, and vowing in his heart an implacable hatred toward the feudal baron, the monk, the monopolist, the bailiff. You can almost see the citizen bewailing the loss of his municipal liberties, and showering maledictions upon the king. The people censure the queen; they are revolted by the reports of ministerial action, and they cry out continually that the taxes are intolerable and revenue payments exorbitant, that crops are bad and winters hard, that provisions are too dear and the monopolists too grasping, that the village lawyer devours the peasant's crops and the village constable tries to play the role of a petty king, that even the mail service is badly organized and the employees too lazy. In short, nothing works well, everybody complains. "It can last no longer, it will come to a bad end," they cry everywhere.

But, between this pacific arguing and insurrection or revolt, there is a wide abyss—that abyss which, for the greatest part of humanity, lies between reasoning and action, thought and will—the urge to act. How has this abyss been bridged? How is it that men who only yesterday were complaining quietly of their lot as they smoked their pipes, and the next moment were humbly saluting the local guard and gendarme whom they had just been abusing—how is it that these same men a few days later were capable of seizing their scythes and their iron-shod pikes and attacking in his castle the lord who only yesterday was so formidable? By what miracle were these men, whose wives justly called them cowards, transformed in a day into heroes, marching through bullets and cannon balls to the conquest of their rights? How was it that *words*, so often spoken and lost in the air like the empty chiming of bells, were changed into *actions?*

The answer is easy.

Action, the continuous action, ceaselessly renewed, of minorities brings about this transformation. Courage, devotion, the spirit of sacrifice, are as contagious as cowardice, submission, and panic.

What forms will this action take? All forms—indeed, the most varied forms, dictated by circumstances, temperament, and the means at disposal. Sometimes tragic, sometimes humorous, but always daring; sometimes collective, sometimes purely individual, this policy of action will neglect none of the means at hand, no event of public life, in order to keep the spirit alive, to propagate and find expression for dissatisfaction, to excite hatred against exploiters, to ridicule the government and expose its weakness, and above all and always, by actual example, to awaken courage and fan the spirit of revolt.

When a revolutionary situation arises in a country, before the spirit of revolt is sufficiently awakened in the masses to express itself in violent demonstrations in the streets or by rebellions and uprisings, it is through *action* that minorities succeed in awakening that feeling of independence and that spirit of audacity without which no revolution can come to a head.

Men of courage, not satisfied with words, but ever searching for the means to transform them into action—men of integrity for whom the act is one with the idea, for whom prison, exile, and death are preferable to a life contrary to their principles—intrepid souls who know that it is necessary to *dare* in order to succeed—these are the lonely sentinels who enter the battle long before the masses are sufficiently roused to raise openly the banner of insurrection and to march, arms in hand, to the conquest of their rights.

In the midst of discontent, talk, theoretical discussions, an individual or collective act of revolt supervenes, symbolizing the dominant aspirations. It is possible that at the beginning the masses will remain indifferent. It is possible that while admiring the courage of the individual or the group which takes the initiative, the masses will at first follow those who are prudent and cautious, who will immediately describe this act as "insanity" and say that "those madmen, those fanatics will endanger everything."

They have calculated so well, those prudent and cautious men, that their party, slowly pursuing its work would, in a hundred years, two hundred years, three hundred years perhaps, succeed in conquering the whole world—and now the unexpected intrudes! The unexpected, of course, is whatever has not been expected by them—those prudent and cautious ones! Whoever has a slight knowledge of history and a fairly clear head knows perfectly well from the beginning that theoretical propaganda for revolution will necessarily express itself in action long before the theoreticians have decided that the moment to act has come. Nevertheless the cautious theoreticians are angry at these madmen, they excommunicate them, they anathematize them. But the madmen win sympathy, the mass of the people secretly applaud their courage, and they find imitators. In proportion as the pioneers go to fill the jails and the penal colonies, others continue their work; acts of illegal protest, of revolt, of vengeance, multiply.

Indifference from this point on is impossible. Those who at the beginning never so much as asked what the "madmen" wanted are compelled to think about them, to discuss their ideas, to take sides for or against. By actions which compel general attention, the new idea seeps into people's minds and wins converts. One such act may, in a few days, make more propaganda than thousands of pamphlets.

Above all, it awakens the spirit of revolt: it breeds daring. The old order, supported by the police, the magistrates, the gendarmes and the soldiers, appeared unshakable, like the old fortress of the Bastille, which also appeared impregnable to the eyes of the unarmed people gathered beneath its high walls equipped with loaded cannon. But soon it became apparent that the established order has not the force one had supposed. One courageous act has sufficed to upset in a few days the entire governmental machine, to make the colossus tremble; another revolt has stirred a whole province into turmoil, and the army, till now always so imposing, has retreated before a handful of peasants armed with sticks and stones. The people observe that the monster is not so terrible as they thought; they begin dimly to perceive that a few energetic efforts will be sufficient to throw it down. Hope is born in their hearts, and let us remember that if exasperation often drives men to revolt, it is always hope, the hope of victory, which makes revolutions.

The government resists; it is savage in its repressions. But, though formerly persecution killed the energy of the oppressed, now, in periods of excitement, it produces the opposite result. It provokes new acts of revolt, individual and collective; it drives the rebels to heroism; and in rapid succession these acts spread, become general, develop. The revolutionary party is strengthened by elements which up to this time were hostile or indifferent to it. The general disintegration penetrates into the government, the ruling classes, the privileged; some of them advocate resistance to the limit; others are in favor of concessions; others, again, go so far as to declare themselves ready to renounce their privileges for the moment, in order to appease the spirit of revolt, hoping to dominate again later on. The unity of the government and the privileged class is broken.

The ruling classes may also try to find safety in savage reaction. But it is now too late; the battle only becomes more bitter, more terrible, and the revolution which is looming will only be more bloody. On the other hand, the smallest concession of the governing classes, since it comes too late, since it has been snatched in struggle, only awakes the revolutionary spirit still more. The common people, who formerly would have been satisfied with the smallest concession, observe now that the enemy is wavering; they foresee victory, they feel their courage growing, and the same men who were formerly crushed by misery and were content to sigh in secret, now lift their heads and march proudly to the conquest of a better future.

Finally the revolution breaks out, the more terrible as the preceding struggles were bitter.

Jean Maitron

The Era of the Attentats

What gave rise to these notorious attacks, for three years a constant theme of press reports, and why did they diminish after the Trial of the Thirty and eventually disappear altogether at the end of 1894? This is a question of historical philosophy rather than of history, variously answered according to individual judgment.

On the theoretical level, we have seen that "propaganda by deed," primarily conceived as a lesson in matters of socialism, came to be considered exclusively as an act of terrorism and was propagated in that form from 1880 to 1888 by the French anarchist groups. Disregarding the events at Montceau les Mines, which had some characteristics of a collective revolt, and the bomb in the Bellecour theater in Lyons, responsibility for which was never claimed, it cannot be said that, at that time, this terrorist propaganda led to effective action. It is not difficult to understand the reasons for this. In essence, they are to be found in two facts: on the one hand, the workers, the object of this propaganda, were too wise in revolutionary experience to indulge themselves in acts only too clearly fruitless; on the other hand, with all the possibilities of legal action available under the state, they must first be used, perhaps combined with some unlawful activity, but without lapsing into a nihilism whose violence barely hid its impotence.

Jean Maitron, *Histoire du Mouvement Anarchiste en France 1880–1914* (Paris, 1955).

It is nevertheless the case that, although displaced in time by some ten years, a terrorist era did begin in 1892. The essentially individual acts involved certainly reflected the traditional kind of anarchist activity; yet why did they come to the fore in 1892 rather than at the time when every single issue of the anarchist press counseled them?

The reason is simple; it was indicated by the accused themselves. It was to avenge Decamps, Dardare, and Léveillé, the victims of police brutality on May 1, 1891, that Ravachol planted his bombs. Once raised to the status of a martyr for anarchy's sake, Ravachol inspired avengers who, martyrs in their turn, engendered new terrorists. . . . Such was the chance cause which lay at the root of the attacks and outrages. . . .

Certain other factors helped to spread the epidemic rather than check it. In this connection, the attitude of socialist groups, particularly the Guesdist party, may be considered. Their hostility could scarcely be distinguished from that of the bourgeois parties and may, by reaction, have reinforced the comrades' solidarity with the propagandists by deed.

Terrorist action also fed upon the corruption among the nation's elected representatives, one third of whom were implicated in the Panama scandal. Well might Drumont write ". . . From the mud of Panama are born men of blood, grotesque, misshapen beings like the monsters which emerged from the silt of the Flood, men prey to a dreadful neurosis, who have killed for killing's sake, destroyed for the sake of destruction."

Lastly, it should also be noted how far the press contributed to a collective psychosis about the attacks. Throughout those troubled years the newspapers maintained a daily dynamite column; they piled on interviews and reports on the subject which to some extent could only encourage the trend.

The reasons for the ending of the outbreak after the murder by Caserio have still to be discussed.

It has been stated that the judicious verdict given at the Trial of the Thirty helped to calm tempers down: this appears incontrovertible. It has also been said that the defensive measures taken against anarchists discouraged the comrades. It is quite true that certain procedures inaugurated at that time had some effect. For example, a report dated April 23, 1894, observes that in Paris and the suburbs "each morning and sometimes even two or three times a day, a policeman goes to these peoples' dwellings" [i.e., those of the anarchists under surveillance] and "takes every care to let it be understood by these people, and even openly shows them, that the police have an eye on them and will not let them out of sight for a single day." However, it was under this system of close watch that two of the most spectacular attacks took place—those carried out by Emile Henry and Caserio. It is therefore clear enough that these preventive measures would have been inadequate in the absence of some weightier reason tending toward the cessation of the attacks. This determinant cause, in my opinion, was essentially inherent in the form taken by the class war at that time. The relationship between the bourgeois-proletariat forces had undergone, within the space of two years, far-reaching changes; a new feeling of collective force which might prove capable of leading to workers' emancipation was gradually redirecting the energies of libertarian propaganda. The new force involved was trade unionism and its panacea—the general strike identified with the revolution. In 1892 the Guesdist syndical federation existed only in a somewhat skeletal form and as a federation was wholly oriented toward reformism and the subjugation of public authority; from 1892 to 1894, there developed a federation of labor resources and in 1895 the anarchist Pelloutier became its general secretary. In 1894, this federation of labor resources held a unique congress, the Congress of Nantes, with the Guesdist syndicates. This represented a first blazing of the trail toward a general labor confederation, which was to be brought into being as an accomplished fact—at least in theory—at the Congress of Limoges in the following year.

It is impossible not to feel some skepticism toward opinions like those of Louzon, who saw the bomb attacks of 1892–1894 as acts of decisive importance in the history of the labor movement "since their operation is like the striking of a gong which roused the French proletariat from the state of prostration and despair into which it had been plunged by the massacres of the Commune; in this way [the attacks] were the prelude to the establishment of the CGT and the mass trade union movement of 1900–1910 . . ." The trade union movement, largely stimulated and inspired by the anarchists, was nothing else but a reaction against the childhood disease of anarchism —terrorism.

On this point, it is worthwhile to trace as closely as possible the slow process of this significant evolution in anarchist thinking. Its basic characteristics are disparagement of propaganda by deed as a factor in social emancipation, exaltation of collective action linked with individual action, and calling the comrades to active militancy within the trade unions.

In the course of 1888, sustained pro-terrorist propaganda in the anarchist press ceased. The first clearly stated counter to a particularly one-sided view of the term "propaganda by deed" is to be found in 1886. An article in *La Révolte* (September 4–10, 1886) is quite precise: "By this expression 'propaganda by deed' three quarters of the comrades mean nothing more than armed demonstrations, executing of exploiters, setting fire to sweatshops, etc. Having developed at the time when the Russian terrorists were unleashing their wonderful war of reprisals against their autocrats, the anarchist movement is more or less permeated by this way of doing things. . . . True, if the movement could establish itself and achieve continual action, that would be wonderful. . . . But, in our view, it would be losing ourselves in illusion and Utopia to believe that such acts could become the aim of a rational, active, sustained propaganda. . . ." The article goes on to point out "how many opportunities for *action* occur every day, perhaps not quite so brilliantly as in our dreams, but just as effectively."

Five years later, in 1891, Kropotkin, no longer content to indicate that other kinds of action existed besides bombs, denounced propaganda by deed, when conceived solely as terrorism, as a mistake. His actual words are: ". . . While the development of the revolutionary spirit gains immensely from individual acts of heroism, it is nonetheless true . . . that revolutions are not made by heroic acts. . . . Revolution is above all a popular movement. . . . That was . . . the mistake of the anarchists in 1881. When the Russian revolutionaries had killed the Czar . . . the European anarchists imagined that, from then on, a handful of fervent revolutionaries, armed with a few bombs, would be enough to bring about the social revolution. . . . A structure founded on centuries of history is not going to be destroyed by a few kilos of explosive. . . ."

After remarking that the mistake was not without its uses, since, in his view, it meant that the anarchists could maintain their ideal in all its purity, Kropotkin nevertheless concluded that the time for it had passed and that it was now necessary "for the anarchist and communist idea to pervade the masses." (*La Révolte*, March 18–24, 1891)

There ought, therefore, to be no cause for surprise that the earliest bombs, far from inspiring enthusiasm, created among the militants some tendency to hold back. Without going so far as to condemn those who plant bombs at the risk of their own lives, *La Révolte* (April 16–22, 1892) admits "that they do more harm than good to the evolution of anarchy." From that time on, during the whole tragic period, *never once* does an anarchist journal unreservedly seek to vindicate terrorism; reading between the lines, judgment has been passed upon it.

The year 1894, therefore, is a notable date in the history of the anarchist movement. Thereafter, without renouncing their principles, the comrades endeavored to assert themselves by other means. The era of individual attacks had ended and that of minorities operating at the heart of the masses was about to begin. . . .

John Most

Advice for Terrorists

I. Attack Is the Best Form of Defense

Since we believe that the propaganda of action is of use, we must be prepared to accept whatever attendant circumstances it involves.

Everyone now knows, from experience, that the more highly placed the one shot or blown up, and the more perfectly executed the attempt, the greater the propagandistic effect.

The basic preconditions of success are methodical preparation, deception of the enemy in question and the overcoming of any obstacles that stand between the one who is to carry out the deed and the enemy.

The expense incurred by such undertakings is, as a rule, quite considerable. Indeed, one could go so far as to say that the possibility of such an action succeeding usually depends on whether the financial means are available to overcome the difficulties. Nowadays, money opens a number of doors one could not break open with an iron bar.

From *Freiheit*, September 13, 1884.

The persuasive clinking of coins turns men blind and dumb. The power of the bank account overrules any ukase.

A man who has no money cannot so much as set foot in "high society" without making himself "suspicious," without being put under surveillance and either summarily arrested or at the least prevented in some other way from carrying out his revolutionary intent. By contrast, by making himself appear elegant and "distinguished," the same man may circulate freely and inconspicuously in those circles where he needs to do some reconnoitering and will even possibly deal the decisive blow, or set in motion some engine of hell concealed beforehand in some good hiding place.

If, then, some comrades are inspired by ideas such as these, if they come to a decision to risk their lives to perform a revolutionary action, and if—realizing that the workers' contributions are but a drop in the ocean—they confiscate the means wherewith to carry out the deed, in our opinion their actions are entirely correct and in no way abnormal.

We are, in fact, firmly convinced that there is no possibility of any noteworthy operations being carried out at all unless the necessary funds have been confiscated in advance from the enemy camp.

Hence, anyone who, while approving an operation against some representative of the modern "order of thieves," at the same time turns up his nose at the manner in which the funds for it are acquired, is guilty of the grossest inconsistency. No one who considers the deed itself to be right can take offense at the manner in which the funds for it are acquired, for he would be like a man rejoicing in his existence who curses his birth. So let us hear no more of this idiotic talk of "moral indignation" at "robbery" and "theft"; from the mouths of socialists, this sort of blathering is really the most stupid nonsense imaginable. Since year in and year out the working people are robbed of everything bar the absolute bare necessities of life, he who wishes to undertake some action in the interests of the proletariat against its enemies is obliged to mix with the privileged robbers and thieves in order to confiscate at least as much as he is able of what has been created by workers, and use it for the correct purposes. In such cases, it is not theft and robbery we are dealing with, but precisely the opposite.

Those, therefore, who condemn financing-operations of the kind we have been discussing, are also against individual revolutionary acts; those who abhor such acts are totally unserious, are deceiving themselves when they call themselves revolutionaries, are unnerving the most active and dedicated pioneers of the proletariat, are playing the whore with the workers' movement, and are, when seen in a clear light, nothing better than treacherous blackguards.

Furthermore, any "illegal" action—whether it is only an action preparatory to some directly revolutionary action or not—may easily precipitate unforeseen circumstances which of their nature only ever present themselves in the middle of a critical situation.

It follows from our argument so far that these secondary circumstances (chance occurrences) cannot be separated off from the action itself and judged according to special criteria.

For example, if a revolutionary, in the process of carrying out an act of vengeance or similar, or of confiscating the means for such an act (money, weapons, poison, explosives, etc.), suddenly finds someone obstructing him, and if this puts the revolutionary in the gravest danger, then he not only has the right, from the usual standpoint of self-defense and self-preservation, to destroy whoever it is has betrayed him by his intervention—for this person's arrival may send him to prison or the gallows—but he even has a duty, for the sake of the cause for which he is fighting, to brush the unexpected obstacle out of his path.

II. When Is the People "Ready" for Freedom?

"Not yet, by a long chalk!" is what the world's blackguards have been answering since time immemorial. Today, things are not so much better as worse in this regard, since we have people agreeing with this sentiment who otherwise behave as if they were working for the highest possible human happiness.

It is easy to understand some crown prince or other declaring that the people is not "ready" for freedom; after all, if he were to say the opposite, he would be showing just how superfluous he is and signing his own death warrant.

In the same way, unless he is going to deny his own right to exist, no aristocrat, bureaucrat, lawyer or other mandarin of the government or the "law" can concede that the people might be "ready." True, we know from the proverb that the world is ruled with unbelievably little wisdom; but however stupid these state layabouts may

From *Freiheit*, November 15, 1884.

be, they still have enough gumption to realize that a people fit for freedom will soon cease to put up with their slavery.

All the clerical and literary preachers whose existence, indeed, entirely depends on being the guardians of the people, and who therefore exert themselves to the utmost to try and befuddle the human brain with their twaddle about the Bible and the Talmud, their newspaper humbug and theatrical garbage, their sophistry and trashy novels, their falsifications of history and their philosophical rubbish—in short, with hundreds of different sorts of hogwash—they will always be trotting out something about the "immaturity" of the people.

The swells and other fat-faced philistines who, though one can read their stupidity on their faces, feel, in their positions as exploiting parasites and state-protected robbers, as happy in this stage of unfreedom as pigs in muck, naturally rub their hands in glee and nod well-contented approval when their mouthpieces, declaiming from their pulpits, lecterns, desks, and podiums, seek to prove to the people that it is not ready for freedom and that therefore it must be plundered, pillaged, and fleeced.

The average man in the street has something of the ape or parrot about him. This explains why it is that hundreds of thousands go round cutting their own throats by squawking to others what those cunning mind-warpers have proclaimed. We are too stupid for freedom—alas, how stupid, stupid, stupid we are!

This is all perfectly comprehensible. What, however, is not comprehensible is that people who make themselves out to be advocates of the proletariat likewise hawk round this hoary old legend about the people's "unreadiness" and the resulting temporary impossibility of allowing it to take possession of its freedom.

Is this just ignorance or a deliberate crime?

Let these people speak for themselves: they show clearly and distinctly enough in both their speeches and writings that:

1. the consequences of modern society will in themselves bring about its destruction.

2. one of the most terrible consequences of the system we have today is the gradually increasing deterioration of large sectors of the population, their physical enervation and spiritual demoralization.

3. today's state of enslavement must be succeeded by a state of freedom.

In other words, what they are saying is this: in the first case, the society we have now is heading for inevitable collapse; in the second case, the people grow steadily more and more wretched (i.e., less and less "ready" for freedom) the longer the present setup persists.

Hence, when such philosophers, despite such statements, exclaim in moving tones that the people is not yet "ripe" for freedom, they cannot do other than concede, in conformity with their own doctrine, that this "readiness" will be even more lacking later on.

Is it, then, that these people are incapable of following the train of their own thought from established fact to resulting conclusion? If this were the case, they would indeed be dunderheads and, at the very least, not sufficiently "mature" to set themselves up as educators of the people. Or is their crippled logic perfectly clear to them, and are they—in order to play the whore with the people—making it dance around on crutches on purpose? If this were the case, they would be criminal blackguards.

Wait!—someone cries in defense of these people—we have found a way of counteracting the degenerating effects of capitalism and making the people ready for freedom despite everything. We *enlighten*.

All well and good! But who has told you that the speed at which things are evolving will leave you enough time to carry out your so-called enlightenment in a systematic way? You yourselves do not believe in that kind of magic.

But what do *you* want?

We provoke; we stoke the fire of revolution and incite people to revolt in any way we can. The people have always been "ready" for freedom; they have simply lacked the courage to claim it for themselves.

We are convinced that necessity is, and will remain, the overriding factor in the struggle for freedom and that therefore hundreds of thousands of men and women will in time appear on the scene as fighters for freedom without ever having heard our call to arms; and we are content, as it were, to construct—by training those who we are able to reach now—sluices which may well prove apt to direct the natural lava-flow of social revolution into practical channels.

As in every previous great social cataclysm, the "readiness" of the people will reveal itself in all its majesty at the moment of conflict—not before, nor after.

And then, too, as always, it will become apparent that it is not the theorists and "enlightened" pussy-footers who will provide the reeling society with a new solid foundation, but those miraculous forces which rise up as if raked up out of the earth at the great moment when they are needed. Practical children of nature who, until that point, have lived quiet and modest existences, reach out suddenly to take steps of which no philosopher in the whole wide world could ever have dreamed in a hundred years. The readiness for freedom is then customarily documented in the most astonishing fashion.

It is, therefore, a piece of monstrous idiocy on the part of any socialist to maintain that the people is not "ready" for freedom.

Everyone who does not number among the exploiters complains that others are more privileged than he. Far and wide, it is clear that the people are dissatisfied with their lot. And if it does not know yet what to replace the present setup with, it will discover it at the moment when something practical can be done in this regard; which is—*immediately*.

III. Action as Propaganda

We have said a hundred times or more that when modern revolutionaries carry out actions, what is important is not solely these actions themselves but also the propagandistic effect they are able to achieve. Hence, we preach not only action in and for itself, but also action as propaganda.

It is a phenomenally simple matter, yet over and over again we meet people, even people close to the center of our party, who either do not or do not wish to understand. We have recently had a clear enough illustration of this over the Lieske affair. . . .

So our question is this: what is the purpose of the anarchists' threats—an eye for an eye, a tooth for a tooth—if they are not followed up by action?

Or are perhaps the "law and order" rabble, all of them blackguards extraordinary à la Rumpff, to be done away in a dark corner so that no one knows the why and the wherefore of what happened?

It would be a form of action, certainly, but not action as propaganda.

The great thing about anarchist vengeance is that it proclaims loud and clear for everyone to hear, that: this man or that man must die for this and this reason; and that at the first opportunity which

From *Freiheit*, July 25, 1885.

presents itself for the realization of such a threat, the rascal in question is really and truly dispatched to the other world.

And this is indeed what happened with Alexander Romanov, with Messenzoff, with Sudeikin, with Bloch and Hlubeck, with Rumpff and others. Once such an action has been carried out, the important thing is that the world learns of it *from the revolutionaries*, so that everyone knows what the position is.

The overwhelming impression this makes is shown by how the reactionaries have repeatedly tried to hush up revolutionary actions that have taken place, or to present them in a different light. This has often been possible in Russia, especially, because of the conditions governing the press there.

In order to achieve the desired success in the fullest measure, immediately after the action has been carried out, especially in the town where it took place, posters should be put up setting out the reasons for the action in such a way as to draw from them the best possible benefit.

And in those cases where this was not done, the reason was simply that it proved inadvisable to involve the number of participants that would have been required; or that there was a lack of money. It was all the more natural in these cases for the anarchist press to glorify and explicate the deeds at every opportunity. For it to have adopted an attitude of indifference toward such actions, or even to have denied them, would have been perfectly idiotic treachery.

Freiheit has always pursued this policy. It is nothing more than insipid, sallow envy which makes those demagogues who are continually mocking us with cries of "Carry on, then, carry on" condemn this aspect of our behavior, among others, whenever they can, as a crime.

This miserable tribe is well aware that no action carried out by anarchists can have its proper propagandist effect if those organs whose responsibility it is neither give suitable prominence to such actions, nor make it palatable to the people.

It is this, above all, which puts the reactionaries in a rage.

IV. The Armament Question

If one suggests the acquisition of rifles, one can be sure to be labeled an "old fogey" by the ultra-radicals, because revolvers are

From *Freiheit*, March 27, 1886.

"more handy." If one had suggested the latter oneself, the other side would no doubt have sung a hymn of praise to ordinary rifles.

If one is inclined to concede the merits of both types of weapon and to give each its due, it is a hundred to one that someone will come along claiming that all firearms are old hat and recommending dynamite.

This explosive, too, is then willingly accepted and emphatically recommended from every quarter, with the single observation that rifles, revolvers, *and* dynamite are better than dynamite alone. What an outcry this causes! Dynamite is now obsolete as well, the mysterious rumor runs, there are other things; and these new miraculous inventions tumble out one after another until finally we are even hearing about bombs that can fly around corners.

We consider that they should go and tell this sort of twaddle to the Marines, and we could perhaps afford to smile at infantility of this ilk, were it not that unfortunately it attracts too much attention to be passed over so lightly.

The immediate consequence of these bickerings and arguments is that some who would otherwise do so do not arm themselves at all. Secondly, they kill all faith in a certain type of weapon and thus frustrate the energy of many armed comrades. In particular however, they lead to the most disastrous confusion.

All of the blithering nonsense that is talked in this regard should be forcefully combatted as soon as and wherever it is heard. What one should be doing, instead of indulging in debates idiotic enough to make the enemies of the proletariat split their sides laughing, is making propaganda on behalf of any sort of arms. Let us for goodness sake allow room for individual preference and talent in this domain as well!

Instead of conceitedly proclaiming that anyone who does not get himself this or that special weapon is a numbskull, we should be glad that members of the proletariat are arming themselves at all.

It also sounds extremely arrogant when people turn up their noses at the workers supposedly "playing at being proper soldiers and sharpshooters," since apart from the fact that nothing of the kind even goes on, so that all of this kind of talk is shown to be the web of trumped-up lies it is, we must not be lured into thinking that drill, and the cultivation of a feeling of "belonging" among those bearing arms, is ludicrous or trivial. . . .

One often hears the view expressed that when the moment for battle comes, the people will take the arms it needs. To be sure, or rather, perhaps! Perhaps, on the other hand, the confiscation of arms will not go quite so smoothly. In any case, this much is certain, that fifty or a hundred well-armed and well-trained people are going to find it easier to clear out an arsenal and ensure that the pickings find their way into the right hands than a crowd of people—no matter how big—who have assembled by pure chance and have only their bare hands to fight with.

Moreover, the actual possession of arms is only half the story; one must also know how to use them. It is easy to shoot, but appreciably more difficult to hit anything.

Far too little credit has hitherto been given to the importance of this fact and not a few revolutionaries have already paid with their lives for having suddenly taken a shot at some representative of "law and order" without first having made himself into a marksman.

For it does take some while, with either a revolver or a rifle, to get the feel of a weapon. Each weapon has, as it were, its own particular characteristics, which need to be studied and respected. Using the first weapon that comes to hand, even the most expert marksman will not be able to score the successes he can achieve with his own gun, which he knows backwards.

The same applies to modern explosives, dynamite, etc.

Numerous incidents—notably in England—have shown just what a fool one can make of oneself if one does not know how to handle these substances properly. Practice, again, must come only after study.

It may be that, at the moment, active revolutionaries comprise only a small minority when compared to the population as a whole, yet this is no reason for telling oneself that there is for the time being little or no point in providing them with proper arms and training, on the grounds that at present they cannot even entertain the idea of declaring war on a hostile world. On the contrary, their firm resolve must be to make up in quality for what they lack in quantity.

The firing line of the proletariat must consist of marksmen, i.e., each man must be sufficiently expert to be able, ultimately, to pick off his man with certainty over the varying distances the weapon covers, and to make every shot a bull's-eye.

While the main bulk of the people will charge against the general hangers-on of the bourgeoisie, the revolutionary marksman must lie in wait in order to be able to pick off an enemy officer or other weighty opponent with every single shot he fires.

Henry David

Prelude to Haymarket

Although it was sometimes proposed that the private-property "beast" might be destroyed by passive measures, the real meaning of the term "all and every means" is best taken as "any and every type of force." For a short while, some of the leaders insisted that if everybody refused to receive and give pay for goods and services, the capitalist system would collapse, and they seriously advocated such action. At the Thanksgiving Day demonstration in 1884, a resolution was adopted to the effect that no man shall either pay or receive pay for anything, and that no man should deprive himself of what he desires if the object of his desire is useful and not being utilized. At the same time, however, a resolution was adopted which recommended the use of force and all types of arms and explosives to wipe out the existing system. Evidently little faith was placed in the first method, for it was quickly abandoned.

"Down with pay," exclaimed the *Alarm*, "and dynamite the man who claims it; and hang him who will not let his energies produce something. This," concluded the writer, "is socialism." "Workingmen of America, learn the manufacture and use of dynamite," advised the *Alarm*. "It will be your most powerful weapon; a weapon of the weak against the strong. . . . Then use it unstintingly, unsparingly. The battle for bread is the battle for life. . . . Death and destruction to the system and its upholders, which plunders and enslaves the men, women and children of toil."

One I.W.P.A. group in the course of discussing the question "How can the idle obtain employment?" proposed that the "unemployed should attack the life and property of those who have robbed them of their labor products and so turn them adrift to starve." Again and again it was asserted that only when the workers "arm themselves and by force acquire the right to life, liberty and happiness" will they secure their "stolen birthright." "Each workingman ought to have been armed long ago," declared the *Arbeiter-Zeitung*. "Daggers and

Henry David, *The History of the Haymarket Affair* (New York, 1936).

revolvers are easily to be gotten. Hand grenades are cheaply . . . produced; explosives, too, can be obtained. . . ." "A number of strikers in Quincy . . . ," observed the same paper, "fired upon their bosses, and not upon the scabs. This is recommended most emphatically for imitation." It was suggested at mass meetings that "If we would achieve our liberation from economic bondage and acquire our natural right to life and liberty, every man must lay by a part of his wages, buy a Colt's navy revolver. . . , a Winchester rifle . . . , and learn how to make and use dynamite. . . . Then raise the flag of rebellion. . . ."

The conviction that force was the sole infallible means to destroy the existing order and inaugurate the glorious new society, together with the consequent constant appeal to and encouragement of its use, was marked by four very general characteristics. No real appreciation of the difference between individual deeds and expressions of mass violence was evident, and both were advised. The use of force was encouraged both for defensive—in resistance to the police, militia, Pinkertons and the like—and aggressive purposes. While every type of violence and every method of destruction was accepted, the use of dynamite and similar explosives was especially encouraged. Finally, unusual stress was placed upon the purely practical aspects of the employment of force.

Thus, the *Alarm* and the *Arbeiter-Zeitung*, frequently following the lead of and reproducing items from the *Freiheit*, published articles on the manufacture of dynamite, gun-cotton, nitroglycerine, mercury and silver fulminates and bombs. They also offered instruction in the use of dangerous explosives. One article in the *Alarm* bore the heading "A Practical Lesson in Popular Chemistry—The Manufacture of Dynamite Made Easy." Another on the manufacture of bombs was subtitled, "The Weapon of the Social Revolutionist Placed within the Reach of All." The files of both papers are liberally studded with such items. The *Arbeiter-Zeitung* ran a notice through December, 1885, and the first three months of 1886 which offered free instruction in the handling of arms to workers "at No. 58 Clybourn Avenue. . . ." And the *Alarm* urged its readers who desired additional information on the manufacture and use of bombs to communicate with it. Sometimes the mad "Revolutionary Catechism" of Nechaev was quoted. Lengthy discussions were frequently published on plans and methods of street-fighting, means of combating the militia, the preparation necessary for revolutionary action, the perpetration of the individual deed, the danger of discovery, and the like.

Upon explosives, and upon dynamite in particular, the greatest emphasis was placed. Dynamite was the great social solvent—it was the "emancipator." The "right of property" could be destroyed, asserted the *Alarm*, and a glorious "free" society inaugurated "simply by making ourselves masters of the use of dynamite, then declaring we will make no further claims to ownership in anything, and deny every . . . person's right to be owner of anything, and administer instant death, by any and all means, to any and every person who attempts to claim personal ownership of anything. This method, and this alone, can relieve the world of this infernal monster called the 'right of property.' "

No article lauding the admirable qualities of dynamite or editorial hymn praising its revolutionary virtues compares with the fantastic and unbelievable contribution of one T. Lizius which was published in the *Alarm* as a letter to the editor:

> Dynamite! Of all the good stuff, this is the stuff. Stuff several pounds of this sublime stuff into an inch pipe (gas or water-pipe), plug up both ends, insert a cap with a fuse attached, place this in the immediate neighborhood of a lot of rich loafers who live by the sweat of other people's brows, and light the fuse. A most cheerful and gratifying result will follow. In giving dynamite to the downtrodden millions of the globe, science has done its best work. The dear stuff can be carried around in the pocket without danger, while it is a formidable weapon against any force of militia, police or detectives that may want to stifle the cry for justice that goes forth from the plundered slaves. It is something not very ornamental but exceedingly useful. It can be used against persons and things, it is better to use it against the former than against bricks and masonry. It is a genuine boon for the disinherited, while it brings terror and fear to the robbers. It brings terror only to the guilty, and consequently the Senator who introduced a bill in Congress to stop its manufacture and use, must be guilty of something. He tears the wrath of an outraged people that has been duped and swindled by him and his like. The same must be the case with the 'servant' of the people who introduced a like measure in the Senate of the Indiana legislature. All the good this will do. Like everything else, the more you prohibit it, the more it will be done. Dynamite is like Banquo's ghost, it keeps on fooling around somewhere or other in spite of his satanic majesty. A pound of this good stuff beats a bushel of ballots all hollow, and don't you forget it. Our lawmakers might as well try to get down on a crater of a volcano or a bayonet as to endeavor to stop the manufacture or use of dynamite. It takes more justice and right than is contained in laws to quiet the spirit of unrest. If workingmen would be truly free, they must learn to know why they are slaves. They must rise above petty prejudice and learn to think. From thought to

action is not far, and when the worker has seen the chains, he need but look a little closer to find near at hand, the sledge with which to shatter every link. The sledge is dynamite.

The campaign of violence included items which ranged from Mrs. Parsons' pointed advice to tramps to learn to use explosives so that they could annoy the rich during hard times, to C. S. Griffin's article on assassination. In the latter, which patently reflects the influence of Nechaev and Russian terrorism, Mr. Griffin declared that

> The moment the abolition of a government is suggested the mind pictures the uprising of a hundred little despotic governments on every hand, quarreling among themselves and domineering over the unorganized people. This fact suggests the idea that the present governments must be destroyed, only in a manner that will prevent the organization or rise of any and all other governments, whether it be a government of three men or three hundred millions. No government can exist without a head, and by assassinating the head just as fast as a government head appears, the government can be destroyed, and by the same process all other governments can be kept out of existence. . . . Those governments least offensive to the people should be destroyed last. . . . He alone is free who submits to no government. All governments are domineering powers and any domineering power is a natural enemy to all mankind, and ought to be treated as such. Assassination will remove the evil from the face of the earth.

The author himself observed that this was the policy of the Nihilists, and in closing said that "Assassination properly applied is wise, just, humane, and brave. For freedom all things are just."

O'Donovan Rossa's Dynamiters

Five years ago O'Donovan Rossa, through the columns of this paper, made known to the Irish people the idea of skirmishing. . . .

From *Irish World*, August 28, 1880.

He did not himself write the address that was published. Rossa called for $5,000. The first notion seemed to rise no higher than the rescue of a few Fenian prisoners then held in English jails. He wanted badly to knock a feather out of England's cap. That sort of theatrical work did not satisfy us.

Nor did it commend itself to some others either. Rossa then said he was willing to burn down some shipping in Liverpool. Why not burn down London and the principal cities of England? asked one of the two whom Rossa, in the beginning, associated with him in the movement. Rossa said he was in favor of anything. The question of loss of life was raised. Yes, said he, who had put forward the idea. Yes, it is war; and in all wars life must be lost; but in my opinion the loss of life under such circumstances would not be one tenth that recorded in the least of the smallest battles between the South and the North. Someone suggested that plenty of thieves and burglars in London could be got to do this job. Here we interposed. Why should you ask others to do what you yourself deem wrong? After all, would it not be yourself that would be committing the sin? Gentlemen, if you cannot go into this thing with a good conscience you ought not to entertain the notion at all.

Here now, two questions presented themselves: (1) Was the thing feasible? (2) If feasible, what would be the probable result?

That the idea could be carried into execution, that London could be laid in ashes in twenty-four hours was to us self-evident. England could be invaded by a small and resolute band of men, say ten or a dozen, when a force of a thousand times this number, coming with ships and artillery, and banners flying, could not effect a landing. Spaniards in the days of the Invincible Armada, and Zulus today, could not do what English-speaking Irishmen can accomplish. Language, skin-color, dress, general manners, are all in favor of the Irish. Then, tens of thousands of Irishmen, from long residence in the enemy's country, know England's cities well. Our Irish skirmishers would be well disguised. They would enter London unknown and unnoticed. When the night for action came, the night that the wind was blowing strong—this little band would deploy, each man setting about his own allotted task, and no man, save the captain of the band alone, knowing what any other man was to do, and *at the same instant strike with lightning the enemy of their land and race. . . . In two hours from the word of command London would be in flames, shooting up to the heavens in fifty different places.* Whilst this would be going on, the men could be still at work. The blazing spectacle would attract all eyes, and leave the skirmishers to operate with impunity in the darkness.

John Devoy

Lomasney

William Mackey Lomasney was one of the most remarkable men of the Fenian movement. A small man of slender build, who spoke with a lisp, modest and retiring in manner, one who did not know him well would never take him for a desperate man, but no man in the Fenian movement ever did more desperate things. He was better known in Cork for his raids for arms in Allport's gunshop and other places after the Rising, than for the part he played at Ballyknockane. They were done in broad daylight and he showed great coolness and daring. When he was arrested he shot the Peeler who had seized him. The Peeler, although severely wounded, did not die and Lomasney was tried for attempted murder. Judge O'Hagan, who had been a Young Irelander and later became Lord Chancellor of Ireland, was the trial judge and undertook to lecture him on the enormity of his crime, but Lomasney turned the tables on him by reminding him that he was himself once a rebel and that he (Lomasney) was only following the example O'Hagan had set in 1848.

The Peeler, a big, powerful man, had knocked Lomasney down and had him under him while they were struggling for possession of Lomasney's revolver. It went off in the struggle and Lomasney had no intention of killing him. O'Hagan was stung by Lomasney's sharp rebuke and imposed a sentence of fifteen years' penal servitude, for which he was severely censured by even the English and the Tory Irish papers. Lomasney took the sentence calmly, although he had only recently been married. It was in Millbank Prison that I first met him, and we became fast friends.

J. Devoy, *Recollections of an Irish Rebel* (New York, 1929).

In America, years later, when the dynamite warfare was on foot, he was warned by the "Triangle" that I was a "traitor" and he must not have anything to do with me, but he told Aleck Sullivan that I was an honest man with a right to my opinions and that he would not obey any order to treat me as a man disloyal to Ireland. Sullivan needed Lomasney to hold his grip on the executive of the organization, which he controlled, so he let the matter drop.

Lomasney then explained his policy and methods to me, and they were entirely different from those of the "Triangle." He wanted simply to strike terror into the government and the governing class and "would not hurt the hair of an Englishman's head" except in fair fight. We then discussed the policy fully and I told him the most he could expect through terrorism was to wring some small concessions from the English which could be taken back at any time when the government's counter-policy of terrorism achieved some success. Lomasney admitted this, but contended that the counter-terrorism would not succeed; that the Irish were a fighting race who had through the long centuries never submitted to coercion; that their fighting spirit would be aroused by the struggle; that the sympathy of the world would eventually be won for Ireland, and that England could not afford to take back the concessions, which could be used to wring others, and that in the end Ireland would win her full freedom.

I freely admitted that if honestly carried out on his lines the policy of terrorism might succeed, but that I utterly disbelieved in the sincerity of those men who were directing it; that they were only carrying on a game of American politics, using the bitter feeling of Irishmen here to obtain control of the organization and turn it into an American political machine to achieve personal purposes. I pleaded for a broader policy that would win the intellect of the Irish at home and abroad and make the race a formidable factor in the counsels of the world, and an ally worth dealing with in England's next big war. I further pointed out to him that the temper of the race would upset all his ideas about "not hurting the hair of an Englishman's head"; that once their blood was up the honest fighting men who would have to carry on the work would kill all the Englishmen they could and that England, having the ear of the world and control of all the agencies of news supply, would see to it that the world was duly shocked.

I wasted my time and made no impression whatever upon him. He was as cool and calm during the argument as if we were discussing the most ordinary subject and, while his manner was animated, there was not the slightest trace of heat or passion in it. He even denied the right of the Home Organization to decide the policy for the whole race when I told him the Supreme Council was as firm as the Rock of Cashel against anything being done within its jurisdiction of which it did not fully approve. He was a fanatic of the deepest dye, and all the harder to argue with because he never got heated or lost his temper.

Such was the man who was blown to atoms under London Bridge with his brother, his brother-in-law, and a splendid man named Fleming, a short time after my talk with him. The explosion only slightly damaged one of the arches, and I have always believed that this was all he intended to do. He was, in my opinion, carrying out his policy of frightening the English government and England's ruling class. And that it did frighten them, as all the other dynamite operations did, there can be no reason to doubt.

PART III

Terrorism in the Twentieth Century

Introductory Note

From the turn of the century to the 1960s, terrorism was mainly the preserve of nationalist-separatist movements and extreme right-wing groups. There were a few major exceptions such as the second wave of left-wing terrorism in Russia (1904–1907) and the industrial and political terrorism indigenous to Spain. But the centers of action were Ireland, Macedonia, Palestine (before and after the Second World War) and, to a lesser degree, some Asian and African countries such as India and Egypt. Terrorist tactics were used by some fascist parties in Central Europe and the Balkans and, after the Second World War, in the struggle which accompanied decolonization, for instance, in Cyprus, Aden, and Algeria. In preparation for their military offensives, North Vietnamese communists used individual terrorism to eliminate their Trotskyite political opponents in the cities and the headmen loyal to the government in the villages. The recrudescence of left-wing terrorism in the 1960s was limited, on the whole, to small sectarian groups; the publicity accorded to their actions was in inverse ratio to their real importance. This is particularly true of groups and individuals in the United States, West Germany, and Japan, which, acting separately or in unison ("Carlos Marighella's multinational terrorism"), frequently had the support of sympathetic governments other than their own.

The use of terrorism as surrogate political warfare is by no means a new phenomenon; a famous precedent was the support Italian fascism lent to the Croatian Ustasha who killed King Alexander in Marseilles in 1934. In the 1960s and 1970s, state-supported terrorism became an established practice, especially in the Middle East and North Africa, with Libya, Algeria, Iraq, South Yemen, and Somalia as the main sponsors, and it was also in evidence on occasion in Latin America (Cuba). There are certain links between multinational terrorism and the Soviet bloc. Some of the terrorist groups of the 1960s tended to the left, others to the right; some defied definition in clear-cut ideological terms and combined concepts and practices of the extreme left and right. Extreme left-wing terrorism was of political significance in Latin America (the Tupamaros in Uruguay, the Argentinian ELP, and the Montoneros), but their activities inevitably resulted in a violent backlash on the part of the extreme right. Historical experience has shown that terrorism has lasted only when it functioned within the framework of a wider political movement (almost always of a nationalist-separatist character) or when it was supported by powerful outside forces (as evidenced in Ulster and by the Basques, Croats, Palestinian Arabs, and other such groups). Furthermore, experience has taught us that while the terrorism of the 1960s and 1970s has professed to fight tyranny, it has hardly ever appeared and has never succeeded where repression is at its greatest. Terrorism is a weapon that can only be used effectually against democratic and ineffective authoritarian regimes.

The Inner Macedonian Revolutionary Organization (IMRO), established in the 1890s to fight the Turks and achieve independence for Macedonia, continued its struggle for four decades but, after the First World War, it became the tool of successive Bulgarian governments for use against internal and external enemies and was itself liquidated when it was no longer needed by its paymasters.

Political terrorism was widely used in the early 1920s in Germany by the precursors of the Nazis; the assassination of Walther Rathenau, foreign minister of the Republic, was the most famous of many terrorist incidents. Other fascist movements such as the Rumanian Iron Guard applied individual terrorism on a wider scale than the Italian fascists and the Nazi party which preferred, on the whole, an open to a covert struggle for power. *Vier Jahre politischer Mord* (Berlin, 1922), a documentary record denouncing the activities of right-wing "patriots," was prepared by a young Heidelberg professor, Emil Julius Gumbel (1891–1966), much to the disgust of the academic authorities who were opposed to such extracurricular activities. After his emigration from Germany, Gumbel taught statistics at Columbia University.

The "Philosophy of the Bomb," a manifesto by a small left-wing Indian group, the Hindustan Socialist Revolutionary Army, was published in January, 1930. It was written by Bhagwat Charan and took issue with Gandhi's policy of nonviolence which guided the Indian Congress party at the time. But terrorism was equally advocated (and more frequently practiced) by extreme right-wing Hindu fundamentalist circles, to which Gandhi's murderer belonged.

The history of the IRA has been related in considerable detail, yet novels and movies (such as, for instance, *The Informer* and *Odd Man Out*) are probably of greater benefit than the official ideological pronouncements in yielding an understanding of the motivation of Irish (and Ulster Protestant) terrorists. Furthermore, any similarity between the theory of ideological pronouncement and practice in the street is usually quite accidental. According to recent doctrinal statements of the IRA, the British army is the sole enemy of the IRA Provisionals and they have nothing in principle against Protestant Irishmen. In actual fact not a single British soldier lost his life in Belfast between September, 1974, and October, 1976, whereas hundreds of Catholic and Protestant civilians were killed in the same period in what is virtually a civil war on sectarian lines. The (anonymous) Easter Week ballad of 1916 and the equally anonymous open letter by an extremist Protestant organization published in a Belfast newspaper in 1972 convey a more accurate impression of the mood prevailing among the warring factions than any lengthy manifestos. In a similar way, the publications of the various Palestinian Arab organizations are no reliable guide to their actions: they dwell in great detail on the strategy of popular resistance and on mass action, whereas the real manifestations of their terrorist tactics, such as the hijacking of planes, are all-but-never discussed. The publications of Iranian terrorists are, in this respect, far more outspoken; the excerpts published here are from Bizham Jazani's (1937–1975) *Armed Struggle in Iran*. According to the official Teheran version the author was shot "while trying to escape from prison." He belonged to the Marxist-Leninist *Siahkal*, a group named after the small town near the Caspian Sea where one of its first armed actions took place in 1971.

Menahem Begin (born 1913) was the leader of the IZL (*Irgun Zvai Leumi*) from 1943 to its dissolution in 1948; he is now head of the Likud party in Israel and prime minister of Israel. In the 1930s, IZL split away from the Hagana, the irregular Palestinian Jewish defense forces. Earlier than other Zionist parties it advocated the establishment of a Jewish state on both banks of the Jordan. The IZL was outflanked by the smaller, more radical, more militant, and, in certain respects, more "left-wing" Stern Gang (Fighters for the Freedom of Israel).

More than any other continent, Latin America has been the scene of terrorist activities during the 1960s and 1970s. The Venezuelan communists had been pioneers in this respect, but it was only after the failure of the various rural guerrilla groups, in particular, Ché

Guevara's small band in 1967, that the terrorist wave reached its highest point. The chief political advocate of "urban guerrilla" was Abraham Guillen; excerpts from his writings can be found in my *Guerrilla Reader*.* More influential, albeit mainly restricted to a discussion of military strategy, was Carlos Marighella's famous *Minimanual*. Marighella, a long-time Brazilian communist, left the party in 1967 because it was not sufficiently militant and was killed in a shoot-out with the police in São Paulo in 1969. "Urbano" was a leader of the Uruguayan Tupamaros, which, prior to their defeat in 1971, were the most successful terrorist group in Latin America. In an interview with Urbano that appeared in a Cuban publication some aspects of the political and tactical approach of the Tupamaros are discussed.

Finally, there are the small terrorist factions that developed out of the remnants of the New Left in the United States, western Europe, and Japan. Their publications, of which *Prairie Fire*, published by the SDS in 1974, and *Das Konzept Stadtguerilla*, published by Baader-Meinhof group in April, 1971, are quite representative, are mainly devoted to statements of general political principles and expectations. No survey of recent terrorist literature would be complete without them, but they do not offer much that is novel in comparison with terrorist groups of previous ages, except for the fact that their activities, like those of the fascist groups of the inter-war period, were directed against democratically elected governments. This might account for the sense of isolation that is distinctly evident beneath the veneer of ultra-radical phraseology.

St. Christowe

Twilight of the IMRO

For fifty years the Macedonians have been spilling blood profusely, their own and their enemies'. I do not believe that the words au-

St. Christowe, *Heroes and Assassins* New York: (Holt, 1935). Reprinted with the permission of the publishers.

* New York: New American Library, 1977.

tonomy, liberty, independence, hold such magic for any other people as they do for the Macedonians. To free peoples the word liberty has lost some of its real signification. They accept it as one of the appurtenances of life, or as one of the necessities, like air, like water. But to the Macedonians liberty has become the highest goal for which man can strive. The *comitadjis*, with all their faults, are not *comitadjis* for the sport of it: Theirs is not a profession. It is true some have become *comitadjis* for sheer adventure, others because it offered them a livelihood, and still others have been forced into the Movement, but most of them have been conscientious lovers of liberty, men that were ashamed to remain a subjugated people in an age of freedom and independence.

And yet at times the *comitadjis have* behaved like gangsters. The last decade of *comitadji* history deals more with internal warfare and self-annihilation than with a consistent and determined pursuit of the goal itself. Since Michailoff's ascent to power the Movement has seen a series of sanguinary spectacles among the *comitadjis* themselves, with an occasional revolutionary act in the enemy camp performed by some terrorist at the cost of his or her life. There is little that is virtuous and humane to distinguish or redeem Michailoff's epoch. The pistol and the dagger have been the solution of all internal conflicts and schisms. Michailoff's reign in IMRO history will go down as one of bloodletting and mutual extermination.

Michailoff is a persuasive talker. He is endowed with a brilliant mind, is patient and kind and modest. He is not an impulsive person and does not jump into fights as does a man of impetuous temperament and belligerent character. On the contrary, he is noted for his cold, rigid logic and his blueprint thinking. He tries every conceivable way of conciliation, but he remains as firm and unyielding as a rock. And when he has talked himself out and has exhausted all other ways of effecting peace and harmony, he invariably seeks recourse in bloodshed. A less rigid, a less adamant attitude, a certain elasticity, and even an occasional compromise, would at least have moderated, if not entirely prevented, the fierce internal clashes and saved the Movement from the discredit, the blemishes, and the final wreck. . . .

. . . Following the wars nearly one half of the Macedonian Bulgars escaped into Bulgaria. Naturally this half was the more virile, the more buoyant ethnically, and from it the Movement derived its principal strength. From this same more vigorous national element the Movement drew its strength afterward also, but where before it was on its own soil, now it was on foreign soil, which makes a great difference. This gave IMRO the features of a foraying, sniping, outlaw society, its bands emerging sporadically in Yugoslav and Greek Macedonia and quickly retreating to their base in Bulgaria for recuperation and re-arming.

When the Serbs and the Greeks took even more drastic measures against these bands, and crossing into either part of Macedonia meant certain death, IMRO transformed itself into a sheerly terroristic society in order to maintain a semblance of revolutionary life in Greek and Yugoslav Macedonia. Thus in its history of forty years the Organization went through three distinct stages of development. First it was a society of secret civilian committees. From these it evolved into a mass organization with a permanent semimilitary armed force —the *comitadjis*. It was as such that Alexandroff attempted to reestablish it and partly succeeded. But as time went on, the Greeks and Serbs destroyed practically every band that crossed over into their jurisdictions, besides putting the local population where such bands were sighted through the most brutal tortures. Under Michailoff, therefore, IMRO went through still another development, becoming a dreaded band of plotting terrorists and depending for its effects almost entirely upon individual heroics.

But in Bulgarian Macedonia and in Bulgaria proper, IMRO was something quite different. Here it was a mass revolutionary organization. But here there was no need whatever for any rebel activity. The *comitadjis* committed no outrages in Bulgaria except against themselves. They made of the Petrich district a kind of *comitadji* Hollywood, with no grinding cameras but with plenty of actors and directors. The old form of *comitadjism*, romantic, picturesque, with its breathless secrecy, its spectral nocturnality, its eerie omnipresence, but with none of the old-time danger that breathed living reality into it, was here recreated. To it were added such modern innovations as whizzing automobiles, telephonic communication, and typewriters.

Michailoff proved himself an able administrator and tax collector as well. He put IMRO on a business basis. The Organization took on the character of a holding corporation, with its finger in all economic enterprises in the district, as well as in most national Macedonian cooperative and commercial ventures in old Bulgaria. Nothing could be done in the Petrich district without permission from IMRO. One could not even build a fence around a field unless one had first consulted with the local IMRO agent. Michailoff appointed schoolteachers, municipal clerks, tax collectors (for the Sofia government), mayors of towns and villages. No one could hold a position with the official government in this territory unless he was *persona grata* to IMRO.

There were no popular elections here; the eleven deputies in the Sofia parliament representing the district were IMRO appointees. The political party machines did not extend into this newly acquired Bulgarian land. Michailoff wanted unity in his "little kingdom" and would not permit the Bulgarian politicians to spread partisan issues and animosities among his people. Partisanship is a serious business in the Balkans. Two Bulgarians belonging to two different parties are like two men of different nationalities. There was one party in Bulgarian Macedonia, and that was IMRO; one political objective, and that was the union of the three parts of Macedonia into a single independent state. Once the Macedonians had attained that objective, they could form as many political parties as they desired and could air their political convictions as much as they wished. Until then, all Macedonians were needed for the struggle, and any one that tried to sow dissension among them or to wean any away from their national duty was an enemy of the cause and would be fought by IMRO.

Emil Julius Gumbel

Organized Murder

The most shocking murders are those which have been committed during periods of complete calm, when there was neither a real nor a fictitious left-wing revolt. Here the excuses and extenuations we have encountered hitherto will not do. We are left with just two methods.

The first method is to say that it is not worth making such a commotion about. The man was mad anyway, he suffered from persecution mania. He was convinced he was going to be killed one

Emil Julius Gumbel, *Vier Jahre politischer Mord* (Berlin, 1922).

day. Is that not proof enough that he knew what his fate was going to be? We can see what sort of people the Left is composed of. By robbing the dead man of his one possession, his good name, they exonerate themselves, by such desecration of the dead, from any responsibility. Nevertheless, the government pledges to hold a thorough enquiry. The periodical reports of how things are proceeding in an orderly fashion grow shorter and shorter. New political problems fill the newspapers and after a while the flood of leaflets abates. Only a few papers continue to cry and yelp. Soon the dead man is forgotten.

Or the murder is made acceptable to the people in advance. The victim must be so inculpated that his assassination is regarded as an act of liberation, an heroic deed. "Germany has finally been freed of a man who brought so much misery to his fatherland." A great deal of detailed work, high culture, masterly preparation and methodical cooperation are involved in bringing about the victim's downfall. "This man is a wrecker. He must be removed. The National United Front alone can help." Thus snarls the press, and goes on snarling until even the last inhabitant of Much-Binding-in-the-Marsh knows it.

Are There Assassination Organizations?

Assassination organizations in the proper sense of the term, i.e., organizations whose sole purpose is political assassination, probably do not exist in present-day Germany. However, there are certainly organizations which condone political assassination either as a secondary aim or as a means to an end. Their true goals, comprising three essentially distinct aims, are nationalist in character. The first is monarchist. This is the first reason why these organizations attack the Republic and, first and foremost, its representatives. At the same time, however, the various organizations that exist disagree both over the form of the future monarchy (whether it should be absolute or constitutional), its scope (Unified German State or return of former rulers), and the person of the monarch himself (whether he should be a Wittelsbach or a Hohenzollern). There is, above all, no sufficiently popular candidate for the throne. This piece of good fortune may perhaps save the Republic, as a similar one saved France in 1870.

The second tendency is the imperialist. The Versailles Peace Treaty dismembered Germany and took away from it territories with

German populations. In view of this, efforts to regain those areas cut off from Germany against their wills and to improve Germany's economic situation are entirely justified. Furthermore, these associations advocate an explicitly imperialist policy, in particular a war of revenge.

The third current within these movements is anti-Semitism, which derives from highly exaggerated ideas of the importance and influence of the Jews.

To a considerable extent, these three aims of policy are not officially acknowledged. In public, they appear more in the guise of professional, scientific, and cultural demands or other political objectives. Some organizations still even insist on maintaining the fiction of political neutrality. In all of them, one finds the most active members are almost always members of the old army.

The three movements are customarily fused. The majority of *Geheimbündler* are simultaneously monarchists, imperialists, and anti-Semites. The organizations' extremist attitudes lead them to believe that by killing one's political opponent one can thereby do away with the ideas he stands for. A second, and essentially different, root-cause of political assassination is an occasional necessity, as it seems, to remove uncomfortable accomplices who, it is feared, may betray the organization.

Secret Communist Organizations

It is beyond question that there have also been secret Communist organizations. This party's mentality, as exemplified in their responsibility for the March, 1921, uprising, makes it barely possible to doubt their existence. But the reports about them have in every single case proved to be grossly exaggerated. In those cases where such organizations have actually existed, a major role has been played by stool-pigeons and provocateurs from right-wing organizations, the reason being that the party as a whole has been heavily infiltrated by stool-pigeons. In Munich, informers have even been uncovered holding positions as district leaders, i.e., officials of the party.

The Social Structure of the *Geheimbünde*

A number of these organizations live only for a short while and then disappear. A series of new ones are then founded. The process appears entirely haphazard and chaotic, yet is in fact very simple. The way in which these organizations fragment into hiking clubs, study groups, sports organizations, regimental associations, rifle clubs, veterans' organizations, officers' federations and organizations of *volkisch*, nationalist and monarchist revival, with some of these groups continually disappearing and new ones emerging, is only intended as a camouflage. It allows the organizations to be continued in the event of a ban, makes it possible for any links to be denied, any identity to be challenged and, furthermore, for any informers who may have crept in to be rendered harmless by a rapid change in the character of the organization. The lines of communication between the leaders and the movement's errand-boys are sometimes very loose. The top leadership must always be in a position to be able to disavow any such connection.

How loose these lines of communication can be kept, without impairing the strong mutual trust that exists, is illustrated by the attack on Harden, when those involved communicated with each other exclusively by post and the instigator of the attack did not even know the name of the superior who was providing him with money. Communications work so well that the authorities have still not succeeded in pinpointing the men who commissioned and funded Rathenau's murder. The maître chefs have been arrested, but not the cooks who actually brewed the whole business up.

A large proportion of the membership is made up of young people. It is students and secondary-school children who comprise the main force of these organizations. Seventeen-year-old grammar-school children played a decisive role in Rathenau's murder. As, despite all the Social Democratic ministers of education we have had, the children of today still study the old textbooks, which are tailored to the emperor and imperial rule, they can hardly escape being convinced that empire is the only true form of government and that the Republic is a regrettable aberration to be corrected as soon as possible. The younger terrorists are therefore acting in absolute good faith and believe themselves to be the true successors of Harmodios and Aristogeiton, and Brutus, if they kill the few Republicans that Germany possesses.

One must not allow the large number of these organizations to mislead one into thinking that they are all independent of each other. Their membership is to a large extent drawn from the same people. One and the same person is often affiliated to ten such organizations under ten different names. The total figure of those belonging to illegal or semi-legal German nationalist organizations would very probably not exceed one quarter of a million. As for arms, the highest estimate would be in the region of a hundred and fifty thousand rifles with ten rounds of ammunition per rifle, and 2,000 light and 500 heavy automatic weapons. It is unlikely that these organizations possess any heavy artillery worth mentioning.

Public Opinion and the Murderers

Even before the victim has stopped twitching, the press begins to make the appropriate noises. "Frightful, frightful," scream the *Local News*, the *Times*, the *Daily Clarion*, the *German Daily News*, etc.: "We condemn political assassination from any quarter." But one can already discern a subdued undertone, which soon becomes increasingly loud: "Is it in fact certain that it was the German nationalists who were responsible?" The crocodile tears fall in torrents. For a few minutes, the government shakes off its lethargy: there will be tough legislation to protect the Republic. The Left level loud accusations against the murderers. Then the undertone grows even more distinct: "We are against such excesses", i.e., we disapprove of people being sincerely and honestly against assassination, we dislike a spade being called a spade and the German nationalist *Geheimbündler* being called murderers.

The murderers escape. The bold headlines in the papers fade away. Committed anti-Republicans easily bend the "Laws for the Protection of the Republic" to suit their own purposes. The newspapers speak of paid assassins sent by a foreign "Communist state": "A German could never do such a thing."

The most interesting aspect is the reaction immediately after the murder. There is great perturbation throughout the country, especially among the workers, and in a few cases among the bourgeoisie, too. Depending on their various attitudes, the workers' parties call for mass action, protest strikes or marches. It is common knowledge that, as a result of the high level of discipline which is generally to be found in the organized socialist parties, a demonstration of this kind can pass off quite peacefully if the police behave sensibly and more especially if they are taken off the streets altogether. Hundreds of marches have shown this to be the case. But for such marches to pass off without event is decidedly not in the interests of those on the

Right. Paid agents provocateurs who deliberately stir up unrest and the provocative behavior of the police ensure that there is disruption. At some point there is a clash between marchers and police. From some direction, the notorious first shot is fired. (Later it proves impossible to discover from which side it came.) Ruthlessly, the well-organized police begin to club, shoot at, beat and trample on the unarmed mass of demonstrators. Dozens of dead marchers—but no dead policemen—are littered over the field of battle. This the press takes as sufficient reason to condemn in the strongest terms the continuing terror from the Left and the excesses not, as one might have thought, of the police, but of the demonstrators, and to conclude that Democracy, Freedom, and the Constitution are under threat—not, one must understand, from the assassins, no, but from the "masses of the workers spurred on by troublemakers." This line of argument is especially effective if, in the course of a demonstration, the workers have destroyed a few symbols of empire.

Easter Week

A Dublin Ballad

Who fears to speak of Easter Week
That week of famed renown,
When the boys in green went out to fight
The forces of the Crown.

With Mausers bold and hearts of gold
And the Countess dressed in green
And high above the G.P.O.
The rebel flag was seen.

Then came ten thousand khaki coats
Our rebel boys to kill,
Before they reached O'Connell Street,
Of fight they got their fill.

Origins unknown.

They'd Maxim guns and cavalry
And cannon in galore;
But it's not our fault that e'er a one
Got back to England's shore.

They shot our leaders in a gaol
Without a trial, they say;
They murdered women and children too
Who in their cellars lay;

They dug their gravc with gun and spade
To hide them from our view
Because they could neither kill nor catch
The Rebels so bold and true.

May the Lord have mercy on three men
Who faced the murderous foe,
There was Dixon, Sheehy-Skeffington
And McIntyre also.

'Twas in a dismal barrack cell
They met their fate so cruel,
Yes, they were shot with no clergy got
To prepare them for their doom.
For six long days we held them off
With odds at ten to one.
And through our lines they could not pass
For all their heavy guns.

And deadly poison-gas they used
To try and crush Sinn Fein
And burn our Irish capital
As the Germans did Louvain.

But we shall love old Ireland
And shall while life remains,
And we shall say, God speed the day
The Rebels shall rise again.

Though Irish slaves and English knaves
Will try us to deceive
Remember those who died for you
And likewise James Connolly's grave.

Freedom Struggle by the Provisional IRA

Quite frankly it suited IRA strategy to carry out selective bombings in Belfast, Derry, and other towns in Occupied Ulster. They see these actions as a legitimate part of war, the targets chosen being military and police barracks, outposts, customs offices, administrative and government buildings, electricity transformers and pylons, certain cinemas, hotels, clubs, dance halls, pubs, all of which provide relaxation and personal comforts for the British forces; also business targets e.g., factories, firms, stores (sometimes under the guise of CO-OPs) owned in whole or part by British financiers or companies, or who in any way are a contributory factor to the well-being of Her Majesty's invading forces, and in certain instances residences of people known to harbor or be in league with espionage personnel or *agents provocateurs* namely the S.A.S., MRF, and S.I.B. In many ways this campaign is reminiscent of that carried out by the underground Resistance in France during World War II.

In all cases IRA bomb squads give adequate warning though these warnings are sometimes withheld or delayed deliberately by the British army as a counter-tactic, with view to making optimum publicity out of the injured and the dead in their propaganda war on the IRA. In no instance has the "warning rule" been violated by the guerrilla forces in sharp contrast with the "no warning" methods used by the Unionist gangs and British army *agents provocateurs.*

The Abercorn Restaurant, McGurk's Bar, Benny's Bar and more recently McGlades Bar are frightening examples of the latter type of instant bombing. Naturally it presents less risk to the bombers in terms of personal safety and lessens the chances of being apprehended. As well as giving warnings, the IRA always claims full responsibility for all military action taken even should this redound

Freedom Struggle by the Provisional IRA (*n.p. n.d.*).

unfavorably on the Republican Movement's popularity; E.B.N.I. and Donegall Street are classic examples of this. Over the years the press has learned to accept the veracity of Irish Republican Publicity Bureau statements, whereas, with the British army's constant propaganda handouts, various versions of incidents and blatant covering-up of tracks have created for them a gross credibility gap.

The effect of the IRA bombing campaign can be gauged in many different ways. Firstly, they have struck at the very root of enemy morale, confining and tying down large numbers of troops and armored vehicles in center city areas, thus relieving much of the pressure on the much-oppressed nationalist areas. In terms of direct financial loss (structural damage, goods, machinery), also in the crippling of industrial output and perhaps worst of all in the scaring-off of foreign capital investments, IRA bombs have hit Britain where she feels it most—in her pocket.

England always found unfortunate soldiers quite dispensable and to a certain extent replaceable, but she always counted in terms of cost to the Treasury. Any peace through the granting of freedom emanating to rebellious colonies from London came by means of calculation—the cost of occupation. Since 1969 a bill of warfare running to at least a conservative £500,000,000 has not gone unnoticed back home in Britain where recent opinion polls showed that over 54 percent of the ordinary people wanted the troops withdrawn forthwith.

Already some 1,500 troops have left Northern Ireland never to return. In many cases death certificates have been issued as for fatal road accident victims to the unsuspecting next-of-kin of soldiers killed in action in a heartless attempt at cooking records and hiding telling manpower losses. Suddenly Northern Ireland has become England's Vietnam. In the knowledge that the will to overcome of a risen people can never be defeated by brute force or even overwhelming odds more enlightened British politicians have seen the light and are themselves thinking along Tone's famous dictum: "Break the connection!"

Great Britain too, of course, has suffered losses other than bomb damage and loss of personnel. Her prestige and credibility in terms of world opinion and world finance have been severely shaken; her duplicity and selective sense of justice have been seriously exposed; her puerile hankering after "holding the last vestige of the Empire" has marked her as a recidivist nation, psychologically vulnerable, unstable, and mentally immature. These considerations have not been lost on the European Common Market countries, especially France and Monsieur Pompidou. Britain's dilemma in Ireland is of her own making and is now seen as a black mark against her in the new capital—Brussels. Time is running out along the Thames.

Ulster: The Counter-Terror

We accept that the press of the world is sick of the sound and sight of Ulster, sick of our orgy of destruction, sick of our rancor and sick of our brutalities. Why, therefore, you ask, should you be interested in the self-delusive ravings of a band of extreme Protestants? A band of men cast in the role of wicked "heavies," the "bad guys" of the story, the narrow-minded bigots of Ulster, the cause of all the present troubles?

Mountains of words have been written about us in the past four years and our role in the affair is cast by the press in a certain way and all comments about us are based upon these assumptions:

That we are narrow-minded. That we are fanatical. That we are similar to the IRA. That we hate all Catholics. That we are repressive, "right wing" fascists. That we cannot be reasoned with.

With all that has been written about the Scots-Irish of Northern Ireland, you would have thought that someone would have eventually grasped the essential truth of it all. The real cause of the bloodshed, the real cause of the hatred. We think you, the press, have done nothing of the sort, and it is high time that you did; for, if nothing else, we do feel you owe our people a little latitude. Just this once.

It seems a lifetime ago that our competent, if partisan, government came under fire from a civil rights movement which, it has to be admitted, did have a justification for many of its grievances. Cast inevitably in the role of St. Bernadette came a pint-sized lady of fiery oratory and poverty-stricken background. How the press loved this little lady, pictured her swinging prettily in a garden as her victories over the repressing, misruling Unionists were announced.

You, the press, made a heroine of this girl and you bear a heavy responsibility for what followed. The blundering, incompetent, and

Statement of Protestant Extremist Group, Dublin *Sunday World* June 9, 1973.

seemingly repressive antics of our leaders confirmed your attitude that she and her associates were right and that we were wrong. The B-Specials, the reactions of our police forces, and the so-called ambush of Burntollet hardened your views which, in turn, hardened ours, and the die was cast.

It is such a pity that you do not consult your history books, for the real truth lies there, repeated over and over again, like a gramophone record. We are a hybrid race descended from men who colonized Scotland from Ireland in the fifth century, and who then colonized Northern Ireland from Scotland in the seventeenth century. Our existence was not placid in Scotland, but that was heavenly compared to our life in Ireland. For four hundred years we have known nothing but uprising, murder, destruction, and repression. We ourselves have repeatedly come to the support of the British crown, only to be betrayed within another twenty years or so by a fresh government of that crown. What is happening now mirrors similar events in the seventeenth, eighteenth, and nineteenth centuries.

We are not good at propaganda and not good at extolling our virtues or admitting our faults. We just stick to our points of view, bow our heads, and pray for it all to die down again for another fifty years or so.

Gradually, however, we have come to realize that this time other factors have come into the age-old conflict of the Scots-Irish versus the Irish-Irish, or if you prefer it that way, the Protestants versus the Catholics in Ireland.

Traditionally the English politicians let us down—betrayal we call it. The Catholics try to overwhelm us so we are caught in between two lines of fire. Second-class Englishmen, half-caste Irishmen, this we can live with and even defeat, but how can we be expected to beat the world revolutionary movement which supplies arms and training, not to mention most sophisticated advice on publicity, promotion, and expertise to the IRA?

We do not have large funds from over-indulgent sentimentally sick Irishmen in America who send the funds of capitalism to sow the seeds of communism here. We do not have the tacit support of the government of Southern Ireland and we do not have the support or interest of the British people.

We are betrayed, maligned, and our families live in constant fear and misery. We are a nuisance to our so-called allies and have no friends anywhere. Once more in the history of our people we have our backs to the wall, facing extinction by one way or another. This is the moment to beware, for Ulstermen in this position fight mercilessly till they or their enemies are dead.

We would like to remind you of a few salient facts: the Russians who condemn our people have millions in slave labor camps and their government is the biggest mass murderer since Adolf Hitler. Edward Kennedy, the heroic night-swimmer of Martha's Vineyard, is hardly in a moral condition to criticize his pet rabbit let alone us. The ruler of Libya is a raving fanatic. If the Unionist government of Northern Ireland was corrupt, it was as pure as the driven snow compared to the government of John Mary Lynch. If the press likes scandals then let them examine the private fortunes of government ministers in the Lynch republic. Fortunes made out of a divine intuition about future planning permissions. If the Protestants in the south of Ireland are so content, why do their numbers dwindle and why do they never complain?

If the Southern Irish government wants us, then it will have to win our hearts, rather than have us as bitterly hostile losers in a bombing war of attrition tacitly backed by them. Their own history should tell them this will never work. Our troubles destroyed their tourist industry, and a few well-planted disease-ridden animals could very rapidly destroy their economic growth. They too are not immune from trouble, and they should not support evil men of violence lest it rebound heavily upon them.

The British army in Ulster has good soldiers who are being set up like dummy targets. The orders of the politicians are tying both hands behind their backs. The British public says: "Send the soldiers home." We say: "Send the politicians and the officers home and leave us the men and the weapons—or, why not send the soldiers home and leave us the weapons and we will send you the IRA wrapped up in little boxes and little tins like cans of baked beans."

The politicians who rule our lives from England do not understand us. They stop the army from defending us properly and stop us from defending ourselves. We do not like these flabby-faced men with pop eyes and fancy accents. . . .

We ourselves are not perfect. We ourselves do not always see eye to eye, but the time is fast coming when the Scots-Irish of Ulster will have to reconsider their future actions. The bloodbath could very soon be a reality, and you who condemned us for it could have precipitated it unjustly on decent people because they jerrymandered a few constituencies to avoid giving power to people who were educated and dedicated to destroying a way of life.

You turned an adulterous little slut into a revolutionary saint; a soft-voiced failed priest fanatic was called a moderate, and you gave a terror organization all the publicity it desired. It was not an *Irish* leader of the IRA who said we were all fit to be bombed but a sick little pop-eyed Englishman with a false name and with no Irish connections whatsoever. We the Scots-Irish are fighting for survival. We think we have been greatly wronged, and we think you should watch the events of the next month with extreme *care*.

Bhagwat Charan

The Philosophy of the Bomb

Recent events, particularly the congress resolution on the attempt to blow up the viceregal special on the 23rd December, 1929, and Gandhi's subsequent writings in *Young India,* clearly show that the Indian National Congress in conjunction with Gandhi has launched a crusade against the revolutionaries. A great amount of public criticism both from the press and platform has been made against them. It is a pity that they have all along been, either deliberately or due to sheer ignorance, misrepresented and misunderstood. The revolutionaries do not shun criticism and public scrutiny of their ideals or actions. They rather welcome these as a chance of making those understand, who have a genuine desire to do so, the basic principles of the revolutionary movement and the high and noble ideals that are perennial source of inspiration and strength to it. It is hoped that this article will help that general public to know the revolutionaries as they are and will prevent it from taking them for what interested and ignorant persons would have it believed them to be.

Let us first take the question of violence and nonviolence. We

Manifesto of the HSRA illegally distributed in various parts of India in January, 1930.

think that the use of these terms in itself is a grave injustice to either party, for they express the ideals of neither of them correctly. Violence is a physical force applied for committing injustice, and that is certainly not what the revolutionaries stand for. On the other hand, what generally goes by the name of nonviolence is in reality the theory of soul force as applied to the attainment of personal and national rights through courting suffering and hoping to finally convert your opponent to your viewpoint. When a revolutionary believes certain things to be his right, he asks for them, pleads for them, argues for them, wills to attain them, with all soul force at his command, stands the greatest amount of suffering for them, is always prepared to make the highest sacrifice for their attainment and also backs his efforts with all the physical force he is capable of. You may coin what other word you like to describe his methods, but you cannot call it violence because that would constitute an outrage on the dictionary meaning of that word. Satyagraha is insistence upon truth. Why press for the acceptance of truth by soul force alone? Why not add physical force to it? While the revolutionaries stand for winning independence by all the forces, physical as well as moral, at their command, the advocate of soul force would like to ban the use of physical force. The question really is therefore not whether you will have violence or nonviolence but whether you will have soul force plus physical force or soul force alone.

The revolutionaries believe that the deliverance of their country will come through revolution. The revolution they are constantly working and hoping for will not only express itself in the form of an armed conflict between the foreign government and its supporters and the people, it will also usher in the new social order. The revolution will bring the death knell of capitalism and class distinction and privileges. It will bring the nation into its own. It will give birth to a new state, a new society. Above all, it will establish the dictatorship of the proletariat and will forever banish social parasites from the seat of political power.

The revolutionaries already see the advent of the revolution in the restlessness of youth, in its desire to get free from the mental bondage and religious superstitions that hold them. As the youth will get more and more saturated with the psychology of revolution, it will come to have a clearer realization of the national bondage and a growing, intense unquenchable thirst for freedom, till, in their righteous anguish, infuriated youth will begin to kill the oppressors. Thus has terrorism been born in the country. It is a phase, a necessary and inevitable phase of the revolution. Terrorism is not complete revolution and the revolution is not complete without terrorism. This thesis can be supported by an analysis of any and every revolution in history. Terrorism instills fear in the hearts of the oppressors, it brings hopes of revenge and redemption to the oppressed masses. It gives courage and self-confidence to the wavering, it shatters the spell of the subject race in the eyes of the world, because it is the most convincing proof of a nation's hunger for freedom. Here in India, as in other countries in the past, terrorism will develop into the revolution and the revolution into independence, social, political and economic. . . .

Gandhi has called upon all those who are nearest to reason to withdraw their support from the revolutionaries and condemn their actions so that our deluded patriots may, for want of nourishment to their violent spirit, realize the futility of violence and the great harm that violent activities have every time done. How easy and convenient it is to call people deluded to declare them to be past reason, to call upon the people to withdraw its support and condemn them so that they may get isolated and be forced to suspend their activities specially when a man holds the confidence of an influential section of the public. It is a pity that Gandhi does not understand and will not understand revolutionary psychology in spite of his life-long experience of public life. It is a precious thing. It is dear to everyone. If a man becomes a revolutionary, if he goes about with his life in the hollow of his hand ready to sacrifice it at any moment he does not do so merely for the fun of it. He does not risk his life because sometimes when the crowd is in a sympathetic mood it cries bravo in appreciation. He does it because his reason forces him to that course, because his conscience dictates it. A revolutionary believes in reason more than anything else. It is to reason and reason alone that he bows. No amount of abuse and condemnation, even [if] it emanates from the highest of the high, can turn him from his set purpose. To think a revolutionary will give up his ideals if public support and appreciation are withdrawn from him is the highest folly. Many a revolutionary has ere now stepped on the scaffold and laid his life for the cause, regardless of the curses that the constitutional agitators rained plentifully upon them. If you will have the revolutionaries suspend their activities, reason with them squarely. This is one way and the only way. For the rest, let there be no doubt in anybody's mind. A revolutionary is the last person on the earth to submit to bullying.

We take this opportunity to appeal to our countrymen, to the youth, to the workers and peasants, to the revolutionary intelligentsia to come forward and to join us in carrying aloft the banner of freedom. Let us establish a new order of society in which political and economic exploitation will be an impossibility. In the name of those gallant men and women who willingly accepted the death so that we their descendents may lead a happier life, who toiled ceaselessly and perished for the poor, defamished [*sic*] and exploited millions of India.

We call upon every patriot to take up the fight in all seriousness. Let nobody toy with the nation's freedom, which is her very life, by making psychological experiments with nonviolence and such other novelties. Our slavery is our shame. When shall we have courage and wisdom enough to be able to shake ourselves free of it? What is our great heritage or our civilization and culture worth if we have not enough self-respect left in us to prevent us from bowing survilance [*sic*] to the commands of foreigners and paying homage to their king and flag.

There is no crime that Britain has not committed in India. Deliberate misrule has reduced us to paupers, has bled us white. As a race and as a people we stand dishonored and outraged. Do people still expect us to forget and forgive. We shall have our revenge, a people's righteous revenge on the tyrant. Let cowards fall back and cling for compromise and peace. We ask not for mercy and we give no quarter. Ours is a war to the end; to victory or death. Long live revolution.

Menahem Begin

The Revolt

At the launching of the revolt we divided the Irgun into a number of sections—in addition to the natural administrative and geographical

Menahem Begin, *The Revolt* (London, n.d.). Reprinted with the permission of the publishers, W. H. Allen.

divisions. We called these sections:

1. A.R.—Army of the Revolution

2. S.U.—Shock Units

3. A.F.—Assault Force

4. R.P.F.—Revolutionary Propaganda Force

We intended, therefore, to have four sections. But reality is stronger than any decisions of a fighting command. The A.R. existed only in theory. It was supposed to serve as a reserve, embracing all the soldiers who were in none of the three remaining sections. But this arrangement never worked. Newcomers passed through it, and after their basic training were transferred to one of the other sections. It had neither officers nor men of its own. It had its day only when we emerged from the underground into the battle with the Arab invaders—when every man in the Irgun was drafted to a regular army unit: section, platoon, company, battalion.

The Shock Units were never actually set up. This was merely a new name given to a unit that had existed before the revolt. It was known—to those that knew of its existence—as the "Red Section" or the "Black Squad." The idea behind this unit was very interesting. It was Yaacov Meridor's idea. He assumed that the struggle for liberation would require men especially trained to operate in the Arab areas, both in Eretz Israel and in the Arab countries. The men chosen were, therefore, brave and dark-skinned. They were given military training and lessons in Arabic. The composition of the "Red Section" was to be kept absolutely secret even from other members of the Irgun. This was the "underground within the underground" idea—which did not succeed. It was daring, but its execution caused a mixture of difficulties, some of them not unamusing. Suddenly the best men, and even officers, began leaving the Irgun. Loyal members who had gone with the Irgun through thick and thin wondered and could not understand. *He*—a deserter? And the deserter would add insult to injury. Not content with loud declarations that he had nothing more to do with the Irgun, he would curse and swear at it. This strange behavior of formerly devoted men and important officers was bound to lower morale in the ranks. It was impossible to explain, or even hint at, the truth. Despite this, however, the deserters were not followed by real ones. Our boys were fortified by the principle we had succeeded in embedding in their hearts: that the ideal is the important thing and not the man. So-and-so had left, such-and-such a one had deserted? What matter? You, the soldier, had taken a historic mission upon yourself out of inner conviction. You had to fulfill it without regard to what anybody might say or do in negation of that mission, whether it were your antagonists or your friends of the day before, or your comrades or your officers. As a soldier of freedom, your supreme commander was the cause itself.

The affair of the "Red Section," though it opened in sorrow, ended in joy and gladness. When the revolt began, all the deserters reappeared in their regular units. There was renewed surprise, but this time it was accompanied by happy relief. Only yesterday that so-and-so had been cursing the Irgun up hill and down dale, and now he was an officer in the front line? They rubbed their eyes. Friendships were re-formed. Much-lowered morale rose up once more.

In the "Red Section" there were many excellent fighters and all, or almost all, looked like Arabs. But it is not only people from the Arab countries who are dark-skinned. There are many Ashkenazi Jews from Europe who are no less dark—and are sometimes darker—than the purest Sephardi. The only two members of the unit I knew personally came from Lodz in Poland. It is true that many of the fighters in the Shock Units sprang from the eastern communities. Hence the story, disseminated particularly by the British press correspondents, of the "Black Squad" of the Irgun, allegedly composed only of Yemenites. This legend was helped along to no small extent by certain Jewish politicians. Wishing to belittle us, these gentlemen whispered, or said aloud, that the *whole* of the Irgun consisted only of Yemenites. Our enemies, who disseminated tales about "black Yemenites" on the one hand and "the scum of Eastern Europe" on the other, were trying to besmirch us. It is a pity that our Jewish political opponents stooped to this nasty "racial" invective so beloved of anti-Semitic propagandists between the wars. The Nazis used to say: "Maybe not all Jews are Communists, but all the Communists are Jews." Similarly, some Zionists said of us: "Not all Yemenites are Irgunists, but all the Irgun people are Yemenites."

Nothing of the sort. In the Shock Units and in all the divisions of the Irgun we had members who came from all Jewish communities and of all classes. We had people from Tunis and Harbin, Poland and Persia, France and Yemen, Belgium and Iraq, Czechoslovakia and Syria; we had natives of the United States and Bokhara, of England, Scotland, Argentina and South Africa, and most of all, of Eretz Israel itself. We were the melting-pot of the Jewish nation in miniature. We never asked about origins: we demanded only loyalty and ability. Our comrades from the eastern communities felt happy and at home in the Irgun. Nobody ever displayed any stupid airs of superiority toward them; and they were thus helped to free themselves of any unjustified sense of inferiority they may have harbored. They were fighting comrades and that was enough. They could, and did, attain the highest positions of responsibility. Shlomo Levi, the first chief of staff in the revolt, is a Sephardi. His brother, "Uzi," on his return from the Eritrea prison camp, became regional commander at Tel-Aviv and commanded thousands of men until he fell, fighting heroically, in the decisive battle for Jaffa. Shimshon, regional commander at Haifa until he was betrayed to the British military authorities, came from Persia. We had a Gideon in Jerusalem, who led the historic operation against the G.H.Q. of the occupation army and led it with consummate bravery and coolness. He was a Sephardi too. Two of the men who went to the gallows, Alkoshi and Kashani, were Sephardim. The "smear" with which our enemies and opponents tried to belittle us was to us a source of pride. People who had been humiliated and degraded became proud fighters in our ranks, free and equal men and women, bearers of liberty and honor. Statistics? We never counted along these lines. But I believe I shall be very near the truth if I say that in the various sections of the Irgun there were no less than 25 percent and no more than 35 percent Sephardim and members of the eastern communities. In the Shock Units, in view of the special emphasis on dark skins, the proportion was probably greater; possibly between 40 and 50 percent.

The members of the Shock Units carried out the early operations of the revolt, but their separate existence was not justified in practical tests. In the course of time and with the deepening of the struggle the Shock Units were united with the Assault Units and became the famous Assault Force of the Irgun, which delivered the heaviest blows against the oppressor and was directly responsible for the disintegration of the mandatory rule in the Eretz Israel. Of the four sections we had planned there remained in practice only two: the Assault Force and the Revolutionary Propaganda Force. And between them there was permanent conflict: every R.P.F. man wanted a transfer to the A.F., and no A.F. man ever agreed to go over to the R.P.F.

This was not the only conflict inside the underground. A fighting underground is a veritable state in miniature: a state at war. It has its army, its police, its own courts. It has at its disposal all the executive arms of a state. Above all, it bore the responsibility for life-and-death not only for individuals, but for whole generations. Nor is it only in this sense that an underground resembles a state. Just as in the ministries and departments of government, so too in the underground and its divisions and sections, there is cooperation and there are quarrels, arising from human nature itself. The regional commanders did not like the "autonomy" granted to the Shock Units and later to the Assault Force. "We" said the regional commanders, "handle all the work in the area under our command. We know what arms we have (or have not). We know our people. Why should we not be in charge of the preparations for battle operations and of the operations themselves?" This argument was quite logical. But the retort of the Assault Force commanders was no less so. "Battle operations," they said, "have often to be prepared very speedily. The regional commander is like a father of many children. He is preoccupied with scores of organization problems. We can only be sure of maximum efficiency if we have direct contact with the local operational officers."

It was not easy to judge between the two sides, particularly as both were seeking only the best means of carrying on the struggle. At times I felt like the judge who had decreed both parties in a dispute to be right and who, when asked by his wife how this could possibly be, replied gently "You are right too, my love!"

This dispute over autonomy that had been granted in the case of the Assault Force went on at the same time as another discussion over autonomy which was not granted. Our Intelligence Service never ceased asking for a certain measure of autonomy. This section did great work during the struggle. While the Assault Force belabored the enemy with iron and lead, the Intelligence fought him with brains. Indeed, the victory over the government forces depended largely on our Intelligence, its revelations, its information and the security belt it built, laboriously and with unerring common-sense, round the fighting underground. Its members, headed by Yoel's deputy and successor, Michael, were anxious for even greater achievements and believed they could obtain them if they were given a measure of freedom of action. Characteristically, they quoted in support of their argument the custom in many countries in which the Intelligence and counter-espionage services are under the direct control of the central government.

Thanks to the understanding and tolerance which all our comrades displayed, we succeeded in overcoming these internecine difficulties, which flowed from the necessary division of labor among many people and their eager desire to succeed in their tasks. It is no exaggeration to say that in the underground we all gained some experience of the machinery of state, with its light and shadow, its virtues and its defects. Generally we overcame the "interdepartmental" problems, but we never succeeded in putting an end to the sacred dispute between the Assault Force and the Revolutionary Propaganda Force.

Platform of the Popular Front for the Liberation of Palestine

1. Conventional War Is the War of the Bourgeoisie. Revolutionary War Is People's War

The Arab bourgeoisie has developed armies which are not prepared to sacrifice their own interests or to risk their privileges. Arab militarism has become an apparatus for oppressing revolutionary socialist movements within the Arab states, while at the same time it claims to be staunchly anti-imperialist. Under the guise of the national question, the bourgeoisie has used its armies to strengthen its bureaucratic power over the masses, and to prevent the workers and peasants from acquiring political power. So far it has demanded the help of the workers and peasants without organizing them or without developing a proletarian ideology. The national bourgeoisie usually comes to power through military coups and without any activity on the part of the masses; as soon as it has captured power it reinforces its bureaucratic position. Through widespread application of terror it is able to talk about revolution while at the same time it suppresses all the revolutionary movements and arrests everyone who tries to advocate revolutionary action.

The Arab bourgeoisie has used the question of Palestine to divert the Arab masses from realizing their own interests and their own domestic problems. The bourgeoisie always concentrated hopes on a victory outside the state's boundaries, in Palestine, and in this way they were able to preserve their class interests and their bureaucratic positions.

The war of June, 1967, disproved the bourgeois theory of conventional war. The best strategy for Israel is to strike rapidly. The enemy is not able to mobilize its armies for a long period of time because this would intensify its economic crisis. It gets complete support from U.S. imperialism and for these reasons it needs quick wars. Therefore for our poor people the best strategy in the long run is a people's war. Our people must overcome their weaknesses and exploit the weaknesses of the enemy by mobilizing the Palestinian and Arab peoples. The weakening of imperialism and Zionism in the Arab world demands revolutionary war as the means to confront them.

2. Guerrilla Struggle as a Form of Pressure for the "Peaceful Solution"

The Palestinian struggle is a part of the whole Arab liberation movement and of the world liberation movement. The Arab bourgeoisie and world imperialism are trying to impose a peaceful solution on this Palestinian problem but this suggestion merely promotes the interests of imperialism and of Zionism, doubt in the efficacy of people's war as a means of liberation, and the preservation of the relations of the Arab bourgeoisie with the imperialist world market.

The Arab bourgeoisie is afraid of being isolated from this market and of losing its role as a mediator of world capitalism. That is why the Arab oil-producing countries broke off the boycott against the West (instituted during the June war), and for this reason McNamara, as head of the World Bank, was ready to offer credits to them.

When the Arab bourgeoisie strive for a peaceful solution, they are in fact striving for the profit which they can get from their role as mediator between the imperialist market and the internal market. The Arab bourgeoisie are not yet opposed to the activity of the guerrillas, and sometimes they even help them; but this is because the presence of the guerrillas is a means of pressure for a peaceful solution. As long as the guerrillas don't have a clear class affiliation and a clear political stand they are unable to resist the implication of such a peaceful solution; but the conflict between the guerrillas and those who strive for a peaceful solution is unavoidable. Therefore the guerrillas must take steps to transform their actions into a people's war with clear goals.

3. No Revolutionary War Without a Revolutionary Theory

The basic weakness of the guerrilla movement is the absence of a revolutionary ideology, which could illuminate the horizons of the Palestinian fighters and would incarnate the stages of a militant political program. Without a revolutionary ideology the national struggle will remain imprisoned within its immediate practical and material needs. The Arab bourgeoisie is quite prepared for a limited satisfaction of the needs of the national struggle, as long as it respects the limits that the bourgeoisie sets. A clear illustration of this is the material help that Saudi Arabia offers Al Fatah while Al Fatah declares that she will not interfere in the internal affairs of any Arab countries.

Since most of the guerrilla movements have no ideological weapons, the Arab bourgeoisie can decide their fate. Therefore, the struggle of the Palestinian people must be supported by the workers and peasants, who will fight against any form of domination by imperialism, Zionism, or the Arab bourgeoisie.

4. The War of Liberation Is a Class War Guided by a Revolutionary Ideology

We must not be satisfied with ignoring the problems of our struggle, saying that our struggle is a national one and not a class struggle. The national struggle reflects the class struggle. The national struggle is a struggle for land and those who struggle for it are the peasants who were driven away from their land. The bourgeoisie is always ready to lead such a movement, hoping to gain control of the internal market. If the bourgeoisie succeeds in bringing the national movement under its control, which strengthens its position, it can lead the movement under the guise of a peaceful solution into compromises with imperialism and Zionism.

Therefore, the fact that the liberation struggle is mainly a class struggle emphasizes the necessity for the workers and peasants to play a leading role in the national liberation movement. If the small bourgeoisie take the leading role, the national revolution will fall as a victim of the class interests of this leadership. It is a great mistake to start by saying that the Zionist challenge demands national unity, for this shows that one does not understand the real class structure of Zionism.

The struggle against Israel is first of all a class struggle. Therefore the oppressed class is the only class which is able to face a confrontation with Zionism.

5. The Main Field of Our Revolutionary Struggle Is Palestine

The decisive battle must be in Palestine. The armed people's struggle in Palestine can help itself with the simplest weapons in order to ruin the economies and the war machinery of their Zionist enemy. The moving of the people's struggle into Palestine depends upon agitating and organizing the masses, more than depending upon border actions in the Jordan valley, although these actions are of importance for the struggle in Palestine.

When guerrilla organizations began their actions in the occupied areas, they were faced with a brutal military repression by the armed forces of Zionism. Because these organizations had no revolutionary ideology and so no program, they gave in to demands of self-preservation and retreated into eastern Jordan. All their activity turned into border actions. This presence of the guerrilla organizations in Jordan enables the Jordanian bourgeoisie and their secret agents to crush these organizations when they are no longer useful as pressure for a peaceful solution.

6. Revolution in Both Regions of Jordan

We must not neglect the struggle in east Jordan, for this land is connected with Palestine more than with the other Arab countries. The problem of the revolution in Palestine is dialectically connected with the problem of the revolution in Jordan. A chain of plots between the Jordanian monarchy, imperialism, and Zionism have proved this connection.

The struggle in east Jordan must take the correct path, that of class struggle. The Palestinian struggle must not be used as a means of propping up the Jordanian monarchy, under the mask of national unity, and the main problem in Jordan is the creation of a Marxist-Leninist party with a clear action program according to which it can organize the masses and enable them to carry out the national and class struggle. The harmony of the struggle in the two regions must be realized through coordinating organs whose tasks will be to guarantee reserves inside Palestine and to mobilize the peasants and soldiers in the border territories.

This is the only way in which Amman can become an Arab Hanoi —a base for the revolutionaries fighting inside Palestine.

Yehoshafat Harkabi

Al Fatah's Doctrine

It is not by sheer accident that the third Fatah pamphlet entitled "The Revolution and Violence, the Road to Victory" is a selective précis of Frantz Fanon's book *The Wretched of the Earth.* Fanon's influence is manifested in other Fatah writings, especially on the psychological impact of Israel on the Arabs and on the transformations that their armed struggle will produce in the Palestinians. "Violence," "violent struggle" and "vengeance" are expressions of great frequency in Fatah literature. The reader of these texts is introduced to a world of simmering frustrated hatred and a drive for unquenchable vengeance.

Violence is described as imperative in wiping out colonialism, for between the colonialist and the colonized there is such a contradiction that no coexistence is possible. One of the two has to be liquidated. (Descriptions of the Arab–Israel conflict as both a zero-sum game and a deadly quarrel are frequent in Arab publications.) Such a conflict is "a war of annihilation of one of the rivals, either wiping out the national entity, or wiping out colonialism. . . . The colonized will be liberated from violence by violence." The "Palestinian revolution" is such a cataclysmic event that it can only be achieved by violence.

Violence liberates people from their shortcomings and anxieties. It inculcates in them both courage and fearlessness concerning death.

Reprinted by special permission from *Adelphi Papers,* No. 53 (December, 1968). Institute of Strategic Studies, London.

Violence has a therapeutic effect, purifying society of its diseases. "Violence will purify the individuals from venom, it will redeem the colonized from inferiority complex, it will return courage to the countryman." In a memorandum to Arab journalists, Fatah stated: "Blazing our armed revolution inside the occupied territory [i.e., Israel, it was written before the Six-Day War] is a healing medicine for all our people's diseases."

The praising of violence as purgative may imply also an element of self-indictment for flaws which will now be rectified, and a desire to exorcize the record of failings. The praising of violence may have as well the function of giving cathartic satisfaction as a substitute for operational action.

Violence, Fatah asserts, will have a unifying influence on people, forging one nation from them. It will draw the individuals from the pettiness of their ego, and imbue them with the effusiveness of collective endeavor, as bloodshed will produce a common experience binding them together. Thus, "the territoriality, [i.e., the fragmentation into different Arab states] which was imposed by imperialism and Arab leaderships and which was sustained by traditional circumstances in the societies, will end."

The struggle, besides its political goals, will have as a by-product an important impact on those who participate in it. It is "a creative struggling" (*Nidalia khallaqa*). Violence, revolutionarism, activism, "the battle of vengeance," "armed struggle," all coalesce in an apocalyptic vision of heroic and just aggression, meting out revenge on Israel. . . .

The parts of Fatah's writings which deal with the phases of war make uneasy reading. Fatah's terminology and formulation may seem both esoteric and highfalutin'. However, what may be more wearisome for the reader who is not versed in such parlance is the generality and abstraction of the discussion. It contains a mixture of a terminology influenced by Marxist literature, attempting to interpret developments in a rational way, with mythical overtones expressed in figures of speech like the "ignition" or "detonation" of a revolution, and leaves the reader wondering how it is to be done.

The organizational stages symbolize the expansion of the circles of those involved in the revolution or war. Stage one is the Formation of the Revolutionary Vanguard. This is achieved by "the movement of revolutionary gathering of the revengeful conscious wills." "The individual of the Revolutionary Vanguard is distinguished by his revolutionary intuition." His task is "to discover the vital tide in his society, for its own sake and for its usefulness for action and movement, and then to realize what obstacles hamper his movement in accordance with history's logic." Thus, "the Revolutionary Vanguard signifies the type of human who interacts positively with the reality [of his predicament], and so elevates himself by his consciousness until he releases himself from reality's grip, in order to pursue the superseding of this reality by another, which differs basically in its values and traits. To take a concrete example, the reality of Arab Palestinian people is fragmented, disfigured, and corrupted, and shows signs of stagnation. However, despite this stagnation and immobility, the historical direction imposes the existence of a current of vitality among the Palestinian people, so long as the Palestinian man treasures vengeance on this reality. As this wish for vengeance grows, the current of vitality congeals in the form of a Revolutionary Vanguard."

The second stage is the Formation of the Revolutionary Organization. In it the Revolutionary Vanguard achieves a psychological mobilization of the Palestinian masses by stimulating their urge for revenge, until "the constructive revolutionary anxiety embraces all the Palestinian Arabs." It is thus called the stage of Revolutionary Embracing. (*Al-Shumul al-Thauri*). Indoctrination of the masses will not precede the staging of the armed struggle but will be achieved by it. "Mistaken are those who advocate the need for rousing a national consciousness before the armed struggle assumes a concrete form. . . . Ineluctably the armed struggle and mass consciousness will go side by side, because the armed struggle will make the masses feel their active personality and restore their self-confidence." The Vanguard will galvanize the masses by means of its example and sacrifice in guerrilla activities.

Fatah's publications state that irresistible might is stored in the Arab masses. They are "latent volcanoes," they are the main "instrument" of the struggle. This explosive capacity has to be activated and this task is allotted to the Vanguard.

The revolution's success is dependent on cooperation between the Vanguard and the masses. "The revolution in its composition has a leadership and a basis, necessitates the accomplishment of a conscious interaction between the basis, which is the masses, and the leadership, in order to ensure the revolution's success and continuation."

The third stage is the Formation of the Supporting Arab Front. Popular support for the "Palestinian revolution" is to be secured in all Arab countries in order to safeguard rear bases in Arab countries for the war, and as a means of putting pressure on the Arab governments not to slacken or deviate from aiding the Palestinian revolution by pursuit of their local interests. The Supporting Arab Front is thus expressed on two levels, the popular and the governmental. The popular support is used as an instrument of pressure against the Arab governments.

In the same publications the overall development of the revolution is divided into two major stages: one, Organization and Mobilization, called elsewhere the Phases of Revolutionary Maturing, comprises the organizational stages already enumerated. The second stage is called that of the Revolutionary Explosion (*Marhal atal-Tafjir al-Thauri*). The stage of the Revolutionary Explosion is described in colorful language: "The hating revengeful masses plunge into the road of revolution in a pressing and vehement fashion as pouring forces that burn everything that stands in their way." In this stage "tempests of revenge" will be let loose. However, the Vanguard should ensure mass discipline to prevent violence going berserk. "The revolution's will should obey its regulating brain."

While the first stage is preparatory, the second is the main interesting stage. Unfortunately, Fatah's description of it is rather rudimentary. Even the question of the timing of its beginning is not clear. Fatah specified: "Our operations in the occupied territory can never reach the stage of the aspired revolution unless all Palestinian groups are polarized around the revolution." Fatah does have an ambition to become the central leader of all the Palestinians, proving that the other movements, which have not matured round what has been described as a Revolutionary Vanguard like itself, are artificial and "counterfeited." Thus the stage of revolution will arrive only when Fatah has mobilized *all* the Palestinians.

Bizham Jazani

Armed Struggle in Iran

THE MAIN FORM OF ADVENTURISM IN THE ARMED MOVEMENT

1. To ignore the objective conditions which are relevant to the growth of the revolutionary movement; to consider the role of the vanguard out of its context; and to peddle the notion that the sensational sacrifice of some elements of the vanguard will immediately (or in a short time) attract the support of the masses, or even encourage their active participation in the struggle, is adventuristic. Such conceptions about armed struggle should be replaced by a Marxist understanding of the dynamics of society and of the revolutionary movement in general. Today, we live in conditions where all factors are combined against the revolution. To believe that all these factors are amenable to change by one single factor, namely, the role of the vanguard—a vanguard in its most elementary form, for that matter—is an unscientific approach to society and to the movement. To persist in such a theory is to deny the role of the masses in the movement. *To deny the masses their role in the movement—although those guilty might vehemently deny this—is the main form of adventurism.*
2. Paying scant attention to revolutionary theory, concentrating only on "practical" and delimited actions, and attention to tactical matters while ignoring strategic questions are all forms of adventurism.

When we fail to recognize that a guerrilla is an informed individual who performs a military assignment armed primarily with revolutionary theory; when we pay little or no attention to political studies and hurriedly try to exploit the excitement caused by a revolutionary action and wish immediately to transform whosoever may join the movement into an exemplary practitioner; and when we imagine that revolutionary theory is merely about tactical questions and sensational literature, then we are only revealing our adventuristic tenden-

Bizham Jazani, *Armed Struggle in Iran*, (1973).

cies, and this can be reflected in the revolutionary movement as a whole.

3. An *absolute* insistence on armed tactics of a particular nature in urban guerrilla struggle; making dogmas out of these tactics and underestimating the value of other tactics besides armed tactics, is only a form of adventurism. To put too much value on sensational tactics, and to pay no attention to tactics that can excite the physical support of the masses for the movement, can alienate the former from the latter and ultimately defeat the movement.

Too much emphasis on the role of the "Fedaee," resorting to constant invocations of "Martyrdom" to offset the absence of a mass movement, and the belief that the sacrifice of blood is sufficient for the start of the revolution are aspects of adventurism.

4. An incorrect knowledge of the potential forces, seeing the struggle merely within the limits of available forces, employing tactics that can only satisfy the latter, disregarding genuine revolutionary forces merely because these will turn to struggle at a later date are deviationary phenomena. Marxist-Leninist organizations are liable to succumb to the temptation of putting aside the special features of their ideology in order to get hold of the available forces offered by certain sections of the petit-bourgeoisie. Such acts can effectively cut the organizations off from the proletariat. This, in effect, means that they will have to make do with a limited force and ignore the potential force in whose hands the revolution will triumph; this is another form of adventurism.

5. Expressions of weariness about the struggle, demonstrations of impatience when the struggle drags on, and complaints about the masses which can turn into pessimism about them is an aspect of adventurism. To employ vengeful tactics in order to offset the absence of a mass movement and to make continuous demands on the members for more and more sacrifices to fill such a vacuum, is a natural consequence of the same thing. To merely examine small tactical matters in an attempt to find the causes of defeat, to explain away the fundamental shortcomings of the movement by looking only at one part of the whole picture, and to blame oneself for the movement's inadequacies is also adventurism.

6. Underestimating the enemy, indulging in self-satisfied expressions because of some victories, exaggerating one's power and ignoring the power of other forces who face the ruling cliques and imperialism is a further form of adventuristic tendency which will prevent us from

making a continuous effort in looking for new tactics, correcting the old ones, and recognizing our shortcomings.

7. Adventurist tendencies can also appear in various other aspects of our work, e.g., in understanding and evaluating the real potentials of different individuals and their political as well as ideological training, in our moral discipline, and in our personal and collective conduct.

The petit-bourgeois deviationary tendency, which manifests itself in the form of leftist and pseudorevolutionary attitudes, is liable to keep us apart from those more straightforward individuals who come to the movement. It can also drive us toward hypocrisy and false humility and prevent us from carrying out fundamental ideological training.

These are the main forms of adventuristic tendencies in groups and organizations attached to the armed movement. The less experienced an organization the more exposed it is to the dangers of these tendencies. Some forms of leftism have a great attraction for inexperienced Marxist individuals, and it is quite true that "leftism" is "an infantile disorder" within the revolutionary working-class movement. Left to itself the disease can spread throughout the whole movement. Those comrades who prescribe the fatal medicine of leftism in order to cure an allegedly "rightist attitude," those comrades who in any way "criticize" a "leftist stand," which in practice is nothing short of an encouragement of this disease, are in effect the most dangerous protagonists of adventurism.

A determined fight against opportunism, in whatever position, the recognition of what are deviationary tendencies and a timely war against them, and a sober defense of revolutionary policy and ideology constitutes the central task facing all elements and groups who are attached to the working classes. Failure to do this is tantamount to leaving the fate of the movement to unforeseen future events. . . .

Armed struggle is bound to grow, despite the inevitable ups and downs which are natural in the development of any movement. Urban guerrilla organizations will expand and armed struggle will assume bigger dimensions and more effective forms. Nevertheless, the following impediments prevent this form of struggle from becoming a mass movement:

a. Urban guerrilla tactics are, from a technical point of view, extraordinarily complicated. In such a struggle every guerrilla will have to be a highly experienced commando. A complete command of the technicalities of struggle against the police—technicalities that continually become more and more complicated—and an extraordinary mobility is an absolute must for every guerrilla. The workers and urban proletariat who have not had sufficient training are unable to use these tactics. The use of these tactics will also be fraught with danger for an ordinary intellectual.

In an urban guerrilla war it is not possible to accept volunteers from among the workers and hope that a few experienced comrades will be able to command them. A commander in such a situation has limited possibilities to guide his men who require leadership at all hours of the day in their various assignments. In such a struggle, every man plays a decisive role in protecting himself and his comrades-in-arms. The great mass of people turn to a struggle in large numbers and suddenly. Hence the above-mentioned features effectively rule out their participation in an urban guerrilla war.

b. Even the largest towns in our country have a limited capacity to accommodate guerrillas. A guerrilla force in Teheran, which is an exceptionally large town, cannot exceed an estimated number of a few hundred—between one to two thousand, if we include the auxiliary units. If we look at the way in which an urban guerrilla unit operates, we will realize that this figure represents an extraordinary force, and is the optimum capacity for military assignments in a town. If the capacity of a town for military actions and concealment is such that the actions of two or more groups overlap each other or cause problems for other groups, thus depriving them of important room for maneuver in the face of possible enemy search-and-destroy operations, then the continuation of a guerrilla existence in that town will become precarious. In such a case the expansion of a guerrilla force is a detrimental factor for us. Those who believe that townspeople will eventually join urban guerrilla organizations in their thousands, or tens of thousands, have, unfortunately, no clear picture of the masses; nor do they have a clear understanding of the characteristics of our struggles. These are the people who occasionally start to murmur about a liberated zone in urban areas.

Urban guerrilla groups and their reserve units (i.e., sympathizers) are formed from conscious and progressive elements. The masses, despite their tremendous size and quality, are unable to partake in urban armed struggle.

c. The intellectuals are better prepared than workers and other proletarians to take part in this struggle. That is why the main force of the urban guerrilla struggle is composed of revolutionary intellectuals.

This composition, with some increase in favor of the workers, will on the whole be maintained through the next stages of the struggle.

In contrast to these limitations and shortcomings, the armed struggle has the following possibilities in the mountains and rural areas.

In the countryside ordinary rural elements can turn to struggle and, after an initial training by experienced cadres, take part in direct actions. There is no impediment to accepting the rural masses into armed combat units, and the reason for dispatching urban guerrilla units to the rural areas is because of the military unpreparedness of the rural population. Not only farmers but also workers and other urban elements can engage in rural armed struggle and develop their potentialities in such a struggle.

The limitations of armed struggle in the towns and its expansion outside does not contradict the primary role of the urban areas in the first stage. In this stage, towns have various advantages over rural areas. These advantages were noted and emphasized by the movement with considerable results. These limitations of urban guerrilla struggle and the possibility of better opportunities in the rural areas, are being analyzed in relation to the armed struggle becoming a mass movement. (Since armed struggle outside the towns is vital to the future of the movement and also because it is very important in the total mobilization of the masses in an armed movement, we have devoted the last chapter of this book to the analysis of this problem.)

Thus the present realities of the situation manifest themselves in two essential ways.

The first is that, parallel to the growth of armed struggle, the urban masses will become active through participation in economic and political movements, the continuation of which will depend on the growth of armed struggle. The second one is that armed struggle will become a mass movement in the rural areas. With the expansion and development of armed struggle in the rural areas, the urban and rural masses will join the struggle. Therefore, we shall in the future—i.e., at the end of the first and throughout the second stages—witness the increase of political and economic protests by the urban population. The expansion of these protests is a result of the growth in social contradictions, and the effect that armed struggle will have on these contradictions in order to reactivate them. . . .

The Effect of Armed Struggle on the People

From the start, the people showed an interest in the guerrillas. Although they had no clear understanding of what a "guerrilla" was, they were thoroughly familiar with the regime. This was the result of a long process of struggle over some generations. The nature of the regime and especially its head, the Shah, was perfectly clear to the masses, not in the form of a political awareness but instinctively. The regime and the Shah's determination to remain in power for such a long time helped this understanding. Therefore, the people's initial reaction to the movement was based on the simple mechanism of "the enemy of the regime is a friend of the people." This mechanism does not always hold good, as it can and has been used by demagogues and the pawns of imperialism to deceive the masses.

Thus even before the nature and characteristics of the "guerrillas" were clear, people displayed favorable sentiments toward them. These were expressed in the form of the various rumors in favor of the guerrillas, although the rumors tended to create a larger-than-life impression about their qualities and numbers. After Siahkal, it was rumored that the northern woods were bristling with guerrillas and the regime's expeditionary force to the north was therefore thought to be on a massive scale. There was, therefore, an exaggerated idea of the enemy's casualties and about the guerrillas' bravery. The news of the guerrillas' defeat was received with incredulity.

It might be said that "rumors" are on a par with lies and fabrication. However, a scientific analysis of "rumors" yields a different picture. In order for rumor to spread quickly and to grow, it needs a suitable social background. The area in which a rumor tends to spread has got to have political, economic and cultural affinity with it. Otherwise not only rumor but even straightforward facts will fail to penetrate the people of that area. Within two days of General Farsio's execution, it was rumored all over the country that he had died immediately (this was in fact the case), whereas the regime was desperately trying to show that he was alive. After this incident, if any of the regime's military political personalities failed to appear in public for a few days, rumor would have it that they had been executed by the guerrillas. . . .

Carlos Marighella

From the "Minimanual"

Personal Qualities of the Urban Guerrilla and How He Subsists

The urban guerrilla is characterized by his bravery and decisive nature. He must be a good tactician and a good shot. The urban guerrilla must be a person of great astuteness to compensate for the fact that he is not sufficiently strong in arms, ammunition, and equipment.

The career militarists or the government police have modern arms and transport, and can go about anywhere freely, using the force of their power. The urban guerrilla does not have such resources at his disposal and leads a clandestine existence. Sometimes he is a convicted person or is out on parole, and is obliged to use false documents.

Nevertheless, the urban guerrilla has a certain advantage over the conventional military or the police. It is that, while the military and the police act on behalf of the enemy, whom the people hate, the urban guerrilla defends a just cause, which is the people's cause.

The urban guerrilla's arms are inferior to the enemy's, but from a moral point of view, the urban guerrilla has an undeniable superiority.

This moral superiority is what sustains the urban guerrilla. Thanks to it, the urban guerrilla can accomplish his principal duty, which is to attack and to survive.

The urban guerrilla has to capture or divert arms from the enemy to be able to fight. Because his arms are not uniform, since what he has are expropriated or have fallen into his hands in different ways, the urban guerrilla faces the problem of a variety of arms and a shortage of ammunition. Moreover, he has no place to practice shooting and marksmanship.

Carlos Marighella, *Handbook of Urban Guerrilla Warfare* (London, n.d.).

These difficulties have to be surmounted, forcing the urban guerrilla to be imaginative and creative, qualities without which it would be impossible for him to carry out his role as a revolutionary.

The urban guerrilla must possess initiative, mobility, and flexibility, as well as versatility and a command of any situation. Initiative especially is an indispensable quality. It is not always possible to foresee everything, and the urban guerrilla cannot let himself become confused, or wait for orders. His duty is to act, to find adequate solutions for each problem he faces, and not to retreat. It is better to err acting than to do nothing for fear of erring. Without initiative there is no urban guerrilla warfare.

Other important qualities in the urban guerrilla are the following: to be a good walker, to be able to stand up against fatigue, hunger, rain, heat. To know how to hide and to be vigilant. To conquer the art of dissembling. Never to fear danger. To behave the same by day as by night. Not to act impetuously. To have unlimited patience. To remain calm and cool in the worst conditions and situations. Never to leave a track or trail. Not to get discouraged.

In the face of the almost insurmountable difficulties of urban warfare, sometimes comrades weaken, leave, give up the work.

The urban guerrilla is not a businessman in a commercial firm nor is he a character in a play. Urban guerrilla warfare, like rural guerrilla warfare, is a pledge the guerrilla makes to himself. When he cannot face the difficulties, or knows that he lacks the patience to wait, then it is better to relinquish his role before he betrays his pledge, for he clearly lacks the basic qualities necessary to be a guerrilla.

The urban guerrilla must know how to live among the people and must be careful not to appear strange and separated from ordinary city life.

He should not wear clothes that are different from those that other people wear. Elaborate and high-fashion clothing for men or women may often be a handicap if the urban guerrilla's mission takes him into working-class neighborhoods or sections where such dress is uncommon. The same care has to be taken if the urban guerrilla moves from the south to the north or vice versa.

The urban guerrilla must live by his work or professional activity. If he is known and sought by the police, if he is convicted or is on parole, he must go underground and sometimes must live hidden. Under such circumstances, the urban guerrilla cannot reveal his activity to anyone, since that is always and only the responsibility of the revolutionary organization in which he is participating.

The urban guerrilla must have a great capacity for observation, must be well informed about everything, principally about the enemy's movements, and must be very searching and knowledgeable about the area in which he lives, operates, or through which he moves.

But the fundamental and decisive characteristic of the urban guerrilla is that he is a man who fights with arms; given this condition, there is very little likelihood that he will be able to follow his normal profession for long without being identified. The role of expropriation thus looms as clear as high noon. It is impossible for the urban guerrilla to exist and survive without fighting to expropriate.

Thus, within the framework of the class struggle, as it inevitably and necessarily sharpens, the armed struggle of the urban guerrilla points toward two essential objectives:

a. the physical liquidation of the chiefs and assistants of the armed forces and of the police;

b. the expropriation of government resources and those belonging to the big capitalists, latifundists, and imperialists, with small expropriations used for the maintenance of individual urban guerrillas and large ones for the sustenance of the revolution itself.

It is clear that the armed struggle of the urban guerrilla also has other objectives. But here we are referring to the two basic objectives, above all expropriation. It is necessary for every urban guerrilla to keep in mind always that he can only maintain his existence if he is disposed to kill the police and those dedicated to repression, and if he is determined—truly determined—to expropriate the wealth of the big capitalists, the latifundists, and the imperialists.

One of the fundamental characteristics of the Brazilian revolution is that from the beginning it developed around the expropriation of the wealth of the major bourgeois, imperialist, and latifundist interests, without excluding the richest and most powerful commercial elements engaged in the import-export business.

And by expropriating the wealth of the principal enemies of the people, the Brazilian revolution was able to hit them at their vital center, with preferential and systematic attacks on the banking network—that is to say, the most telling blows were leveled against capitalism's nerve system.

The bank robberies carried out by the Brazilian urban guerrillas hurt such big capitalists as Moreira Salles and others, the foreign firms which insure and reinsure the banking capital, the imperialist companies, the federal and state governments—all of them systematically expropriated as of now.

The fruit of these expropriations has been devoted to the work of learning and perfecting urban guerrilla techniques, the purchase, the production, and the transportation of arms and ammunition for the rural areas, the security apparatus of the revolutionaries, the daily maintenance of the fighters, of those who have been liberated from prison by armed force and those who are wounded or persecuted by the police, or to any kind of problem concerning comrades liberated from jail, or assassinated by the police and the military dictatorship.

The tremendous costs of the revolutionary war must fall on the big capitalists, on imperialism, and the latifundists and on the government too, both federal and state, since they are all exploiters and oppressors of the people.

Men of the government, agents of the dictatorship and of North American imperialism principally, must pay with their lives for the crimes committed against the Brazilian people.

In Brazil, the number of violent actions carried out by urban guerrillas, including deaths, explosions, seizures of arms, ammunition, and explosives, assaults on banks and prisons, etc., is significant enough to leave no room for doubt as to the actual aims of the revolutionaries. The execution of the CIA spy Charles Chandler, a member of the U.S. Army who came from the war in Vietnam to infiltrate the Brazilian student movement, the military henchmen killed in bloody encounters with urban guerrillas, all are witness to the fact that we are in full revolutionary war and that the war can be waged only by violent means.

This is the reason why the urban guerrilla uses armed struggle and why he continues to concentrate his activity on the physical extermination of the agents of repression, and to dedicate twenty-four hours a day to expropriation from the people's exploiters.

Technical Preparation of the Urban Guerrilla

No one can become an urban guerrilla without paying special attention to technical preparation.

The technical preparation of the urban guerrilla runs from the concern for his physical preparedness, to knowledge of and apprenticeship in professions and skills of all kinds, particularly manual skills.

The urban guerrilla can have strong physical resistance only if he trains systematically. He cannot be a good fighter if he has not learned the art of fighting. For that reason the urban guerrilla must learn and practice various kinds of fighting, of attack, and personal defense.

Other useful forms of physical preparation are hiking, camping, and practice in survival in the woods, mountain climbing, rowing, swimming, skin diving, training as a frogman, fishing, harpooning, and the hunting of birds, small and big game.

It is very important to learn how to drive, pilot a plane, handle a motor boat and a sailboat, understand mechanics, radio, telephone, electricity, and have some knowledge of electronic techniques.

It is also important to have a knowledge of topographical information, to be able to locate one's position by instruments or other available resources, to calculate distances, make maps and plans, draw to scale, make timings, work with an angle protractor, a compass, etc.

A knowledge of chemistry and of color combination, of stamp-making, the domination of the technique of calligraphy and the copying of letters and other skills are part of the technical preparation of the urban guerrilla, who is obliged to falsify documents in order to live within a society that he seeks to destroy.

In the area of auxiliary medicine he has the special role of being a doctor or understanding medicine, nursing, pharmacology, drugs, elementary surgery, and emergency first aid.

The basic question in the technical preparation of the urban guerrilla is nevertheless to know how to handle arms such as the machine gun, revolver, automatic, FAL, various types of shotguns, carbines, mortars, bazookas, etc.

A knowledge of various types of ammunition and explosives is another aspect to consider. Among the explosives, dynamite must be well understood. The use of incendiary bombs, of smoke bombs, and other types is indispensable prior knowledge.

To know how to make and repair arms, prepare Molotov cocktails, grenades, mines, homemade destructive devices, how to blow up bridges, tear up and put out of service rails and sleepers, these are requisites in the technical preparation of the urban guerrilla that can never be considered unimportant.

The highest level of preparation for the urban guerrilla is the center for technical training. But only the guerrilla who has already passed the preliminary examination can go on to this school—that is to say, one who has passed the proof of fire in revolutionary action, in actual combat against the enemy.

The Urban Guerrilla's Arms

The urban guerrilla's arms are light arms, easily exchanged, usually captured from the enemy, purchased, or made on the spot.

Light arms have the advantage of fast handling and easy transport. In general, light arms are characterized as short-barreled. This includes many automatic arms.

Automatic and semi-automatic arms considerably increase the fighting power of the urban guerrilla. The disadvantage of this type of arm for us is the difficulty in controlling it, resulting in wasted rounds or in a prodigious use of ammunition, compensated for only by optimal aim and firing precision. Men who are poorly trained convert automatic weapons into an ammunition drain.

Experience has shown that the basic arm of the urban guerrilla is the light machine gun. This arm, in addition to being efficient and easy to shoot in an urban area, has the advantage of being greatly respected by the enemy. The guerrilla must know thoroughly how to handle the machine gun, now so popular and indispensable to the Brazilian urban guerrilla.

The ideal machine gun for the urban guerrilla is the Ina 45 caliber. Other types of machine guns of different calibers can be used—understanding, of course, the problem of ammunition. Thus it is preferable that the industrial potential of the urban guerrilla permits the production of a single machine gun so that the ammunition used can be standardized.

Each firing group of urban guerrillas must have a machine gun managed by a good marksman. The other components of the group must be armed with .38 revolvers, our standard arm. The .32 is also useful for those who want to participate. But the .38 is preferable since its impact usually puts the enemy out of action.

Hand grenades and conventional smoke bombs can be considered light arms, with defensive power for cover and withdrawal.

Long barrel arms are more difficult for the urban guerrilla to transport and attract much attention because of their size. Among the long barrel arms are the FAL, the Mauser guns or rifles, hunting guns such as the Winchester, and others.

Shotguns can be useful if used at close range and point blank. They are useful even for a poor shot, especially at night when precision isn't much help. A pressure airgun can be useful for training in marksmanship. Bazookas and mortars can also be used in action but the conditions for using them have to be prepared and the people who use them must be trained.

The urban guerrilla should not try to base his actions on the use of heavy arms, which have major drawbacks in a type of fighting that demands lightweight weapons to insure mobility and speed.

Homemade weapons are often as efficient as the best arms produced in conventional factories, and even a cut-off shotgun is a good arm for the urban guerrilla.

The urban guerrilla's role as gunsmith has a fundamental importance. As gunsmith he takes care of the arms, knows how to repair them, and in many cases can set up a small shop for improvising and producing efficient small arms.

Work in metallurgy and on the mechanical lathe are basic skills the urban guerrilla should incorporate into his industrial planning, which is the construction of homemade weapons.

This construction and courses in explosives and sabotage must be organized. The primary materials for practice in these courses must be obtained ahead of time to prevent an incomplete apprenticeship—that is to say, so as to leave no room for experimentation.

Molotov cocktails, gasoline, homemade contrivances such as catapults and mortars for firing explosives, grenades made of tubes and cans, smoke bombs, mines, conventional explosives such as dynamite and potassium chloride, plastic explosives, gelatine capsules, ammunition of every kind are indispensable to the success of the urban guerrilla's mission.

The method of obtaining the necessary materials and munitions will be to buy them or to take them by force in expropriation actions especially planned and carried out.

The urban guerrilla will be careful not to keep explosives and materials that can cause accidents around for very long, but will try always to use them immediately on their destined targets.

The urban guerrilla's arms and his ability to maintain them constitute his fire power. By taking advantage of modern arms and introducing innovations in his fire power and in the use of certain arms, the urban guerrilla can change many of the tactics of city warfare. An example of this was the innovation made by the urban guerrillas in Brazil when they introduced the machine gun in their attacks on tanks.

When the massive use of uniform machine guns becomes possible, there will be new changes in urban guerrilla warfare tactics. The firing group that utilizes uniform weapons and corresponding ammunition, with reasonable support for their maintenance, will reach a considerable level of efficiency. The urban guerrilla increases his efficiency as he improves his firing potential.

The Shot: The Urban Guerrilla's Reason for Existence

The urban guerrilla's reason for existence, the basic condition in which he acts and survives, is to shoot. The urban guerrilla must know how to shoot well because it is required by this type of combat.

In conventional warfare, combat is generally at a distance with long-range arms. In unconventional warfare, in which urban guerrilla warfare is included, the combat is at close range, often very close. To prevent his own extinction, the urban guerrilla has to shoot first and he cannot err in his shot. He cannot waste his ammunition because he doesn't have large amounts, so he must save it. Nor can he replace his ammunition quickly, since he is part of a small group in which each guerrilla has to take care of himself. The urban guerrilla can lose no time and must be able to shoot at once.

One fundamental fact, which we want to emphasize fully and whose particular importance cannot be overestimated, is that the urban guerrilla must not fire continuously, using up his ammunition. It may be that the enemy is not responding to the fire precisely because he is waiting until the guerrilla's ammunition is used up. At such a moment, without having time to replace his ammunition, the urban guerrilla faces a rain of enemy fire and can be taken prisoner or be killed.

In spite of the value of the surprise factor which many times makes it unnecessary for the urban guerrilla to use his arms, he cannot be allowed the luxury of entering combat without knowing how to shoot. And face to face with the enemy, he must always be moving from one position to another, because to stay in one position makes him a fixed target and, as such, very vulnerable.

The urban guerrilla's life depends on shooting, on his ability to handle his arms well and to avoid being hit. When we speak of shooting, we speak of marksmanship as well. Shooting must be learned until it becomes a reflex action on the part of the urban guerrilla.

To learn how to shoot and to have good aim, the urban guerrilla must train himself systematically, utilizing every apprenticeship method, shooting at targets, even in amusement parks and at home.

Shooting and marksmanship are the urban guerrilla's water and air. His perfection of the art of shooting makes him a special type of urban guerrilla—that is, a sniper, a category of solitary combatant indispensable in isolated actions. The sniper knows how to shoot, at close range and at long range, and his arms are appropriate for either type of shooting.

THE FIRING GROUP

In order to function, the urban guerrillas must be organized in small groups. A group of no more than four or five is called *the firing group*.

A minimum of two firing groups, separated and sealed off from other firing groups, directed and co-ordinated by one or two persons, this is what makes a *firing team*.

Within the firing group there must be complete confidence among the comrades. The best shot and the one who best knows how to manage the machine gun is the person in charge of operations.

The firing group plans and executes urban guerrilla actions, obtains and guards arms, studies and corrects its own tactics.

When there are tasks planned by the strategic command, these tasks take preference. But there is no such thing as a firing group without its own initiative. For this reason it is essential to avoid any rigidity in the organization in order to permit the greatest possible initiative on the part of the firing group. The old-type hierarchy, the style of the traditional left doesn't exist in our organization.

This means that, except for the priority of objectives set by the strategic command, any firing group can decide to assault a bank, to kidnap or to execute an agent of the dictatorship, a figure identified with the reaction, or a North American spy, and can carry out any kind of propaganda or war of nerves against the enemy without the need to consult the general command.

No firing group can remain inactive waiting for orders from above. Its obligation is to act. Any single urban guerrilla who wants to establish a firing group and begin action can do so and thus become a part of the organization.

This method of action eliminates the need for knowing who is carrying out which actions, since there is free initiative and the only important point is to increase substantially the volume of urban guerrilla activity in order to wear out the government and force it onto the defensive.

The firing group is the instrument of organized action. Within it, guerrilla operations and tactics are planned, launched, and carried through to success.

The general command counts on the firing groups to carry out objectives of a strategic nature, and to do so in any part of the country. For its part, it helps the firing groups with their difficulties and their needs.

The organization is an indestructible network of firing groups, and of coordinations among them, that functions simply and practically with a general command that also participates in the attacks; an organization which exists for no purpose other than pure and simple revolutionary action.

Interview with "Urbano"

The way of armed struggle is adopted when one is fully convinced that it is the way to overthrow those who hold on to power—that power that gives them all their profits, privileges, and pleasures at the cost of the efforts of others.

At this point, I would like to return to the second part of my question, that concerning the urban nature of the armed struggle.

I'll begin by saying that the decision to take the way of armed struggle was in no way dependent on the specific geographical characteristics of our country. It is a matter of concept. Otherwise, those countries lacking the geographical conditions favorable to rural guerrilla warfare, for example, would have to discard armed struggle in the process of a revolution.

There was a time when the urban guerrillas were looked upon as

From *Cuba Socialista*, December, 1970/January, 1971.

units to provide logistic support—communications, weapons, funds, etc.—for what should be the main nucleus: the rural guerrillas. This concept was discussed by the MLN on the basis of an analysis of our national situation—in which the possibilities for rural guerrilla warfare are practically nil, as we have neither vast jungles nor mountains—and some previous experiences, and we came to the conclusion that the development of urban struggle was possible, thanks to some very interesting, specific conditions.

We studied the French resistance to Nazi occupation; the Algerian struggle—which, even though it developed mainly in the mountains, had its counterpart in the cities—and an example which, as a result of its methodology, its being strictly limited to the urban areas, was extremely useful to the Movement: the struggle waged by the Jews against the English, reference to which is made in a booklet entitled *Rebellion in the Holy Land.*

On the basis of these facts, it was considered feasible to begin the experiment in Latin America, of a guerrilla force whose action would be centered in the cities instead of in the countryside.

Comparatively speaking, what are the advantages and disadvantages, as far as your organization is concerned, of urban and rural guerrilla warfare?

We believe that urban struggle has a number of advantages over rural struggle and that, in turn, the rural struggle also presents certain advantages over the urban struggle. However, the important thing, at this stage of the game, is the proof that the nucleus can come to life, survive, and develop within the city, and all this in keeping with its own laws. It is true that we are operating right in the mouth of the enemy, but it is also true that the enemy is gagging on us. We are faced with the inconvenience of having to lead a dual life, in which we carry on a public activity—whenever we are able to—yet, in reality, are somebody else altogether. But we have the advantage of having a series of indispensable resources at hand which rural guerrillas must engage in special operations to obtain: food, ammunition, weapons, and communications. The same thing applies with respect to the environment: our adaptation to it comes almost naturally.

Adaptation to the environment is another interesting factor. We, the urban guerrillas, move about in a city which we know like the palm of our hand, in which we look like everybody else, and where we go from one place to another with the same ease as do the other million people who live in it.

However, the rate of our losses, in relation to our experiences in

Montevideo, shows a marked increase. Every week, every two weeks, every month, the number of comrades who are captured increases. Were it not for a very strong Tupamaros-people relationship, this might mean that the organization would be decimated.

However, the multiplication of the Movement is so great that it makes for an easy, rapid replacement of these losses.

Losses are relatively high in a city. For example, a person in hiding is identified by the police because his features were not disguised effectively enough; a house that serves as a base of operations begins to attract attention; a person in hiding is detected by the police, goes into a house, the house is raided, and he and other comrades are captured; or a comrade is captured with a document that belongs to the organization or an expropriated weapon on his person.

In other words, there are a number of mechanisms which, in a city, make it possible, beginning from a starting point, to unravel part of the skein. Hence, losses could be described as something inevitable, no matter what security measures are adopted in urban guerrilla warfare.

That is why the replacement of those who are captured, technological and political development and the training of military cadres are the burning issue. The loss of cadres and the loss of infrastructures are a necessary evil which the urban guerrilla force has to face.

I repeat, the replacement of those cadres, the replacement of the infrastructure, is the greatest problem.

Hasn't the organization, in view of the specific conditions that exist in Uruguay, thought of reversing the usual roles and developing some type of rural guerrilla unit that would serve as support or complement to the urban guerrilla action?

The tactical plan contemplated by the organization at present includes extending the war to the interior of the country. A series of actions that were planned recently, which included cutting off communications—tearing down telephone poles, etc.—have been carried out. Many of these actions will eventually be planned within the characteristics of the urban struggle. In other words, even though these actions will be carried out in the countryside, they will have characteristics not so much of rural guerrilla action but rather of a commando raid—that is, going out, completing the operation, and returning, if possible, to normal, everyday life.

The Uruguayan guerrillas have brought into play a number of resources of ingenuity and imagination that make them rather unique.

Could you tell us how important these resources are to the Movement's operational effectiveness and some cases where they have been particularly useful?

Yes, we believe that acute discernment and ingenuity play an important role in urban guerrilla warfare. Since the urban guerrilla always operates in enemy territory, always moves on enemy ground, since he must carry on his work near one of the repression's bases, he must, of necessity, depend on a series of resources which, given the circumstances, are of vital importance.

One example is his use of the same methods employed by the forces of repression.

In the case of the Banco Francés e Italiano, for example, one of our "messengers" arrived at the bank, followed by comrades posing as members of the Intelligence Corps and police liaison men; they entered the bank when the door was opened to let in the "messenger" who customarily arrived at the bank at that time. Once inside the building, the group announced that the Tupamaros had placed a bomb on the premises, everybody was rounded up, and then we told them who we were and that we intended to carry out an action.

That was the first stage of the operation. The second stage consisted of opening the vault. Three of the bank's officials had one key to the vault each. However, they were not in the bank at that moment. But there was a practically surefire way to bring them there. We found one of them, told him that the general manager had committed suicide and that there was chaos in his office, and asked him to please come with us. Then we visited the man who was supposed to have killed himself and told him the same story about the other one. The same procedure was employed with the third man. In this particular case, it was impossible to locate the third party, and, as a result, 380 million pesos remained safely ensconced in the vault, but we took with us a number of documents that proved that the bank was engaged in fraudulent operations and which practically determined the bank's closing.

The documents led to an investigation by the Department of Revenue. We were pretty unhappy about not having been able to get to the 380 million pesos so we tried a new raid, in which we were to pose as revenue agents who were to participate in the work of investigation.

These are examples of ingenuity, which are of the utmost importance in any type of urban action. Something quite similar happened in the taking of the navy garrison.

Two comrades posing as security agents asked to see an official to clear up some incident. While someone went to find him, two soldiers walking along the side of the building were intercepted by one of our comrades impersonating an agent of the investigation department. The comrade demanded that they produce their identification papers, and a heated argument ensued in which the soldiers tried to justify their presence there even though they carried no identification. Needless to say, the two "soldiers" also belonged to our organization. At the right time, everybody went into action, the guards were subdued and the rest of the comrades who were to carry out the operation went into the building.

A similar procedure was employed for getting into the police headquarters in Pando. The action was carried out by two comrades who posed as army officers who were bringing in two captured Tupamaros.

Only a few days separated this action from the one at the El Mago supermarket, which took place the same day the government closed all the branch banks to keep the Movement from getting funds, and it had similar characteristics. Our comrades went into the supermarket posing as security agents looking for a Tupamaro who was working there. The supermarket's administration did a beautiful job of cooperating with us, rounding up all the employees to clear up the situation.

We have staged a number of raids this way.

Then there was a time when we got our weapons by raiding private collections. We used to forge search warrants, and one of our comrades dressed in a policeman's uniform would show the order and ask to be let in. This went on until the Minister of the Interior put an end to this wave of seizures from weapons collectors by announcing that weapons could only be seized provided an order signed by him was presented to the collector.

This, in turn, forced us to forge new orders, bearing his "signature" of course, so we could remove the weapons in question.

Prairie Fire—Political Statement of the Weather Underground, 1974

Armed struggle has come into being in the United States. It is an indication of growth that our movement has developed clandestine organizations and that we are learning how to fight.

The development of guerrilla organization and armed activity against the state is most advanced in the black community, where the tradition and necessity for resistance is highest. The crises of the society provide the training grounds; for Third World People the conditions of prison, the army, the streets and most oppressive jobs produce warriors, political theorists, and active strategists.

The Black Liberation Army—fighting for three years under ruthless attack by the state, the fighters in prisons, and recently the Symbionese Liberation Army are leading forces in the development of the armed struggle and political consciousness, respected by ourselves and other revolutionaries.

At this early stage in the armed and clandestine struggle, our forms of combat and confrontation are few and precise. Our organized forces are small, the enemy's forces are huge. We live inside the oppressor nation, particularly suited to urban guerrilla warfare. We are strategically situated in the nerve centers of the international empire, where the institutions and symbols of imperial power are concentrated. The cities will be a major battleground, for the overwhelming majority of people live in the cities; the cities are our terrain.

We believe that carrying out armed struggle will affect the people's consciousness of the nature of the struggle against the state. By beginning the armed struggle, the awareness of its necessity will be furthered. This is no less true in the U.S. than in other countries throughout the world. Revolutionary action generates revolutionary consciousness; growing consciousness develops revolutionary action. Action teaches the lessons of fighting and demonstrates that armed struggle is possible.

Prairie Fire, n.p., 1974.

We are building a foundation. In four years of armed work, we have come to appreciate the complexity of doing it right and the difficulty of sustaining it. These are contradictions we are working with:

—We live in a whirlwind; nonetheless, time is on the side of the guerrillas. Fighting the enemy is urgent, and we have a duty to do all we can. Yet it takes time to win the people's trust; it takes time to build an organization capable of surviving the hunt; it takes time to recover and learn from mistakes, to prepare, train, study, and investigate. This is an observation. It is not offered as an argument for delay.

—There is constant resolution between carrying forward the struggle and the necessity of preserving valuable cadre and supporters. Sometimes this is not a matter of choice—the guerrillas are forced, because of the torture and murder committed by the repressive apparatus, to escalate and move beyond what can be immediately sustained.

—Armed struggle brings the resistance to a sharper and deeper level of development. The greater the resistance, the greater will be the force and scope of the state repression brought to bear upon the people. When resistance is at a high level, the enemy takes measures against the people. But treading lightly will not assuage the rulers. Violent repression is built into the status quo. Guerrilla strategy has to resolve the contradiction between the necessary progress of the struggle and what the people can sustain at any given time.

—Armed actions push forward people's consciousness and commitment; they are a great teacher and example. Yet they must be clearly understandable to the people, identify our enemy precisely, and overcome his massive lies and propaganda.

Attacks by the Weather Underground have been focused and specific. These actions were a catalyst for thousands of politically directed armed actions between 1970 and 1972, almost all of which complemented mass struggles.

These bombings were carried out by the Weather Underground:

—To retaliate for the most savage criminal attacks against black and Third World people, especially by the police apparatus:

- Haymarket police statue, Chicago, October, 1969, and October, 1970
- Chicago police cars, following the murder of Fred Hampton and Mark Clark, December, 1969
- New York City Police Headquarters, June, 1970

- Marin County Courthouse, following the murder of Jonathan Jackson, William Christmas, and James McClain, August, 1970
- Long Island City Courthouse, in Queens, in solidarity with prison revolts taking place in New York City, October, 1970
- Department of Corrections in San Francisco and Office of California Prisons in Sacramento, for the murder of George Jackson in San Quentin, August, 1971
- Department of Corrections in Albany, N.Y., for the murder and assault against the prisoners of Attica, September, 1971
- 103rd Precinct of the New York City police, for the murder of 10-year-old Clifford Clover, May, 1973

—To disrupt and agitate against U.S. aggression and terror against Vietnam and the Third World:

- Harvard war research Center for International Affairs, Proud Eagle Tribe (women's brigade), October, 1970
- U.S. Capitol, after the invasion of Laos, March, 1971
- MIT research center, William Bundy's office, Proud Eagle Tribe (women's brigade), October, 1971
- The Pentagon, after the bombing of Hanoi and mining of the harbors of North Vietnam, May, 1972
- Draft and recruiting centers
- ROTC buildings
- ITT Latin America headquarters, following the fascist counter-revolution in Chile, September, 1973

—To expose and focus attention against the power and institutions which most cruelly oppress, exploit and delude the people:

- National Guard Headquarters, Washington, D.C., after the murders at Jackson State and Kent State, May, 1970
- Presidio Army Base and MP Station, San Francisco, July 26, 1970
- Federal Offices of HEW (Health, Education and Welfare), (women's brigade), San Francisco, March, 1974
- Liberation of Timothy Leary from California Men's Colony, San Luis Obispo, September, 1970

Mass struggle and movements are not mere spectators in revolutionary war; armed struggle cannot become a spectacle. It is the responsibility of mass leaders and organizations to encourage and support revolutionary armed struggle in open as well as quiet ways. Actions are more powerful when they are explained and defended. The political thrust of each armed intervention can be publicly championed and built on. Parallel mass support will further both the mass and military struggle.

There are many faces to militant resistance and fighting, a continuum between guerrilla and mass work. An examination of recent history points to: *acts of resistance* . . . draft-card burnings, sabotage in the military, on the job, in government, and attacks on the police; *mass demonstrations* . . . Marches on the Pentagon, Stop the Draft Week, African Liberation Day rallies, International Women's Day marches, Chicano Moratorium marches; *demands for control and power through seizures of institutions* . . . community control of hospitals and schools, occupations of land such as Wounded Knee, or symbols such as the Statue of Liberty, People's Park, prison rebellions and takeovers; *clandestine propaganda* . . . spray painting, pouring blood on draft files, the Media, Pa., FBI ripoff; *popular rebellion* . . . Watts, Detroit, Chicago, Cleveland, Newark; *outrage expressed violently and collectively* . . . Jackson/Kent/Cambodia, bank burning at Isla Vista, TDA's, Days of Rage.

There are connecting lines between these different forms of fighting. All are forms of resistance by the people and forms of attack against the state. Militancy and armed struggle are consistent threads in revolutionary movements—they cannot be wished or forced away. They will continue to be practiced as long as imperialism exists. Together they constitute the fullness of revolutionary war.

The greater part of the revolution remains before us. We need to evaluate our strengths and weaknesses to go on from here. Our present strategy is rooted in our interpretation of the struggles of the last fourteen years.

RAF (Baader-Meinhof Group)

The Concept of the Urban Guerrilla

If we are correct in saying that American imperialism is a paper tiger, i.e., that it can ultimately be defeated, and if the Chinese Communists

Rote Armee Fraktion (RAF), *Das Konzept Stadtguerilla*, April, 1971.

are correct in their thesis that victory over American imperialism has become possible because the struggle against it is now being waged in all four corners of the earth, with the result that the forces of imperialism are fragmented, a fragmentation which makes them possible to defeat—if this is correct, then there is no reason to exclude or disqualify any particular country or any particular region from taking part in the anti-imperialist struggle because the forces of revolution are especially weak there and the forces of reaction especially strong.

As it is wrong to discourage the forces of revolution by underestimating their power, so it is wrong to suggest they should seek confrontations in which these forces cannot but be squandered or annihilated. The contradiction between the sincere comrades in the organizations—let's forget about the prattlers—and the Red Army Fraction, is that we charge them with discouraging the forces of revolution and they suspect us of squandering the forces of revolution. Certainly, this analysis does indicate the directions in which the fraction of those comrades working in the factories and at local level and the Red Army Fraction are overdoing things, if they are overdoing things. Dogmatism and adventurism have since time immemorial been characteristic deviations in periods of revolutionary weakness in all countries. Anarchists having since time immemorial been the sharpest critics of opportunism, anyone criticizing the opportunists exposes himself to the charge of anarchism. This is something of an old chestnut.

The concept of the "urban guerrilla" originated in Latin America. Here, the urban guerrilla can only be what he is there: the only revolutionary method of intervention available to what are on the whole weak revolutionary forces.

The urban guerrilla starts by recognizing that there will be no Prussian order of march of the kind in which so many so-called revolutionaries would like to lead the people into battle. He starts by recognizing that by the time the moment for armed struggle arrives, it will already be too late to start preparing for it; that in a country whose potential for violence is as great and whose revolutionary traditions are as broken and feeble as the Federal Republic's, there will not—without revolutionary initiative—even be a revolutionary orientation when conditions for revolutionary struggle are better than they are at present—which will happen as an inevitable consequence of the development of late capitalism itself.

To this extent, the "urban guerrilla" is the logical consequence of the negation of parliamentary democracy long since perpetrated by its very own representatives; the only and inevitable response to emergency laws and the rule of the hand grenade; the readiness to fight with those same means the system has chosen to use in trying to eliminate its opponents. The "urban guerrilla" is based on a recognition of the facts instead of an apologia of the facts.

The student movement, for one, realized something of what the urban guerrilla can do. He can make concrete the agitation and propaganda which remain the sum total of left-wing activity. One can imagine the concept being applied to the Springer Campaign at that time or to the Heidelberg students' Cabora Bassa Campaign, to the squads in Frankfurt, or in relation to the Federal Republic's military aid to the *comprador* regimes in Africa, in relation to criticism of prison sentences and class justice, of safety legislation at work and injustice there.

The urban guerrilla can concretize verbal internationalism as the requisition of guns and money. He can blunt the state's weapon of a ban on communists by organizing an underground beyond the reach of the police. The urban guerrilla is a weapon in the class war.

The "urban guerrilla" signifies armed struggle, necessary to the extent that it is the police which make indiscriminate use of firearms, exonerating class justice from guilt and burying our comrades alive unless we prevent them. To be an "urban guerrilla" means not to let oneself be demoralized by the violence of the system.

The urban guerrilla's aim is to attack the state's apparatus of control at certain points and put them out of action, to destroy the myth of the system's omnipresence and invulnerability.

The "urban guerrilla" presupposes the organization of an illegal apparatus, in other words apartments, weapons, ammunition, cars, and papers. A detailed description of what is involved is to be found in Marighella's *Minimanual for the Urban Guerrilla*. As for what else is involved, we are ready at any time to inform anyone who needs to know because he intends to do it. We do not know a great deal yet, but we do know something.

What is important is that one should have had some political experience in legality before deciding to take up armed struggle. Those who have joined the revolutionary left just to be trendy had better be careful not to involve themselves in something from which there is no going back.

The Red Army Fraction and the "urban guerrilla" are that fraction and praxis which, because they draw a clear dividing line between themselves and the enemy, are combatted most intensively. This presupposes a political identity, presupposes that one or two lessons have already been learned.

In our original concept, we planned to combine urban guerrilla activity with grass-roots work. What we wanted was for each of us to work simultaneously within existing socialist groups at the work place and in local districts, helping to influence the discussion process, learning, gaining experience. It has become clear that this cannot be done. These groups are under such close surveillance by the political police, their meetings, timetables, and the content of their discussions so well monitored, that it is impossible to attend without being put under surveillance oneself. We have learned that individuals cannot combine legal and illegal activity.

Becoming an "urban guerrilla" presupposes that one is clear about one's own motivation, that one is sure of being immune to "Bild-Zeitung" methods, sure that the whole anti-Semite-criminal-subhuman-murderer-arsonist syndrome they use against revolutionaries, all that shit that they alone are able to abstract and articulate and that still influences some comrades' attitude to us, that none of this has any effect on us.

PART IV

Interpretations of Terrorism

Introductory Note

The study of terrorism has given rise to a great many theories and interpretations because terrorism itself has varied so much in character, origins, and causes. Some of these interpretations are discussed in my *Terrorism* (Boston: Little, Brown; and London: Weidenfeld, 1977). The excerpts presented in this section are fairly typical of their kind. Lucien de la Hodde, a member of many French secret societies of the 1830s and 1840s, was the chief police spy of the period; his life reads like that of a character in a Balzac novel. In a book published in 1850, after his role as informer had been revealed, he listed the reasons which, in his view, impelled people to join a revolutionary movement. Sometimes this sounds like a caricature, at others the resemblance to the original is uncomfortably close. A more detached view was taken by Cesare Lombroso (1835–1909), the most respected student of criminology of the second half of the nineteenth century who devoted several books to political crimes and their putative causes. Emma Goldman (1869–1940), one of the patron saints of anarchism, argued, not without reason that it was quite wrong to assume that all terrorists were anarchists; most of them were not. As for those anarchists who had opted for violence, Emma Goldman claimed that intolerable pressure had driven them to commit acts of despair. The views of Marx and Engels, Lenin and Trotsky about terrorism are documented in some detail. With them we reach the contemporary period. No one should be deterred by the fact that there is no "general scientific theory" of terrorism, let alone universal agreement about its character. A general theory is *a priori* impossible because the phenomenon has so many different roots and manifestations. But this is not to say that all the theories are equally true and deserve the same measure of respect. On the whole, terrorism is not a complicated issue and its basic patterns are not shrouded in secrecy. Chalmers Johnson is Professor of Political Science at the University of California, Los Angeles; Paul Wilkinson teaches at University College, Cardiff; until his recent retirement,

Feliks Gross was Professor of Politics at Brooklyn College; Dr. Hans Josef Horchem is head of the *Bundesamt fuer Verfassungsschutz* in Hamburg.

Lucien de la Hodde

The Disaffected

Whatever may be done to the contrary, it is very certain that no form of government among us will ever escape the pest of conspiracies; for there is always a large class of men who think that the government under which they live is the worst one that they could have; and as these men also think that all our insurrections have been the work of secret societies, these societies are hence held by them in very particular esteem.

But, in fact, not one of our revolutions during the last sixty years has been the work of conspirators. However blasphemous this assertion may appear to the grumblers of the mob, we hold it to be . . . true.

There is but one maker of revolutions in France, and that is Paris; idle, sophistical, disappointed, restless, evil-minded Paris. We all know her. But this Paris does not overthrow the government on a fixed day, and according to a settled plan; for every time she takes the initiative she is crushed at once. Witness the affair of June, 1832; of May, 1839; and several other similar affrays. To meet with success, it is necessary that the bourgeoisie, either in a fit of passion, as in 1830, or from a misdirection of ideas, as in 1848, should set the insurrection in motion. And above all, Providence itself must permit one of those incomprehensible contingencies—such, for instance, as that of sovereign power giving way to a revolt without the test of a combat.

This Paris, which is always lying in wait to seize power by the throat and strangle it, is composed of the following elements, viz:

1. *The Youth of the Schools* (as they are called)—It is the nature of these gentlemen to be opposed to the government. The most of

Lucien de la Hodde, *History of Secret Societies* (New York, 1864).

them would consider it ridiculous to have the same ideas as their neighbor, the bourgeois, who defends the existing order of things, because they give him and his family the means of an honest livelihood. And then schoolboys, we know, are fond of noise, fracas, and sudden events, and, indeed, they expect to be recognized by such traits. Everyone has heard of their traditions of the Pré aux Clercs; they are a species of puerility which would be amusing if these young men, as well by their real courage as from the prestige which is accorded them, and from the facility with which they become instruments in the hands of the factious, did not, in fact, possess a considerable weight in our revolutions. The majority of students, it is well known, are occupied in the study of law, of medicine, or some other science, and not in reforming the government at the point of the bayonet; hence, in speaking of the youth of the schools, we mean only those of whom the anarchical journals take it upon themselves to be the interested flatterers—those who parade at the clubs, political meetings, and other rude places. The students who are occupied with their studies have never had the honor of attracting the attention of our patriot editors.

The youth of the schools have their chiefs, some of whom have never taken the papers, and others have ceased to take them for the last ten years, for they go directly to the *pure* fountainhead, to the offices of the papers themselves, and there receive their instructions When an order of the day is given, they hasten to all the estaminets in the Latin quarter of the town, where they are sure to meet with their fellows—some of the youths of the schools frequent such places, too; the leaders resort thither, also, and then are distributed those documents which, at one and the same time, enlighten the faithful and invite the curious.

Rumors have spread that the schools are to be removed beyond the limits of Paris; and it is certain that the government might thus cut off *one* of the arms of the insurrectional Briareus. The English, who have a genius for order and public tranquility, have long since excluded from their capital this interesting but rather dangerous portion of the community. Besides the political question involved, it is a sufficient reason for the government that those students who now spend their time at billiards, or in revolutionary maneuvers, would be much better off in the provinces under the eyes of their parents than at Paris, and that those who really wish to devote themselves to study have no need of the too numerous distractions of the capital.

2. *The Imbeciles*—In this class are included lawyers without cli-

ents, doctors without patients, writers without readers, merchants without customers, and all that troupe of hopeful men, who, having studied their parts in the politics of the newspapers, aspire to enact them as men of the state. Some few of them are indeed capable of the posts to which they aspire, but they find it intolerable to arrive at them like the rest of the crowd, by diligence and perseverance. Others of their number are not capable, and these are by far the most ardent and ambitious. They are all imbecile, for they fail in the first evidence of strength, which is patience. The organizers of secret societies and schemers of insurrection come from this class.

3. *The Gypsies*—These exist everywhere, and especially among us—a class of imaginative persons who have an utter horror of ordinary life. The generality of mortals usually understand that pleasure and repose are the rewards only of labor and privation, but the gypsies expect never to work and always to enjoy. As this kind of life, however, in order to be conveniently practiced, requires some fat rents, which they have not, they are obliged to have recourse to the expedient of establishing a sort of vagrancy, of which the obscurest estaminets become the courts of miracles. The provinces count but a few of these individuals, for they generally alight upon the capital, the only place where idleness flourishes and where certain wickednesses thrive at their ease. To determine from what quarter this variety of the social world comes is not easy; it comes from no matter where, from the highest as well as the lowest. Some few of them remain very nearly honest men, especially if they are not of too excitable a temperament or are wanting in the courage of crime; but the greater part of them have the instincts of debauchees, which they gratify at all hazards.

It is in this class that are found the chiefs of sections, the commandants of barricades, etc.

4. *The Sovereign People* (that is to say, the workmen of Paris, either native or those who have become acclimated in the suburbs)—Brave by nature, and a fighter by habit, the workman expects to make a fortune out of every political tumult. A lofty sentiment of independence, acquired by the reading of revolutionary rhapsodies, renders him impatient of the restraints of authority. He never likes the master by whom he is employed, generally detests all others, and the rich and the dignitaries of the government he considers himself bound to execrate. This is not a mere portrait of our own inventing, for M. Louis Blanc, who will recognize some of his own workmanship in it, declares that the people is gross and brutal. Now there is but one

people for M. Louis Blanc and men of his like, and that people is the people of Paris. This organizer of labor adds, it is true, that it is not the fault of the people that they are so. Agreed. But it is something very astonishing that with two such important qualities, courage and intelligence, the people of Paris should remain so deplorably deficient in polish. Those socialists who are candid frankly confess the fact, and if they would open their eyes and confess the whole truth, they would acknowledge that they themselves are the cause of it.

It is useless to deny that this workman, gross, brutal, quarrelsome, ignorant of his duty, in opposition always to the law, is not in the majority in Paris; we mean, of course, of those who are wheedled by the patriots—those who are told, and really believe it themselves, that they alone are the masters of the destinies of the country.

5. *The Fly-Catchers*—This is a class of persons who are rather to be pitied than condemned. They are good men at bottom, but they listen to M. Bareste, maker of almanacs, who tells them that the country is horribly governed; to M. Proudhon, that detestable mystifier, who tells them that property is theft; to M. Ledru-Rollin, a millionaire overwhelmed with debts, who tells them that the patriots are dying from hunger. Through foolish or shameless newspapers, they are made to see every day that black is white, and white black; the same falsehood presented in a hundred different ways, the same deception practiced in a hundred different forms, is offered to them every morning, in the most natural manner in the world—with the most perfect air of assurance; the friends are near to support the cause; the papers of the opposite opinion are never read, because *they* are *sold;* if good advice happens to be given, *that* comes from a renegade or a spy; and thus a large mass of honest men give themselves up to foolish schemes, harassing miserably their own lives, and those of others. From the National Guard which introduces the Republic with the shout of "Hurrah for reform!" down to the innocent citizen who swallows everything that is told him, they are fly-catchers, political and socialist, from every class of society, and of every shade and variety of color and complexion.

These honest souls serve as the lever, as the plastron, or as the make-weights of the revolutions.

6. *The Disaffected*—This class, also, is composed of an infinitude of elements; but we design especially to speak of those persons who, by the fall of former governments, have been injured either in their fortunes or affections. They never take a part in the insurrection as mere common soldiers; some are led into it for the sake of excite-

ment, and others for a consideration. These latter, men practiced in the routine of political life, are too skillful to leave any traces of their maneuvers. Instructions, advice, material aid, everything of this kind, reaches its destination among them only from the third or fourth person. The police alone has been able to follow this train of bribes and intrigues into its obscure shades; but thus far it has seldom been able to detect the plotters in the fact.

These men, who are the very leprosy of the body politic, are incontestably the most dangerous of all others to every government.

7. *Political Refugees*—This class of men is a virus with which France has become inoculated, and which adds to her revolutionary maladies. The abettors of revolt from all countries, drawn among us by an imprudent generosity on our part, are constantly busied in fomenting insurrections; knowing well that a disturbance in France is a signal to other countries.

8. *The Bandits*—The social condition of a country is always very much disturbed during revolutionary times, and it is then, in particular, that malefactors have rare picking. A few good men, it is true, during the disturbances of February, posted up notices of "Death to Robbers!" but this did not prevent the Duchess of Orleans' shawls from being stolen, nor the wine casks of M. Duchatel from being emptied, nor the jewels of the family of Orleans from being sold throughout Europe. That some few of the mob endeavored to preserve the police cannot be denied; we render justice to whom it is due. But what a fine pretension is here set up! Ah! we must know these fellows who live upon the wealth of others. No sooner does the disturbance break forth, than, seized with patriotic zeal, they rush with a lantern in one hand and a musket in the other, demanding only to be posted at the best places, reserving the time and mode of action to themselves.

But robbers are not the only ones who profit by an insurrection. There are a few well-meaning men, it is true, who, after having shouted, "Hurrah for the charter! Hurrah for reform!" and having borne the brunt of the fight, then withdraw, in all the pride of integrity, to die in their garrets; but there are some very accomplished rascals, on the other hand, who, when the revolution is over, are found living in comfortable ease on their suddenly acquired rents. Indeed, it is beyond a doubt that the thieves, robbers, and assassins of Paris never fail to furnish some of the *heroes* of our revolutions.

Such, then, are the eight divisions of the forces which are usually employed in an insurrection. Sometimes they may be seen all assembled together; but this depends upon circumstances; for, if the affair appears to be badly managed, some of the forces draw off, but when things take a favorable turn, and success seems probable, then the whole army may be found drawn up in line.

Cesare Lombroso

The Militants

We suffer above all from our defective economic order. Not that it is really worse than that of our fathers; indeed, famine, which formerly carried off millions of victims, today accounts for only a few hundreds, and our working women have more linen to wear than the proudest of *châtelaines* in former times. But the needs of the people have increased to an extent disproportionate with their incomes, together with a repugnance for the means of satisfying them; charity, as dispensed by the convents and monasteries, is still the most widespread remedy for acute poverty, though it does not so much relieve the need for basic necessities as cause irritation to the natural pride of modern man. As for co-operatives, their field of action is too limited; indeed, in our country districts, they are almost altogether lacking.

Even if both sources of assistance were fruitful and efficient they would not suffice to calm our people, because social and economic fanaticism, blind and violent like all fanatical movements, is rising . . .

This is because the ideals of religion, of family life and of patriotism, together with those of local loyalties, inherited rank, caste, and *esprit de corps*, have disappeared before our eyes.

And since men have always need of some ideals, they now cling to economic betterment, as positive and relevant to the necessities of life, and not subject, like the others now discredited, to the ruthless logic of modern analysis. Here they concentrate all the energies formerly disseminated among the others; so that, if we no longer feel the

Cesare Lombroso, *Gli Anarchisti*, Chap. 1 (Turin, 1895).

advantages of those ideals overthrown (such as generosity, tolerance, and the spirit of self-sacrifice), sufficient relics of the old order remain to make us realize the injuries and constraints we suffered from it. Thus, if history has duly punished the two higher social strata, history has not wiped out all the evils they engendered; we still have to endure them and those that have succeeded them. Feudal arrogance and overbearing behavior, for instance, religious hypocrisy and intolerance, etc., continue in many places together with, and in addition to, the arrogance of the third estate.

Theocratic dominance faded from our customs long ago, at least to all appearance; but try to bring into the open some question into which, even remotely, that of religion enters, such as, for instance, that of divorce, or anti-Semitism, or the suppression of the clerical schools, and you will see the opposition that is aroused, of course disguised in the most diverse forms, even the most liberal; bringing into play individual freedom, respect for womanhood, the protection of children, and so on. The domination of the military class, too, has not been with us for many centuries; but nevertheless, try to sound this note, if not to members of the general public at any rate in official or semi-official circles, and you will inevitably create hostility toward yourself. The state finances show millions spent on the maintenance of hundreds of gold-braided, useless generals, while meager salaries are meted out to impoverished teachers who merely receive unprofitable praise, and promises never carried out. Meanwhile, approaching bankruptcy is blatantly disregarded, as is, worse still, the starvation of the exhausted peasantry.

The same can be said of patriotic and aesthetic ideals; they are undermined, it is true, but go and tell the French common people to have done with its hatred for the Italians, the English, and half the rest of the world; tell the Italian middle classes how ridiculous they are with their false adoration of the classics, which, in fact, they neither appreciate nor understand, while on their altar they waste the best hours of their sons' lives: and they will pretend not to understand you, or will be scandalized.

Against the greed for gain of the industrialists, the fourth estate, which protests about everything, is already raising its voice; maintaining that there is no kind of proportion between the profits and the amount of labor expended by the three upper levels of society, and the scanty gains and hard work which are their own lot.

This is all the more felt and vigorously proclaimed now where poverty is least in evidence, because it is easiest there to create a reaction. The poor Indians, dying by millions of hunger, have no strength to react, nor can the Lombards who are dying of pellagra. On the other hand, the peasants of Germany and the Romagna, who are relatively better off than the rest, like the workers of Australia, have more strength of initiative and are able to protest on behalf of those poorer than themselves. And in fact the anarchists are not among the poorest of the workers, indeed many of them are comparatively well off.*

And then, it is undeniable that, whether under the form of a republic or a monarchy, at least for the Latin races, all our social and governmental institutions are a great, conventional sham, as we all admit in our hearts but deny with our lips.

Faith in parliamentary government, which every day lays bare its dismal impotence, is a falsehood; false is our faith in the infallibility of the heads of state, who are often inferior to the least of us; and false our faith in a form of justice which, weighing heavily on the shoulders of honest men, strikes at scarcely 20 percent of the true culprits, the majority of whom are of low intelligence and leaves the rest free, obeyed and admired, amid the weak and innocent destined to be their victims.

We no longer possess even a hands'-breadth of dominion over the sea that surrounds us; we have not cleansed our uncultivated lands, and we are playing the fool like children in an area no better than a desert which may cost us much blood, without bringing us the slightest gain.

* According to statistics, certainly neither exact nor impartial, from the Paris prefecture, there are 500 anarchists in Paris (they themselves claim that there are 7,500 in Paris and 4,000 in France. Of the 500 there are two classes, the propagandists and the real initiates: among the propagandists there are 10 journalists, 25 printers, and 2 proofreaders; among the skilled workers 17 tailors, 16 shoemakers, 20 workers in the food industries, 15 cabinetmakers, 12 barbers, 15 mechanics, 10 bricklayers, and 250 belonging to various professions, viz: 1 architect, 1 ex-doorkeeper, 1 singer, 1 bank messenger, 1 insurance agent, etc. These figures are doubtless incomplete. In any case, they cannot represent excessive poverty, nor do they in the case of H. Dupont, one of the leaders and a rich man, nor in that of Prince Kropotkin, nor Gori and Molinari, professional men and landowners, nor in the Bohemian bomber Drexken, a member of a very rich family.

Dubois, in *Le péril anarchiste* (1893), calculates the anarchists in France as numbering 20,000 to 30,000, the majority of them sedentary workers; shoemakers, carpenters, weavers and mineworkers, followed by dyers and upholsterers; therefore, not by any means indigent.

Against the deep-seated evils that are gnawing at our vitals—against pellagra, alcoholism, and superstition, against legal injustice and ignorance in our educational system, we react with theatrical demonstrations, rhetorical phrases, and bureaucratic formulas, winning time, if possible, if not to make matters worse, at least to give an impression of dealing with them.

The society of the capital, headed like that of Japan by a Mikado and a Shogun is ravaged by a crowd of wretched rhetoricians, who on a small scale sum up all the ills of Italy.

We have a clergy, powerless in theory but in fact still influential over the two extremes of the social structure—the common people and the aristocracy—a caste that officially has inherited the power but not the prestige of both, and which is scarcely superior to them in abilities or in energy; so that mediocrity dominates everywhere, and unconscious of its own ineptitude strives to achieve some effect, without forseeing or caring about the outcome.

This is why, for want of any solid basis from his education, the young man seizes upon any new idea, however erroneous and ill-adapted to the times, if it reminds him of a remotely glimpsed antiquity. Whoever doubts this should remember the classicism of the revolutionaries of '89 and read Vallés' book: *Le bachelier et l'insurgé*. He will see there how greatly this education, so out of key with modern times, contributes to the formation of unsettled and rebellious youth.

This abuse of classical education prompts our ready agreement to set up a monument or celebrate a centenary rather than to inaugurate a school or an industry, or to drain a swamp. And from this education is derived that adoration of violence which has been the point of departure of all our revolutionaries, from Cola da Rienzi to Robespierre.

". . . All our classical education," writes Guglielmo Ferrero (*Riforma sociale*, 1894), "what is it if not a continual glorification of violence, in all its forms? Beginning with the apotheosis of the assassinations committed by Codrus or by Aristogeiton and leading up to the regicides headed by Brutus. And all the history of the Middle Ages and all modern history, and the history of our Risorgimento itself, as it is taught today almost everywhere, what is it if not the glorification, from a particular point of view, of brutal and violent acts? Has not a poet, regarded by everyone as the moral representative of the new Italy, felt able to write, amid general applause:

Steel and wine I must have . . .
Steel to strike down the tyrants,
Wine to celebrate their obsequies

"Here the evil is so deep-seated that all parties are in agreement: the clericals give cheers for Ravaillac's stabbing of Henry IV; the conservatives for the mass shooting of the *communards* of 1871; and the republicans at Orsini's bombs; all are of one mind in celebrating the sanctity of violence when it turns out useful to themselves. The new hero of the last years of this century is neither a man famed for great learning nor a great artist, but Napoleon I."

Emma Goldman

The Psychology of Political Violence

To analyze the psychology of political violence is not only extremely difficult but also very dangerous. If such acts are treated with understanding, one is immediately accused of eulogizing them. If, on the other hand, human sympathy is expressed with the *Attentäter*, one risks being considered a possible accomplice. Yet it is only intelligence and sympathy that can bring us closer to the source of human suffering and teach us the ultimate way out of it.

The primitive man, ignorant of natural forces, dreaded their approach, hiding from the perils they threatened. As man learned to understand Nature's phenomena, he realized that though these may destroy life and cause great loss, they also bring relief. To the earnest student it must be apparent that the accumulated forces in our social and economic life, culminating in a political act of violence, are similar to the terrors of the atmosphere, manifested in storm and lightning.

To thoroughly appreciate the truth of this view, one must feel intensely the indignity of our social wrongs; one's very being must

Emma Goldman, *Anarchism and Other Essays* (London, 1910).

throb with the pain, the sorrow, the despair millions of people are daily made to endure. Indeed, unless we have become a part of humanity, we cannot even faintly understand the just indignation that accumulates in a human soul, the burning, surging passion that makes the storm inevitable.

The ignorant mass looks upon the man who makes a violent protest against our social and economic iniquities as upon a wild beast, a cruel, heartless monster, whose joy it is to destroy life and bathe in blood; or at best, as upon an irresponsible lunatic. Yet nothing is further from the truth. As a matter of fact, those who have studied the character and personality of these men, or who have come in close contact with them, are agreed that it is their super sensitiveness to the wrong and injustice surrounding them which compels them to pay the toll of our social crimes. The most noted writers and poets, discussing the psychology of political offenders, have paid them the highest tribute. Could anyone assume that these men had advised violence, or even approved of the acts? Certainly not. Theirs was the attitude of the social student, of the man who knows that beyond every violent act there is a vital cause.

Björnstjerne Björnson, in the second part of *Beyond Human Power*, emphasizes the fact that it is among the anarchists that we must look for the modern martyrs who pay for their faith with their blood, and who welcome death with a smile, because they believe, as truly as Christ did, that their martyrdom will redeem humanity.

François Coppée, the French novelist, thus expresses himself regarding the psychology of the *Attentäter:*

> The reading of the details of Vaillant's execution left me in a thoughtful mood. I imagined him expanding his chest under the ropes, marching with firm step, stiffening his will, concentrating all his energy, and, with eyes fixed upon the knife, hurling finally at society his cry of malediction. And, in spite of me, another spectacle rose suddenly before my mind. I saw a group of men and women pressing against each other in the middle of the oblong arena of the circus, under the gaze of thousands of eyes, while from all the steps of the immense amphitheater went up the terrible cry, *Ad leones!* and, below, the opening cages of the wild beasts.
>
> I did not believe the execution would take place. In the first place, no victim had been struck with death, and it had long been the custom not to punish an abortive crime with the last degree of severity. Then, this crime, however terrible in intention, was disinterested, born of an abstract idea. The man's past, his abandoned

> childhood, his life of hardship, pleaded also in his favor. In the independent press generous voices were raised in his behalf, very loud and eloquent. "A purely literary current of opinion" some have said, with no little scorn. *It is, on the contrary, an honor to the men of art and thought to have expressed once more their disgust at the scaffold. . . .*

That every act of political violence should nowadays be attributed to anarchists is not at all surprising. Yet it is a fact known to almost everyone familiar with the anarchist movement that a great number of acts, for which anarchists had to suffer, either originated with the capitalist press or were instigated, if not directly perpetrated, by the police.

For a number of years acts of violence had been committed in Spain, for which the anarchists were held responsible, hounded like wild beasts, and thrown into prison. Later it was disclosed that the perpetrators of these acts were not anarchists, but members of the police department. The scandal became so widespread that the conservative Spanish papers demanded the apprehension and punishment of the gang leader, Juan Rull, who was subsequently condemned to death and executed. The sensational evidence, brought to light during the trial, forced Police Inspector Momento to exonerate completely the anarchists from any connection with the acts committed during a long period. This resulted in the dismissal of a number of police officials, among them Inspector Tressols, who, in revenge, disclosed the fact that behind the gang of police bomb throwers were others of far higher position, who provided them with funds and protected them.

This is one of the many striking examples of how anarchist conspiracies are manufactured.

That the American police can perjure themselves with the same ease, that they are just as merciless, just as brutal and cunning as their European colleagues, has been proven on more than one occasion. We need only recall the tragedy of the eleventh of November, 1887, known as the Haymarket Riot.

No one who is at all familiar with the case can possibly doubt that the anarchists, judicially murdered in Chicago, died as victims of a lying, bloodthirsty press and of a cruel police conspiracy. Has not Judge Gary himself said: "Not because you have caused the Haymarket bomb, but because you are anarchists, you are on trial."

The impartial and thorough analysis by Governor Altgeld of that blotch on the American escutcheon verified the brutal frankness of Judge Gary. It was this that induced Altgeld to pardon the three anarchists, thereby earning the lasting esteem of every liberty-loving man and woman in the world. . . .

But, it is often asked, have not acknowledged anarchists committed acts of violence? Certainly they have, always however ready to shoulder the responsibility. My contention is that they were impelled, not by the teachings of anarchism, but by the tremendous pressure of conditions, making life unbearable to their sensitive natures. Obviously, anarchism, or any other social theory, making man a conscious social unit, will act as a lesson for rebellion. This is not a mere assertion, but a fact verified by all experience. A close examination of the circumstances bearing upon this question will further clarify my position.

Let us consider some of the most important anarchist acts within the last two decades. Strange as it may seem, one of the most significant deeds of political violence occurred here in America, in connection with the Homestead strike of 1892.

During that memorable time the Carnegie Steel Company organized a conspiracy to crush the Amalgamated Association of Iron and Steel Workers. Henry Clay Frick, then chairman of the company, was intrusted with that democratic task. He lost no time in carrying out the policy of breaking the union, the policy which he had so successfully practiced during his reign of terror in the coke regions. Secretly, and while peace negotiations were being purposely prolonged, Frick supervised the military preparations, the fortification of the Homestead Steel Works, the erection of a high board fence, capped with barbed wire and provided with loopholes for sharpshooters. And then, in the dead of night, he attempted to smuggle his army of hired Pinkerton thugs into Homestead, which act precipitated the terrible carnage of the steel workers. Not content with the death of eleven victims, killed in the Pinkerton skirmish, Henry Clay Frick, good Christian and free American, straightway began the hounding down of the helpless wives and orphans, by ordering them out of the wretched company houses. . . .

If such a phenomenon can occur in a country [India] socially and individually permeated for centuries with the spirit of passivity, can one question the tremendous, revolutionizing effect on human character exerted by great social iniquities? Can one doubt the logic, the justice of these words:

> Repression, tyranny, and indiscriminate punishment of innocent men have been the watchwords of the government of the alien domination in India ever since we began the commercial boycott of English goods. The tiger qualities of the British are much in evidence now in India. They think that by the strength of the sword they will keep down India! It is this arrogance that has brought about the bomb, and the more they tyrannize over a helpless and unarmed people, the more terrorism will grow. We may deprecate terrorism as outlandish and foreign to our culture, but it is inevitable as long as this tyranny continues, for it is not the terrorists that are to be blamed, but the tyrants who are responsible for it. It is the only resource for a helpless and unarmed people when brought to the verge of despair. It is never criminal on their part. The crime lies with the tyrant."*

Even conservative scientists are beginning to realize that heredity is not the sole factor molding human character. Climate, food, occupation; nay, color, light, and sound must be considered in the study of human psychology.

If that be true, how much more correct is the contention that great social abuses will and must influence different minds and temperaments in a different way. And how utterly fallacious the stereotyped notion that the teachings of anarchism, or certain exponents of these teachings, are responsible for the acts of political violence.

Anarchism, more than any other social theory, values human life above things. All anarchists agree with Tolstoy in this fundamental truth: if the production of any commodity necessitates the sacrifice of human life, society should do without that commodity, but it cannot do without that life. That, however, nowise indicates that anarchism teaches submission. How can it, when it knows that all suffering, all misery, all ills, result from the evil of submission?

Has not some American ancestor said, many years ago, that resistance to tyranny is obedience to God? And he was not an anarchist even. I would say that resistance to tyranny is man's highest ideal. So long as tyranny exists, in whatever form, man's deepest aspiration must resist it as inevitably as man must breathe.

Compared with the wholesale violence of capital and government, political acts of violence are but a drop in the ocean. That so few resist is the strongest proof how terrible must be the conflict between their souls and unbearable social iniquities.

High-strung, like a violin string, they weep and moan for life, so

* *The Free Hindustan.*

relentless, so cruel, so terribly inhuman. In a desperate moment the string breaks. Untuned ears hear nothing but discord. But those who feel the agonized cry understand its harmony; they hear in it the fulfillment of the most compelling moment of human nature.

Such is the psychology of political violence.

Marxism and Terrorism

INTRODUCTORY NOTE:

Marx and Engels believed in revolution, not in individual terror. They ridiculed Heinzen, regarded Most as a semi-educated charlatan, and bitterly attacked Bakunin. They were pro-Irish but emphatically condemned the terrorist activities of the Fenians (such as the Clerkenwell prison explosion in 1867) and of the "Invincibles" (including the Phoenix Park murder in 1882). Engels thought that the bombs of the Irish dynamiters and the French anarchists were counterproductive. Their attitude toward the Russian revolutionary terrorists of the 1870s and 1880s was more positive. When Plekhanov published "Our Differences" in 1884, Engels dryly noted that the *Narodniki* were "after all the only people in Russia who were doing something." Earlier, in 1879, he had anticipated a "decisive movement" in Russia. The agents of the government had committed incredible atrocities: "Against such wild beasts one ought to defend oneself to the best of one's ability with *Pulver* and *Blei*. Political murder is the only way open to intelligent and decent people of strong character to defend themselves against the agents of unheard-of despotism" (*La Plebe*, March 30, 1879). Marx's comment on the assassins of Alexander II in 1881 is worth recalling: "They were sterling people through and through." They had been simple, businesslike, and heroic, and had endeavored to show Europe that their chosen modus operandi was specifically Russian and historically inevitable. One could as much moralize about their action, or for against, as about the earthquake of Chios. "Russia is the France of this century," Engels told Lopatin, the Russian emigré. And, in a letter to Vera Zasulich, he wrote that the revolution might break out any day in Russia, for just a push was needed. Perhaps Blanqui and his fantasies had been right after all—with regard to Russia, of course. Perhaps a small conspiracy could overthrow an entire society. Perhaps this was one of the few cases in which a handful of people could "make" a revolution. Engels later admitted that he and Marx had exaggerated the prospects for terrorism in Russia: it had no future, after all.

The Bolsheviks and their allies did not oppose terrorism in principle; total rejection of terrorism was philistine, Lenin wrote. But terrorism was advisable only at the right time and place and if it were to proceed "together with the people." There were endless polemics between Lenin and the Social Revolutionaries (who believed in terrorism) about what "together with the people" really meant. Both Lenin and Trotsky had strong misgivings about the indiscriminate use of terror by the SR: it was a specific kind of struggle practiced by the intelligentsia (Lenin); it was "our national Russian achievement" in an ironic vein, (Trotsky). It made organizational and political work among the people more difficult. "Easy tactics" had never proved their worth. Patient organization and propaganda were needed. Terrorism was only likely to spread harmful illusions that the Czarist autocracy could easily be defeated. In a revolutionary situation, on the other hand, the bomb could be used as well as other weapons of guerrilla warfare and terrorism. Interestingly, Trotsky noted after the failure of the first Russian revolution of 1905 that, though terrorism was dead in Russia, it might have a future in what would be called in later years the "Third World"; it was "part of the political awakening" in these countries.

The attitudes of communist parties toward individual terrorism have been somewhat ambiguous ever since. On the doctrinal level, they have always considered terrorism fundamentally opposed to the teachings of Marxism-Leninism. But in practice, individual communist parties have occasionally engaged in terrorist tactics in the struggle for power. This is true with regard to Spain after the First World War, Bulgaria and Germany in the 1920s, and, of course, Vietnam and some Latin American countries. But it is equally true that terrorism was never regarded by the communists as their main and most telling weapon. In this respect they differed from some other radical groups which genuinely believed that terrorism was a cure for all society's ills.

Marx to Engels

December 14, 1867

Dear Fred,

The last exploit of the Fenians in Clerkenwell was a very stupid thing. The London masses, who have shown great sympathy for Ireland, will be made wild by it and driven into the arms of the government party. One cannot expect the London proletarians to allow themselves to be blown up in honor of the Fenian emissaries. There is always a kind of fatality about such a secret, melodramatic sort of conspiracy.

Engels to Marx

December 19, 1867

The stupid affair in Clerkenwell was obviously the work of a few specialized fanatics; it is the misfortune of all conspiracies that they lead to such stupidities, because "after all something must happen, after all something must be done." In particular, there has been a lot of bluster in America about this blowing up and arson business, and then a few asses come and instigate such nonsense. Moreover, these cannibals are generally the greatest cowards, like this Allen, who seems to have already turned Queen's evidence, and then the idea of liberating Ireland by setting a London tailor's shop on fire!

Engels to Marx

December 29, 1867

As regards the Fenians you are quite right. The beastliness of the English must not make us forget that the leaders of this sect are mostly asses and partly exploiters and we cannot in any way make ourselves responsible for the stupidities which occur in every conspiracy. And they are certain to happen. . . .

Marx to Paul and Laura Lafargue

March 5, 1870

Here, at home, as you are fully aware, the Fenians' sway is paramount. Tussy is one of their head centers. Jenny writes on their behalf in the *"Marseillaise"* under the pseudonym of J. Williams. I have not only treated the same theme in the Brussels *"Internationale,"* and caused resolutions of the Central Council to be passed against their jailers. In a circular, addressed by the Council to our corresponding committees, I have explained the merits of the Irish Question.

You understand at once that I am not only acted upon by feelings of humanity. There is something besides. To accelerate the social development in Europe, you must push on the catastrophe of official England. To do so, you must attack her in Ireland. That's her weakest point. Ireland lost, the British "Empire" is gone, and the class war in England, till now somnolent and chronic, will assume acute forms. But England is the metropolis of landlordism and capitalism all over the world.

Engels to Karl Kautsky

February 7, 1882

. . . I therefore hold the view that *two* nations in Europe have not only the right but even the duty to be nationalistic before they become internationalistic: the Irish and the Poles. They are most internationalistic when they are genuinely nationalistic. The Poles understood this during all crises and have proved it on all the battlefields of the revolution. Deprive them of the prospect of restoring Poland or convince them that the new Poland will soon drop into their lap by herself, and it is all over with their interest in the European revolution.

Engels to Eduard Bernstein

June 26, 1882

. . . Therefore all that is left to Ireland is the constitutional way of gradually conquering one position after the other; and here the mysterious background of a Fenian armed conspiracy can remain a very effective element. But these Fenians are themselves increasingly being pushed into a sort of Bakuninism. . . . Thus the "heroic deed" in Phoenix Park appears if not as pure stupidity, then at least as pure Bakuninist, bragging, purposeless *"propagande par le fait."* If it has not had the same consequences as the similar silly actions of Hödel and Nobiling, it is only because Ireland lies not quite in Prussia. It should therefore be left to the Bakuninists and Mostians to attach equal importance to this childishness and to the assassination of Alexander II, and to threaten with an "Irish revolution" which never comes.

One more thing should be thoroughly noted about Ireland: never praise a single Irishman—a politician—unreservedly, and never identify yourself with him before he is dead. Celtic blood and the customary exploitation of the peasant (all the "educated" social layers in Ireland, especially the lawyers, live by this alone) make Irish politicians very responsive to corruption. O'Connell let the peasants pay him as much as £30,000 a year for his agitation. In connection with the Union, for which England paid out £1,000,000 in bribes, one of those bribed was reproached: "You have sold your motherland." Reply: "Yes, and I was damned glad to have a motherland to sell."

Engels to J. Becker in Geneva

December 16, 1882

. . . The anarchists commit suicide every year and arise anew from the ashes every year; this will continue until anarchism is persecuted in earnest. It is the only socialist sect which can really be destroyed by persecution. For its perpetual resurrection is due to the fact that there are always would-be great men who would like on the cheap to play an important role. It seems as if anarchism were specially made for this purpose. But to run a risk—that is no go! The present persecutions of anarchists in France, therefore, will harm these people only if they are not just pretense and police humbug. Those who are bound to suffer are those poor fellows—the miners of Montceau. Incidentally, I have got so used to these anarchist buffoons that it seems quite natural to me to see alongside the real movement this clownish caricature. The anarchists are dangerous only in countries like Austria and Spain, and even there only temporarily. The Jura too with its watchmaking, which is always carried on in scattered cottages, seems to have been destined to become a focus of this nonsense, and your blows will probably do them good.

Engels to P. Inglesias in Madrid (Draft)

March 26, 1894

. . . As for the anarchists, they are perhaps on the point of committing suicide. This violent fever, this salvo of insane outrages, ultimately paid for and provoked by the police, cannot fail to open the eyes even of the bourgeoisie to the nature of this propaganda by madmen and provocateurs. Even the bourgeoisie will realize in the long run that it is absurd to pay the police and, through the police, the anarchists, to blow up the very bourgeois who pay them. And even if we ourselves are now liable to suffer from the bourgeois reaction against the anarchists, we shall gain in the long run because this time we shall succeed in establishing in the eyes of the world that there is a great gulf between us and the anarchists.

Marx and Engels: Report of the Hague Congress of the International, July, 1873

In the student unrest Bakunin discovers "an all-destroying spirit opposed to the state . . . which has emerged from the very depths of the people's life"; he congratulates "our young brothers on their revolutionary tendencies. . . . This means that the end is in sight of this infamous Empire of all the Russias! . . ."

The Russian people, Bakunin continues, are at present living in conditions similar to those that forced them to rise under Czar Alexei, father of Peter the Great. Then it was Stenka Razin, the Cossack brigand chief, who placed himself at their head and showed them "the road" to "freedom." In order to rise today the people are waiting only for a new Stenka Razin; but this time he

> "will be replaced by the legion of declassed youth who are already living the life of the people . . . Stenka Razin, no longer an individual hero but a collective one" [!] "consequently they have an invincible hero behind them. Such a hero are all the magnificent young people over whom his spirit already soars."

To perform this role of a collective Stenka Razin, the young people must prepare themselves through ignorance:

> "Therefore abandon with all speed this world doomed to destruction. Leave its universities, its academies, its schools and go among the people," to become "the midwife of the people's self-emancipation, the uniter and organizer of their forces and efforts. Do not bother at this moment with learning, in the name of which they would blind you, castrate you. . . . Such is the belief of the finest people in the West. . . . The workers' world of Europe and America calls you to join them in a fraternal alliance. . . ."

Citizen B——— acclaims here for the first time the Russian brigand as the type of true revolutionary and preaches the cult of ignorance to young Russians under the pretext that modern science is merely official science (can one imagine an official mathematics, physics, or chemistry?), and that this is the opinion of the finest people in the West. Finally he ends his leaflet by letting it be understood that through his mediation the International is proposing an alliance to these young people, whom he forbids even the *learning* of the Ignorantines. . . .

By the law of anarchist assimilation Bakunin assimilates student youth:

> "The government itself shows us the road *we* must follow to attain *our* goal, that is to say, the goal of the people. It drives *us* out of the universities, the academies, the schools. We are grateful to it for having thus put us on such glorious, such strong ground. Now we stand on firm ground, now we can do things. And what are we going to do? Teach the people? That would be stupid. The people know themselves, and better than we do, what they need" (compare

> the secret statutes which endow the masses with "popular instincts," and the initiates with "the revolutionary idea"). "Our task is not to teach the people but to rouse them." Up to now "they have always rebelled in vain because they have rebelled separately . . . we can render them invaluable assistance, we can give them what they have always lacked, what has been the principal cause of all their defeats. We can give them the unity of a universal movement by rallying their own forces."

This is where the doctrine of the Alliance, anarchy at the bottom and discipline at the top, emerges in all its purity. First by rioting comes the "unleashing of what are today called the evil passions" but "in the midst of the popular anarchy, which will constitute the very life and energy of the revolution, there must be an organ expressing unity of revolutionary idea and action." That organ will be the universal "Alliance," Russian section, the *Society of the People's Judgment.*

But Bakunin is not to be satisfied merely with youth. He calls all brigands to the banner of his Alliance, Russian section. . . .

In the second leaflet, "The Principles of Revolution," we find a development of the order given in the secret statutes for "not leaving a stone standing." Everything must be destroyed in order to produce "complete amorphism," for if even "one of the old forms" be preserved, it will become the "embryo" from which all the other old social forms will be regenerated. The leaflet accuses the political revolutionaries who do not take this amorphism seriously of deceiving the people. . . .

Here, then, the existence of the *international brothers*, so carefully concealed in the West, is exposed before the Russian public and the Russian police. Further the leaflet goes on to preach systematic assassination and declares that for people engaged in practical revolutionary work all argument about the future is

> "criminal because it hinders *pure destruction* and delays the march of revolution. We believe only in those who show their devotion to the cause of revolution by deeds, without fear of torture or imprisonment, because we renounce all words that are not immediately followed by deeds. We have no further use for aimless propaganda that does not set itself a definite time and place for realization of the aims of revolution. What is more, it stands in our way and we shall make every effort to combat it. . . . We shall silence by force the chatterers who refuse to understand this."

These threats were addressed to the Russian émigrés who had not bowed to Bakunin's papal authority and whom he called doctrinaires.

> "We break all ties with political émigrés who refuse to return to their country to join our ranks, and, until these ranks become evident, with all those who refuse to work for their public emergence on the scene of Russian life. *We make exception for the émigrés who have already declared themselves workers of the European revolution.* From now on we shall make no further repetitions or appeals. . . . He who has ears and eyes will hear and see the men of action, and if he does not join them his destruction will be no fault of ours, just as it will be no fault of ours if all who hide behind the scenes are cold-bloodedly and pitilessly destroyed, along with the scenery that hides them."

At this point we can see right through Bakunin. While enjoining the émigrés on pain of death to return to Russia as agents of his secret society—like the Russian police-spies who would offer them passports and money to go there and join in conspiracies—he grants himself a papal dispensation to remain peacefully in Switzerland as "a worker of the European revolution," and to occupy himself composing manifestos that compromise the unfortunate students whom the police hold in their prisons.

> "While not recognizing any other activity but that of destruction, we acknowledge that the forms in which it manifests itself may be extremely varied: poison, dagger, noose, etc. The revolution sanctifies all without distinction. The field lies open! . . . Let all heads that are young and healthy undertake at once the sacred work of killing out evil, purging and enlightening the Russian land by fire and sword, joining fraternally with those who will do the same thing throughout Europe."

Let us add that in this lofty proclamation the inevitable brigand figures in the melodramatic person of Karl Moor (from Schiller's *Robbers*), and that No. 2 of *The People's Judgment*, quoting a passage from this leaflet, calls it straight out "*a proclamation of Bakunin's.*" . . .

Engels: Enemies of the Russian Revolution

There were three major explosions within fifteen minutes in London on January 24 [1885] around two in the afternoon which caused more damage than all previous ones together and which killed at least seven people and perhaps as many as fifteen, according to other estimates. . . .

Who profits from these explosions? Who has the most interest in these otherwise purposeless false alarms the victims of which were not just simple policemen and bourgeois but also workers, their wives and children? Who indeed? The few Irishmen driven to despair in prison partly through government brutality who, according to conjecture, did plant the dynamite? Or the Russian government which cannot achieve its aim [an extradition treaty] without exerting extraordinary pressure on the British government and people, fanning public opinion to blind and mad rage against the dynamiters? . . .

This way of struggle has been dictated to the Russian revolutionaries by dire necessity, by the action of their enemies. They are responsible to their people and to history for the means they apply. But the gentlemen in western Europe who needlessly parody this struggle like schoolchildren, who reduce the revolution to actions à la Schinderhannes* and who direct their arms not against their real enemies but against the public in general, these gentlemen are not the heirs and successors of the Russian revolutionaries but their worst enemies. . . .

Kaiserlich Russische Wirkliche Geheime Dynamitraete, published in *Der Sozialdemokrat*, January 29, 1885.

Engels to V. I. Zasulich in Geneva

April 23, 1885

What I know, or think I know, about the situation in Russia leads me to believe that the Russians are approaching their 1789. Revolution must break out within a certain time, but it may break out any

* Schinderhannes, head of a famous gang of robbers in eighteenth-century Germany.

day. Under these conditions the country is like an unexploded mine which only needs the fuse to be lit. This is especially so since March 13th.* It is one of those exceptional circumstances when a handful of people can succeed in making a revolution. With one small push they can topple a whole system which is in a precarious state of balance (to use Plekhanov's metaphor) and can liberate with one action, insignificant in itself, explosive forces which will subsequently be impossible to contain. And if ever the Blanquist vision of using a small explosion to shock a whole society had any foundation, then it is in Petersburg. Once the powder is set alight, once the forces are unleashed and potential national energy is transformed into action (also one of Plekhanov's favorite and most successful images), the people who light the fuse will be caught in the explosion which will seem a thousand times stronger than they. The explosion will occur where it may, subject to economic forces and economic resistance.

Let us suppose that these people imagine that they can seize power. What of it? Let them only make the breach which will destroy the dike, then the flood will swiftly put an end to their illusions. But if these illusions were to give them greater strength of will, would it be worth complaining about? People boasting that they have made a revolution are always convinced next day that they did not know what they were doing and that the revolution they have made is not at all the one they wanted to make. This is what Hegel called the irony of history, the irony which very few historical figures have escaped. Look at Bismarck, an unwilling revolutionary, and at Gladstone, who in the end became caught up in his beloved monarch's ideas.

It is important for Russia to be given a push so that revolution may break out. Whether the signal is given by this faction or that, whether it will take place under this flag or that, is of little importance. Be it even a palace conspiracy, it will be swept away the very next day. Where the situation is so tense, where revolutionary elements have gathered to such a degree, where day by day the economic situation of the vast mass of the people is becoming less bearable, where every stage of social development from the primitive commune to modern heavy industrialization and powerful financiers is represented, and where all these contradictions are held together by the force of despotism which has no equal, despotism that the young, the embodiment of the reason and worth of the nation, are finding harder

* Engels has in mind the murder of Alexander II on March 13, 1881 ED.

and harder to bear—there, in such a country, it is well worth initiating a 1789, for a 1793 will not be long in following.

Engels: Russian Terrorism in Perspective

At the time [the late 1870s] there were two governments in Russia, that of the Czar and that of the Central Committee of the terrorist conspirators. The power of the alternative government increased daily. The overthrow of Czarism seemed imminent; a revolution in Russia was bound to deprive European reaction of its strongest pillar, its reserve army, and to give the political movement in the West a new, tremendous impetus and, moreover, to provide infinitely better conditions for its action. No wonder that Marx advised the Russians not to hurry too much with their "jump into capitalism." The Russian revolution did not come. Czarism prevailed over terrorism which had driven into its arms the classes which preferred law and order. . . .

We shall not quarrel with these people, only a few hundred altogether, who thought that the Russians were the chosen people because as the result of their self-sacrifice and courage they had compelled Czarism to consider capitulation. But we need not share their illusions. The time of the chosen peoples has gone forever.

Nachwort zu "Soziales aus dem Volksstaat" (Berlin, 1894).

Lenin: Why the Social Democrats Must Declare War on the SR.s

. . . the Socialist Revolutionaries, by including terrorism in their program and advocating it in its present-day form as a means of political struggle, are thereby doing the most serious harm to the movement, destroying the indissoluble ties between socialist work and the mass of the revolutionary class. No verbal assurances and vows can disprove the unquestionable fact that present-day terrorism, as

Written in June-July, 1902. First published in 1923 in the magazine *Prozhektor*, No. 14.

practiced and advocated by the Socialist Revolutionaries, is *not connected in any way* with work among the masses, for the masses, or together with the masses; that the organization of terroristic acts by the party distracts our very scanty organizational forces from their difficult and by no means completed task of organizing a revolutionary *workers'* party; that *in practice* the terrorism of the Socialist Revolutionaries is nothing else than *single combat*, a method that has been wholly condemned by the experience of history. Even foreign socialists are beginning to become embarrassed by the noisy advocacy of terrorism advanced today by our Socialist Revolutionaries. Among the masses of the Russian workers this advocacy simply sows harmful illusions, such as the idea that terrorism "compels people to think politically, even against their will" (*Revolutsionnaya Rossiya*), or that "more effectively than months of verbal propaganda it is capable of changing the views . . . of thousands of people with regard to the revolutionaries and the meaning [!!] of their activity," or that it is capable of "infusing new strength into the waverers, those discouraged and shocked by the sad outcome of many demonstrations," and so on. These harmful illusions can only bring about early disappointment and weaken the work of preparing the masses for the onslaught upon the autocracy.

Lenin: Revolutionary Adventurism

In their defense of terrorism, which the experience of the Russian revolutionary movement has so clearly proved to be ineffective, the Socialist Revolutionaries are talking themselves blue in the face in asseverating that they recognize terrorism only in conjunction with work among the masses, and that therefore the arguments used by the Russian Social Democrats to refute the efficacy of this method of struggle (and which have indeed been refuted for a long time to come) do not apply to them. Here something very similar to their attitude toward "criticism" is repeating itself. We are not opportunists, cry the Socialist Revolutionaries, and at the same time they are shelving the dogma of proletarian socialism, for reason of sheer opportunist criticism and no other. We are not repeating the ter-

Iskra, August-September, 1902.

rorists' mistakes and are not diverting attention from work among the masses, the Socialist Revolutionaries assure us, and at the same time enthusiastically recommend to the party acts such as Balmashov's assassination of Sipyagin, although everyone knows and sees perfectly well that this act was in no way connected with the masses and, moreover, could not have been by reason of the very way in which it was carried out—that the persons who committed this terrorist act neither counted on nor hoped for any definite action or support on the part of the masses. In their naiveté, the Socialist Revolutionaries do not realize that their predilection for terrorism is causally most intimately linked with the fact that, from the very outset, they have always kept, and still keep, aloof from the working class movement, without even attempting to become a party of the revolutionary class which is waging its class struggle. Over-ardent protestations very often lead one to doubt and suspect the worth of whatever it is that requires such strong seasoning. Do not these protestations weary them?—I often think of these words, when I read assurances by the Socialist Revolutionaries: "by terrorism we are *not* relegating work among the masses into the background." After all, these assurances come from the very people who have already drifted away from the Social Democratic labor movement, which really rouses the masses; they come from people who are continuing to drift away from this movement, clutching at fragments of any kind of theory.

The leaflet issued by the "Party of the Socialist Revolutionaries" on April 3, 1902, may serve as a splendid illustration of what has been stated above. It is a most realistic source, one that is very close to the immediate leaders, a most authentic source. The "presentation of the question of terrorist struggle" in this leaflet "coincides in full" also "with the party views," according to the valuable testimony of *Revolutsionnaya Rossiya*.

The April 3 leaflet follows the pattern of the terrorists' "latest" arguments with remarkable accuracy. The first thing that strikes the eye is the words: "we advocate terrorism, not in place of work among the masses, but precisely for and simultaneously with that work." They strike the eye particularly because these words are printed in letters three times as large as the rest of the text (a device that is of course repeated by *Revolutsionnaya Rossiya*). It is all really so simple! One has only to set "not in place of, but together with" in bold type—and all the arguments of the Social Democrats, all that history has taught, will fall to the ground. But just read the whole leaflet and you will see that the protestation in bold type takes the name of the masses in vain. The day "when the working people will emerge from the shadows" and "the mighty popular wave will shatter the iron gates to smithereens"—"alas!" (literally, "alas!") "is still a long way off, and it is frightful to think of the future toll of victims!" Do not these words "alas, still a long way off" reflect an utter failure to understand the mass movement and a lack of faith in it? Is not this argument meant as a deliberate sneer at the fact that the working people are already beginning to rise? And, finally, even if this trite argument were just as well founded as it is actually stuff and nonsense, what would emerge from it in particularly bold relief would be the inefficacy of terrorism, for *without* the working people all bombs are powerless, patently powerless.

Just listen to what follows: "Every terrorist blow, as it were, takes away part of the strength of the autocracy and transfers [!] all this strength [!] to the side of the fighters for freedom." "And if terrorism is practiced systematically [!], it is obvious that the scales of the balance will finally weigh down on our side." Yes, indeed, it is obvious to all that we have here in its grossest form one of the greatest prejudices of the terrorists: political assassination of itself "transfers strength"! Thus, on the one hand you have the theory of the transference of strength, and on the other—"not in place of, but together with". . . . Do not these protestations weary them?

But this is just the beginning. The real thing is yet to come. "Whom are we to strike down?" asks the party of the Socialist Revolutionaries, and replies: the ministers, and not the Czar, for "the Czar will not allow matters to go to extremes" (How did they find that out??), and besides "it is also easier" (this is literally what they say!): "No minister can ensconce himself in a palace as in a fortress." And this argument concludes with the following piece of reasoning, which deserves to be immortalized as a model of the "theory" of the Socialist Revolutionaries. "Against the crowd the autocracy has its soldiers; against the revolutionary organizations its secret and uniformed police; but what will save it . . ." (what kind of "it" is this? The autocracy? The author has unwittingly identified the autocracy with a target in the person of a minister whom it is easier to strike down!) ". . . from individuals or small groups that are ceaselessly, and even in ignorance of one another[!!], preparing for attack, and are attacking? No force will be of avail against elusiveness. Hence, our task is clear: to remove every one of the autocracy's brutal oppressors by the only means that has been left [!] us by the autocracy—

death." No matter how many reams of paper the Socialist Revolutionaries may fill with assurances that they are not relegating work among the masses into the background or disorganizing it by their advocacy of terrorism—their spate of words cannot disprove the fact that the actual psychology of the modern terrorist is faithfully conveyed in the leaflet we have quoted. The theory of the transference of strength finds its natural complement in the theory of elusiveness, a theory which turns upside down, not only all past experience, but all common sense as well. . . .

Nor does the leaflet eschew the theory of excitative terrorism. "Each time a hero engages in single combat, this arouses in us all a spirit of struggle and courage," we are told. But we know from the past and see in the present that *only* new forms of the mass movement or the awakening of new sections of the masses to independent struggle really rouses a spirit of struggle and courage *in all.* Single combat however, inasmuch as it remains *single combat* waged by the Balmashovs, has the immediate effect of simply creating a short-lived sensation, while indirectly it even leads to apathy and passive waiting for the next *bout.* We are further assured that "every flash of terrorism lights up the mind," which, unfortunately, we have not noticed to be the case with the terrorism-preaching party of the Socialist Revolutionaries. We are presented with the theory of big work and petty work. "Let not those who have greater strength, greater opportunities and resolution rest content with petty [!] work; let them find and devote themselves to a big cause—the propaganda of terrorism among the masses [!], the preparation of the intricate [the theory of elusiveness is already forgotten!] . . . terrorist ventures." How amazingly clever this is in all truth: to sacrifice the life of a revolutionary for the sake of wreaking vengeance on the scoundrel Sipyagin, who is then replaced by the scoundrel Plehve—that is big work. But to prepare, *for instance,* the masses for an armed demonstration—that is petty work. . . .

Lenin: A Militant Agreement for the Uprising

It seems to us, therefore, a gross exaggeration for *Revolutsionnaya Rossiya* to assert that "the pioneers of the armed struggle were swal-

Vperyod 7, 1905.

lowed up in the ranks of the roused masses. . . ." This is the desirable future rather than the reality of the moment. The assassination of Sergei in Moscow on February 17, which has been reported by telegraph this very day, is obviously an act of terrorism of the old type. The pioneers of the armed struggle have *not yet* been swallowed up in the ranks of the roused masses. Pioneers with bombs evidently lay in wait for Sergei in Moscow while the masses (in St. Petersburg), without pioneers, without arms, without revolutionary officers, and without a revolutionary staff "flung themselves in implacable fury upon bristling bayonets," as this same *Revolutsionnaya Rossiya* expresses it. The separateness of which we spoke above *still exists*, and the individual intellectualist terror shows all the more strikingly its inadequacy in face of the growing realization that "the masses have risen to the stature of individual heroes, that mass heroism has been awakened in them" (*Revolutsionnaya Rossiya*). The pioneers should submerge among the masses *in actual fact*, that is, exert their selfless energies in real inseparable connection with the insurgent masses, and proceed with them in the literal, not figurative, symbolical, sense of the word. That this is essential can hardly be open to doubt now. That it is possible has been proved by the Ninth of January and by the deep unrest which is still smoldering among the working class masses. The fact that this is a new, higher, and more difficult task in comparison with the preceding ones cannot and should not stop us from meeting it at once in a practical way.

Fighting unity between the Social Democratic Party and the revolutionary democratic party—the Socialist Revolutionary Party, might be one way of facilitating the solution of this problem. Such unity will be all the more practicable the sooner the pioneers of the armed struggle are "swallowed up" in the ranks of the insurgent masses, the more firmly the Socialist Revolutionaries follow the path which they themselves have charted in the words, "May these beginnings of fusion between revolutionary terrorism and the mass movement grow and strengthen, may the masses act as quickly as possible, armed cap-à-pie with terrorist methods of struggle!"

"The masses took to arms themselves," *Revolutsionnaya Rossiya* wrote in connection with the Ninth of January. "Sooner or later, without doubt, the question of arming the masses will be decided." "That is when the fusion between terrorism and the mass movement, to which we are striving by word and deed in accordance with the entire spirit of our party tactics, will be manifested and realized in the most striking manner." (We would remark parenthetically that we would gladly put a question mark after the word "deed"; but let us proceed with the quotation.) "Not so long ago, before our own eyes, these two factors of the movement were separate, and this separateness deprived them of their full force."

What is true is true! Exactly! Intelligentsia terrorism and the mass movement of the working class *were separate, and this separateness deprived them of their full force.* That is precisely what the revolutionary Social Democrats have been saying all along. For this very reason they have always been opposed to terrorism and to all the vacillations toward terrorism which members of the intellectualist wing of our party have often displayed. For this reason precisely the old *Iskra* took a position against terrorism when it wrote: "The terrorist struggle of the *old type* was the riskiest form of revolutionary struggle, and those who engaged in it had the reputation of being resolute, self-sacrificing people. . . . Now, however, when demonstrations develop into acts of open resistance to the government . . . the old terrorism ceases to be an exceptionally daring method of struggle. . . . Heroism has now come out into the open; the true heroes of our time are now the revolutionaries who lead the popular masses, which are rising against their oppressors. . . . The terrorism of the great French Revolution . . . began on July 14, 1789, with the storming of the Bastille. Its strength was the strength of the revolutionary movement of the people. . . . *That* terrorism was due, not to disappointment in the strength of the mass movement, but, on the contrary, to unshakable faith in its strength. . . . The history of *that* terrorism is exceedingly instructive for the Russian revolutionary."

Yes, a thousand times yes! The history of *that* terrorism is instructive in the extreme.

Lenin: A Tactical Platform for the Unity Congress

We are of the opinion, and propose that the Congress should agree:

1. that the party must regard the fighting guerrilla operations of

March, 1906.

the squads affiliated to or associated with it as being, in principle, permissible and advisable in the present period;

2. that the character of these fighting guerrilla operations must be adjusted to the task of training leaders of the masses of workers at a time of insurrection, and of acquiring experience in conducting offensive and surprise military operations;

3. that the paramount immediate object of these operations is to destroy the government, police and military machinery, and to wage a relentless struggle against the active Black Hundred organizations which are using violence against the population and intimidating it;

4. that fighting operations are also permissible for the purpose of seizing funds belonging to the enemy, i.e., the autocratic government, to meet the needs of insurrection, particular care being taken that the interests of the people are infringed as little as possible;

5. that fighting guerrilla operations must be conducted under the control of the party and, furthermore, in such a way as to prevent the forces of the proletariat from being frittered away and to ensure that the state of the working class movement and the mood of the broad masses of the given locality are taken into account.

Trotsky: The Collapse of Terrorism (I)

Individual terrorism as a method of political revolution is a specifically Russian feature. Of course, the murder of "tyrants" is almost as old as the institution of "tyrants" and poets in almost every age have composed many odes in honor of those who liberate by means of the knife. But systematic terror that sets itself the task of removing satrap after satrap, minister after minister, monarch after monarch, "Ivan after Ivan," as was formulated by a certain member of the "People's Freedom Movement" of the 80s as a program of terror, this terror, which adapts itself to the bureaucratic hierarchy of absolutism and founds its own revolutionary bureaucracy, is an original product of the Russian intelligentsia. Naturally there must be profound reasons for this and one must seek them firstly in the nature of Russian autocracy and secondly in the nature of the Russian intelligentsia.

So that the idea of mechanically annihilating absolutism may gain

Przeglad Socyal-demokratyczny, May 1909.

popularity, the state apparatus must present itself as being completely set apart from the organization of force, as not having any roots in the organization of society. But Russian autocracy appeared to the revolutionary intelligentsia as precisely this. Its historical foundation was based on this very illusion. Czarism was founded under pressure from more cultured Western states. To survive competition it had to fleece the masses without mercy and, by so doing, tear up the economic ground from under the feet of even the privileged classes. They were not even successful in raising themselves to the political level of their counterparts in the West. And in the nineteenth century the powerful pressure of the European currency exchange was added to this. As the sums it lent Czarism increased, so did Czarism's direct relation to the economic conditions of its own country decrease. It armed itself with European military technology at Europe's expense and thus grew into a (relatively speaking) self-sufficient organization raising itself above all other classes of society. From this grew the idea of using dynamite to blow this superstructure of foreign origin sky-high.

It was the intelligentsia which felt the call to undertake this task. Like the state it had developed under the direct influence of the West; as had its enemy, it too had outrun the economic development of the country. The state had done so technologically, the intelligentsia ideologically. At the time when revolutionary ideas were developing more or less parallel with broad revolutionary forces in older European societies, in Russia the intelligentsia, accustomed to the West's ready-made cultural and political ideas, was spiritually revolutionized before the economic development of the country could give birth to revolutionary classes on which it could have counted for support. Under such conditions nothing remained for it but to increase its revolutionary enthusiasm by using the explosive strength of nitroglycerine. It was thus that the terrorism of the classic "People's Freedom Movement" arose. In two or three years it reached its zenith, then rapidly fizzled out to nothing, having burnt in its own fire the supply of military force which the intelligentsia, so weak in numbers, could have mustered.

The Socialist Revolutionaries' terror is due both in general and particular to the same historical causes: on the one hand, the "self-contained" despotism of the Russian state and, on the other, the "self-contained" revolutionary character of the Russian intelligentsia. But twenty years have not passed in vain and the second wave of terrorists are already emerging as imitators noted by the press as historically behind their time. The capitalist period of "*Sturm und Drang*" of the 80s and 90s created and nurtured a numerous industrial proletariat, penetrated the strong defenses of the village, and closely linked it to the factory and the town. There was no revolutionary class behind the "Peoples Freedom Movement," the Socialist Revolutionaries just did not want to see the revolutionary proletariat or at least they did not know how to value its historic significance.

Of course one can easily select from the Socialist Revolutionaries' literature several dozen quotations to the effect that they would create terror, not instead of the struggle of the masses but together with the struggle of the masses. But these quotations bear witness only to the struggle which came to be fought between the ideologists of terror and the Marxists, the theoreticians of the mass struggle. This does not alter the facts, however. By its very nature terrorist work demands the kind of concentration of energy on "the great moment," the evaluation of the significance of personal heroism and finally the "hermetic" secrecy of conspiracy which, if not logically, then psychologically, absolutely exclude agitation and organization among the masses. For the terrorist only two fruitful points exist in each political field—the government and the fighting organization. "The government is ready to make temporary peace with the existence of all other movements," wrote Gershuni to his friends who were awaiting the death sentence, "but it has decided to concentrate all its strength on crushing the Socialist Revolutionary party." "I fervently hope," wrote Kalyaev at the very same time, "that our generation, with the fighting organization at its head, will make an end to autocracy."

Everything that is not understood by terrorism is only a condition of war and, even at best, a subsidiary means. In the blinding flames of exploding bombs, distinctions between political parties and boundaries of class struggle disappear without trace. And we hear the greatest romantic and finest exponent of the new terrorism, Gershuni, demanding of his friends "not to split up either the revolutionary ranks or those of the opposition."

"Not instead of the masses, but together with the masses." Terrorism is, however, too "absolute" a form of struggle to be content with playing a relative and subordinate role in any party. Conceived in the absence of a revolutionary class, born as a consequence of lack of faith in the revolutionary masses, terrorism can best support its own existence only by exploiting the weakness and disorganized state of the masses by belittling their achievements and magnifying their defeats. During Kalyaev's trial, the lawyer Zhdanov said of terrorists, "They have seen how impossible it is against modern weapons for the masses, armed with pitchforks and boathooks, those hallowed weapons in the people's armory, to destroy present-day Bastilles. After the Ninth of January [1905] they now know to what this leads; against machine guns and rapid-fire-arms they set revolvers and bombs; these are the barricades of the twentieth century." The revolvers of solitary heroes replace the people's boathooks and pitchforks; bombs replace barricades. Such is the true formula of terrorism. And whatever subordinate place "artificial" party theoreticians may give it, terrorism will always hold the advantage; in fact, the fighting organization which the official party hierarchy puts beneath the Central Committee appears unavoidably to be above it, above the party and all its work until a cruel fate places it below the police department. It is just because of this that the downfall of the police conspirators' fighting organization will be the unavoidable signal for the political downfall of the party.

Trotsky: The Collapse of Terrorism (II)

Terrorism in Russia is dead, thanks to Bakai, that counterrevolutionary double agent, a terrorist Anabaptist who helped to transform terrorists into corpses in Warsaw and who now with his godfather, Burtsev, is trying to provoke a spark of life from the corpse of terrorism. If, however, he can succeed in creating the conditions needed for a second double agent organization in the style of Azev, it will be (at best) less than a tenth as successful as the first.

Revolutionary terrorism has removed itself far to the east—to the regions of the Punjab and Bengal. There, the slow political awakening of a 300 million-strong nation provides a sympathetic atmosphere in which it can flourish. The ruling class there appears to be even more absolute in its despotism over society, even more foreign and a matter of "chance," for the politico-military apparatus of the East Indies was exported from England together with calico and business ledgers. That is why the Indian intelligentsia, accustomed from its

Der Kampf, November, 1911. Translated here from the Russian.

school days to communicate with the ideas of Locke, Bentham, and Mill, and in its ideological evolution having left behind the political development of its country, is naturally predisposed to seek the strength it lacks in the bottom of an alchemist's retort. Perhaps other Eastern countries, too, may be fated to live through a period of flourishing terrorism. But in Russia it is already considered to be the property of history. . . .

Our class enemies are in the habit of complaining against our terrorism. What they mean by terrorism is not always clear. They would particularly like to brand with the name of terrorism all those acts of the proletariat directed against their interests. In their view, strikes are the chief method of terrorism. The threat of a strike, the economic boycott of a blood-sucking boss, the organization of a strike picket, and the moral boycott of a traitor in their own ranks they call by the name of terrorism. If one understands as terrorism every act that brings fear to the enemy or causes him to suffer damage, then of course the class war is none other than terrorism. One may only question whether bourgeois politicians have the right to pour onto proletarian terrorism the floods of their moral indignation when their whole state apparatus, with its laws, police, and army, is none other than the apparatus of capitalist terror.

One must say, though, that when they reproach us with terrorism, they are trying, however bad the reasoning, to give this word a more narrow and direct meaning. The merciless beating-up of an employer, the threat of setting fire to a factory or killing its owner, an armed attempt on the life of a minister are all terrorist acts in the true meaning of the word. However, anyone who knows anything about the true nature of international social democracy must be aware that it has always fought implacably against this type of terrorism. . . .

Only a thinking and well-organized working class is capable of sending strong representatives who will be vigilant on behalf of proletarian interests to parliament. However, it is not necessary to have the organized masses behind one simply to kill an important official. Recipes for making explosives are available to all and a Browning can be obtained anywhere.

Firstly, there is the social struggle, the ways and means of which forcibly flow from the very nature of the ruling social order; secondly there is purely mechanical coercion, the same everywhere, obvious in its external form (murder, explosion, etc.) but which is quite harmless to the social structure.

Even the most minor strike brings social consequences in its wake; it strengthens the confidence of the workers, helps the trade unions to grow, and often even succeeds in taking over the machinery of production. The murder of a factory owner only results in police action and makes no change in the social significance of the owners.

Whether or not a terrorist attempt, even a "successful" one, throws ruling circles into confusion will depend on concrete political circumstances. In any case this confusion must only be of short duration; the existence of the capitalist state does not depend on its ministers and cannot be destroyed with them. The classes which it serves can always find new people; the mechanism will remain whole and will continue to function.

But a far worse confusion can be caused by attempting to carry a terrorist action into ranks of the working masses themselves. If one can achieve one's aims armed only with a pistol, what is the point of the efforts of class struggle? If a thimbleful of gunpowder and a tiny piece of lead are enough to shoot the enemy through the neck, what need is there for class organization? If the thunder of an explosion can intimidate high personages, what is the need for a party? What is the point of meetings, mass agitation, and elections when it is so easy to aim at the minister's bench from the parliamentary gallery?

The reason why individual terrorism is, in our view, not permissible is precisely because it lowers the political consciousness of the masses, causes them to acquiesce in their own lack of strength, and directs their gaze and hopes to a great avenger and liberator who may come one day to do their work for them.

Anarchist prophets of the "propaganda by deed" may discuss to their hearts' content the elevating and stimulating influence of terrorist attempts on the masses. Theoretical considerations and political experience prove the exact opposite. The more "effective" terrorist acts are, the greater the impression they make, the more the attention of the masses is concentrated upon them, the more will the masses' interest in self-education decline.

But the smoke of the explosion is drifting away, panic is subsiding, the murdered minister's successor is here; once again life settles into its old rut. The wheels of capitalist exploitation turn round as before, only police repression becomes more brutal and shameless and, as a result, in place of burnt-out hopes and artificially aroused awareness we have disillusionment and apathy.

Reactionary attempts to stop strikes and the mass movement generally have always and everywhere ended in failure. Capitalist society needs an active, mobile, and intelligent proletariat; it cannot, therefore, keep it bound hand and foot for long. On the other hand, the anarchist program of action has always shown that the state is more strengthened by the use of physical destruction and the mechanics of repression than are terrorist groups. . . .

Before it is raised to the level of being a method of political struggle, terrorism appears in the form of isolated acts of revenge. So it was in Russia, the classical country of terrorism. The flogging of political prisoners roused Vera Zasulich into giving vent to the general feeling of indignation by her attempt on the life of General Trepov. This example was imitated in the circles of the revolutionary intelligentsia, which did not have the support of the masses behind it. What started as an instinctive feeling of revenge developed from 1879 to 1881 into an entire system. Anarchist attempts in western Europe and America always flare up after government atrocities, for instance, after the shooting of strikers or after executions. The search to find expression for the feeling of revenge is always an important psychological source of terrorism.

It is not necessary to expand the fact that the Social Democrat has nothing in common with those moralists who, on the occasion of every terrorist attempt, pontificate triumphantly about the "absolute value" of human life. They are the same people who in other circumstances, in the name of other absolute values, for example, the honor of the nation or the prestige of the monarchy, are ready to push millions of people into the hell of war. Today their hero is the minister who gives orders to shoot unarmed workers in the name of the most sacred right of property. Tomorrow, when the hand of the desperate unemployed clenches into a fist or takes up a weapon, they will mouth empty words about the inadmissibility of violence.

Whatever moral eunuchs and pharisees may say, the feeling of revenge has its right. The working class has greater moral probity because it does not look with dull indifference at what is happening in this, the best of all worlds. The proletariat's unsatisfied feeling of revenge should not be extinguished; on the contrary, it should be aroused again and again; it should be deepened and directed against genuine examples of every kind of wrong and human baseness. This is the task of the Social Democrat.

If we rise against terrorist acts, it is only because individual revenge does not satisfy us. The account that we must settle with the capitalist status quo is too great to present to an official calling himself a minister. We must learn to see the monstrous evidence of the class structure in all crimes against the individual, in every attempt to maim or stifle a human being, body and soul, so that we may direct all our strength toward a collective struggle against this class structure. This, then, is the method by which the burning desire for revenge can achieve its greatest moral satisfaction.

J. B. S. Hardman

Terrorism: A Summing Up in the 1930s

Terrorism is a term used to describe the method or the theory behind the method whereby an organized group or party seeks to achieve its avowed aims chiefly through the systematic use of violence. Terroristic acts are directed against persons who as individuals, agents, or representatives of authority interfere with the consummation of the objectives of such a group. Destruction of property and machinery or the devastation of land may in specific cases be regarded as additional forms of terroristic activity, constituting variations of agrarian or economic terrorism as a supplement to a general program of political terrorism. The term does not appear to be applicable to violent clashes or even to systematic resorts to violence in conflicts of an industrial nature, such as may occur between workers struggling to secure recognition and status as an organized body and employers who fight these efforts; nor does it apply when violence results from the fact that racketeers have gained a foothold in an industry. Such phenomena may be described as manifestations of intimidation rather than of terrorism.

Intimidation differs from terrorism in that the intimidator, unlike the terrorist, merely threatens injury or material harm in order to

"Terrorism" by J. B. S. Hardman. Reprinted by permission of the publisher from *The Encyclopedia of the Social Sciences*, Edwin R. A. Seligman, Editor-in-Chief, Alvin Johnson, Associate Editor. Volume XIV, pages 575–579.

arouse fear of severe punishment for noncompliance with his demands. The intimidator will resort only to the degree of violence needed to insure collection of tribute or to force certain persons to abstain from committing overt or covert acts. Having committed a crime or engaged in criminal practices, usually through hired underlings, a racketeer or an employing company whose anti-union labor "protective" machinery has been apprehended in unlawful acts will seek the protection of the law through influential politicians, purchasable attorneys, and accommodating judges. The attitude of the political terrorist is entirely different. He imposes the punishment meted out by his organization upon those who are considered guilty or who are held to interfere with the revolutionary program; thus he serves notice that his organization will be satisfied with nothing short of removal of the undesired social or governmental system and of the persons behind it. The terrorist does not threaten; death or destruction is part of his program of action, and if he is caught his behavior during trial is generally directed primarily not toward winning his freedom but toward spreading a knowledge of his doctrines. Intimidation and the practices of violence resulting from it are a logical consequence although an extreme manifestation of the struggle among persons or conspiratorial groups for pecuniary reward in an acquisitive society based upon vested rights and the possession of capital wealth. Terrorism is a method of combat in the struggle between social groups and forces rather than individuals, and it may take place in any social order. Those who appear on the terroristic scene, whether as protagonists or as victims, stand as representatives of social groups or of systems of government. Violence and death are not intended to produce revenue or to terrorize the persons attacked but to cause society or government to take notice of the imminence of large-scale struggles. The terroristic act committed in secrecy by one person or several is conceived as the advance notice of what may be expected from mass action. It is usually employed where other methods of propaganda are not permitted.

Resort to terrorism is not the exclusive monopoly of political organizations and parties. A group of any other character seeking the relocation of power may deem it expedient to use terror and may organize for this purpose. The nature of the power contested may vary greatly; it may be the dominance of one nation over another or the oppression of one economic class by another. A conflict between the supporters of two substantially different systems of government may also call forth terroristic tactics. Terrorism as a method is always characterized by the fact that it seeks to arouse not only the reigning government or the nation in control but also the mass of the people to a realization that constituted authority is no longer safely entrenched and unchallenged. The publicity value of the terroristic act is a cardinal point in the strategy of terrorism. If terror fails to elicit a wide response in circles outside of those at whom it is directly aimed, it is futile as a weapon in a social conflict. The logic of terroristic activity cannot fully be understood without a proper evaluation of the revealing nature of the terroristic act.

Terrorism differs in several important aspects from such phenomena as mob violence, mass insurrection and governmental terror. Terror practiced by a government in office appears as law enforcement and is directed against the opposition, while terrorism in its proper sense implies open defiance of law and is the means whereby an opposition aims to demoralize a governmental authority, to undermine its power and to initiate a revolution or counterrevolution. While the terrorist party makes no pretense at legality, legitimate government must at least formally adhere to law. In the absence of directly supporting legislation governmental terror is made to appear as justified by a declaration that a state of emergency exists, usually followed by the issuance of special decrees. The moral and political justification of the terrorism of a revolutionary or counterrevolutionary party, on the other hand, proceeds from its consideration of existing government as a usurper of the people's power or of the historic rights of a certain dynasty or class.

Although it is based upon the practice of violence, terrorism differs essentially from what is described as mob violence. Terrorism is carried on by a narrowly limited organization and is inspired by a sustained program of large-scale objectives in the name of which terror is practiced; mob violence, although it may conceivably break out in response to a terroristic act, is ordinarily unplanned and uncontrolled, brought into action by some immediate and not necessarily rational motivation and follows no precise program.

Mass insurrection is ideologically most akin to terrorism, but it too is not necessarily premeditated and is likely to occur without painstaking preliminary preparation. The initiation of a mass insurrection may be one of the objectives of a party which employs terrorism as a revolutionary method; in such a case the relation between the two may be one of means to an end. Generally, however, the two phenomena are not linked in the theory of revolutionary strategy. In a situation where mass insurrection as a means of attaining certain political aims is within the realm of possibility the terrorist method appears unnecessary, although it is not impossible that the removal of a conspicuous representative of the functioning government might prove the starting point for mass action or at least accelerate its pace. The Blanquist conception of revolutionary insurrection seems to be related to terrorism in the importance it attributes to detailed preparation and to the conspirative methods. Likewise the careful preparation of revolutionary forces appears in Bolshevik theory to be a revolutionary weapon similar in type to terrorism. But in addition to the essential distinction that neither Blanquism nor Bolshevism lists terror among its chosen instrumentalities of action, there are vital differences between the three concepts. The Blanquists conceived of armed insurrection as the task of a well-organized and strictly disciplined band of trained fighters who might carry out their purpose whenever success seemed reasonably certain. Once successful, the revolutionary party would proceed to enforce its program, whether or not the latter had gained a substantial degree of acceptance among the people. Blanqui's army of insurrectionists throughout the long period of his leadership between the 1840s and the 1870s at no time claimed more than a few thousand men. Blanquism, in practice if not in theory, is the technique of a *Putsch* or coup d'état. Differing entirely from this concept is the Bolshevik idea of armed insurrection, which regards the latter at the most as a link in a chain of revolutionary circumstances, a final weapon to be employed only after all preliminary measures have been completed. The frequently quoted statement, ascribed to Trotsky, that a few well-trained, select shock troops may at a propitious time seize the government and change the course of history represents neither Trotsky's nor Lenin's ideas of a revolutionary overturn. Bolshevik evolutionary strategy is rooted in the acceptance of mass movements as the basic force which will effect the shift of social power from the capitalist class to that of the workers. Lenin repeatedly stressed the need of winning the masses to the party's ideas before a decisive action could be precipitated.

Terrorism as a means of achieving national emancipation was exemplified in the so-called Anglo-Irish war led by Sinn Feiners between 1919 and 1921. Its objective was forcibly to eradicate English control in Ireland and to establish Irish unity. Destruction of the property of the English government and of conspicuous Irish sympathizers with English rule, shooting of police, attacks on police barracks, and ambushing of British soldiery with bombs, rifles, and revolvers were among the means used in this internal struggle. Terrorism in this particular case bordered on guerrilla warfare and it was based upon the expectation that the noncombatant population would fall into line with the victorious side; terroristic means were used to force the issue. The revolutionary party claimed its justification in the right of the Irish people to national self-determination and made its terroristic practices appear as retaliatory action against the British reign of terror in Ireland.

Terrorism as a revolutionary technique was for many years an accepted tenet of anarchism. The writings of Bakunin with their emphasis upon violence as a method of achieving social change were the inspiration if not the actual source of this doctrine. The idea of "the propaganda of the deed" was developed in the years following Bakunin's death by Kropotkin, Brousse, and others, who stressed the failure of generally accepted methods and the educative and publicity value of acts of terrorism. This theory was translated into action principally in the last two decades of the nineteenth century, especially in the Latin countries. In Germany and Austria-Hungary, where the anarchist movement was relatively weak, there were only a few *attentats*, but police measures proved quite ineffectual in France, Spain, and Italy in dealing with the assassination of many government officials. Among the anarchists in the United States Johann Most was the foremost exponent of terrorism, while the outstanding attempts to propagandize by the deed were the assassination of McKinley by Czolgosz and the shooting of Frick by Alexander Berkman. The method advocated by the syndicalists is one of direct mass action rather than of individual terror.

The fullest expression of the theory and practice of terrorism is to be found in the functioning of the famous Russian revolutionary organization—the executive committee of the *Narodnaya Volya* (People's Will), formed in 1879. Its spectacular activity began in the late 1870s under the name of its predecessor, a society called *Zemlya i Volya* (Land and Freedom), and it attracted attention with the shot fired by Vera Zasulich at General Trepov, the commandant of St. Petersburg, as an act of revolutionary revenge for the flogging of the revolutionist Emelyanov, which the general had ordered. In 1879 Solovev made an unsuccessful attempt to shoot the czar and in the following year a revolutionary workman, Khalturin, succeeded in dynamiting the czar's dining room at the Winter Palace, where the royal family was to entertain a large official assemblage; they were saved only by an accidental delay in the opening of the function. In 1881, however, Alexander II was killed by a bomb. Such an effective start encouraged the *Narodnaya Volya* (also called *narodniki*) and its activity spread despite the efforts of the government to exterminate the organization at all costs. As in the case of all revolutionary movements, it was not governmental persecution but popular reaction which determined its future.

The party's own view of its method of action was expressed in paragraph 2, section D, of its program, which defines destructive and terroristic activity as follows: "Terroristic activity, consisting in destroying the most harmful person in the government, in defending the party against espionage, in punishing the perpetrators of the notable cases of violence and arbitrariness on the part of the government and the administration, aims to undermine the prestige of the government's power, to demonstrate steadily the possibility of struggle against the government, to arouse in this manner the revolutionary spirit of the people and their confidence in the success of the cause, and finally, to give shape and direction to the forces fit and trained to carry on the fight" ("*Programma Ispolnitelnago Komiteta*, 1879 g." [Program of the Executive Committee, 1879], reprinted in *Sbornik programm i programmnikh statey partii "Narodnoy Voli"* [Geneva, 1903] p. 3–8.)

The motivation of the party's recourse to the terroristic method was, as frequently stated, that at that time it appeared the only possible way of achieving political change. The purpose of this change was explained in paragraph I, section V, of the same program: "By this overturn, in the first place, the development of the people will be to proceed independently and in line with its disposition, and, in the second place, many purely socialist principles common to us and the people will gain recognition and be supported in our Russian life."

The spokesmen of the party stressed the following principles of their movement: that the use of terror was not an end in itself but only a means to effect the transference of power from the government to the people; that the party proposed to seize and retain power only until a form of popular government could be determined upon by a constituent assembly; and that it would not decree revolutionary reforms and impose its desires upon the people but on the contrary would aid the latter to express its own will, to which the party would submit.

This political program, unusual for its modesty and self-negation, sounds crudely naïve and almost unbelievable in an era of historic struggles between fascism, on which declining capitalism stakes its own survival, and communism, the fighting essence and pragmatic realization of classical socialism. But in its time and situation this self-negation of the terrorists had roots in the specific conditions of Russian life. The psychology of terrorism is that of romantic messianism. The Russian terrorists imagined that because certain conditions of landownership forced the Russian peasant community to adhere to a quasi-collectivist form of land utilization, the peasants were the carriers of the purely socialist principle germane to the very nature of the Russian people. These potential socialists were supposedly awaiting an energetic impulsion from the revolutionists, and the explosion of a bomb thrown at a cruel czarist officer was expected to awaken the people from their lethargy. But although many bombs were exploded and numerous officials and members of the ruling order assassinated, the masses failed to respond. Their passivity and total lack of rebelliousness at first spurred the terrorists to more and more daring ventures. The program of the party called for widespread mass activity to arouse the peasants, the workers, and the professionals. Essentially, however, terroristic activity produced results contrary to its professed purpose, for it centered party activity on the one tangible thing, organization of the terror, to the exclusion of all other contemplated work; and it fostered in the intelligent elements among the masses as well as among the revolutionists the idea that revolution was the task of the self-sacrificing terrorist. Terroristic activity thus was the joint product of trust in a metaphysical, peculiar fitness of a certain people for socialism or its contemporary equivalent, the "good life," and of distrust in the capacity of the people to organize a fight for the economically comprehensible things which at all times were the leaven of organization. The fact that the forces of the terrorists were generally recruited from young students and the descendants of the economically depressed elements of the nobility may account in part for the romantic orientation of the movement; but it is likewise true that this romantic aspect attracted the intelligentsia and left the peasants and workers cold. Support of terroristic activity came for the most part from the liberal bourgeoisie, a group which everywhere abounds in lovers of vicarious experience.

Terrorism was revived in 1901 when the Socialist Revolutionary party came into existence and proceeded to carry on the tradition of the older movement. But in the meantime economic development had led to the rise of a working class. Industrial changes, defeat in war, and a complicated international situation which had repercussions in politics and finance made terrorism appear outmoded as a revolutionary method, although it still aroused admiration. The rising mass movement and the spread of nationwide economic and political strikes made terror irrelevant and unnecessary. Moreover the government had learned how to place its agents at the core of the central fighting organization of the party; the provocateur Azef, for example, instigated several assassinations of members of the czarist family. These factors together with the opening of the Duma led the party to abandon terrorism in 1906. Three years later, however, this resolution was revoked, and terroristic activity continued until the World War.

Terroristic methods were tried once again in Russia, after the revolution of 1917, upon the cessation of the temporary political alliance of the Socialist Revolutionary party with the Bolsheviks, when the former declared war on the Soviet regime. The assassination of the German ambassador to Russia, calculated to create an international conflict embarrassing to the Bolsheviks, and finally an attempt upon Lenin's life were the outstanding results of the campaign. But the "propaganda by the deed" failed to achieve its aim; the masses of the people did not respond, seeing no reason for joining a movement which appeared to hold no promise for them.

As a complete revolutionary tactic terrorism has never attained real success. Governments, whether conservative or revolutionary, are not inclined to retreat before acts of terror directed against key persons. The will to power is not weakened by the exercise of power, and positions made vacant through the explosion of bombs are readily filled. On the other hand, the will to revolution requires a stronger force than the heroism of isolated individuals or even of small, well-organized groups. The art of revolution must be sustained by the interested will of a large proportion of the population and by concerted mass operations.

Feliks Gross

Causation of Terror

Whether an assassination is vindicated by public opinion and ultimately legitimated depends upon the historical context. This is also important for determining whether the sociological situation is conducive to political-ideological assassination or to systematic terror.

We shall limit ourselves here primarily to the factual material already presented in this study. The cases which were discussed occurred at certain times and in certain political cultures. The causative factors might be different in other political cultures and in other periods of time. Furthermore, a moral distinction must be made between terror applied against a domestic autocracy or against a foreign occupying power and terror directed against representatives of democratic institutions.

In the Polish and Russian cases, two major socio-political conditions could be identified from past experience which resulted in terroristic response: (a) oppressive foreign rule and conquest, or (b) oppressive domestic rule without any expectation of institutionalized, legalized avenues of change. We may call this a dead-end situation.

What is meant by "oppressive"? It means acts of physical brutality, including murder, limitations of freedom, humiliation of persons, economic exploitation, denial of elementary economic opportunities, and confiscation of property. Definitions cannot illustrate the humiliation and deprivation the Armenians and Bulgarians suffered under Turkish rule, or the Serbs under Croatian Ustasha government, or the Jews in Germany, or the areas of eastern Europe occupied by the Germans or Soviets. The moral, political, and economic subordination of ethnic groups or of a nation by extreme coercive measures, to the point at which an oppressed people views such conditions as no

Feliks Gross: "Political Violence and Terror in 19th and 20th Century Russia and Eastern Europe," in J. F. Kirkham (ed.), *Assassination and Political Violence* (Washington, D.C., 1969).

longer tolerable, results—under certain circumstances—in situations in which revolutionary committees may favor the choice of violence as the only adequate response.

The chances of such a response are enhanced under foreign occupation. We shall call this factor "sociological," because essentially it arises out of ethnic or class subordination or stratification as well as from foreign control of political and social behavior through extreme coercive measures.

The case of Poland prior to 1918 is quite illustrative. In Galicia, the Austrian-occupied part of Poland, tactical terror was absent, while in the Russian part terror was directed against important government representatives. Russian rule was oppressive and autocratic relative to the rule in Galicia, because the latter enjoyed a large measure of autonomy and individual political rights. Later, terror was revived by the Polish underground fighters during the brutal German occupation.

In the Balkan area, the systematic terror at first employed against Turkish officials in Macedonia was later institutionalized by the terroristic organizations of IMRO. Their terroristic activities continued, but without their former sociological justification. The Armenian terrorism of the Dashnaks was primarily a response to Turkish massacres and persecutions. During World War II, terrorism in the Balkans was reactivated in a similar way.

The condition generating terroristic action was usually that of a certain high-intensity threshold level of oppression, which theoretically at least could be measured by the enormity of oppressive acts, such as destruction of households, massacre of the subjugated people, the number of persons of the subjugated ethnic group who were political prisoners, and the limitations imposed on freedom of movement and freedom of expression. Arbitrary values can be assigned to each type of oppression and a composite index formed of all those types of occurrences. Yet a quantitative index cannot express the qualitative nature of human suffering and humiliation. Difficult as it is to evaluate the nature of oppression, however, the fact that there are various intensity levels seems to be obvious. Fascist Italian rule, for example, oppressive as it was, was less oppressive for the Jewish people than that of the Nazis. . . .

The experience of a century in violent political behavior (terror and political assassination) in Russia and eastern Europe, including the Balkans, suggests some rather striking but tentative findings, or hypotheses:

1. Assassinations and individual terror have appeared or increased in the past in eastern Europe (including the Balkans) in periods of intensification of ethnic tensions (Yugoslavia, Rumania, Bulgaria, Poland). Socio-economic tensions before or during the terror did not result in tactics of individual violence.

2. Ideological-political inequalities and tensions rather than social and economic conditions contributed to revolutionary situations in which terror was waged by underground parties in Russia (in the 19th and early 20th centuries). In Russian revolutionary theory, terror and violence were primarily legitimated as tactics toward achievement of political objectives (representative government, democracy, or dictatorship) and not of socio-economic goals.

How long does terror last as a systematic tactic? In the past, the duration has varied. The longest duration of tactics of individual terror in Russia and eastern Europe was about 40 years (IMRO), and of mass terror in Europe 600 years (Inquisition).

Once terror begins it is very difficult to arrest it. Assassination calls for vengeance or retaliation, as terror releases counter-terror. A tragic chain of reciprocity, once initiated, cannot be easily stopped, since it is motivated by strong emotions. A short, tentative table of the durations of terroristic actions illustrates this. The data on duration are not precise, but are gross approximations,

Duration of Tactics of Individual Terror Against Autocracy and Foreign Rule (Approximations)

Polish Socialist Party under Russian occupation	4–5 years
Armenian Dashnaks	25–30 years
Russian Populists and Social Revolutionaries	30 years
IMRO (Internal Macedonian Revolutionary Organization) (periods of struggle against foreign rule and domestic moderate governments before and after two Balkan wars and World War I)	40 years (and more)

Duration of Terroristic Tactics Against Democracy and Moderate Governments (Approximations)

Croatian Ustasha	35 years
Macedonian IMRO (2nd period)	20 years
Rumanian Iron Guard	15 years

Both terror and mass terror have had periods of long duration. Once the terroristic group is institutionalized, terror activity becomes a part of "institutional" behavior; it creates values of its own, and has its own discipline and routines. Institutions, especially bureaucracies of mass terror, have a tendency to perpetuate and extend the life of their organization. They resist termination. After institutionalization, professionalization of terroristic parties appears. Terroristic activity for those who are actively engaged in it becomes a full-time occupation; their livelihood depends on the party. This tactic requires careful preparation, planning, and deadly skills. It necessitates secrecy, which again conflicts with regular, daily, 8-hour employment.

In most of the cases discussed in this essay, the core of the terroristic organization became professional. As the years passed—some of those organizations lasted for two or even three revolutionary generations—this type of revolutionary activity became a way of life.

Once the socio-political situation changed, at least in the cases of the Russian social revolutionaries and the Poles, the revolutionaries knew how to terminate their terroristic activities. They became members of representative institutions and channeled their energies into building a short-lived democratic society. But some could hardly adjust to new conditions. In other cases, however, as in the case of certain sections of the Macedonian IMRO, the objectives were changed and terroristic activities did not cease. The professionals continued to apply terror in internal and external struggles.

The extension of the duration of terroristic tactics was also dependent on the response in the social base, i.e., the response of the social class the party claimed to represent, or in other cases, the response of social or ethnic groups. Some of the terroristic parties had stronger support than others. At certain times, the terroristic activities of the underground movement in Poland had, in the cities at least, broad national support. IMRO at the turn of the century, in its terroristic activities against the Turks, had the support of the Bulgarian peasantry. The Black Hand of Serbia had strong influence in the army and among the younger educated classes. This class or ethnic support contributed to the strength of the terroristic parties and to their duration.

But the major factors of duration were: (1) the sociological situation within which the party operated; (2) the nature of the party organization and its ideological appeal; and (3) the personalities of the party's leadership and militants, as well as its recruits of new members.

Once terror was initiated in one country, the news was disseminated abroad, so that violence was emulated elsewhere. In eastern Europe, the Russian "people's will" and the Social Revolutionary Party were influential outside of the country. Since the 1890s their tactics had been assimilated by revolutionary parties in eastern Europe, the Balkans, and Russian Armenia. A kind of political style developed, which to a certain extent was a result of terroristic tactics. This type of tactics imposed—as a condition of individual and group survival—a certain style of political behavior, even a style of personal life. After the situation had changed and the way of life of the militants had been modified, something yet remained of the past.

Those who fought against autocracy by way of assassination were frequently men and women of high principles and education. For some, this was a tragic and traumatic experience that left lasting impressions. The terroristic fascist and authoritarian parties moved from terror to massacres, mass terror, and genocide, which have changed the history and destiny of nations and contributed to the formation of hostile attitudes and painful memories which are difficult to eradicate or alter. Yet after World War II, mankind did recover rather miraculously from this ghastly past, even if on a superficial level only.

The use of terror, violence, and political assassination on a systematic scale, directed against democratic and free societies, debilitates slowly the entire political fabric and erodes representative institutions. It forces, sooner or later, a resolute action in defense of democracy, which may also result in limitation of freedom and establishment of repressive measures that are contradictory to democracy; or, an intimidated populace may yield to a vocal and aggressive minority.

Democracy, by definition, is a political system in which respect for a dissenting minority and government by consent, not by violence, are fundamental premises. Democracies, conceived as governments of free peoples, never have developed adequate ways of combatting continuous systematic violence, and particularly individual tactical terror and assassination. Free societies view individual political assassination as an exceptional, isolated occurrence. We believe that a country in which a citizen enjoys freedom and relative welfare should be free of violence. Current experience seems not to confirm fully such an assumption. Political violence has appeared, even in societies in which personal freedom was a supreme value.

It is of paramount significance to understand better the conditions that are conducive to political assassination, because the control of such conditions suggests that a humane policy of prevention is far more preferable and workable than a policy of repression. Political situations can be manipulated, however, and small terroristic groups may operate for a time in a democratic society by using their political rights as a shield.

The lessons of the past are a message of warning: once the politics of violence and terror is established, it is difficult to reestablish representative institutions that will function as well as they did previously. Violence creates conditions in which an arrogant and brutal minority can seize power and rule over an intimidated and passive population for many years.

Only a few great civilizations, and even these for rather short periods in history, were able to maintain governments based on democratic legitimacy, free elections, government by consent, and the protection of dissident minorities. Democracies decline by the slow erosion of faith in the efficacy of their institutions and by means of violence. An understanding of the conditions in which individual violence grows, the ways by which it can be controlled by democratic means, the setting of limits for violent political behavior, and defining the conditions under which force must be used to protect representative institutions, are areas requiring calm judgment, investigation, serious thinking, and the advocacy of wise and humane proposals.

Paul Wilkinson

Pathology and Theory

Thomas Kuhn has argued that "later scientific theories are better than earlier ones for solving puzzles in the often quite different environments to which they are applied." He states that the more recent theories can be distinguished from earlier ones by the following cri-

Paul Wilkinson, *Political Terrorism* (London, 1974). Published with the kind permission of the publishers, Macmillan, London.

teria: "accuracy of prediction, particularly of quantitative prediction; the balance between esoteric and everyday subject matter; and the number of different problems solved." Other factors which are less useful but nevertheless important, Kuhn suggests, are scope, simplicity, and compatibility with other specialties. Now it must be clearly admitted that in the terms of Kuhn's rigorous criteria there is as yet no adequate and generally accepted scientific theory of political violence or of political terrorism. Much the most valuable insight yielded by modern analysts of political violence belongs to a far older tradition of statecraft and political wisdom, a tradition which it is most foolish to despise. Moss, in his excellent pioneering study of urban guerrillas, illustrates its relevance when he observes: "many people fail to observe what de Tocqueville pointed out more than a century ago in his classic study of the French Revolution: that, ironically, uprisings often begin at the moment when things are getting better, and there is a genuine possibility of peaceful reform." And it is no reflection on Peter Calvert to note the pure Machiavellianism of some of his generalizations in *A Study of Revolution*: "Revolutionaries aim to create an impression of power, invincibility and effectiveness, representing themselves as a force which must inevitably assume supremacy. . . . This may not reach the people but it tends to reach government very quickly! . . . a substantial number of governments collapse from internal disillusion and decay . . . because government tries to use the views of the revolutionaries for its own purposes and in so doing rots its own structure." Crozier also forged some propositions about terrorism in a revolutionary context which stand up well to extensive comparative investigation: that terrorism is generally "the weapon of the weak"; that it is usually a useful auxiliary weapon rather than a decisive one; and that revolutionary terrorism seems to be a strategy most suited to national liberation struggles against foreign rulers, and to use by relatively small conspiratorial movements lacking any power base. Our comparative analysis suggests two further generalizations: first, that terrorism is highly unpredictable in its effects; and second, that terroristic violence can escalate until it is uncontrollable, with terrible results for society.

Nevertheless there are some interesting attempts at a more ambitious general theory, and these will now be examined. One of the most influential is the relative deprivation theory of civil violence, sometimes termed frustration-aggression theory. One of its proponents asserts: "the necessary precondition for violent civil conflict is relative deprivation, defined as actors' perception of discrepancy between their value expectations and their environment's apparent value capabilities. This deprivation may be individual or collective." There are at least four models of relative deprivation: rising expectations may overtake rising capabilities; capabilities may remain static while expectations rise; general socio-economic malaise may actually bring about a drop in capabilities while expectations remain constant; and finally there is the classic *F*-curve phenomenon in which, for a period, capabilities keep pace with rising expectations and then suddenly drop behind (a situation identified with the French revolutionary situation by de Tocqueville). Gurr has elaborated a number of propositions which attempt systematically to relate the level of frustration-aggression (or anger) which is likely to be expressed in civil violence to governmental responses, social control, and prevailing ideologies and beliefs. Some of his formal propositions are pitched at such a high level of generality that it is hard to see how they could be invalidated. For example: "the more intensely people are motivated toward a goal or committed to an attained level of values, the more sharply is interference resented and the greater the consequent instigation to aggression" and "the strength of anger tends to vary inversely with the extent to which deprivation is held to be legitimate." Gurr also holds that historical traditions and beliefs sanctioning violence, and the absence of institutional mechanisms permitting the expression of nonviolent hostility, increase the likelihood and magnitude of civil violence. Of more specific relevance to a theory of terrorism is Gurr's contention that the deprived require "some congruent image or model of violent action" to trigger them into violence. He suggests that a terrorist act can be used as such a demonstration effect.

Yet because of its concentration on frustration-aggression and its "instinctual" overtones, relative deprivation theory has very little to say about the social psychology of prejudice and hatred and, in particular, about the ways in which such hatreds are learned or acquired. There is widespread agreement in the literature that such hatreds and fanaticisms play a major role in encouraging extreme violence. Contemporary fanaticisms might not evince the monstrous and murderous elements present in the Nazi movement. Nevertheless, racial and religious hatreds have been whipped up in the course of numerous contemporary conflicts; for example in the Middle East, among Northern Irish extremists of both sides and among the Bengalis. As we have noted, there are now ideologues of the extreme left as well as the extreme right who follow Sorel and Fanon in believing collective violence to be creative and cathartic. A more recent development has been the calculated fostering of generational hatreds, a glorification of violence in youth culture. A recent (1972) publication aimed at the "alternative" or "underground" movements declares: "the bombings and the campus riots are not the start of the revolution, they are the defense against an increasing external threat. . . . The bombs of the Angry Brigade and the Weathermen are the result of the constant attempts to destroy it. They are a warning to the death culture. The private property of our parents has become the target for a symbolic vengeance for the lives that have been wantonly destroyed."* A slogan in one illustration in the book declares: "An' when yer smashin' th' state, kids, don't fergit t'keep a smile on yer lips an' a song in yer heart!"

How important is relative deprivation as a determinant of civil violence? Feierabend, Feierabend and Nesvold, in their comparative study of violence covering eighty-four countries, conclude that "socio-economic frustration" is positively related to conditions of internal political-unrest. But they find that it is only one among a number of other important correlates such as a rapid rate of modernization, the coerciveness of the regime, and the presence of strong minority group populations. Their findings concerning what they term "systematic conditions of political unrest" are of some interest and are quoted in full:

a. Political instability is negatively related to indicators of social and economic development.
b. Political instability is positively related to level of systemic frustration, measured in terms of the ratio (gap) between social wants and social satisfactions within society.
c. Political instability is positively related to rapid rate of modernization. This relationship holds both for static measures of instability and trends over time.
d. Political instability is positively related to the level of need achievement within society and especially to increases in need achievement levels between 1925 and 1950.

* M. Farren, E. Barker *et al.*, *Watch Out Kids* (London: Open Gate Books, 1972).

e. Political instability is curvilinearly related to level of coerciveness of political regime: the probability of a high level of political instability increases with mid-levels of coerciveness, insufficient to be a deterrent to aggression, but sufficient to increase level of systemic frustration.
f. Political instability is linearly related to fluctuations in coerciveness of the political regime.
g. The presence of strong minority populations serves to increase political instability beyond what would be predicted by the fluctuations in coercion.
h. The higher the level of socio-economic frustration, the higher the level of coerciveness necessary to act as a deterrent to aggression.
i. The probability of a high level of political instability is greatest with a combination of high levels of socio-economic frustration, high levels of fluctuation in coerciveness, and mid-level coerciveness of the political regime.

It is a long step, however, from theorizing about the conditions for political instability and civil violence in general* to a theory of revolutionary terrorism, the subject of the present study. There are at least three main avenues which may provide some progress toward the building of useful theories of revolutionary terrorism. First, we can, as several political scientists have urged, concentrate on its essentially *political* preconditions, on structures of power and mobilization processes and their interrelationship. It is a key premise of this approach that revolutionary violence stems directly from conflicts within and between a country's political institutions. Revolutionary violence is seen as basically the product of conflict about legitimacy, political rights, and access to power. It often results from the refusal or incapacity of a government to meet certain claims made upon it by a powerful group or a coalition of groups. Feliks Gross places primary stress on political factors in his theoretical models of the causation of terror. He has proposed two models; one for the causation of tactical terroristic acts against domestic autocracy or foreign rule, and one for the causation of individual violence as a tactic against democratic institutions.

Gross defines three "seminal" antecedents for terror against for-

* For a valuable discussion see "Civil Violence and the International System," Parts I and II, *Adelphi Papers*, Nos. 82 and 83 (London: International Institute for Strategic Studies, 1971).

eign rule or autocracy. The first is a widely perceived condition of oppressive rule, and by oppressive Gross means cruel, brutal, exploitive, arbitrary, and humiliating. If the rulers are foreigners then this generally provides an intensification of perceived oppression which Gross terms "sociological" because it "arises out of ethnic or class subordination or stratification as well as from foreign control..." Yet this "sociological" factor is not a sufficient cause of terror. Two other antecedent conditions must exist: an organized group with terroristic tactics and ideology must be available, and there must be activist individuals "willing to make a political choice and respond with direct action and violence to conditions of oppression." The antecedent conditions for terror against democracy are different. First there must be either an erosion of shared democratic values, a state of anomie, or a crisis of democratic institutions. Secondly, a terroristic organization must exist. Thirdly, there will be a pre-assassination phase directed at subverting and defaming democratic leaders and institutions. And lastly there must be activist personalities prepared to initiate terror. The models are in both cases entirely dependent upon subjective and contingent factors. They should be regarded, as Gross suggests, as no more than useful distillations of causal variables. He suggests an additional general hypothesis of note: assassination and individual terror begin or increase at periods of rising ethnic tensions and ideological-political inequalities rather than as a result of socio-economic strains.

Another very influential political hypothesis concerning the causation of terrorism is that put forward by Hannah Arendt suggesting that acts of extreme revolutionary violence in modern states may be a form of desperate revolt against "rule by Nobody," the anonymity of the bureaucratic state. When Simone Weil castigated the "bureaucratic machine which excludes all judgment and all genius" and which tends "to concentrate all powers in itself," she was attacking communist dictatorships. Yet we would surely be justified in taking into account the alienating and atomizing effects of all modern highly bureaucratized social systems. Orvik may be correct in suggesting that the apparently all-pervasive nature of government in post-industrial societies has rendered the insurrection and the *coup d'état* practically obsolete. In these conditions small extremist groups will be tempted to try assassination as an alternative weapon of social change. Crick has pointed out that, "in an age of bureaucrats, tyrannicide is plainly less useful than terror."

The second main line of advance toward a theory of revolutionary terrorism is concentration upon the terrorists themselves; their recruitment and induction into terrorism, their personalities, beliefs and attitudes, and their careers. The invention of revolutionary terrorism implies the invention of a new profession, the professional terrorist. One of the most thoroughgoing explorations of the terrorist in modern literature is that of Malraux in his novel *La Condition humaine*. Konig, the repressive police chief serving Chiang Kai-shek in Shanghai in early 1927, is portrayed as a man seeking to erase the memory of his own humiliation at the hands of the Russians by wholesale murder and torture: "My dignity is to kill them." But even this is not enough; he feels driven to humiliate his victims before their death, just as he was humiliated by his Russian captors. Malraux's archetypal revolutionary terrorist is portrayed in the character of Ch'en, a Westernized young Chinese who creates his own personal ideology of terrorism. Malraux suggests that Ch'en resorts to professional terror to escape from his private anguish, his extreme loneliness, and the fact that he needs to serve a cause and yet lacks faith in anything except his own power to destroy. Though he begins his terrorist career by murdering a sleeping man as an act of revolutionary duty, the political motives or purposes of his acts become increasingly irrelevant for him. Ch'en becomes consumed by terrorism as an end in itself. He can only forget himself by becoming a lonely executioner and sacrificing his own life: "*Il fallait que le terrorisme devint une mystique. Solitude, d'abord: que le terroriste décidât seul, exécutât seul . . .*" In his famous play, *Les Justes*, Camus distinguishes between the cynically opportunist terrorist (represented by Stepan) and the genuinely idealist revolutionary (Kaliaev) who believes that an act of assassination may be justified in the furtherance of the revolutionary crusade. In presenting the clash of these two attitudes to revolutionary action, Camus implies that there must be clearly defined *limits* to violence, limits that we transgress at our peril. Kaliaev, the revolutionary idealist, comes to believe that it is only permissible to kill in furtherance of "the cause" provided the terrorist is prepared to sacrifice his own life. But is this convincing? Does a terrorist's self-immolation in some way extenuate his taking another's life?

Marx is quite candid about the strange bedfellows that accompany every revolution: "In every revolution there intrude at the side of its true agents, men of a different stamp; some of them survivors of, and devotees to, past revolutions without insight into the present movement, but preserving popular influence by their honesty and courage or by the sheer force of tradition, others mere brawlers . . ." We should be warned against any crude attempts to stereotype terrorists. There is much evidence to support the view that some revolutionaries are impelled by passionate idealism and conviction. As one authority on anarchism observes, "for many anarchists, the belief in education, cooperation and peaceful persuasion goes hand in hand with a belief in direct action and even with active involvement in schemes for assassination," and he cites the case of the Spanish educationalist Francisco Ferrer in illustration. Nor should we assume that political terrorism is the pursuit of the less intelligent or less able. On the contrary, there is considerable evidence that revolutionary terrorism attracts the highly educated, and that the university student body is one of its major sources of recruitment. Dr. David Hubbard's portrait of the typical American hijacker as a suicidal schizophrenic with criminal or psychopathic tendencies *may* have some practical use as the basis for a crude "hijacker profile" for use by security officers at U.S. airports. But as it is aimed at the criminal or psychopathic hijacker it is of no use in identifying the explicitly political terrorist. Thus, for example, the Japanese who perpetrated the massacre at Lydda Airport were hardly noticed when they boarded the aircraft at Rome and their luggage in the hold was not searched. And indeed on what evidence could the authorities have suspected them? Far more questionable is a recent attempt to stereotype terrorists as "sociopaths" using the Wechsler intelligence measurement scales. There is not a shred of evidence to substantiate the claim that political terrorists are below average in abstract thinking: indeed it could be argued that with many terrorists the reverse is the case; they are prepared to sacrifice all humane considerations and often their lives for the sake of abstractions. Nor is it proven that terrorists are educationally retarded.

Political terrorism cannot be understood outside the context of the development of terroristic, or potentially terroristic, ideologies, beliefs and life-styles. Most influential has been the tradition of romantic individualism developed by Goethe, Humboldt, Schiller, and Stefan George in Germany. They posited a heroic genius forced into conflict with society or into isolation by the philistinism of the world. Max Stirner elaborated this individualism into a cult of the self-assertive egoist which in its amorality and anti-intellectualism anticipated certain currents in modern existentialism. The existentialist idea, so powerfully articulated by Camus and Sartre, that it is only through our own *actions* or *acts of will* that we can escape from despair, has been enormously pervasive. Under certain conditions such beliefs can become powerfully conducive to acts of terrorism. They can create a kind of politics of will and glorification of action for its own sake of the kind which Marinetti and the Futurists expounded. In the age of industrial organizations, machines, and mass armies, extremists of Left and Right may come to feel that all effective forms of symbolic action are exhausted. They may become convinced that acts of terrorism are the only means of asserting individual will and power. The culmination of this politics of the blood is an utterly amoral aestheticization of politics: *"Qu'importe les victimes, si le geste est beau?"** The fact is that for some, though by no means all, terrorists extreme violence is primarily undertaken as an act of self-assertion and self-expression. Paradoxically, therefore, acts of terrorism which occur as acts of will (though often given a post-facto political rationalization by others) are not truly political; they are antipolitical.

It is this writer's view that the psychology and beliefs of terrorists have been inadequately explored to date, although such a study could be a valuable aid to advance in the subject. Much more influential, yet disappointingly fruitless, has been the third avenue of approach via military and insurgency theory. Although, as we have noted, the French have evolved a military doctrine of revolutionary power, and although "insurgency studies" have had a certain vogue in American social science, remarkably little of the literature on guerrilla war and insurgency contributes directly to a theory of terrorism. The most influential theoretical model of the role of revolutionary terrorism in internal war is Thornton's. Following Crozier, Thornton accepts that terrorism is normally associated with the initial phase of internal war, that is as a preliminary to full-scale guerrilla operations. But Thornton's model is sufficiently flexible to allow for the fact that terror can be employed simultaneously with guerrilla and conventional war phases. . . . In his exposition of the consolidation phase Thornton does concede that the new incumbents will generally use "a considerable degree" of enforcement terror, but argues that this is not connected with the internal war situation. He argues that terror generally reaches its maximum in the initial stage when "the incumbents, if they have not previously detected the movement, must now

* Words of Laurent Tailhade on hearing that an anarchist bomb had been thrown in the Chamber of Deputies.

launch their maximum enforcement attack if they hope to stifle the movement. At this stage, therefore, both agitational and enforcement terrors will be at a maximum." The deficiencies of Thornton's model as the basis for a theory of terrorism are quite obvious. In fairness, Thornton does not make ambitious claims for the model. It is clearly only appropriate in certain archetypal internal war situations and does not really fit the many cases of struggles waged almost entirely by means of terrorism. Many of these, as we have observed, simply do not conform to the phasing of the model. Thornton does not offer any purchase on problems of terrorist motivation, or for identifying the conditions conducive to the adoption of revolutionary terrorism.

A surprising lacuna in strategic studies of revolutionary terrorism is the absence of a full treatment of weapon availability and supply and of the implications of new weapon technology for terrorism. Sir Frank Blackaby, at the British Association meeting (general section) in 1972, hinted at the nightmare possibility of a terrorist group seizing control over a nuclear device and attempting to blackmail government and society. So far these weapons have been successfully monopolized by states: the rapid proliferation of nuclear expertise and the recently announced American development of a "pocket" nuclear weapon device make this threat considerably more credible. Practically every other kind of weapon, short of nuclear, is potentially obtainable from the arms dealers or from sympathetic or neutral states. Peter Calvert comments interestingly on the effects of the technical improvement of weapons which enable persons to kill one another at relatively greater distances. He suggests that this increase in distance is sufficient to prevent the aggressive instinct of the user from being controlled by the normal restraints of face-to-face fighting. Calvert observes, "though this gives advantage to the defense where forces are evenly matched, it also enables one deviant to kill a very large number of people single-handed." The case of Villain, Jaurès's assassin, would suggest the truth of this claim. Villain confessed that he had been unable to go through with his first attempt at assassination because of the look of goodness and serenity he saw in his victim's eyes. Is the intensification of terror directly related to the physical distance of the terrorist fighter from his target?

Kent Layne Oots and Thomas C. Wiegele

Terrorist and Victim

Psychiatric and Physiological Approaches from a Social Science Perspective

Most of those in the medical profession who have attempted to understand terrorism have done so from a psychiatric or psychological perspective. To the social scientist, the methods of psychiatry often appear to be impressionistic and even idiographic in the extreme. Because the overriding concern of the psychiatrist is the personality of the individual, and subjects are interviewed and treated one at a time, the literature does not contain any full-scale, quantitative studies from which to develop general theories of terrorism.*

Definitions of terrorism vary, but it can at least be agreed that terrorism is violence. Medical studies of violence have, at times, been less than perfect in their methodology. Coleman (1974, pp. 676–678) discusses the problems surrounding two theories of violent behavior. The first of these theories posited that the existence of the *xyy* chromosome caused "super-maleness" and violent tendencies. According to Coleman (1974, p. 677) the violent *xyy* male is a myth and a modern version of demonology. The second controversy resulted from the claim that violence often results from psychomotor (temporal lobe) epilepsy. This theory was used to justify the removal of certain brain tissues from psychomotor epileptics even though the studies from which the theory was developed lacked sufficient methodological safeguards and produced results of dubious quality

* The reader interested in the general applicability of psychiatry to the social sciences in general and political science in particular is directed to Rogow (1971).

Reprinted excerpts from *Terrorism, An International Journal,* Vol. 8, No. 1, 1985 with the kind permission of the editor.

(Coleman, 1974, p. 678). These approaches to the study and control of violence, along with several others, Coleman has labeled the "New Phrenology" (1974, p. 681).

Coleman's argument is well taken. It does not suggest that medical studies of violence in general or terrorism in particular are irrelevant or based on superstition. It does, however, illustrate the necessity of choosing a methodology sufficiently rigorous to test the hypotheses under consideration. Thus, social scientists must be cautious in applying studies from the field of medicine in developing their understanding of terrorism. In short, while many consider medicine to be a "hard science," not all medical researchers are "hard scientists."

II. The Terrorist

The Psychiatry of the Terrorist. Many attempts have been made to explain violence and terrorism from a psychiatric or psychological perspective (Marcus, 1974; Kaplan, 1978; Toch, 1969; and Moyer, 1976a, 1976b). Hubbard (1975) used the psychiatric method in his interviews with fifty-two American and Canadian skyjackers and members of the FIQ and the Black Panthers.

Forensic psychiatrist Franco Ferracuti reviewed four theories of revolutionary violence. The first, the "Olson Theory," is a rational choice theory which holds that participants in revolutionary violence base their behavior on a rational cost-benefit calculus, concluding that violence is the best available course of action under the given social conditions. The second theory is the psychological theory or frustration-aggression theory. The third theory, a systemic theory of revolutionary violence, holds that revolution results from an imbalance in the social system. Finally, there is the Marxist theory of revolution (Ferracuti, 1982, pp. 138–139).

None of these four theories is adequate for explaining terrorism, according to Ferracuti. A better approach, he argues, would be a subcultural theory which takes account of the fact that terrorists live in their own subculture with their own value systems (Ferracuti, 1982, p. 139).

Murray S. Miron used the techniques of psycholinguistics to study the audiotapes produced by the Symbionese Liberation Army (SLA). Miron (1976, p. 16) concluded that "the oppression of which these people speak is the oppression of their own guilt. Incapable of managing that guilt they project the source of their oppression outward to the world around them." Miron's point is that the SLA terrorists had to justify their actions to themselves. They could overcome their guilt only by convincing themselves that some other entity (society) was really responsible for their actions. In Miron's view, terrorists must convince themselves that they have no choice, that there is no other way, and that therefore some other entity is ultimately responsible for their violence.

Miron's findings parallel those of Guttman (1979, p. 525), who argues, "The terrorist asserts that he loves only the socially redeeming qualities of his murderous act, not the act itself." The conscience of the terrorist, by this logic, is turned against those who oppose his violent ways, not against himself (Guttman, 1979, p. 525). The terrorist has projected his guilt outward.

The claim the terrorist must make in order to absolve his own guilt is that he is only doing what he must do, that he has no other choice under the circumstances. In reality, however, other options are open to the terrorist. It is the liberal audience which legitimizes the terrorist by accepting this mixture of murder with morality (Guttman, 1979, pp. 525–526).

The audience is invaluable, and, in fact, terrorist actions are aimed more at the audience than at the immediate victims. It is, after all, the audience that may have to meet the terrorist's demands. Moreover, the terrorist requires a liberal rather than a right-wing audience for success. Liberals make the terrorist respectable by accepting the ideology which the terrorist alleges informs his acts. The terrorist also requires liberal control of the media for the transmission of his ideology (Guttman, 1979, pp. 521–523).

Guttman's point of view may be more in line with left-wing rather than right-wing terrorism, and not all terrorism is left-wing. Ferracuti and Bruno (1981, p. 199) point out that between 1969 and 1980 2,017 persons were indicted for political crimes (terrorist acts) in Italy. Fifty-five percent of these terrorists were left-wing and forty-five percent were right-wing. Furthermore, there is a distinctive psychological pattern among right-wing terrorists.

Ferracuti and Bruno (1981, p. 209) list nine psychological traits common to right-wing terrorists:

1. Ambivalence toward authority.
2. Poor and defective insight.
3. Adherence to conventional behavioral patterns.

4. Emotional detachment from the consequences of their actions.
5. Disturbances in sexual identity with role uncertainties.
6. Superstition, magic, and stereotyped thinking.
7. Etero- and auto-destructiveness.
8. Low-level educational reference patterns.
9. Perception of weapons as fetishes and adherence to violent subcultural norms.

The above set of traits make up what Ferracuti and Bruno (1981, p. 209) call an "authoritarian-extremist personality." They conclude (1981, p. 209) that right-wing terrorism may be more dangerous than left-wing terrorism because "in right-wing terrorism, the individuals are frequently psychopathological and the ideology is empty: ideology is outside reality, and the terrorists are both more normal and more fanatical."

David G. Hubbard (1971, 1979, 1983) has been one of the most prolific psychiatrists writing on the phenomenon of terrorism. Hubbard's (1979) work examined why hierarchical authority, i.e., the committee decision-making structure common to most large organizations, is ineffective against the terrorist. First, management is supposed to produce smooth and efficient operating systems and is not equipped to deal with catastrophic emergencies such as terrorism. Second, committees are not an efficient way to make decisions when quick decisions are needed. Third, the hierarchical nature of the system, which impels the senior man to take control of the situation in crisis conditions produces several problems. Conflicts among committee members come out into the open. The senior man cannot control events and is no more prepared to deal with a crisis than is the committee. Furthermore, the senior man is usually a high-ranking political figure and his position elevates the event and makes it unduly important. Even if the committee remains in control, the terrorist will refuse to submit to its authority. In short, the governed do not consent to the actions of their governors (Hubbard, 1979, pp. 108–110). Hubbard concludes that the whole system of committee governance works against fast action in a crisis because recommendations for quick action, rather than careful study, are out of line with the psychology of large organizations (Hubbard, 1979, p. 110).

A Physiological Model of Terrorist Contagion. Several recent attempts have been made to understand how terrorism diffuses from one area to another, i.e., the contagion effect of terrorism (Heyman and Mickolus, 1980a, 1980b; Heyman, 1980; Hamilton and Hamilton, 1983; and Midlarsky, Crenshaw, and Yoshida, 1980).

Hamilton and Hamilton (1983) use three models of contagion: a Poisson model (no contagion effect), contagion, and reversible contagion. Heyman (1980) uses adjacency maps to study the diffusion of terrorism from one area to another. Midlarsky, Crenshaw, and Yoshida (1980) use both Poisson and negative binomial models of the contagion process.

At the core of studies of the diffusion of terrorism is the assumption that terrorist behavior can be easily imitated, especially given the fact that terrorist activity generates international publicity (Midlarsky, Crenshaw, and Yoshida, 1980, p. 279). The methods, demands, and goals of terrorists are instantly made available to other susceptible people, i.e., potential terrorists.

Beer (1981) develops a contagion model of war in the international system based on an analogy with epidemiology. Beer (1981, p. 1) begins with the premise that the infection of war spreads much like a disease wherein the effects of contagion bring a clustering of violence. Like disease, war spreads at the points of contact between states (Beer, 1981, pp. 52–53).

In the model developed in this chapter an argument is made that terrorism also spreads like a disease. Direct contact among carriers (terrorists) and the susceptible population (potential terrorists) is not necessary, however, since the media provide exposure to the disease (terrorism).

Several other studies shed some light on exactly how terrorism spreads. Scharff and Schlottman (1973, p. 287) report that already angered individuals become more aggressive after they are exposed to verbal reports of violence. Their research suggests that susceptible people in an angry state who are predisposed to violence may actually become violent if they are exposed to violence. Thus, this paper argues that a potential terrorist who is angry about some aspect of the sociopolitical environment could be led to commit an act of terrorism by media reports of the exploits of actual terrorists. Our scenario brings the phenomenon of terrorist contagion down from the regional and group focuses to the level of the individual terrorist.

The work of Watts (1981) and Watts and Sumi (1976, 1979) resembles that of Scharff and Schlottman, but these researchers bring in an additional element of relevance to political analysis, namely pre-existing political attitudes. Watts and Sumi (1979) point out the importance of pre-existing attitudes to the physiological arousal response of individuals to visually presented violent stimuli. The attitudes interact with the stimulus to produce a specific physiological response. Moreover, the attitudes of the respondent mediate the physiological response to produce two different types of physiological arousal. Some individuals become aroused in a violence-accepting way; others in a violence-rejecting way. The direction of the response, especially whether the heart rate decreases (accepting) or increases (rejecting), depends in large part on the pre-existing attitudes toward violence (Watts and Sumi, 1979, pp. 551–552). It is important to keep these directional differences in mind as the physiological model of terrorist contagion is developed. Potential terrorists have a predisposition (attitudinal preference) for violent solutions, and, therefore, media presentations of terrorist events arouse them in a violence-accepting way.

The work of Watts and Sumi (1979) is especially valuable in that it points out some of the attitudinal correlates of violence-accepting arousal. The study made use of college students and developed attitudinal measures on three scales. The Mach IV scale was used to test for Machiavellianism, interpersonal manipulativeness, among the subjects. The violence ideology scale measured approval toward various types of social violence. The traditionalism scale measured attitudes toward social conventionalism. All three of these scales were hypothesized to correlate with stimulus intake (violence-acceptance) when visual presentations of violence were made (Watts and Sumi, 1979, pp. 546–547).

The results of the study are illuminating. The correlations between heart rate and the Mach IV scale were −.35 for males and −.17 for females. The traditionalism scale correlated with heart rate at −.42 for males and −.06 for females. The violence ideology scale correlated with heart rate at −.41 for males and −.25 for females. The correlations were not as strong for females as for males; however, a negative correlation is indicative of a lowered heart rate and does indicate that violence-accepting arousal is associated with all three scales.

Since the argument is made in this paper that potential terrorists become aroused in a violence-accepting way by media presentations of terrorism, we should also consider whether terrorists may hold the attitudes measured by the three scales discussed above. There are no data on the subject. Nonetheless, some preliminary comments can be offered. Traditionalism could be a part of the terrorist's attitudes, although, ordinarily it would not. It is more likely to be a factor in terrorism conducted by conservative forces rather than left-wing forces. Violence ideology would, with some modifications, seem to be a part of the attitudes of terrorists. Terrorists must, by the nature of their actions, have an attitude which allows violence. However, the types of violence sanctioned by the terrorist may differ from those in the study by Watts and Sumi (1979).* Machiavellianism may be a part of the terrorist's attitudes. Terrorism, insofar as it is an effort to manipulate the authorities, the media, and the public, is a Machiavellian act. Indeed, since terrorists use their immediate victims as symbols and objects in their struggle for public goods, terrorists are manipulating their victims as well as the press, the public, and the authorities. The victims become game pieces to the terrorists. There is very little affect, either negative or positive, in the terrorist's relationship with his hostages. Since people are to be used by the terrorist in pursuit of public goods, they have very little other value to the terrorist.

Westermeyer's (1973) study of the phenomenon of "amok" violence in Southeast Asia argues that amok may be epidemic rather than endemic. Episodes of amok violence tend to cluster: they are not distributed randomly. Moreover, there is a contagion effect in the methods of amok violence as amok individuals have moved from the use of bladed weapons to the use of grenades as their chosen weapon. Amok has also spread from nation to nation in Southeast Asia and to other, more distant cultures which have had contact with Southeast Asian society. Amok, therefore, is epidemic and is a learned behavior transmitted from one person to another (Westermeyer, 1973, pp. 873–874).

Westermeyer's work points out that violence can be transmitted from person to person. A susceptible person who witnesses such violence, whether in person or through the media, is not only led to commit a violent act, but can learn the method of violence as well.

Laborit (1978, pp. 738–745) lists several types of aggression which occur in animals:

* For a list of the components of the violence ideology scale as well as the traditionalism scale, see Watts and Sumi (1979), p. 547.

1. Predatory aggression arises from a basic need, hunger.
2. Competitive aggression occurs when two objects occupying the same space seek the same object.
3. Defense of territory results from competition with intruding organisms for "satisfying objects."
4. Intermale aggression results from the sexual instinct.
5. Hierarchy formation is the end result of competitive aggression.
6. Defensive aggression is a response to a painful stimulus.
7. Anxiety or irritability aggression results from frustration and is relieved only by gratification.

Laborit goes on to argue that all forms of aggression except predatory aggression are learned behaviors. Learned forms of aggression are reinforced by the resulting gratification (Laborit, 1978, p. 746).

If aggression is a learned behavior, then terrorism, a specific type of aggressive behavior, can also be learned. Potential terrorists can learn the methods, the goals, and the rhetoric of actual terrorists and be inspired or aroused by their exploits. Moreover, potential terrorists can see the results of terrorist activity, i.e., what measure of gratification can be achieved through the terrorist act. The potential terrorist need not experience gratification himself; he need only see that terrorism has worked for others in order to become aggressively aroused. Modern communications systems make it possible for potential terrorists to learn the methods and achievements of a large number of actual terrorists, and to become aroused again and again.

What takes place among potential terrorists is collective learning wherein large numbers of susceptible individuals learn simultaneously, either directly or vicariously.

Cannon (1929) developed the theory of the "fight or flight" response of the human body, noting that when an individual is under stress the heart rate increases, the lungs operate more efficiently, adrenaline and sugar are released into the bloodstream, and the muscles become infused with blood.

Stegenga (1978) and Davies (1980) have pointed out the role of the brain in producing physiological arousal and aggression. The seat of aggressive behavior in the brain is the limbic system, the emotional part of the brain (Stegenga, 1978, p. 53). Because conflict behavior inevitably involves emotion, it involves the limbic system (Davies, 1980, p. 32).

Stimulation of specific parts of the limbic brain produces specific types of aggression. The hypothalamus and the amygdala are most closely associated with irritability aggression (Stegenga, 1978, p. 54); and most acts of terrorism are classifiable as irritability aggression.

Davies (1980, p. 34) points out that experimental research has shown that specific types of aggression can be induced in animals through electrical stimulation of specific parts of the brain. Cats, for example, have been made to attack rats by means of electrical stimulation and have ceased their attacks when the stimulation was turned off.

Under normal conditions, stimulation of the limbic system takes place through the bloodstream. Specifically, androgens (male hormones) carried by the bloodstream tend to increase feelings of aggression and hostility while estrogens (female hormones) tend to decrease such feelings (Stegenga, 1978, p. 55). In addition to the sex hormones (steroids), catechlomines, secreted by the endocrine glands, also affect aggressive behavior. Dopamine, a catechlomine, produces noradrenalin and norepinephrine, which in turn produce adrenaline and epinephrine. Epinephrine and norepinephrine increase the body's metabolic rate and prepare it to meet a challenge, i.e., epinephrine and norepinephrine are the chemical stimulants of the fight or flight response. Moreover, experimental work on animals has demonstrated that when the body is under prolonged stress, as is the potential terrorist who is repeatedly aroused by media accounts of terrorism, norepinephrine is stored up in the brain (Davies, 1980, pp. 38–42).

The release of these hormones and therefore the stimulation of the limbic system and the physiological arousal of the individual are linked to events in the environment, i.e., they usually result from an external stimulus (Stegenga, 1978, p. 56). The denial of political goals and media presentations of terrorist activities constitute the external stimuli necessary to set the potential terrorist on the way to aggressive physiological arousal.

Stegenga (1978, p. 54) points out that certain parts of the limbic system also inhibit violence and aggression. The internal balance of the limbic brain determines, in part, the extent of aggressiveness that an individual will exhibit. The neurophysiological model of aggression also speaks to the issue of how terrorism can be controlled. If the neurophysiological model is accepted* then social remedies may not work because, as Stegenga (1978, p. 59) puts it:

> Sociological remedies always presuppose a normally functioning brain: but much violence is done by individuals with abnormally functioning brains that are damaged or diseased or simply badly and perhaps unalterably programmed. Some combination of sociological and biological remedies seems necessary if violence is to be controlled.

If the neurophysiological model of aggression is realistic, there is no basis for the argument that terrorism could be eliminated if its sociopolitical causes were eliminated. Such an argument only accounts for half of the problem. Even if some concept of equal justice and dignity could be agreed upon and instituted worldwide, there is no guarantee that equality would satisfy those whose brains have malfunctioned.

Some studies have also pointed out that high frustration and arousal may lead to aggressive behavior and that aggression, when acted out, may produce some relief from the state of arousal (Grings and Dawson, 1978, pp. 101–102).

The fight or flight response in modern society is rarely relieved by either fight or flight. Most individuals cannot run away from their problems nor can they fight simply because they are angry. Relief from a state of physiological arousal is generally not possible. The potential terrorist, however, is, in all likelihood, a frustrated individual who has become aroused and has repeatedly experienced the fight or flight syndrome. Moreover, after these repeated arousals, the potential terrorist seeks relief through an aggressive act and also seeks, in part, to remove the initial cause of his frustration by achieving the political goal which he has hitherto been denied.

This model points logically to several conclusions. First, social scientists who seek to understand terrorism should take account of the possibility that biological or physiological variables may play a role in bringing an individual to the point of performing an act of terrorism. Second, social scientists should be mindful of the role of the individual in the terrorist act. Third, psychiatrists, psychologists,

* See Stegenga (1978, pp. 60–61) for a discussion of the methodological and theoretical problems which make the neurophysiological model tentative rather than conclusive.

and medical researchers who seek to understand terrorism should attempt to account for the influence of sociopolitical variables since the political system is the real target of terrorism, and it is some perceived political condition that the terrorist seeks to change. Fourth, physiological and sociopolitical variables may interact in the terrorist act and may reinforce each other. These conclusions point toward a broader, interdisciplinary understanding of terrorism. It is often said, and often true, that social phenomena do not usually fall into neat disciplinary categories.

V. Theoretical Considerations

Social scientists seeking to understand how terrorism affects its victims must have better information than is currently available. Obtaining that information requires the construction of suitable data bases. The psychiatric method, i.e., interviewing an individual, is not adequate to the task. To obtain this sample, social scientists could design a survey questionnaire, which with the aid of law enforcement officials and former victims, could be administered to all victims of political terrorism. Such a survey would also have to be designed with the aid of medical personnel in order to be certain that it would give the social scientist a better understanding of the psychophysiological state of the victim. A large sample would give social scientists an indication of what problems are most common to victims of terrorism and how much variation there is from one individual to another.

The physiological responses of terrorists and their victims are another area of concern to social scientists. The collection and coding of a large number of medical profiles of victims would provide some clues as to the physiological changes brought on by terrorist victimization. Such a method would not, however, give any indication of the state of the victim during the terrorist event itself.

The state of the victim during an attack could be measured during simulations of terrorist events. However, the responses would not be as pronounced during a simulation as they would be during an actual terrorist event.

The physiological response of the terrorist is an area which lends itself to experimental study by social scientists. Subjects could be deprived of some good and then exposed to media coverage of various terrorist events. Tests could then be conducted on their level of aggression, and their physiological level of arousal could be measured.

The study of the physiological and psychiatric aspects of both terrorists and victims will require social scientists to look beyond their own disciplines. Such studies will require the assistance of those in the medical professions who are familiar with the phenomenon. Interdisciplinary work which mixes the careful attention to the individual found in medicine with the manipulation of large data bases by social scientists may provide major theoretical breakthroughs in understanding terrorism.

Terrorism is a phenomenon that requires social scientists to consider numerous variables in developing an understanding. If the physiological model of terrorist contagion is correct, terrorism is a psychiatric, physiological, and political phenomenon. Social scientists must be sensitive to the fact that biological and psychiatric variables may influence and be influenced by the sociopolitical variables which form the subject matter of the social sciences.

The reverse is also true. Medical professionals who seek to understand terrorism must remember that terrorism is political violence with a political goal and a political cause. Terrorism must be treated as a special case of the general class of violence. No understanding of terrorism can be considered complete or even realistic until both biological and sociopolitical variables are included.

At this time it is impossible to say what form a complete theory of terrorism might take. It is, however, obvious that a number of methods and variables from a number of disciplines will be needed to develop even a preliminary theory.

REFERENCES

Beer. F. A. 1981. *Peace Against War*. San Francisco: W. H. Freeman and Company.

Cannon, W. B. 1929. *Bodily Changes in Pain, Hunger, Fear and Rage*. Second edition. Boston: Charles T. Bradford Company.

Coleman, L. S. 1974. "Perspectives on the Medical Study of Violence." *American Journal of Orthopsychiatry* 44: 675–687.

Davies, J. C. 1976. "Ions of Emotion and Political Behavior." In *Biology and Politics*. A. Somit, ed. Paris: Mouton. Pp. 97–125.

Davies, J. S. 1980. "Biological Perspectives on Human Conflict." In *Handbook of Political Conflict: Theory and Research*. T. R. Gurr, ed. New York: The Free Press. Pp. 19–61.

Eitinger, L. 1977. "The Stress of Captivity." In *The Dimensions of Victimization in the Context of Terroristic Acts.* R. D. Crelinsten, ed. Montreal: International Centre for Comparative Criminology. Pp. 69–85.

Ferracuti, F. 1982. "A Sociopsychiatric Interpretation of Terrorism." *The Annals of the American Academy of Political and Social Science* 463: 129–140.

Ferracuti, F., and F. Bruno. 1981. "Psychiatric Aspects of Terrorism in Italy." In *The Mad, the Bad and the Different: Essays in Honor of Simon Dinitz.* I. L. Barak-Glantz and C. R. Huff, eds. Lexington: Lexington Books. Pp. 199–213.

Foreman, P. B. 1953. "Panic Theory." *Sociology and Social Research* 37: 295–304.

Grings, W., and M. E. Dawson, 1978. *Emotions and Bodily Responses: A Psychophysiological Approach.* New York: Academic Press.

Guttman, D. 1979. "Killers and Consumers: The Terrorist and His Audience." *Social Research* 46: 517–526.

Hamilton, L. C., and J. D. Hamilton. 1983. "Dynamics of Terrorism." *International Studies Quarterly* 27: 39–54.

Heyman, E. 1980. "The Diffusion of Transnational Terrorism." In *Responding to the Terrorist Threat: Security and Crisis Management.* R. Shultz and S. Sloan, eds. New York: Pergamon. Pp. 190–244.

Heyman, E., and E. Mickolus, 1980a. "Imitation by Terrorists: Quantitative Approaches to the Study of Diffusion Patterns in Transnational Terrorism." In *Behavioral and Quantitative Perspectives on Terrorism.* Y. Alexander and J. M. Gleason, eds. New York: Pergamon. Pp. 175–228.

Heyman, E., and E. Mickolus, 1980b. "Observations on Why Violence Spreads." *International Studies Quarterly* 24: 299–305.

Hubbard, D. G. 1971. *The Skyjacker: His Flights of Fantasy.* New York: Macmillan.

Hubbard, D. G. 1975. "A Glimmer of Hope: A Psychiatric Perspective." In *International Terrorism and Political Crimes.* M. C. Bassiouni, ed. Springfield, Ill.: Charles C. Thomas. Pp. 27–32.

Hubbard, D. G. 1979. "A Story of Inadequacy: Hierarchical Authority Versus the Terrorist." In *Political Terrorism and Business: The Threat and Response.* Y. Alexander and R. A. Kilmarx, eds. New York: Praeger. Pp. 106–112.

Hubbard, D. G. 1983. "The Psychodynamics of Terrorism." In *International Violence.* Y. Alexander and T. Adeniran, eds. New York: Praeger. Pp. 45–53.

Kaplan, A. 1978. "The Psychodynamics of Terrorism." *Terrorism* 1: 237–257.

Laborit, H. 1978. "The Biological and Sociological Mechanisms of Aggression." *International Social Science Journal* 30: 727–749.

Marcus, A. 1974. "Some Psychiatric and Sociological Aspects of Violence." *International Journal of Group Tensions* 4: 254–268.

Midlarsky, M. I., M. Crenshaw, and F. Yoshida. 1980. "Why Violence Spreads: The Contagion of International Terrorism." *International Studies Quarterly* 24: 262–298.

Miron, M. S. 1976. "Psycholinguistic Analysis of the SLA." *Assets Protection* 1: 14–19.

Moyer, K. E. 1976a. *The Psychobiology of Aggression.* New York: Harper & Row.

Moyer, K. E., ed. 1976b. *Physiology of Aggression and Implications for Control.* New York: Raven Press.

Ochberg, F. M. 1978. "The Victim of Terrorism: Psychiatric Considerations." *Terrorism* 1: 147–168.

Ochberg, F. M. 1979. "Preparing for Terrorist Victimization." In *Political Terrorism and Business: The Threat and Response*. Y. Alexander and R. A. Kilmarx, eds. New York: Praeger. Pp. 113–122.

Quarantelli, E. L. 1954. "The Nature and Conditions of Panic." *American Journal of Sociology* 60: 267–275.

Rogow, A. A. 1971. "Some Psychiatric Aspects of Political Science and Political Life." In *Social Psychology and Political Life: Problems and Prospects*. G. Abcarian and J. W. Soule, eds. Columbus, Ohio: Charles E. Merrill. Pp. 185–209.

Roth, W. T. 1977. "Psychosomatic Implications of Confinement by Terrorists." In *The Dimensions of Victimization in the Context of Terroristic Acts*. R. D. Crelinsten, ed. Montreal: International Centre for Comparative Criminology. Pp. 41–60.

Scharff, W. H., and R. S. Schlottman. 1973. "The Effects of Verbal Reports of Violence on Aggression." *The Journal of Psychology* 84: 283–290.

Selye, H. 1956. *The Stress of Life*. New York: McGraw-Hill.

Silverstein, M. E. 1979. "Counterterrorist Medical Preparedness: A Necessity for the Corporate Executive." In *Political Terrorism and Business: The Threat and Response*. Y. Alexander and R. A. Kilmarx, eds. New York: Praeger. Pp. 123–128.

Sloan, S. 1981. *Simulating Terrorism*. Norman: University of Oklahoma Press.

Stegenga, J. A. 1978. "The Physiology of Aggression (and of Warfare?)." *International Journal of Group Tensions* 8 (3/4): 51–67.

Tinklenberg, J. R., P. Murphy, and P. Murphy, 1977. "Adaptive Behavior of Victims of Terrorism." In *The Dimensions of Victimization in the Context of Terroristic Acts*. R. D. Crelinsten, ed. Montreal: International Centre for Comparative Criminology. Pp. 92–107.

Toch, H. 1969. *Violent Men: An Inquiry into the Psychology of Violence*. Chicago: Aldine.

Watts, M. W. 1981. "Psychophysiological Analysis of Personality/Attitude Scales: Some Experimental Results." *Political Methodology* 7 (1): 81–102.

Watts, M. W., and D. Sumi. 1976. "Attitudes and Physiological Response to Audiovisual Display of Aggressive Social Behavior." Paper presented to the annual meeting of the Midwest Political Science Association, Chicago, April 29–May 1.

Watts, M. W., and D. Sumi. 1979. "Studies in the Physiological Component of Aggression-Related Attitudes." *American Journal of Political Science* 23 (3): 528–558.

Westermeyer, J. 1973. "On the Epidemicity of Amok Violence." *Archives of General Psychiatry* 28: 873–876.

Daniel E. Georges-Abeyie

Women as Terrorists

Information on women as terrorists is sketchy at best. Walter Laqueur takes cognizance of the fact that women have participated in almost all guerrilla movements but have been most prominent in small urban guerrilla groups in the United States and West Germany, and particularly in Korea, where they constituted more than a quarter of the Communist revolutionary cadre.* W. Middendorff and D. Middendorff note the dearth of reliable criminological studies of German terrorists and suggest two reasons for this absence of information:

> firstly because there are not enough terrorists to enable statistical empirical research and secondly because the terrorists constantly resist any psychological and psychiatric examination, and they completely refuse to answer any questions. . . .†

Charles A. Russell and Bowman H. Miller's excellent study in this volume provides one of the most comprehensive reviews of variables associated with terrorism.

Various mass-media sources as well as social-control sources, primarily the Federal Bureau of Investigation (FBI) and the International Association of Chiefs of Police (IACP); also concluded that women have played a relatively secondary role in terrorist violence, as well as in terrorist groups, although there have been some notable exceptions.‡ These exceptions are discussed by Russell and

* Walter Laqueur, *Terrorism* (Boston, 1977).

† W. Middendorff and D. Middendorff, "Changing Patterns of Female Criminality," mimeograph (Freiburg, n.d.).

‡ Federal Bureau of Investigation, *Uniform Crime Reports* (Washington, DC: U.S. Department of Justice, 1977). In 1978 the FBI noted that the percent change for violent crime perpetrated by women over the time span 1968–77 was +72.0, while the respective percent change for property crime was +121.3.

Excerpts reprinted from Yonah Alexander (ed.) *Perspectives on Terrorism.*

Miller, who note that women have occupied an important position in West German terrorist movements, especially in the Baader-Meinhof organization and the Movement Two June where they have constituted one-third of the operational personnel.

Other exceptions to the relatively low-level participation of women as terrorist leaders or as members of terrorist groups include:

1. Leila Khalid and Fusako Shigenobu, leaders in the Popular Front for the Liberation of Palestine (PFLP) and the Japanese Red Army (JRA), respectively. Together they were instrumental in arranging the initial PFLP training of JRA and West German cadres in Lebanon during the early 1970s.
2. Ellen Mary Margaret McKearney, a runner for the Irish Republican Army (IRA) bombers operating in England.
3. Norma Ester Arostito, cofounder of the Argentine Montoneros. She also served as their chief ideologue until her death in 1976.
4. Genoveve Forest Tarat, who played a key role in the 12 December 1973 Basque Fatherland and Liberty Movement (ETA-V) operation that resulted in the assassination of Spanish Premier Admiral Carrero Blanco. She also participated in the 13 September 1974 bombing of a Madrid restaurant, the Café Rolando, which resulted in eleven dead and seventy wounded.
5. Margherita Cagol, the now-deceased wife of Italian Red Brigades leader Renato Curcio, who played an important role in the organization and quite possibly led the Red Brigades commando team that freed Curcio from Rome's Casale Monferrato jail on 8 February 1975.
6. Bernardine (Bernadette) Rae Dohrn, active in the Weather Underground (WU).
7. Mario Torres, wife of Carlos Torres, of the Armed Forces of National Liberation (FALN). They were possibly coleaders and cofounders of this Puerto Rican movement.
8. The Symbionese Liberation Army (SLA) women, including Angela Atwood, Camilla Christine Hall, Emily Mantague Schwartz Harris, Nancy Ling Perry, Mary Alice Landles, and Patricia Solytsik (alias Mizmoon-Zoya).

EXPLANATIONS FOR FEMALE MEMBERSHIP IN TERRORIST ORGANIZATIONS

Many varied, and at times, extreme explanations have been offered for female involvement in terrorist activities. Here are the most common: (1) revolutionary and terrorist activity offers excitement; (2) danger is both an attraction as well as a repellant; (3) terrorist violence is tied to causes which initially may appear legitimate; (4) terrorist organizations provide an opportunity for upward mobility, in leadership and in an active role in formulating the group's policies, opportunities that are absent or extremely limited in the white male-dominated world of legitimate activity; (5) terrorist organizations offer change and a renunciation of the current male-dominated chauvinistic mores; (6) the traditional American stereotype of women as weak, supportive, submissive, silent, and of lower intelligence and drive is absent in the philosophies of many terrorist organizations; (7) membership in a terrorist organization is the natural outgrowth of membership in extreme feminist organizations; (8) women are by nature more violent and dangerous than men, and terrorist organizations provide an outlet for this tendency; (9) women are rejecting stereotypic roles and thus adopting traditional male roles that include revolutionary and terrorist violence; (10) hormonal disturbances, caused by excessive sexual freedom and particularly by having sexual relations before maturity, affect these women; (11) economic, political, and familial liberation due to the trend toward greater justice and equality for women plays a role; (12) a continuation of natural selection, or the survival of the fittest, has an influence; (13) middle-class white Anglo-Saxon Protestant (WASP) restraints, in regard to mind-sets (ideas and attitudes) as well as behavior, are rejected.

Many of these explanations appear extreme and even laughable. But, perhaps, there is some merit to a less extreme interpretation of some of the correlates to these and other theories of this specific form of female criminality. There can be little doubt that the North American and Western European terrorist organizations with female leadership or sizable numbers of female cadres proselytized female homosexuality and bisexuality as well as pansexualism and feminist ideology—factors not present in most South American, African, Asian, and Eastern European terrorist groups. We must not, however, confuse associative factors for causal models. Unfortunately, the data in respect to female involvement in terrorist and guerrilla organizations are rudimentary at best. Each of the above-cited explanations can and should be developed into hypotheses and tested by means of various social science research techniques. Several of the previously cited explanations grounded in the changing socio-economic role-set ascribed to women offer fruitful areas for social science research. This writer would also contend that terrorism by women may, in part, be tied to the same systemic structural-functional changes in society that have brought about uncertainty in female role-sets and a possible increase in female criminality in general.

Toward a Theory of Women as Terrorists

The following is a rudimentary attempt at a formulation of a theory of women as terrorists. It must be stressed that this theory is rudimentary at best, but it does present the known variables associated with female terrorist behavior.

Proposition One: *Women, except for a few notable exceptions, have played a relatively minor role in terrorist violence in the last thirty years.* Official arrest and suspect data reveal a relatively minor level of female participation in terrorist activity.

Proposition Two: *Although women, except for a few notable exceptions, have played a relatively minor role in terrorist violence in the last thirty years, one may expect female participation, both as free-lance nonmovement-oriented terrorists as well as members of terrorist organizations, in terrorist incidents to increase dramatically in the future.* Changing role-sets ascribed to women will place them more directly into the mainstream of academia and corporate enterprise. These changes in the expected belief and activity patterns of women will result in direct conflict with the more traditional female role-sets: wife, mother, and passive, gentle, noncompetitive beauties of moderate or low intelligence and low aspirations. With women entering the labor force as well as the academic world at an accelerating rate, the system with its limited resources and rewards will frustrate women who have attained all of the socially defined attributes usually tied to success, such as proper speech, aggressive personalities, superior technical training, and high levels of education; these highly skilled women will perceive the reality of blocked opportunity while becoming more conscious of their unique exclusion from the system of rewards, thus fostering and reinforcing demands for sociostructural change of both a socialist and feminist nature.

We must also realize that as new employment fields open up for women, they will acquire new skills, some of which may be used in terrorist acts. Combat or combat-support units in the "New Army" train women to shoot guns and handle explosives, while new opportunities in various local, state, and federal-level control agencies also open up similar training. Women currently taught to work on farms, in forests, and in mines learn skills in the storage and discharge of explosives.

Proposition Three: *Female input in terrorist acts is tied in part to feminist demands and practices.* Feminist organizations, or organizations with socialistic principles, allow for increased opportunities to women for upward mobility. This upward mobility more likely is determined by a woman's innate or learned skills and leadership qualities than by the sex-linked, stereotyped characteristics often found in more traditional male-dominated organizations. Female input in groups that champion feminist and socialistic objectives is likely to be considerable. If such demands should exceed society's capacity to deliver reform, then violence or the threat of violence is probable by radical organizations.

Proposition Four: *Contemporary female terrorists are likely to exhibit male personality or physical traits.* The demand for immediate change and the ability to compete forcefully in the labor market and in the classroom are traits often viewed as masculine. Thus, those who assert markedly radical demands for structural-functional change in regard to role-sets assigned to women, or any oppressed majority or minority, may be viewed as masculine in character. Women who lack the characteristics and traits that society considers appropriate—gentleness, passivity, nonviolent personalities, seductiveness, physically attractive faces and figures—may seek success in some nonfeminine realm, by displaying aggression, unadorned faces and bodies, toughness, or other masculine qualities.

Masculine or feminine characteristics are often culturally defined. Female terrorists of the future can be expected to exhibit fewer of the characteristics usually defined as masculine, because clear divisions between sex-linked roles no longer will exist.

Proposition Five: *Terrorist acts by females now and in the future will become more instrumental and less expressive.* There can be little doubt that terrorist acts by females have often been expressive in character. However, as more women join terrorist groups with well-defined political goals and objectives, women will carry out fewer incidents of so-called expressive violence, or violence that does not appear to be conducive to goal achievement. There is no reason to believe that trained female terrorists will function in a manner different from trained male terrorists.

The claim that terrorism by women is often tied to the liberation of their imprisoned mates is no different from much of the terrorism perpetrated by their male counterparts. In fact, most acts of terrorism by either female or male terrorists have not been tied to the liberation of loved ones. However, male terrorism has not been totally immune to the act of struggling for the liberation of imprisoned lovers: one must recall that the Uruguayan government's most effective counter-terrorism strategy against the Tupamaros, or Movimento de Liberacion Nacional (MLN), was the wholesale arrest of the loved ones, wives, and families of the male-dominated guerrillas of the MLN movement. The government then waited for the Tupamaros to attack the jails and prisons which held their families, on the theory that during the attack the guerrillas would be slaughtered.

A theory, therefore, that attempts to explain women as terrorists would read as follows: one may expect a considerable amount of female terrorists in organizations that exhibit and preach feminist or socialistic principles. These organizations and, thus, sizable numbers of female cadres may exist in societies undergoing dramatic challenge to, or change in, their present economic system. Trained female terrorists can be expected to function in a manner similar to their male counterparts. And female terrorists most likely will serve as integrated cadres in both socialistic and nationalistic struggles, and not as autonomous legions of Amazon-oriented warriors.

The Outlook for Female Participation in Terrorism

Most criminal-justice experts who specialize in the study of terrorism agree that conditions are favorable for increased terrorist activity throughout much of the world and that women will play an increasingly dynamic and important role. What is debatable is whether or not female terrorism is and will continue to be more emotive and less instrumental than male terrorism, or terrorism that is carried out by groups predominantly male in both ideology and membership. The emancipation of women from the household and related domestic functions, their increased opportunity and expectations in the worlds of enterprise and academia brought about by the reorganization of the workplace, and feminist pressures on women's role in the nuclear family will no doubt produce a woman who is both willing and able to take her rightful place in all aspects of society and culture, including revolutionary and terrorist activities.

The classic factors conducive to terrorist violence remain: (1) a self-conscious, segregated, ethnic, cultural or religious minority;* (2) which feels itself to be economically deprived or politically oppressed—a feeling exacerbated by the effect of modern communications—with poor job opportunities, lacking in voting rights, but encouraged to believe that change is coming and then is disappointed; (3) in a situation of unemployment or inflation; (4) externally encouraged; (5) with an historical "them" to blame; (6) and with frustrated elites to provide leadership and to overcome the natural distaste, of all save the psychopathic fringe, to initiate violence by giving it an ideological justification; (7) in a society with at least an oral tradition of democracy and upward mobility.†

To these factors we must add feminist demands, both logical and irrational, requiring serious response and gratification by societies with a history of nonresponse to nonviolent pressure, including the so-called western democracies. If we are to comprehend more fully the role of women as terrorists, we must recognize that women comprise a self-conscious, dynamic sector of our society which often perceives itself to be an oppressed majority—a majority oppressed not only because of race, religion, ethnicity, or national origin but also because of sex. That oppression mirrors all of the factors that Burton and Laqueur have listed as classic conditions conducive of terrorist violence. Future research might attempt to examine more fully the correlates of female terrorism, the conditions conducive to terrorist and revolutionary violence, feminism, socialism, and the traditional and changing modes of female criminality.

* A. Burton, *Urban Terrorism: Theory, Practice and Response* (New York: 1975), 249.

† Walter Laqueur, *Terrorism* (Boston, 1977).

Chalmers Johnson

Perspectives on Terrorism

On March 25–26, 1976, the Department of State sponsored a conference of some 200 American and foreign specialists on the problems of terrorism. The intent of the conference was to pose and display the numerous controversies that exist in this field, not to resolve such differences or to formulate new policy. Thus, this report on the work of the conference does not attempt to assert a preferred definition of terrorism, a correct breakdown of the types of terrorism, a consensus on the causes of terrorism, or an indicated set of remedies for the elimination of terrorism. Instead, it seeks to promote analytical sophistication and control by contrasting the arguments on the various sides of these issues.

It might seem lame, even academic, to begin with so mundane a concern as definitions, but to think so overlooks the important fact that the U.S. Draft Convention on Terrorism of 1972 failed in the United Nations largely because of definitional questions. "It appears," writes one authority and member of the conference, "that the failure to obtain approval of the instrument at the United Nations was due in part to an unnecessary confusion among states as to what the 1972 U.S. Draft Convention sought to control and, more importantly, what it did not prohibit." (Jordan J. Paust, "A Survey of Possible Legal Responses to International Terrorism: Prevention, Punishment, and Cooperative Action," *Georgia Journal of International and Comparative Law*, Vol. 5 [1975], p. 432.) We shall return to this problem. First, a few formal definitions.

Terrorism is political, goal-oriented action, involving the use or threat of extraordinary violence, performed for psychological rather than material effect, and the victims of which are symbolic rather than instrumental. Here is a perfectly adequate definition, one that was offered to the conference by a speaker. But it raises questions. Does this definition exclude assassinations of political leaders performed for material and only incidentally for psychological effect? Does an attempt to outlaw terrorism, in short, also outlaw tyrannicide?

Let us try another definition. "Terrorism," writes Paust, "involves the intentional use of violence or the threat of violence by the precipitator(s) against an instrumental target in order to communicate to a primary target a threat of future violence. The object is to use intense fear or anxiety to coerce the primary target into behavior or to mold its attitudes in connection with a demanded power (political) outcome. It should be noted that in a specific context the instrumental and primary targets could well be the same person or group. Also, terror can be caused by an unintended act, but the community does not seek to perceive such activity as 'terrorism'; nor does it seek to regulate terror caused by conduct which does not include intense coercion or acts and threats of violence. It is often difficult to draw the parameters of the subjectivities and intensities of coercion. The crucial factor is that the task of deciding between the permissible and impermissible labels of a particular coercive process should be guided by community expectations and all relevant policies and features of context" (pp. 434–435).

This seems to say that terrorism is terrorism when some (but which?) people think that it is terrorism. Or, as one conference member quoted Raymond Aron, "An action of violence is labeled 'terrorist' when its psychological effects are out of proportion to its purely physical result" (*Peace and War*, London, 1966, p. 170). One conference participant declared the whole problem to be tautological: "Intrinsically, terrorism is a state of mind. Political terrorism, presumably, is the state of mind of political actors who are paralyzed by the threat of unpredictable attack. No one has ever attempted to document systematically the existence of such a state of mind in besieged officials or activists, few of whom would admit to it in any case. So by default the concept has come to be employed to characterize the kinds of actions which are assumed to induce 'terrorism.' The definitional problem of circularity is obvious."

Rather than reciting more—and there are many more—formal definitions, let us turn to some of Aron's "purely physical results." The fact that terrorism is not easily isolable from wars, accidents, disasters, and so forth, and that its definition depends in part on the subjective intent of the actor and on the perceptions of his audience obviously complicates any attempt to count and to measure the changing incidence of terrorist acts. Several sophisticated statistical analyses were nonetheless offered to the conference.

One of these counted terrorist incidents for the 1961–1970 decade in 87 countries, based on reports in the *New York Times*. The operational definition of terrorist incidents used in this study excluded "assumptions about what effects the users hope to accomplish by their actions, or about how their would-be victims react" and was made up of three elements. These are: the employment of destructive violence, its use against political targets, and the sporadic and clandestine nature of the acts. The latter element was felt to be necessary to exclude terrorism, planned or unplanned, which is intrinsic or incidental to "an ongoing movement of armed revolution." Thus, in this particular study, terrorist acts occurring during the final stages of the Algerian conflict or during the Vietnam war were not counted. Given this research design, the author concluded that during the decade of the sixties terrorist events occurred in 63 of the 87 countries at a cost of approximately 4,600 lives. The author stated during the conference that, in his opinion, this loss of life was relatively minor compared to the three quarters of a million people who lost their lives in all forms of civil strife during the 1960s or in light of the city of Chicago's murder rate of nearly one thousand per annum. The mention of these comparisons, however, returned the debate at once to the psychological dimensions of the definitional problem, since it was pointed out repeatedly that the general population's ability to predict the probabilities of involvement in civil strife, murder, or even accidental death is much more accurate than with regard to terrorist incidents. The varying rates of different forms of violence are therefore politically incommensurable.

Another statistical study took up "international and transnational terrorist incidents" that occurred between January 1, 1968, and December 31, 1975. It found that there were 913 such incidents, including 123 kidnappings, 31 barricade and hostage episodes, 375 cases of the use of explosive devices, 95 armed assaults or ambushes, 137 hijackings of aircraft and other means of transportation, 59 incendiary attacks or cases of arson, 48 assassinations, and 45 cases of other forms of violence. According to comments offered to the conference, some 800 people have been killed and 1,700 injured in international terrorist incidents since 1968.

The most important finding of this study was that a rapid rise in the number of terrorist incidents has been taking place. Between 1965 and late 1968 the number of cases remained below 50 per year. The rate jumped to well over 100 during 1969–1970, fell back to around 75 during 1971, ascended steeply to over 200 during 1973, and then declined slightly to around 175 per annum by the end of 1975. The conference was in general agreement that terrorist incidents, according to the most elementary definition, have increased at a very rapid rate since 1968 and that the problem remains acute.

Despite their differences in time frame and in methodology, these two statistical studies agreed vaguely on one point and closely on another. The loose agreement was on geographical distribution of terrorist incidents: they occur most commonly in western and NATO Europe, followed closely by Latin America and more distantly by North America. In other words, terrorism is most common in democratic nations, least common in authoritarian regimes, and intermediate in frequency in "mixed regimes" (meaning, roughly, the underdeveloped nations, or the Third World, or the nations with poorly institutionalized political systems). Terrorism is, however, more lethal in mixed regimes (i.e., there are more killed casualties), least lethal in autocratic regimes, and intermediately lethal in democratic regimes.

The point on which these studies are in strong agreement is that terrorism is a low-risk activity for terrorists. The analysis of data from the 1960s revealed that terrorists were themselves casualties in only 14 percent of all cases—a much lower figure than in two alternative forms of violent political activity, rioting and guerrilla warfare, where rioters and guerrillas characteristically sustain more casualties than security forces or noncombatants. Nonetheless, this study concluded that "one cannot identify even one unambiguous instance in the last fifteen years of a campaign of political terrorism which led directly or indirectly to revolutionary change of the kind championed by the left." The analysis of the 1965–1975 period does not disaggregate data on the question of terrorist risk but concludes, "Briefly put, the record shows that transnational terrorists have generally been rather successful in avoiding capture (or, if caught, in escaping punishment) and in meeting at least some of their proximate objectives." Despite direct disagreement on the significance of the data, these two statistical studies of recent terrorism lead to a definition of terrorism close to that of Aron's quoted earlier: "The achievement of disproportionately large effects from the employment of minimal resources is . . . what political terrorism is all about."

The intrinsic limitations of statistical studies—what to count?—lead us back to the main definitional problem in the analysis of terrorism: the subjective intent of the terrorists and the psychological effect of their actions on governments, the public, or some other audience. It was phrased at the conference in these terms: "one man's terrorist is another man's freedom-fighter." Although attempts to separate means from ends and disputes about political justifications for otherwise unjustifiable deeds is as old as rebellion itself, it should be remembered that these were the issues that caused the defeat of the Draft Convention on Terrorism of 1972. There are ways of resolving the problem short of conceding that, indeed, one man's terrorist is another's freedom-fighter, but first it is well to note the political potency of such rhetoric.

One conference participant took pains to show that the contemporary wave of political terrorism began in 1944 with the onset of Jewish terrorism against the British in Palestine. He reviewed the activities of the *Irgun Zvai Leumi* and the Stern Gang, including the murder of Lord Moyne on November 6, 1944, the murder of Count Bernadotte on September 17, 1948, the blowing up of the King David Hotel in Jerusalem on July 22, 1946, and the hanging of two British army sergeants whose bodies were found at the end of July, 1947. He concluded that this terrorist campaign successfully contributed to the British decision of December 11, 1947, to give up the Palestine Mandate. "Today," he added, "when Palestinian Arab terrorism has become a major problem, the relevance of Zionist terrorism thirty years ago is inescapable." Here, starkly posed for Americans who support the democratic government and accomplishments of Israel, is the problem of the justification of terrorism.

Regardless of past instances of terrorism and their outcomes, the conference held generally that an international law convention outlawing terrorism was desirable and could obtain ratification if properly drafted. It was pointed out, for example, that both the customary law of war and its practice have already prohibited any form of violence against noncombatants, and that the intentional use of a strategy which produces terror that is not incidental to lawful combat operations has been condemned by both international and domestic war crimes tribunals.

Although the legal specialists attending the conference recommended a new international law convention on terrorism, there was some confusion about the status of the international law that already exists. In 1970, the United Nations General Assembly enacted its Declaration of Principles of International Law Concerning Friendly Relations and Cooperation Among States in Accordance with the Charter of the United Nations. This document states, on the one hand, that "Every state has the duty to refrain from organizing, instigating, or participating in acts of civil strife or terrorist acts in another state or acquiescing in organized activities within its territory directed toward the commission of such acts," while, on the other hand, it obligates states to assist peoples struggling for the realization of their "right to self-determination and freedom and independence." In light of these ambiguities and the poor track record of nations in ratifying or conforming to international conventions, the conference participants were only mildly interested in general international law attempts to resolve the freedom-fighter vs. terrorist dispute. It was noted that there are already on the books the 1963 Tokyo Convention on Offenses and Certain Other Acts Committed on Board Aircraft, the 1970 Hague Convention for the Suppression of the Unlawful Seizure of Aircraft, the 1973 Montreal Convention for the Suppression of Unlawful Acts Against the Safety of Civil Aviation, the 1973 UN Convention on the Prevention and Punishment of Crimes Against Diplomats (only nine ratifications to date and not in force), and the 1971 OAS Convention to Prevent and Punish Acts of Terrorism Taking the Form of Crimes Against Persons and Related Extortion that are of International Significance.

Turning directly to the question of whether a terrorist could ever also be a freedom-fighter, most conference participants thought, "No, he could not." A majority of the discussants held that an end that requires unjust means is not a just end and that terrorism cannot contribute to a just end if terrorization is the intent of the actor. One participant sought to sustain this line of argument by distinguishing terror and terrorism. Terror often accompanies the high-intensity violence of international or revolutionary war, but it is uncontrolled and epiphenomenal. "Terrorism on the other hand is a deliberate policy of waging terror for political ends: it is the systematic and calculated use of terrorization and is explicitly rationalized and justified by some philosophy, theory, or ideology, however crude."

When terrorism is defined in this way, it can be distinguished from freedom-fighting. One certain mark of terrorism in this sense is the use of terror by members of the ideological group against each other to maintain secrecy, obedience, and loyalty (compare the Japanese Red Army's 1972 lynchings of its own members). Thus, the above participant continued:

> Let us strip away the masks of terrorist illusions and expose the deathhead of murder beneath. Terrorists are fond of using romantic euphemisms for their murderous crimes. They claim to be revolutionary heroes yet they commit cowardly acts and lack the heroic qualities of humanity and magnanimity. They profess to be revolutionary soldiers yet they attack only by stealth, murder and maim the innocent, and disdain all rules and conventions of war. They claim to bring Liberation when in reality they seek power for themselves. Some claim that their violence ennobles them: history shows that it is totally corrupting and ultimately is turned against the revolutionary society itself. They frequently profess that they administer "revolutionary justice": in truth they make war on all ethics and legality and substitute the whim of their own tyranny.

Not all participants in the conference agreed with this view. Concurring that the special subjective mentality of terrorists is their defining characteristic, one commentator nonetheless maintained that terrorism itself is only a tactic of the "hate collectives" that remain a constant factor in twentieth-century history. The "hate collectives" are fundamental; terrorism is only one manifestation of them. "Their tactics are dictated by technology and mass response, or lack of response. If a 1930s-type world depression recurred, we might see 'Carlos,' alias Ilich Ramirez of the Great OPEC Snatch, shift to electoral politics and win votes just as Hitler did with phenomenal success from 1928–1932."

Perhaps this is as far as we can go with definitions. Terrorism is, like criminality, a matter of behavior *and* intent. It is doubtful that where both the behavior and the intent to terrorize are present any lasting political benefit can result. Beyond that, more light can be shed on the problem by turning to the types, causes, and consequences of terrorism.

TYPOLOGIES

Typologies like taxonomies, are intended to display differences within a class of phenomena, differences that may be intrinsic to the class and which therefore tell us something about the dynamics of development of the class, or differences that may have been obscured by the crude grouping into one category of superficially similar but, in fact, utterly different phenomena. Typologizing is related to analysis in the chemical sense: the division of a substance into its constituent parts and the attempt to reveal the relationship that they have with each other. One practical benefit of typologies of terrorism is that they may help tailor countermeasures to particular types and thereby make them more effective (for example, capital punishment may be recommended for some terrorists and not for others, since in some cases capital punishment seems to attract suicidally inclined individuals).

Typologies are based upon observation of differences and upon the attempt to discover the principles causing the differentiation. Thus, one of the simplest, observation-based typologies of terrorist movements distinguishes four species in the genus terrorism: ethnic (including religious, linguistic, regional, or other particularistic movements), nationalistic (irredentist or anticolonial), ideological (including anarchist, radical leftist, orthodox communist, extreme rightist, and others), and pathological (including groups that attack public targets for apparently private, biographical reasons: for example, the Manson gang). What are the principles that inform this typology? Several conference participants offered suggestions. One saw two differentiating principles at work. First, movements differ according to their "legitimacy potential," meaning that a terrorist organization may be formed of a minority that is never likely to attract significant popular support, or it may be formed of a minority that has the potential of becoming a mass movement. Second, terrorist organizations differ by their principal audiences and by the reactions that they aim to create through terrorist deeds. It may be true that the victims of terrorism are only symbolic, but it is necessary to ask, symbolic of what? An elite? A race? A government? A class?

Do terrorist groups ever have a "legitimacy potential"? The answer seems to vary according to the degree to which a terrorist group is committed or drawn exclusively to the tactic of terrorism, and according to the degree to which a terrorist group is only part of or an offshoot of a larger movement of authentic revolution. Those groups explicitly committed to acts of terrorism are likely to degenerate into criminal gangs, as has happened often in the past. In the case of terrorist organizations that are part of a wider politico-military scheme of revolution, several conference participants drew attention to the use of terrorism as an aspect of revolutionary strategy in Algeria, Indochina, Latin America, and elsewhere. In these cases the resort to terrorism is not necessarily evidence of a low legitimacy potential. Terrorism may be pursued in the hope of producing a damaging overreaction by the defending side or as a means of purging and hardening the ideologically defined "people" in preparation for revolutionary war. One panelist suggested that revolutionary war strategies today plan for four broad phases: the creation of a clandestine subversive apparatus; terrorism, whether rural or urban; guerrilla or mobile warfare; and the "revolutionary final offensive."

One use of typologies is to help explain what a movement is by isolating what it is not. Thus, one conference participant offered a fourfold typology of all forms of terrorism, his intent being to identify the form that was of immediate concern. First, there is incidental terrorism, a by-product of all forms of war. In these cases the intent to terrorize is allegedly not present, and such terrorism is uncontrolled. Second is repressive terrorism by a state against its own people. Such terrorism is intended to quell opposition, and it is normally not internationalized by its perpetrators, although it may be in instances of imperialist conquest. Third is sub-revolutionary terrorism, which refers to small, uncoordinated acts of protest with no strategic significance. And fourth and of primary concern to the conference is revolutionary terrorism, meaning coordinated activity by terrorist brotherhoods (sometimes including sisters, despite the rigidities of the English language) intended to bring about basic political and social change. A subtypology was offered in terms of the target regimes of revolutionary terrorism: terrorism against an indigenous autocracy, against foreign rule, against totalitarianism, and against liberal democracy. Only the last was said at present to be the target of transnational terrorism.

It should be apparent that there are almost as many typologies of terrorism as there are analysts and that there is little agreement on the principles that should inform either the construction of a typology or the assignment of a particular instance of terrorism to one or another category. Given this situation (which is a sign as much of the complexity of the subject as of human idiosyncracy), it seems most profitable to settle here for the classic typology used in the study of all movements of rebellion and revolution—one formed according to the diversity of motivation or ideology displayed by terrorist groups. Using this standard, one participant presented a sixfold typology of terrorist groups:

1. Minority Nationalist Groups (for example, both wings of the IRA, the Basque ETA, the Palestinian Al Fatah, the Quebec FLQ).
2. Marxist Revolutionary Groups (for example, Trotskyist, Maoist, and Guevarist groups such as the Venceremos Brigade or the Tupamaros).
3. Anarchist Groups (for example, the MIL in Spain).
4. The "Syndicalism of Immaturity" (for example, Weathermen, Baader-Meinhof gang, and Symbionese Liberation Army).
5. Neo-Fascist and Extreme Right-Wing Groups (for example, the Avanguardia Nazionale and Ordine Nuovo in Italy).
6. Ideological Mercenaries (for example, the Japanese Red Army, or the Black September).

By far the most important typological distinction discussed by the conference concerned "international terrorism," which was defined as terrorism that "transcends national boundaries, through the choice of a foreign victim or target, commission of the terrorist act in a foreign country, or effort to influence the policies of a foreign government. The international terrorist strikes abroad, or at a diplomat or other foreigner at home, because he believes he can thereby exert the greatest possible pressure on his own or another government or on world opinion." This category of terrorism has been rising in frequency at a dramatic rate, cannot be controlled by relying on domestic security forces and criminal processes, and is occurring in part because of support from foreign governments. Examples include the hijacking and destruction in the Middle East of three transatlantic airliners on September 6, 1970, by the Popular Front for the Liberation of Palestine; the attacks on Lod Airport and the Munich Olympics; kidnappings and murders of U.S. and other diplomats in Brazil, Argentina, Guatemala, and elsewhere; terrorist abductions and hostage cases in Port-au-Prince, Khartoum, Guadalajara, Cordoba, Santo Domingo, Kuala Lumpur, Beirut, and other places; the April, 1975, seizure of the German embassy in Stockholm by the Baader-Meinhof gang; and most recently the Vienna OPEC, South Moluccan, Balcombe Street, and Herrema cases.

Within this general category of terrorist incidents, a further distinction can be made in terms of who is calling the shots. For some conference participants, the term "international terrorism" was reserved for terrorist actions that are carried out by individuals or groups controlled by a sovereign state, including one-time "contract jobs" undertaken on behalf of governments by a group that normally operates independently. The term "transnational terrorism" was reserved for terrorist actions undertaken by autonomous non-state groups, whether or not they enjoy some degree of support from sympathetic states. Although the conference was deeply concerned about international terrorism in this restricted sense, including the possibility of an increase in "surrogate warfare" between states that literally employ loose brotherhoods of free-lance terrorists to commit acts against other nations, it was generally believed that this category of terrorism is controllable. Nonetheless, the maintenance of "subversive centers" for the training and operational support of transnational terrorists was seen as a major cause of the increase in their activities. It was, therefore, the category and various ramifications of transnational terrorism—which threatens innocent people who are in no way parties to whatever dispute or grievance motivates the terrorists, and which is carried out by groups that are beyond or free of the control of sovereign governments—that was of primary concern to the conference. Having isolated this category, it is necessary next to turn to an analysis of its causes—and to the controversial subject of the causes of terrorism in general.

CAUSES

The conference was in general agreement that the causes of terrorism must be divided into two general classes—direct causes and permissive causes—although there was some disagreement about the nature or importance of direct causes. Direct causes refer to grievances or frustrations, such as neocolonialism, ethnic dependence, or other alleged victimization of a group of people that may lead activists to resort to political violence. Permissive causes are those factors that make terrorism possible, even easy, and that therefore recommend it as a tactic for extremists. All of the conference participants were agreed that this distinction should not be made too rigidly, since lack of alternatives to terrorism could be understood as either a direct or an enabling cause. Similarly, the availability of publicity through news media was seen as a permissive cause in most cases, but it was also recognized that publicity leads to a contagion or imitation effect, which can in turn become a direct cause of subsequent acts of terrorism. Thus, the direct and permissive causes may differ between a single terrorist act and a cycle or epidemic of terrorism.

Most conference participants believed that the direct causes of terrorism had remained relatively constant in recent times and that the rise in transnational terrorist incidents was due almost entirely to changes in the permissive causes. Before turning to the latter subject, however, let us dwell somewhat longer on direct causes. Many members of the conference doubted that the direct causes of terrorism could be discovered in political or socio-economic conditions. They were skeptical of the argument that the way to stop terrorism was to "remove its causes," particularly when in concrete cases the causes seemed more psychological or pathological than socio-political. It was noted, for example, that in the Lod Airport massacre of May, 1972, the terrorists were Japanese, recruited and trained through agents in North Korea, supported by funds from West Germany, given final training in Syria and Lebanon, armed in Italy, and sent to a destination unknown to them in advance by the Popular Front for the Liberation of Palestine. The sole surviving terrorist, Koza Okamoto, has testified that he became involved primarily because of the influence of his elder brother, and he has shown signs of severe mental disorientation in captivity. In this case the "direct" causes of the incident seem unlikely to have been removed even if the Arab-Israeli conflict were somehow resolved. One conference participant observed that West Germany alone has over ninety terrorists in prison, and he urged that serious research be undertaken on these individuals to produce a more adequate profile or syndrome of their motives. (Certainly, the suicidal component in terrorists' motivations was highlighted by the recent suicide of Ulrike Meinhof.)

The disagreement about direct causes was not settled at the conference. Some participants maintained that the direct causes of terrorism were to be found in the major social movements of the postwar era, particularly decolonization, and one individual argued that a decline in terrorism could be expected because decolonization was virtually complete. It was also said in this connection that the shock value of terrorism had been attenuated through over-use and that this too was conducive to a decline in terrorism. Some participants speculated that terrorism might be directly related to cyclical fluctuations in the overall economic climate—economic upturns allegedly promote terrorism by heightening expectations, while economic downturns may dampen revolutionary ardor through the numbing effects of general adversity—and one contributor thought that extra-cyclical worldwide economic strains, such as the quadrupling of oil prices, might have something to do with the rise in terrorism by overtaxing the capabilities of local regimes to govern effectively. Another participant ventured that the increasing bureaucratization of the world was a direct cause; terrorism was thought to relate to bureaucracy as tyrannicide does to tyranny. Still another participant returned to the theme of the lack of alternatives: "Revolutionaries in Western countries have adopted terroristic tactics *because* they are revolutionaries in societies where the great majority of the population finds the status quo tolerable. In the poorer and weaker nations of the Third World, discontent is sufficiently widespread that revolutionaries have much more promising material with which to work than high explosives."

Despite these conjectures about direct causes, the predominant concern of the conference was with permissive causes. These were phrased by many spokesmen in terms such as "resentment, means, publicity, and low-risk" or "feasibility, efficacy, and popularity," but the most persuasive disaggregation of permissive causes was, to this writer, the "three T's": targets, technology, and toleration. Transnational terrorism has been on the increase over the past eight years because of the availability of new targets, new technology, and new toleration. Let us briefly analyze each of these categories.

By new targets we mean vulnerabilities or bottlenecks in advanced, open, industrial societies that make suitable targets for terrorist attack. These include large aircraft, supertankers, international power grids and pipelines, transportation hubs, commercial and communications centers, motorcades, offshore oil rigs, liquified natural gas facilities, nuclear power facilities, and computerized information and management systems. The very existence of a complex and interdependent modern world seems to have contributed to the advance of terrorism by offering the terrorist a plethora of vulnerable targets. Some speakers expressed despair concerning any society's ability to defend such targets, but it was argued in rejoinder that the analytical solution to this problem was to build sufficient redundancy into modern systems so as to avoid vulnerable bottlenecks. For example, transportation systems should seek a mix of automobile, public transit, waterborne, and short and long-range air transport in order to avoid offering critical vulnerabilities, just as communications should be diversified among ground lines, microwave, satellite, and other technologies.

There are two aspects to new technology: new weapons and new means whereby the terrorist can capture global attention. In addition to the traditional arsenal of time bombs, machine guns, and plastic explosives, modern technology has contributed the miniaturized letter bomb; the man-portable guided missile (such as the Soviet SA-7 heat-seeking rocket); chemical, biological, and radiological agents; and the potentiality of the use of nuclear weapons. Two SA-7's were captured in the hands of Arab terrorists at the end of a runway in Rome in 1973, and radioactice iodine was employed in a terrorist incident in Austria in 1974. One conference participant wrote, "The development and deployment of man-portable, precision-guided munitions and their likely acquisition by political extremists represents the most serious new terrorist threat. We probably will see the use of these weapons by terrorists within the next decade."

Equal to or greater in importance than new weaponry in the growth of terrorism is the global expansion of mass media of communications. Every commentator mentioned it as a fundamental permissive cause of terrorism, and much of the attention of the conference was taken up by problems of how to control the media. One conference participant wrote, "Among all the technological advances in recent years, the development of satellite communications, and in particular, their upgrading in 1968 to include a television capability have unquestionably been among the most important in making transnational activity attractive to terrorist groups." Since public attention to his cause is usually one of the terrorist's key objectives, communications advances have been critically valuable to him. Several participants noted the desirability of preventing a terrorist group's "kidnapping" of the media—as occurred in the SLA case in California—but it was also observed that attempts to control the media might only lead to an escalation in the scale of terrorist attacks. Media contribute publicity for a particular terrorist cause, contagious triggering of other terrorists' decisions to act, training of terrorists through a "media-fed pool of experience and inspiration," and international linkages among terrorist organizations.

Under the category of new toleration, we include direct and indirect support by nations of terrorist organizations, toleration through fear of retaliation among law-abiding nations, the frustration of efforts to elicit international cooperation in carrying out countermeasures, and the increased legitimization of "revolutionary" activities. Conference participants devoted considerable attention to so-called subversive centers for the training and support of terrorists. By far the most important of these is the Soviet Union and related East European regimes, but also listed and described by various authorities are Libya, Cuba, China, North Korea, Algeria, the Popular Democratic Republic of Yemen, Tanzania, the Republic of the Congo (Brazzaville), Zaire, Egypt, Syria, Iraq, Lebanon, and, recently retired from the business (but apparently not from state terrorism), Chile. Such centers supply terrorists with funds, arms, training, documentation, and operational support.

In a somewhat different category is the "humanitarian" aid supplied to the revolutionaries in Mozambique, Guinea-Bissau, and Angola by Sweden, Denmark, Holland, Norway, Finland, and the World Council of Churches. Although not consisting of guns, this assistance has contributed to the climate of toleration of terrorist acts. In still another category are France and Switzerland, which have become involuntary hosts to all manner of foreign dissident groups because of their heritage of strong rights of political asylum and of protection of democratic freedoms. And in still a third category are those nations that are inhibited by political or commercial interests from offending governments that support or condone terrorism. They may also be concerned that if they convict and imprison terrorists, this will attract more terrorists to their territories seeking, through further violence, to free their comrades.

For all of these reasons, international efforts to stop terrorism have been weak, and this toleration of terrorism has contributed to its spread. One recent study indicates that since 1968, an international terrorist involved in a kidnapping has an 80 percent chance of escaping death or capture, a close to even chance that all or some of his ransom demands will be granted, and the virtual certainty that he will receive worldwide publicity. For all crimes of terrorism the average sentence for the small proportion of terrorists caught and tried is less than eighteen months.

In addition to the direct causes and the "three T's," one final factor that appears to be promoting the spread of transnational terrorism should be mentioned. This is the proliferation of antiterrorist authoritarian governments. Rigid and effective authoritarian rule may be fostering transnational terrorism by closing the main target systems to dissidents and forcing them to operate abroad. One panelist speculated that the situation today of various Latin American revolutionaries (particularly those from Brazil, Chile, Uruguay, and Post-Peronist Argentina) may be somewhat parallel to that of Palestinian terrorists in the late 1960s. Being frustrated in their attempts to pressure Israel directly, the Palestinians sought to dramatize their cause by attacking more accessible societies. Similarly, Latin American revolutionaries, frozen out in their own societies, may be preparing to enter the transnational terrorist arena with attacks in North America.

Consequences

Terrorism appears to be flourishing, despite some comments to the contrary at the conference. Several participants noted the disturbing precedent of the international recognition during 1974 of the Palestine Liberation Organization as the sole legitimate representative of the Palestinian people. Beginning with recognition at the Islamic nonaligned and Rabat summit meetings and continuing at the 1974 UN General Assembly session, the PLO has been allowed to open offices in some fifty nations, and five UN-affiliated international agencies (ILO, WHO, UPU, ITU, and UNESCO) have granted it observer status. At the same time, some conference participants felt that this recognition had caused a decline in the PLO's sponsorship of terrorism; and they also suggested that the media, playing an international "linkage" role, had helped to bring about this change.

Another major consequence of terrorist activity, already mentioned in a different connection, has been the spread of authoritarianism and a reduction in the number of democracies. Several regimes faced with terrorist campaigns have managed to overcome them but have also lost their democratic institutions in the process. The best example is probably Uruguay, which between 1968 and 1971 was ravaged by the Tupamaros. Between April and August, 1972, however, President Juan-Maria Bordaberry broke the movement by proclaiming a "state of internal war" and giving the army and police complete freedom in their choice of methods. The Tupamaros are now gone, but democracy has not returned.

Few positive international steps have been taken to diminish terrorist activity, although by far the most important of these was the

U.S.-Cuba memorandum of understanding concerning hijackers of aircraft and vessels that was signed in 1973. Another achievement was the virtual elimination of aircraft hijacking in the United States through the use of physical inspection of all passengers and their hand baggage. The expense of this program argues against its extension to all exposed systems, but it may become necessary to consider some comparable measures such as the X-raying of mail at vital points. The problem of using capital punishment against terrorists was debated at the conference, with strong views being expressed on both sides of the issue and no consensus emerging.

Also discussed was the policy, in force in the United States, of publicly declaring in advance that a government will not negotiate with terrorists under any circumstances, versus the policy of reserving one's options and tailoring responses to particular cases. Members of the conference who had had direct experience in dealing with terrorists advocated the policy of no negotiations, arguing that it prevented the spread of terrorism and worked as a deterrent. Some participants doubted this and suggested that the seizure of a Soviet embassy in a Western capital would be a hard test of the policy. One commentator offered the thought that "In some countries political terrorism may evolve into a specific bargaining tactic, a mechanism of regular influence for groups which have no other effective leverage on the centers of power," but this view was not seconded at the conference. The dilemma of multinational corporations faced with kidnappings of their executives was discussed, including their inability to retain personnel if an absolute policy of no concessions is adopted. All participants seemed to support a ban on insurance against terrorist kidnappings—for obvious reasons—and a ban on allowing tax credits for ransom payments.

In lieu of an effective international convention against terrorism, the experienced speakers at the conference stressed the need for an enhanced intelligence capability against terrorists and the necessity of timely exchanges of intelligence information among cooperating security forces. It was through intelligence that the terrorists armed with SA-7's were apprehended at the edge of the airport in Rome before they could destroy their intended Israeli Airlines target. American conference participants, in particular, asserted that their need for counterterrorist intelligence was rising at precisely a time when political circles were making efforts to prevent or restrict their abilities to collect such intelligence.

The main issue in the general area of consequences that divided the conference was whether or not terrorism could be suppressed. Some thought that it could not be eliminated and warned against the dangers of overreaction. They felt that domestic criminal processes were adequate to deal with the problem, and that new countermeasures were not indicated. Others vehemently disagreed and cited the cost of not dealing with terrorism or of naively believing that terrorism could not thrive in an open society with few structurally generated grievances. Commentators from Great Britain stated that with respect to Ireland, Britain had in effect been experimenting with a policy of tolerating terrorism and that the results had been disastrous. Others said that the costs of believing that "the cure could be worse than the disease" could be, on the one hand, a terrorist victory and the probable establishment of a totalitarian regime, or, on the other hand, a military-authoritarian reaction leading to the more or less permanent suspension of civil liberties.

Those who felt that terrorism could and must be suppressed candidly acknowledged that the problem is less the defeat of terrorism than the avoidance of measures that may foreclose the rights and liberties characteristic of open, pluralistic societies. It was argued that terrorism can be suppressed through "special powers," but that these inevitably entail a temporary curtailment or suspension of certain liberties. For example, censorship and detention without trial may be necessary. In order to insure that these measures do not lead to authoritarianism, it was stressed that special powers must be voted by parliaments—on the analogy of special powers enacted "for the duration" of a war against an external enemy—and that elected assemblies must act in order to retain their sovereignty. "Paradoxically, then," wrote one analyst, "the proclamation of a 'state of emergency,' martial law, or a 'state of internal war' by the elected assembly, retaining its own sovereignty and therefore its right to revert to normal procedures, may be the only way of avoiding the military-authoritarian takeover. Sovereign assemblies that fail to act in good time clearly do so at their peril, if recent history is any guide."

Another theme of this discussion was the need to retaliate against nations that train and support international terrorists as surrogates. This point was made particularly with regard to the Soviet Union and Cuba. It was argued that political countermeasures were possible within the framework of the détente relationship, so long as that relationship were more realistically understood by the Western nations. Enhanced international intelligence on the matter of communist support of terrorists was clearly called for.

A variety of speakers at the end of the conference indicated that the gathering had succeeded in airing most significant points of view and in alerting the diverse groups and agencies represented at the conference to the special problems that the field posed. It was recommended that further conferences might address specific questions set in advance. Speakers also drew attention to the need for intensive work in the future on the actual techniques of procedure in barricade and hostage situations and on the psychodynamic characteristics of terrorists.

PART V

The Last Decade

Hans Josef Horchem

European Terrorism: A German Perspective

German Terrorist Organizations

"Red Armee Faction" (RAF) and "Movement of 2nd of June." The RAF is the oldest and most dangerous German terrorist organization. In June 1980 the RAF took over the remaining cadre of the second German terrorist group, the "Movement of 2nd of June."

The RAF retained its structure and its system of organization after the unification with the "Movement of 2nd of June." Hierarchical order does not exist and decisions are made collectively. In an attack every member has to fight unto death.

The commando unit includes only 20 people. The attack against Hanns Martin Schleyer was made with only 20 members of the RAF, in spite of the fact that extensive logistic preparations were necessary.

The commando unit is living underground and depends on the "legal environment," which includes approximately 200 people. In the seventies the legal units were organized in "Anti-Fascist Groups" or in "Committees against Isolation-Torture." These names don't exist anymore. But the supporters of these groups compose a reservoir for illegal activities in the future.

Enough money is available. The "war booty" of the "Movement of 2nd of June" after the kidnapping of the Austrian industrialist Palmers in November 1977 is now in the hands of the RAF. Of the original 4 million Deutschmark the RAF has spent about 2 million Deutschmark.

The RAF propagates only one thing, that is armed conflict, and

Reprinted excerpts from *Terrorism: an International Journal* Vol. 6, No. 1, 1982 with the kind permission of the editor.

tries to win comrades-in-arms for this. "The armed campaign is the highest form of class struggle." The leading force and the avant-garde of the class struggle is not the working class but the "revolutionary intelligence."

Already in 1971 the RAF said in its publication "Close the Loopholes of the Revolutionary Theory—Build up the Red Army": "It is not the organizations of the industrial working class, but the revolutionary sections of the student bodies that are today the bearers of the contemporary conscience." The industrial proletariats inside the developed capitalist countries have changed into an "aristocracy of workers." Therefore a true revolutionary cannot rely on them anymore.

The long-range strategy of the RAF was then and is today aimed at "U.S. imperialism" and its chief ally in Europe, the Federal Republic of Germany.

The "Revolutionary Cells" (RZ). The third organization of German left-wing terrorism is the RZ. Until 1980 their attacks were directed only against objects. Last year the RZ admitted that also human beings could be hurt by the attacks. With the killing of Hans-Herbert Karry (Minister of Finance of Hesse) on December 19, 1980 the RZ gained a new profile. In a letter of confession the murderers claimed that the attack on Karry was meant only to be "punishment." They wanted to shoot him in the knees. They killed him only because it was too dark to aim correctly. The RZ obviously wanted to follow the Italian example.

From the beginning the policy of the RZ was to distinguish their strategy from the political concept of the RAF. They opposed the theory of the RAF that only student elites should guide the revolution. They emphasized that each action should be fed back to the "masses." Each single revolutionary activity should be tied up and brought into contact with existing conflicts in society. Operating on the basis of these principles, the RZ developed the so-called "contact theory." . . .

German Right-wing Terrorism. Right-wing terrorism has two roots. One is the NPD which is still the strongest force in German right-wing extremism, at least in numbers. The NPD (National Democratic Party) is undergoing a continuing process of decline. In the last 15 years it has lost 20,000 members. Today it has only 7,000 members. This process of decay worked to bolster some small neo-Nazi-groups which are the second root of the present German right-wing terrorism. Young members of the NPD went into the ranks of these neo-Nazi groups and made their organizations more militant.

Neo-Nazi groups which became a hotbed for terrorism are the "Aktionsgemeinschaft Nationaler Sozialisten" (The "Führer" is a former lieutenant of the Bundeswehr, Michael Kühnen, now in jail) and the "Deutsche Aktionsgruppen" (head of this organization is a former lawyer, Manfred Roeder, now on trial in Stuttgart-Stammheim).

Two other right-wing extremist organizations, which later embraced terrorism, were the "Wehrsportgruppe Hoffmann" and the "Volkssozialistische Bewegung Deutschlands/Partei der Arbeit" (VSBD/PdA). The "Wehrsportgruppe Hoffmann" has been destroyed; Hoffmann and some of his followers are expecting prosecution in Nuremberg. The VSBD/PdA and its youth organization, "Junge Front," were forbidden and declared illegal by the Federal Minister of the Interior on January 26, 1982. During searches much propaganda material was found and, in Berlin, a small quantity of firearms. The leader of the organizations, Friedhelm Busse, was arrested. . . .

Terrorism in Italy

Left-wing Organizations. The terrorism that is now endemic in Italy evolved gradually, from the ideological extremism of the revolutionary generation of 1968, through the "Hot Autumn" of labor unrest in the Turin-Milan-Genoa industrial triangle, through the first guerrilla skirmishes in the "piazzas," to the ambushes in the middle of the seventies with attacks against journalists and judges who were shot in the knee. The year 1976 saw a series of "executions." In March 1978, the former Prime Minister Aldo Moro was kidnapped, his bodyguards and his driver were shot and Moro later was murdered.

In the field of Italian left-wing terrorism one has to distinguish between two "systems." On the one hand are the closely knit underground "columns" of the Red Brigades, who, making the factories of northern Italy their initial target, carried out sensational, military-style actions. In 1979–80 a southern "column" with headquarters in Naples grew forth. On the other hand, there are the smaller armed factions (with 115 different names to date) and the suburban "autonomous collectives" that are systematically engaged in spreading violence in the form of full-scale guerrilla warfare.

There were 702 terrorist attacks in Italy in 1975, 1198 in 1976, 2128 in 1977, 2395 in 1978. In 1979 it slipped slightly to 2366, in 1980 to 1264, and in 1981 it dropped to 924.

In 1980, the Italian police forces discovered 36 terrorist hideouts and in the first half of 1981 twelve. They arrested about 700 people. In the second half of 1981 more police raids against terrorists were made. They led to other 35 hideouts and to other hundreds of arrests. The terrorist organization Prima Linea (Front Line) was virtually broken up. The Red Brigades were down, though definitely not out.

In 1981 and 1982, the police succeeded in arresting leading functionaries of the Red Brigades. In April 1981, Mario Moretti, a 42-year-old former manager of an electrical plant in Milan, was arrested on a Milan street together with his comrade, Professor Fenzi. Moretti was probably the "general" of the Milan "column" of the Red Brigades. On January 10, 1982, the police arrested Professor of Criminology Giovanni Senzani in a hideout near Rome. Senzani was the "chief ideologist" of the Red Brigades.

After the rescue of General Dozier, who was kidnapped on December 17, 1981, the number of arrests of members of the Red Brigades escalated. About 50 "Brigadists" were arrested and 10 bases were rounded up. Among the arrested people were Antonio Savasta, leader of the kidnappers and "officer" of the "column" of the Red Brigades of Verona and Venice, and Luigi Scricciolo and his wife Paola. Scricciolo was a leading functionary of the UIL, a trade union of the Socialist-Republican Party.

There were two reasons for the success of the police in the case of General Dozier. On the one hand, the morale of the Red Brigades had gone down since the successful raids which the police made in 1980 and 1981. On the other hand, more and more jailed "Brigadists" were willing to cooperate with the police and confessed. The discipline and the fighting spirit have been waning and the in-fighting between different factions inside the organization has increased. No doubt the Red Brigades still have the power to carry out large-scale operations, which require coordination with terrorist forces in other parts of the country. But its members no longer want an armed clash when they are cornered by the police.

Right-wing Organizations. Investigations of right-wing terrorists in Italy in the beginning suffered from a certain preoccupation of magistrates and judges. The first big terrorist attack in Italy, for instance, with extremely widespread consequences occurred on December 12, 1969. In the main banking area of the Milan Bank of Agriculture a detonating bomb killed 16 persons. Afterward two trails were followed by the security agencies in investigating this assault. One "red trail" led to the group "March 22," a group of anarchists headed by Pietro Valpreda. The other one, a "black trail," led to a group of extreme rightists which was charged with other successful and unsuccessful attempts. The proceedings against this latter group were not opened until March 1972. At that time, the main suspects of these two groups were candidates in parliamentary elections: Valpreda on the ballots of the extreme left-wing Manifesto Group, the journalist Pino Rauti on the ballots of the Neo-Fascisti.

In November 1973, the neo-fascistic combat group "Ordine Nuovo" was dissolved after a jury in Rome had found thirty accused guilty. They had wanted to reestablish the fascist party. "Ordine Nuovo" had been established during the fifties; Pino Rauti was one of its most active leaders.

A successor organization of "Ordine Nuovo," "Ordine Nero" (black order), has committed several attempts since March 1974. The group claimed responsibility for the assult at the Rome-Munich express train on August 4, 1974, which caused twelve people to die, and for a bomb attack in the city of Brescia on May 28, 1974, which killed eight and injured about 100 persons.

"Ordine Nero" was also responsible for the bomb attack in the main station of Bologna on August 2, 1980. No less than 86 persons were killed. Leaders of the "Ordine Nero" (Professor Paolo Signorelli, Sergio Calore, Aldo Tisei) were indicted on account of this massacre.

The main characteristics of politically motivated terrorism in Italy are, on one hand, its partially anarchistic root, and on the other hand the fact that extreme left and extreme right groups are fighting each other and that some groups are terrorist assault parties of political organizations working overtly. Both wings of terrorism aim at paralyzing and destroying the governmental institutions. At least from time to time, there was an infiltration of anarchistic terrorist groups by terrorists with extreme rightist motivations. The melding of such forces has made the investigations of terrorist attacks more complicated. All of these characteristics set Italian terrorism off from terrorism in the Federal Republic of Germany.

The fascist position in Italy is in the longer term far more dangerous to democracy than are German terrorists. In Italy right-wing terrorism has a kind of constituency in the neo-fascist party MSI. This organization has provided the Italian fascists with a vehicle capable of mobilizing some mass support, and has channeled funds and weapons to clandestine terrorist groups. Almirante, the head of the MSI, believes that "history is made neither by the masses, nor by ideas, nor by 'silently working' forces, but by the elites, who, from time to time, assert themselves." It is therefore no surprise to find today's Italian fascists adopting the characteristic tactics of modern terrorism. But there is a rather different pattern in the fascists' choice of targets. They mainly concentrate on immigrants and their property, or on left-wing offices and personnel, or on Jewish targets, depending on the ideological character of the target group. One particularly worrying feature of fascists' bomb attacks is that the perpetrators appear to have no inhibitions about causing mass slaughter in public places. Unlike the neo-Marxist revolutionaries of the extreme left, they do not appear worried about turning the working class against them. They see the masses as too corrupted by democracy and socialism to be able to save themselves. Salvation, in their eyes, can come only from the fascist leader and his elite storm-trooper vanguard. . . .

TERRORISM IN SPAIN

Left-wing Organizations. Political terrorism in Spain has roots in autonomist traditions of certain parts of the country and is a heritage of the authoritarian form of government during the Franco era. It has specific Spanish characteristics, such as direct assaults against the state security forces with the use of small firearms. Such assaults aimed at police forces repeatedly lead to escalation in the conflict between the two sides and could easily assume the status of a special war between security forces and terrorist organizations.

The motto of Spanish terrorists is "the worse, the better." The more unrest they create, the harder becomes retaliation. This again increases the mutual hatred. A Spanish anarchist tradition is covered in the contemporary robe of Marxist-Leninist theories.

Two left-wing organizations, which reached the highest level of their activities in the seventies, have since been almost destroyed. The FRAP (Revolutionary Anti-Fascistic Patriotic Front) was first noted in 1973. It was an avant-garde of a Maoist party (PCF/ML) established in industrial cities, which listed mainly students of universities and colleges as members. In the spring of 1975 the group started firing at Spanish police officers patrolling the highways. Several malicious killings occurred. The second important left-wing terrorist organization was the GRAPO (Revolutionary Anti-Fascist Group of October 1). It too was a "military arm" of Maoist-Communist splinter groups. At its zenith the GRAPO had about 200 members. In 1979 most of them were arrested.

At the end of the seventies a few attacks by right-wing individuals who had links to the neo-Fascist party "Fuerza Nueva," occurred in Madrid, but did not have lasting effects.

The ETA. The members of the ETA are the "lost sons" of the Basque Nationalist Party (PNV), a bourgeois Catholic organization mainly of middle-class people. ETA is the abbreviation of "Euskadi ta Askatasuna": Basque country and freedom.

The present situation of the ETA is understandable only with regards to the historical development. It started when a group of the party's youth section, Euzko-Gaztedi, traveled to Paris in 1957 to persuade the leadership of the PNV living in exile there to embark upon an armed struggle. The youngsters failed. Disappointed, they returned home and drew close to a circle of university students who published a clandestine journal called *Ekin* (Action). Before long the police moved in and broke up the group. A new organization was needed, and ETA was born on July 31, 1959. The members had at first a fundamentally patriotic conviction. They were democratic.

ETA's first assembly took place in May 1962. There the first timid steps toward terrorism were made, inspired especially by the example of Fidel Castro. A Spanish Basque, José Echevarrieta Ortiz, studying law in Paris, had read the works of Mao Tse-tung and tried to influence the ETA with his theories. The founders of the ETA had to call a further assembly in March 1963. Since then, ETA has confused nationalism and ideology, and endless feuding and splits are taking place.

In 1964, the third assembly finally broke with the old nationalist

PNV, and ETA defined itself as an "anti-capitalist" and "anti-imperialist" movement. The black French sociologist Frantz Fanon through his book *The Wretched of the Earth* wielded great influence.

In the summer of 1965 the ETA assembly met in Brussels. The leaders had come into contact with orthodox Communist party members, and a debate had begun as to whether it was advisable or not to link the ETA with the PCE.

The founders of the movement had to fight not only the influence of the powerful PCE but also the Trotskyists, who made a determined effort to infiltrate the ETA.

For the fifth assembly in December 1966 the ETA met for the first time in Spain. Only 45 people came together. Possibly 13 of them were strongly inclined toward communism. Discussions were continued in March 1967 in a tiny fishing village near San Sebastian.

In the meantime the police had uprooted almost the entire organization. In 1969, the famous trial at Burgos started. This gave ETA enormous publicity and attracted a new and younger generation of enthusiasts. Among them was Eduardo Moreno Bergareche, born 1950, who prepared the ideological position papers for the sixth assembly held in Hasparren, France, in the summer of 1973.

No more than 20 people were present, but they formally adopted on behalf of the whole organization the principles of "democratic centralism."

The following months showed that it was impossible to turn ETA into a Marxist-Leninist vanguard party. Moreno Bergareche became the head of the faction called ETA (politico-militar) which believed the armed struggle pursued by "militarists" should go hand in hand with a more general "political-military" program aimed at strengthening the movement among the workers. The other wing of the movement called itself ETA (militar). In 1976, Moreno Bergareche was murdered by members of ETA (militar).

The two wings of ETA are supported by two political parties. ETA (politico militar) is backed by Euskadiko Ezkerra (EE), i.e., Basque Left. The principal candidates of this party are Juan Maria Bandrés, a lawyer from San Sebastian, who had under Franco defended ETA suspects in the courts, and Mario Onaindia, who at the Burgos trial had been sentenced to death. They dismissed ETA (militar) as an "elitist" organization and rejected terrorism as "non-revolutionary." In the elections of March 1979 Bandrés was actually elected and took his seat in the Cortes.

While ETA (politico militar) renounced violence and participated in elections, ETA (militar) did not. ETA (militar) is backed by Herri Batasuna (HB), i.e., people's unity. In the elections of March 1979 HB won three seats in the Lower House and one in the Senate with something like 15 percent of the vote (172,000). The majority of the Basques, however, voted for the PNV, which came into the lower house with 7 deputies. In the municipal elections which followed in April the PNV won 1,084 places to 260 of HB, leaving the EE with 85. The great cities of Bilbao, San Sebastian, and Vitoria all have PNV mayors. The HB does not attend meetings of the regional parliament in Vitoria.

In the sixties ETA had about 60 to 70 activists. In the beginning of the seventies this number went down to 40. Today both wings of the ETA probably have about 200 members altogether.

Since 1968 ETA has made about 3,000 attacks. Three hundred and twenty-five people have been killed; more than 50 percent of this number were police officers and members of the armed forces. Since 1976 almost all of the murders were committed by ETA (militar). The most spectacular action was the assassination of the then Spanish Prime Minister Carrero Blanco on December 20, 1973, in Madrid. In the late summer of 1980 ETA (politico militar) agreed to an "armistice" with the Basque government. In March 1981 the Executive Committee of ETA (militar) met in a small village in southern France. The leader of ETA (militar), Txomin Iturbe Abasolo, suggested that ETA (militar) should also agree to an "armistice." His demand was rejected. It is expected, however, that in the near future negotiations between the government in Vitoria and ETA (militar) will succeed. The kidnapping of the Spanish-German industrialist José Lipperheide in January, 1982, was called a "mistake" by the ETA; ransom was not paid.

Michael S. Radu

Terror, Terrorism, and Insurgency in Latin America

The mainland states of Latin America, from Mexico to Argentina, continue to play a particularly important role in the history of contemporary political violence. The omnipresence of the Brazilian Carlos Marighella's "Mini-Manual of Guerrilla Warfare" in the hideouts of such different groups as the ETA, IRA, PLO, and Baader-Meinhof Gang is a demonstration of Latin America's importance as a source for terrorist theory and practice, just as the myth of Ernesto "Che" Guevara is a demonstration of Latin America's role as a source for the theory and practice of guerrilla warfare around the world. . . .

Patterns and Methods of Terrorism in Latin America

In "Thirty Questions to a Tupamaro," one of the most famous texts of a well-known Latin American terrorist group, a revolutionary asked to give a detailed definition of the Tupamaro strategy replies: "I cannot give you a detailed strategy. However, one can give some general strategic principles by the day, month, and year as one develops them."* This answer is a classic example of the character of some of the most influential and politically violent groups in Latin America and elsewhere in the world. On the one

* "30 Preguntas a un Tupamaro," in Angel Gutierrez, ed., *Los Tupamaros en la década de los anos sesenta* (Mexico City: Editorial Extemporaneos, 1978), p. 152.

Reprinted excerpts from *Orbis*, Spring 1984, with the kind permission of the editor.

hand, by practically dismissing the very notion of strategy by making it dependent on circumstances that may change daily, the Tupamaro is in fact manifesting his group's lack of strategy as a long-term military process with clearly defined goals. On the other hand, his answer defines the very essence of many a Latin American (and Middle Eastern, West European, or American) "revolutionary" as emotional, voluntaristic, personalistic, and decisively constrained by the imminence of pure action. An examination of the Tupamaros "Programme for Government," with its naive and incoherent attempt to make promises without any discussion of how to fulfill them, is another example of the voluntaristic character of violent Latin American groups. At the tactical and organizational levels, however, the sophisticated middle-class leaders of the Tupamaros were among the most coherent and articulate of the Latin American revolutionaries. They treated with supreme contempt the unorganized, chaotic violence and banditry evident, for example, in the Colombian disturbances of the 1950s.

The absence of any well-defined sense of long-term political or military aims that characterizes the Tupamaros is shared by many a Latin American terrorist group, as well as by such groups as the German Baader-Meinhof Gang and the Italian Brigatte Rosse, which have as their main goal the disruption of society rather than the defeat of the established government's military. All such groups operate only in the immediate present—today is far more important, significant, and symbolic than tomorrow.

This particular relationship between terrorist actions and time, in which the latter is of strictly immediate importance, is a characteristic of the Southern Cone countries (Chile, Uruguay, and Argentina), the most Westernized, middle-class-dominated, least "typical" Latin American states. Outside the Southern Cone, particularly among the pre-1979 FSLN (Sandinista Front for National Liberation) in Nicaragua and the ERP (People's Revolutionary Army) in El Salvador, terrorism as indiscriminate or civilian-directed violence tended to be characteristic of middle-class, as opposed to peasant- or worker-led, groups. While the Latin American middle-class revolutionary groups tend to be the most violent and indiscriminate, peasants and workers, particularly the latter, tend to be the most consistent, future-oriented, and discriminate in their nonmilitary violence.

Some Sociological Aspects of Latin American Terrorism

The most striking characteristics of Latin America's politically violent groups are the middle- or upper-middle-class background of their leaders and the direct relationship between the social and educational status of a group and the kind of terrorist acts it commits. The most prominent terrorist leaders in Latin America, from Miguel Enriquez and Pascal Allende of the Chilean MIR (Movement of the Revolutionary Left) to Raul Sendic of the Tupamaros, Mario Firmenich of the Montoneros, and Roberto Santucho of the Argentine ERP, not to mention the almost exclusively middle-class and well-to-do membership of the Nicaraguan FSLN, all come from social and educational groups well above the average. They are often products of universities subsidized by the state and have had only scant contact and experience with either the marketplace or the job market. In other words, prominent Latin American terrorists, like their West European counterparts, are economically, educationally, and socially pampered. One of the remaining myths of the liberal Western imagination is that the Latin American revolutionary leader or activist is a member and representative of the downtrodden masses. The archetypical leftist Latin American revolutionary is a rebel, but a rebel in the Camusian sense of being a rebel against his own class background and interests. The Latin *guerrillero* leader or terrorist chief is a socially suicidal character, a destroyer of the world and the values of his own childhood and adolescence, a rebel against himself as well as his upbringing. . . .

Universities and Violence

Such considerations apart, the role of Latin American universities in linking the philosophical ideas of the past, Marx, and Lenin with revolutionary practice is decisive, as is the tendency to apply a distorted version of Christian utopianism to reality. In both cases, the revolutionary leaders' elitism, "liberation theology," or utopianism exacts a price in blood as they test their ideas in the real world. Both must be examined to understand the psychological, social, and political origins of political violence in Latin America.

Ever since colonial times the university in Latin America has been considered a place where the normal relationship between a social institution and the government is suspended. Even the most reactionary Latin American military dictatorships accept the principle of university autonomy, which has by now become more of a cultural habit than a matter of policy in most countries south of the Rio Grande. Although in many practical ways autonomy is an absurd and artificial notion, it is also widely supported. As a result, regardless of the political and social role they were playing, the universities were free of government interference. Islands of autonomy supported by the taxpayers of poor countries, Latin American universities became revolutionary training grounds subsidized by antirevolutionary governments by the late 1950s and early 1960s. There, and in the Catholic-run universities and high schools, the children of the middle class and selected representatives of the lower classes were able, without social or financial cost, to become the cadres of revolution. The price for their being imbued with international revolutionary ideas was paid by the very governments they sought to eliminate. . . .

The Church and Violence

The impact of the Roman Catholic Church on Latin American revolutionary and terrorist thinking has been considerable and is, to a large extent, similar to that of Leninism and elitism. Theoretically, "liberation theology" is at the same time a contemporary expression of the age-old Catholic hostility to capitalism, private enterprise, and individualism, which are seen as "exploitative" or morally wrong, and an expression of the historic coalition between church and state in Latin lands. It should, however, be pointed out that the connection between the Church and revolution or terrorism has never been an institutional one—that is, the Church as such has never supported revolution in a Latin American country, although important sectors of it have. At the same time, the Church has very seldom officially condemned, either at the national or the Vatican level, the actions of particular members or groups within it.

Conclusion and Trends

The failure of the Castroite guerrilla *foci* in the rural areas during the 1960s has resulted in a decade of alternative revolutionary attempts in Latin America, based mostly in the cities of the relatively affluent countries of the Southern Cone. A largely middle-class phenomenon, urban political violence in Uruguay, Chile, and Argentina generally took the form of terrorism and served as a model for similar groups in Western Europe. By the mid-1970s, however, the ineffectiveness of the Southern Cone terrorist approach had become obvious and forced a reassessment of revolutionary strategy. With increasing frequency, attempts were made to incorporate techniques of political mobilization borrowed from the orthodox Communist parties and principles of guerrilla warfare taken from the Chinese and the Vietnamese.

The results of this reassessment were a decline in the number of ideological disputes within the violent Left, since all its factions were able to contribute to a new approach to violence, and an increasing similarity in the modus operandi of most of the violent groups on the continent. This was reinforced by the formalization of the coordination among violent leftist groups across national lines demonstrated by the April 1983 meeting in Esmeralda, Colombia, attended by the Salvadoran FMLN, Sendero Luminoso, the Guatemalan EGP (Guerrilla Army of the Poor), the Colombian M-19 (19th of April Movement), and the Venezuelan Bandera Roja. In addition, the FMLN, initially through the PRTC, has established operational groups in Honduras that pose as Honduran *guerrilleros* but are in fact under direct Salvadoran control; Sendero Luminoso has apparently established "branches" in Colombia and Venezuela; and the Colombian M-19 has created an Ecuadoran operations group led by its own members.

In light of these trends, and of the increasingly close ties between Latin American guerrilla groups and similar groups in Western Europe and the Middle East, it appears likely that more practical and operational cooperation at the international level will develop, with the Latin Americans playing a prominent role. This implies that tactical and theoretical changes in the revolutionary Left in Latin America will soon be adopted by non-Latin groups. The use of indiscriminate terror can thus be expected to decline, while the use of political fronts and mobilizational efforts and the internationalist accent of most politically violent groups throughout the world can be expected to increase.

Ariel Merari

The Future of Palestinian Terrorism

About seven years ago, Salah Khalaf ("Abu Ayad"), one of the prominent leaders of FATAH, gave a series of interviews to French journalist Eric Rouleau, which were later published as a book entitled *Palestinien sans Patrie* (Fayolle, 1978). In a gloomy and possibly prophetic statement, Abu Ayad said during one of those interviews: "The Fedayun, after their expulsion from Jordan, have no other 'stronghold' but Lebanon. If they surrender it, they would lose achievements of many years of struggle. Although the Palestinian revolution will always exist, a crushing defeat in Lebanon will endanger it for a long time to come."

More than two years after the September 1982 Palestinian expulsion from Beirut and about a year after Arafat's evacuation of Tripoli, the PLO is, indeed, in deep trouble.

The Lebanese war affected mainly the Palestinian groups that belonged to the PLO. The extra-PLO groups (the late Abu Nidal's FRC and the two factions that split from the late Wadi Hadad's PFLP-Special Operations) were influenced indirectly, for the most part. But it is the PLO groups that constitute the bulk of the Palestinian terrorist capabilities.

Major Factors Influencing Palestinian Terrorism

Three main factors influence present and near-future Palestinian terrorism: (a) the geographic dispersal of PLO forces, (b) the internal struggle, and (c) the likelihood of political achievements.

The Geographic Dispersal of Forces. As a result of the PLO's evacuation of their state-within-a-state in Lebanon, most of the Palestinian fighting force has been scattered throughout the Arab world.

Reprinted from *Terrorism, Violence, Insurgency (TVI) Journal,* Winter 1985, with the kind permission of the editor.

Although the exact distribution is constantly changing, due primarily to FATAH's effort to reestablish bases in Lebanon and to the buildup of forces in Jordan, the following list is fairly accurate:

Lebanon—8,000 of all groups (2,000 in Beirut and the rest mostly in Syrian-controlled areas)
Syria—2,000–3,000 (all rejectionist groups)
Jordan—2,000 (PLA and FATAH loyalists)
North Yemen—1,500 (mainly FATAH loyalists)
Algeria—1,500 (mostly FATAH loyalists)
PDRY—800–900 (FATAH, PFLP)
Iraq—800 (ALF and some FATAH loyalists)
Tunisia—500 (FATAH loyalists)
Sudan—300 (FATAH loyalists)
Egypt—500 (PLA)

The dispersal has reduced FATAH's control of the other groups, thus increasing their ability to assume independent positions and to challenge Arafat's line. Internal control within FATAH itself must have been weakened as well, if only because of the organizational difficulties involved in administering several thousand men scattered over several countries. It also created a situation in which thousands of young men, accustomed to relatively comfortable lives in Lebanon, have to be constantly reminded of what purpose is being served by their being kept far away from their families, under less than ideal conditions.

The Rift Within the PLO. The May 1983 eruption of the rebellion inside FATAH led to further ripples of splitting within several groups, as well as to the formation of three major blocks. FATAH rebels themselves have suffered from internal struggles among the three leaders. Nimr Saleh, Abu Khaled al-Amla, and Abu Musa, although the latter, with Syrian support, seems to have the upper hand. Gibril's PFLP-GC split during the siege of Tripoli, when a group of 100 to 150 members led by "Abu Jaber," the organization's head of "Central Security," joined Arafat's camp. The PLF has yielded no less than three factions: Arafat supporters, rejectionists, and middle-of-the-roaders.

The *Arafat followers* make up the largest faction (more than 8,000 active members) and exercise the greatest control over Palestinian institutions and resources. This group includes most of the FATAH, the pro-Iraqi ALF, and a faction of PLF led by Abu al-Abbas. The rebel camp (the rejectionists), calling itself the "National Revolutionary Alliance," includes Abu Musa's FATAH secessionists, the Syrian protégé Saiqa, Gibril's PFLP-GC, and the PPSF. With about 4,500 men, this is the second largest block in terms of manpower. The third formation, which assumed the name "Democratic Alliance," consists of the radical left-wing groups, PFLP and DFLP (with a combined strength of about 2,000 active members). Its political importance, however, surpasses its numerical power. Both the "Democratic Alliance" and "Revolutionary Alliance" are severe critics of Arafat leadership, the domination of Arafat's men over the PLO's organs and decision-making processes, and, most important, his political orientation. However, whereas FATAH rebels, with strong Syrian backing, are determined to remove Arafat, stop any political overtures, sever relations with Jordan and Egypt, and tie the PLO exclusively to radical Arab countries such as Syria, Libya, and Algeria, the "Democratic Alliance" attaches supreme value to the PLO's independence of Arab countries' patronage, would do much to maintain the PLO's integrity and, recognizing Arafat's symbolic value, favor his remaining in office.

The Likelihood of Political Achievements. The third factor that affects the future course of Palestinian terrorism is the chance for political advancement of the Palestinian cause. Despite face-saving statements to the contrary, most Palestinians, including Arafat's followers, view the war in Lebanon as a serious setback. This traumatic experience, however, has probably only highlighted and exacerbated undercurrent feelings that existed for years before the war. Twenty years after the writing of the politically uncompromising Palestinian National Covenant, which emphasized armed struggle as the only way to achieve Palestinian national goals, doubts about the wisdom of totalistic demands and the effectiveness of the violent struggle as the main instrument seem to have permeated the thinking of some Palestinian leaders and, conceiveably, the sentiments of part of the rank and file. A political breakthrough might offer the disappointed an alternative to the return to puritanical struggle advocated by the rejectionists.

The chance for a political light at the end of the tunnel is, however, rather slim. The minimal condition for such a development is the support of Israel, Jordan, and the PLO. All three are unwilling or unable to promote this course of action.

Despite some vocal opposition from a small left-wing minority, the two major Israeli parties, Labor and the Likud, agree on the principle of no negotiation with the PLO, although they are open to talks with Jordan. Israel is still committed to the Autonomy Plan and rejects the possibility of an independent Palestinian state altogether.

For Jordan, with more than 50 percent of its population of Palestinian origin and the memory of the 1970–1971 internal war between the PLO and the Jordanian army still strong, a Palestinian state would pose an even greater threat to the Hashemite throne than Israel. The present flirtation between debased Arafat and Syrian-threatened Hussein is a matter of temporary political convenience rather than a true case of common long-range interests. Quite likely, therefore, Jordan will undermine any effort for a political breakthrough toward Palestinian independence, although it is hardly necessary for Jordan to do a job that others do so well for it.

Arafat seems to represent the only party that is truly interested in a political advancement toward Palestinian independence. Yet he is clearly unable to assume an unequivocal position in this regard as long as he entertains the slimmest hope for PLO unity. Thus, even in the recent PNC meeting in Amman, Arafat merely voiced vague support for a political initiative while reiterating the centrality of the armed struggle in promoting the Palestinian cause.

Altogether, it seems that despite some rhetoric, the likelihood of political achievements on the part of the PLO is very small.

Terrorist Activity

Three sectors of Palestinian terrorist activity should be considered separately: (1) terrorist activity from within Israel and the Administered Territories; (2) terrorist activity launched against Israel from territories of neighboring Arab countries; and (3) international terrorism.

Terrorism Inside Israel. Terrorism inside Israel has always been a top priority for the PLO. The limiting factors in this sector have been the efficiency of Israeli security services and the PLO's limited capabilities, rather than motivation. In numbers of incidents, there has been some decline in Palestinian terrorist activity from inside Israel and the territories since the 1982 war, attributable to the increased difficulty of smuggling weapons and explosives as well as to the disruption of the "Western Sector Apparatus," the PLO organ in charge of terrorist activity in Israel. In 1980, 232 incidents were recorded in Israel and the Administered Territories; in 1981, 159; in 1982, 203 (about two-thirds of them in the first half of the year, before the war); and in 1983, 173 incidents. Most of the incidents have consisted of placing improvised explosive charges in public sites and throwing molotov cocktails at Israeli vehicles in the Territories, which usually cause little or no damage. The most spectacular incident—the hijacking of a bus on April 13, 1984—resulted in the death of the four perpetrators and one passenger. The PLO has recently invested great effort in reorganizing the "Western Sector Apparatus," whose headquarters was moved to Amman under the direction of Halil al-Wazir ("Abu Jihad"). In the long run, however, there is no reason to expect a significant change in the pattern or volume of terrorist activity in this sector.

Terrorist Attacks from Neighboring Countries. Before the war, the most spectacular terrorist attacks in Israel were initiated from neighboring countries. These consisted of incursions of specially trained terrorist teams, sent to stage barricade/hostage events or to carry out random mass killings, and of artillery and Katyusha rocket shelling of Israeli border settlements. Almost all of these attacks were launched from Lebanese territory. These types of activity were used sparingly prior to the war, at least by the major organizations, for fear of fierce Israeli retaliation in the form of a massive ground attack on the Palestinian stronghold in Lebanon. The war deprived the PLO of its main base for these attacks, but at the same time it relieved the PLO of the deterrence factor.

The great need of salient achievements after the PLO defeat in the war and the intergroup competition exacerbated by the internal rift have led to recent efforts by the PLO to carry out spectacular actions in this sector. These efforts, however, have been greatly hampered by the attitude of neighboring Arab countries. Egypt and Jordan actively try to prevent this kind of activity, and Syria supports it only on the condition that it not be committed directly from Syrian territory. In Lebanon, despite intensive guerrilla-type activity against Israeli forces (mostly by local Shi'ites), the presence of those forces and the South Lebanese Army belt have proven effective barriers to attacks against Israeli territory. Thus, postwar terrorism initiated in neighboring countries has so far consisted of several attempted incursions, all but one of them foiled, and several improvised Katyusha rockets fired from Lebanon or from Jordan by squads that came from bases in Syrian territory.

Despite the meager achievements thus far, some small number of these attempts are likely to succeed. The chance of success will, of course, increase if Syria, Jordan, and Egypt change their present policies (which is not very likely) or if Palestinian terrorists manage to reentrench in South Lebanon after the Israeli evacuation.

International Terrorism. Since 1974, the PLO has by and large refrained from international terrorist activity. The international terrorist attacks after that year have been carried out mainly by the extra-PLO groups, Abu Nidal's FRC, Abu Ibrahim's May 15, and Salim Abu Salem's PFLP—Special Command. PLO member organizations have reserved international operations for special occasions (e.g., to express dissatisfaction with the Israeli-Egyptian peace process). Present conditions, however, resemble in some important respects those of the period which led to the height of international Palestinian terrorism in the early 1970s. Both then, after their expulsion from Jordan, and now, the PLO had suffered a humiliating blow that caused internal morale problems, and in both situations the PLO had lost its former operational bases, which imposed limitations upon activity in the other arenas. It is surprising, therefore, that so far the PLO has not resorted to large-scale international terrorism. Although in the months following the war, Abu Ayad expressed a few threats of reviving the Black September Organization (BSO) and resorting to international terrorism, such threats have not been repeated. The factual picture is similar. In 1982 there were 34 international terrorist incidents perpetrated by Palestinian groups, 34 such events in 1983, and 32 in 1984, only five of the latter directed against Israeli interests (as compared to 66 international incidents in 1973, at the peak of Black September activity).

Nevertheless, it should be remembered that 14 months elapsed between September 1970 and the first appearance of BSO in November 1971. In the present case, it can be argued that throughout most of the postwar period, the Palestinian groups have been very busy resettling in their new bases and waging internal battles. In the absence of a political advance that might engage the rank and file in support of the PLO leadership, the latter's need for spectacular violent activity will presumably be high. Furthermore, Arafat, who is constantly accused by his opponents of deserting the course of armed struggle, will be under pressure to prove the contrary. Since terrorist activity inside the Israeli Territories and across the borders is largely contained, returning to international terrorism is quite attractive for the PLO. It seems to be only a question of time.

Aaron D. Miller

Portrait of Abu Nidal

Terrorist Casts Long Shadow

Abu Nidal left a calling card last fall in an interview with the German magazine *Der Spiegel*. "I can assure you of one thing," he said. "If we have the chance to inflict the slightest harm to Americans, we will not hesitate to do it. In the months and years to come, the Americans will think of us."

Americans may indeed be thinking of Abu Nidal following recent events. His real name is Sabri Khalil al-Banna, and he is one of those on whom Libyan leader Muammar Khadafy will most likely depend to carry out his campaign to attack American interests. It is clear that the Libyans are supporting Abu Nidal, and he is linked to last December's bloody attacks at the Rome and Vienna airports, only the most recent example of the mayhem that he has made his life's work.

Here is a snapshot of the man who describes himself as America's enemy: His politics are those of revenge and revolution on a grand scale. He seeks through terror a retributive and perfect justice that can never be achieved. He moves through a shadowy inter-connected world of international and Arab terrorist networks that have given him a mystique larger than life. And yet through all of this there is something very ordinary, small and marginal about him—something that seems to reinforce the fact that terror, no matter how brutal, is only a symptom of a failed cause and of the frustrations of a desperate man.

Reprinted from the *Washington Post*, March 30, 1986, with the kind permission of the author.

Perhaps even more frightening than the man himself is his relationship to those Arab regimes willing to tolerate his excesses. In a world where assassinations and violence have become legitimate tools of political struggle, Abu Nidal and those like him provide important services in the never-ending fight for influence and power. He is not simply a product of the Arab-Israeli conflict but of an intra-Arab struggle in which ideology is subordinated to regime survival and personal vendetta. How else can we explain that a man who in 1976 tried to kill the Syrian foreign minister could be operating out of Damascus seven years later?

Who is this elusive figure and what is the nature of the environment in which he operates? Is he simply the hired gun of state-sponsored terrorism, or is he the genuine revolutionary he claims to be?

One of the most frustrating aspects of dealing with Abu Nidal is that so little is known about him. Even in the murky subterranean world of international terrorism, he is a mystery. Despite two recent interviews, rumors still abound that he is dead or incapacitated and that his operations are run by committee. In a recent interview, Abu Nidal claimed that he had undergone plastic surgery. His interviewers usually ask him for some proof of his identity and wonder themselves whether he is who he claims to be. During one interview, Abu Nidal reportedly ripped open his shirt to show an inquisitive journalist scars from a much rumored heart operation.

His method of operation only enhances his image as a secretive shadowy force likely to appear anywhere at any time. The entire Abu Nidal organization is tightly compartmentalized and may not number more than a few hundred. The structure of the organization further obscures the links between operations and the master command. Capitalizing on the shadowy terrorist network in Europe and the Middle East, Abu Nidal further covers his tracks. Thus, in the Rome and Vienna operations, the terrorists could have been trained in Lebanon, acquired Libyan confiscated Tunisian passports, and obtained weapons in Europe.

The same difficulties apply to analyzing his recruiting style. Many of his recruits are probably young Palestinians, with varying levels of educations and places of origin. Abu Nidal can draw from disillusioned and radicalized Palestinian refugees in camps and shantytowns from Beirut to Amman. He can also use his European connections to recruit from more sophisticated Palestinian students on the continent. In traditional Middle Eastern style, he may also make effective use of an extended network of family relations and friends. According to Yossi Melman, an Israeli journalist who has published an account of Abu Nidal, the attempted assassination of the Israeli ambassador to Britain may have involved one of Abu Nidal's cousins.

What we do know about Abu Nidal's early years suggests unremarkable origins. Born in Jaffa, Palestine, in the late 1930s to an affluent family, he attended French and Islamic schools before the outbreak of the 1948 Arab-Israeli war. Here accounts of his life vary significantly. Melman claims that his family moved first to Nablus. Because of the family's declining fortunes, he attended a government school and later went to Cairo University to study engineering. Afterwards he worked for a time in Saudi Arabia.

In a 1985 interview, on the other hand, Abu Nidal claims that his family moved first to Gaza as refugees where he was recruited by ARAMCO to work in Saudi Arabia. Here he claims he was arrested, tortured, and expelled from the country. This account, however, would have been far more marketable in revolutionary circles as Abu Nidal set out to validate his credentials as a militant Palestinian nationalist. It also presents an image of a young, educated, middle-class Palestinian-disillusioned with the passivity of his parents generation and eager to deny his middle-class roots in order to pursue the struggle to "liberate Palestine."

By the mid-1960s, al-Banna was drawn into the politics of the Palestinian resistance movement where he fell in with Yasir Arafat's Fatah organization. Here he apparently adopted his *nom de guerre* (Abu Nidal, Father of the Struggle) and developed, during King Hussein's bloody suppression of the Palestinian fedayeen in September 1970, a deep hatred for the Hashemites. It was during these years as well that he also began to develop links with other radical Palestinian groups committed to the use of international terror. He may also have maintained ties with Fatah's own terrorist arm, Black September. By 1971 he had been appointed PLO representative in Baghdad. It is here that he became intrigued with the radical approach of the Iraqi Ba'th and more disillusioned with what he perceived to be establishment PLO policies.

By 1973 the stage was set for a formal break with Arafat and Fatah. Several events seemed to converge to push him away from Fatah. At a time when Fatah was beginning to limit its involvement in international terrorism, Abu Nidal was just getting started—carrying out attacks against the Saudi embassy in Paris and an attempted hijacking at the Rome airport. He had been greatly influenced by the earlier activities of Black September, and became convinced that transnational terrorism had to play a central role in Palestinian strategy.

At about the same time, the October 1973 war and the possibilities of movement on the diplomatic front had prompted Arafat to begin cultivating a more respectable international image and to adopt a more flexible political program. Abu Nidal vehemently opposed any tempering of the PLO's commitment to the armed struggle and felt excluded from the diplomatic and political world in which the PLO began to operate. He was not alone in his opposition. This tactical shift in Fatah's policies created a real dilemma for those in the movement committed to the PLO's maximalist goals. In 1974, George Habbash's PFLP temporarily left the PLO's executive committee to protest what it saw as Arafat's accommodationist policies.

Unlike Habbash, however, Abu Nidal did not return. That year the break with Arafat became final amidst accusations that Abu Nidal was implicated in a plot to eliminate Fatah's top leadership, although Abu Nidal claims that the rift was triggered by Fatah's campaign to kill its own people. Abu Nidal was tried and sentenced to death in absentia. The break with Arafat was now complete and a vendetta sworn against Fatah that would become a key component of Abu Nidal's *raison d'etre.*

For the next nine years, Abu Nidal would operate out of three Middle Eastern capitals—Baghdad, Damascus, and Tripoli, not coincidentally regimes that were in the forefront of opposition to any Arab-Israeli accommodation. For the Iraqis, with whom he cooperated closely until they broke with him and expelled him in the early 1980s, he offered a useful tool in their campaign against their archrival Syria. In fact, after the Syrian move into Lebanon in June 1974, Abu Nidal adopted the name Black June as a cover for his anti-Syrian activities—undertaking attacks against a range of Syrian and Palestinian targets.

For the Syrians, with whom he still maintains ties, Abu Nidal became an asset in Assad's efforts to pressure Jordan and the PLO. As Arafat's dialogue with Jordan's King Hussein intensified, so did Abu Nidal's anti-PLO and Jordanian activities. In 1983, Abu Nidal's organization was thought to have been involved in the assassination of Issam Sartawi, the PLO's leading advocate of accommodation with Israel; he is also thought to have been involved in the murder of Fahd

Qawasmeh, a moderate West Bank mayor deported by the Israelis. This attack, occurring in broad daylight in a residential area of Amman, was doubtless intended as a not-so-subtle message to King Hussein that there would be a price to pay for ignoring Damascus' interests on Arab-Israeli issues. Throughout 1985, Abu Nidal continued to attack Jordanian diplomats and airline facilities.

Finally, for Libya, with whom he has been strengthening ties since mid-1984, Abu Nidal became another hit man for Khadafy's terror squads. His choice of an Egyptian airliner in the recent Malta hijacking and recent operations in Europe coincide with Libya's support for international terrorism. Indeed a look at Abu Nidal's recent operations —culminating in the December 1985 attacks in Rome and Vienna suggests that he has—while not severing his Syrian connection—brought his tactics into closer alignment with Libyan interests. In a September 1985 interview in Kuwait he claimed to fully support Egypt's Revolutionaries, a group that has claimed responsibility for killing Israeli diplomats in Cairo. Such operations coincide with Libya's goal of embarrassing Mubarak and creating tension between Israel and Egypt.

But what of Abu Nidal's goals and objectives? What does he hope to achieve and what do his patrons hope to gain?

In following Abu Nidal's trail over the past decade, one fact is unmistakable. The violence and terror he sows is not directed at any achievable political goal. While Abu Nidal pursues tactical ends—publicity, intimidation—he does not seek to use terror to achieve Palestinian rights or a state in his lifetime or even in that of his children. For him the struggle against Zionism and all of its supporters is timeless and continues without regard for accommodation, compromise, or negotiation. "The fact that the Zionists have taken my Arab homeland is for me more than a crime," Abu Nidal asserted last fall. "For me it would be a crime if we permitted the Zionists to leave our homeland alive." It is here, in a world of grievances that can never be addressed, of injustices that can never be righted and of unending vengeance that Abu Nidal operates—impervious and opposed to all forms of accommodation or moderation.

Within this view of revolution and terrorism, however, Abu Nidal has pursued two basic objectives. First, he has sought to challenge Fatah, and Arafat in particular, by maintaining that he is the legitimate heir to Fatah's original policies. Much of the ideological rationalization for his policies rests on his accusations that Arafat is deviating from the principles of the total destruction of the "Zionist entity" and the pursuit of true Arab unity.

It would be misleading, however, to suggest that Abu Nidal's only enemy is Arafat and the Israelis. Coincident with his total opposition to the Arab establishment is his virulent hostility to "bourgeois and pro-imperialist" Arab regimes whom he views as corrupt and venal. Although Jordan is a particular object of his hatred, Hussein is not alone. "My enemies are the slovenly and chaotic states of our Arab society, as well as the suppression and seduction of our young generation," Abu Nidal recently declared. Like other Arab revolutionaries of the 1950s and 1960s, Abu Nidal places a high premium on the importance of overthrowing these regimes as a prerequisite to Arab unity and thus the liberation of Palestine.

Abu Nidal, however, does not exist in a vacuum and it is crucial to understand the intra-Arab and international environment in which he operates. In a sense it is this Arab and international support that elevates him from the garden-variety terrorist to the transnational terrorist league in which he plays. The Arab states that have backed Abu Nidal-Iraq at one time, Syria and now Libya—and the East Europe bloc nations did not create him; he is not simply a kind of Palestinian or "have Kalashnikov, will travel." Nonetheless, the support these states provide is vital to the effectiveness of his operations. While there is clearly a transnational terrorist network from which a man like Abu Nidal could benefit, his ability to operate and survive for over a decade and a half is directly linked to the assistance he derives from external sources.

The Libyan connection is only the latest of Abu Nidal's tactical alliances, and it's no coincidence that the states that have most actively supported Abu Nidal over the past 10 years are those that have historically been most opposed to reconciliation with Israel. They have also at one time or another been involved in major confrontations with those moderate states—Egypt and Jordan—that have been pushing for peace with Israel. It is also these states that have been most adept at using terror not only in the Arab arena but abroad as well in the service of their own goals. Although Abu Nidal's Arab support is thus relatively tightly circumscribed, there was always a market for his services. When Arab states' interests and behavior shift, as in the case of Iraq in the early 1980s or in the case of Syria, 1984–1985, Abu Nidal moves on to another patron. Thus, it is possible for Abu Nidal operatives to train in the Bekaa Valley and yet be given false passports, money, and weapons by Libya.

The lessons drawn from studying Abu Nidal and his world are not heartening ones. Indeed the consistency and effectivenesss of his operations lead to the conclusion that his brand of terrorism is likely to remain a permanent feature of the Middle East's political landscape. Even more sobering is the recognition that Abu Nidal's terror has become very much a permanent fixture of shifting rivalries between Arab regimes. He remains effective because he is willing and able to provide services for a variety of patrons.

Nonetheless, in the end there are limits to what Abu Nidal can hope to achieve. He represents no constituency with any real power, he can never achieve anything positive for Palestinians. He can only destroy and intimidate until he himself is destroyed. More like him may follow, but their legacy will not be any more enduring.

Hizballah

"Open Letter to Downtrodden in Lebanon and the World"

[Editor's note: Hizballah is the most extreme Shiite terrorist group in Lebanon.]

We declare frankly and clearly that we are a nation that fears only God and that does not accept tyranny, aggression, and humiliation. America and its allies in and the Zionist entity that has usurped the sacred Islamic land of Palestine have engaged and continue to engage in constant aggression against us and are working to constantly hu-

Text of open letter addressed by Hizballah to downtrodden in Lebanon and the world, pointing out in its projections and path on occasion of the first anniversary of the martyrdom of Raghib Harb, the symbol of Islamic resistance and the paramount martyr.

miliate us. Therefore, we are in a state of constant and escalating preparedness to repel the aggression and to defend our religion, existence, and dignity.

They have attacked our country, destroyed our villages, massacred our children, violated our sanctities and installed over our heads criminal henchmen who have perpetrated terrible massacres against our nation. They are still supporting these butchers who are Israel's allies and preventing us from determining our destiny with our free will. . . .

We Have No Alternative to Confrontation

Thus, we have seen that aggression can be repelled only with sacrifices and dignity gained only with the sacrifice of blood and that freedom is not given but regained with the sacrifice of both heart and soul.

We have opted for religion, freedom, and dignity over humiliation and constant submission to America and its allies and to Zionism and their Phalangist allies. We have risen to liberate our country, to drive the imperialists and the invaders out of it and to determine our fate by our own hands.

We could not endure more than we have endured. Our tragedy is more than 10 years old and all we have seen so far are the covetous, hypocritical, and incapable. . . .

Our Basic Enemies

Our people could not withstand all this treason and decided to confront the imams of infidelity of America, France, and Israel. The first punishment against these forces was carried out on 18 April and the second on 29 October 1983. By that time, a real war had started against the Israeli occupation forces, rising to the level of destroying two main centers of the enemy's military rulers. Our people also escalated their popular and military Islamic resistance to the point where they forced the enemy to make its decision on phased withdrawal—a decision that Israel was compelled to adopt for the first time in the history of the so-called Arab-Israeli conflict.

For the sake of the truth, we declare that the sons of Hizballah's nation have come to know well their basic enemies in the area: Israel, America, France, and the Phalange.

OUR OBJECTIVES IN LEBANON

Our sons are now in a state of ever-escalating confrontation against these enemies until the following objectives are achieved:

Israel's final departure from Lebanon as a prelude to its final obliteration from existence and the liberation of venerable Jerusalem from the talons of occupation.

The final departure of America, France, and their allies from Lebanon and the termination of the influence of any imperialist power in the country.

Submission by the Phalange to just rule and their trial for the crimes they have committed against both Muslims and Christians with the encouragement of America and Israel.

Giving all our people the opportunity to determine their fate and to choose with full freedom the system of government they want, keeping in mind that we do not hide our commitment to the rule of Islam and that we urge to choose the Islamic system, which alone guarantees justice and dignity for all and prevents any new imperialist attempt to infiltrate our country.

ISRAEL MUST BE WIPED OUT OF EXISTENCE

As for Israel, we consider it the American spearhead in our Islamic world. It is a usurping enemy that must be fought until the usurped right is returned to its owners.

This enemy poses a great danger to our future generations and to the destiny of our nation, especially since it embraces a settlement-oriented and expansionist idea which it has already begun to apply in occupied Palestine and it is extending and expanding to build Greater Israel, from the Euphrates to the Nile.

Our struggle with usurping Israel emanates from an ideological and historical awareness that this Zionist entity is aggressive in its origins and structure and is built on usurped land and at the expense of the rights of a Muslim people.

Therefore, our confrontation of this entity must end with its obliteration from existence. This is why we do not recognize any cease-fire agreement, any truce or any separate or nonseparate peace treaty with it.

Escalating Islamic Resistance

When speaking of usurping Israel, we must pause before the phenomenon of Islamic resistance which sprang from the occupied Lebanese territories to impose a new historic and cultural turn on the course of the struggle against the Zionist enemy.

The honorable Islamic resistance which has inscribed and continues to inscribe the most magnificent sagas against the Zionist invasion forces, which has destroyed by the faith of its strugglers the myth of invincible Israel, which has been able to place the usurping entity into a real dilemma as a result of the daily military, economic, and human attrition it inflicts on this entity, forcing its leaders to acknowledge the severe resistance they face at the hands of the muslims. . . .

This Islamic resistance must continue, grow, and escalate, with God's help, and must receive from all Muslims in all parts of the world utter support, aid, backing, and participation so that we may be able to uproot this cancerous germ and obliterate it from existence.

Murray J. Leaf

The Punjab Crisis

The key to understanding the tragic sequence of events from the attack on the Golden Temple to the assassination of Indira Gandhi lies in seeing how the legitimate and resolvable problems bundled into the argument about federalism became submerged in the fundamentally unresolvable demands and ideas associated with separatism and terrorism. What happened in Punjab, beginning with the declaration of President's Rule in 1980, was the progressive disenfranchisement of the mainstream of the population, the middle ground of political

Reprinted excerpts from *Asian Survey*, Vol. XXV, No. 5, May 5, 1985, with the kind permission of the editor.

opinion. The first method by which the moderates were deprived of a political voice was the use of President's Rule to topple state governments unfavorable to central policies. By insisting on a state government that was loyal to her above all and measuring the loyalty by lack of objections to her policies, Mrs. Gandhi necessarily deprived those who favored alternative policies of the power to speak through established government organs with a force appropriate to their local political strength. Of course, Badal and others continued to speak as members of the legislative opposition, but this power too was attacked in several ways. One was intimidation. As early as August 1980 Mrs. Gandhi was quoted in the press as having told her Congress supporters that "Opposition parties were creating a situation similar to the one obtaining before June 1975." This could hardly be taken otherwise than as a threat to return to the practices of the Emergency.*

It is difficult in retrospect to determine exactly when the first re-use to preventive detention occurred, but a UPI story carried in the American press in April 1983 said that 600 "militant Sikhs" from the Akali Party had been arrested to "avert a threatened highway blockade" as part of a protest against Mrs. Gandhi's policies.† The blockade took place anyway and in the course of it 200 more were arrested and 20 killed in a police "firing." Later, in 1984, Harchand Singh Longowal, as president of the Sikh Gurudwara management committee, was placed under arrest prior to the attack on the Golden Temple but released by the time of the attack under terms of the law. The law was then amended to increase the power of detention, and he was rearrested immediately after the attack. At the time of Mrs. Gandhi's assassination, and through the subsequent elections, virtually the entire body of mainstream Akali politicians was in jail—including Badal and Longowal. Such tactics—silencing political opposition in the interest of "unity"—obviously have the effect of denying a voice to the constituencies represented by the silenced politicians. When these politicians represent the moderate middle ground of the political spectrum and their constituencies represent the bulk of the working population of a state, the result can only be to leave the political stage to politicians and constituencies at the fringes.

A second method of disenfranchisement was unresponsiveness. There can be no doubt that repeated and complete explanations were

* *The Tribune* (Chandigarh), August 12, 1980.

† *Dallas Times Herald* (Dallas), April 3, 1983.

made of the Punjab view of its problems and their solutions, but the central government, either in the person of Mrs. Gandhi herself or her close advisors, never publicly acknowledged them as serious or legitimate. The most common response was to ignore them; an almost equally common response was to treat them as a smokescreen by "rich farmers" to oppress the "poor." Since the average size of a farm holding in Punjab is about 2.56 hectares, and the average farmer cultivates his land with his own efforts and would consider "luxury" the possession of a battery-powered cassette player and an electric fan, this was very hard to take as anything but a thinly disguised threat (to impose even more punitive land ceilings). About the nearest Mrs. Gandhi came to a direct response to the Punjab farmers' concerns (which were shared widely in other states) was to convene a large "farmer's rally" in March 1981 in an effort to compete with a similar rally being organized by Charan Singh to promote his national farmer's party. In her address to the rally, as described in the press, Gandhi was quoted as promising to "solve" the farmers' problems, but also as having "referred to [farmer] agitations in certain areas and said while some of their demands were justified it was impossible to fulfill others, which only served the interests of big landlords." She also "pointed out that 25% of the allocation [in the forthcoming sixth five-year plan] had been earmarked for the rural sector."* Since over 80% of the population is rural and about half of these are farmers, the number is not likely to have been particularly impressive. The press had something of a field day describing the clothing and appearance of those attending, suggesting very strongly that there were very few real farmers among them. They appeared to have been mainly Congress Party workers and supporters, and have been brought to the rally by a massive government transportation effort. All of this was underlined in the descriptions of the subsequent opposition rally. Although the estimated 200,000 in attendance were only a tenth the number of Mrs. Gandhi's crowd, they did indeed appear to be farmers who were poor and who had come by their own means.

The third method by which Mrs. Gandhi disenfranchised the Punjab mainstream was the most dangerous, and ultimately was self-destructive. It was this that created the current misunderstanding of the issues in the West, as indeed in much of India outside of Punjab. In place of addressing the economic and political issues, she used her

* *The Tribune* (Chandigarh), February 17, 1981.

superior access to national and international media to consistently describe the opposition as religious fanatics who advocated secession and separatism motivated by "communalism" and "regionalism." To substantiate these characterizations she and her supporters much more often referred to the actions and statements of the extremists than to those of the moderates. Among those unacquainted with the details of the area, the characterization won short-term support for her position. Who could not support a prime minister who was acting in favor of national unity against dissolution and disorder, and in favor of reason and progress against irrationality, selfishness, and fanaticism? Within Punjab the characterization appeared to be intended (as, for different reasons, were the anti-Hindu actions of Bhindranwale) to drive a wedge between the rural Sikhs and urban Hindus and thus between the two major parties (Akali and Jan Sangh) who had to unite to defeat the Congress. In the end it became a self-fulfilling prophecy. It had the logical effect of magnifying the extremists and discouraging the moderates even though they never actually ceased to try to present their case. It had the political effect of tapping the well of prejudice that is available whenever there are religious and ethnic differences and of gaining widespread acceptance in India and the world for the idea that the conflict was indeed communal and religious—that the anger of the Punjabis was irrational and antinational and that tolerating it would be tantamount to allowing India to drop back into the eighteenth century. Punjabis in their turn were aware of this misrepresentation of their concerns and its acceptance, and it only increased their frustration and anger. It also evidently increased the willingness to tolerate (or perhaps unwillingness to root out) the likes of Bhindranwale, and finally to accept him as a legitimate Sikh martyr, a person who gave his life for no other reason than to expose and resist danger to the survival of the community.

The Attack on the Golden Temple

There doesn't seem to be any serious doubt that Bhindranwale was the main organizer of a terrorist campaign that was responsible for the random murder of several hundred innocent Hindus and that in publicly wearing arms and defiantly proclaiming his willingness to use them he was making himself a target for retribution. Moreover, by setting up his headquarters in the Golden Temple he was in effect daring the authorities to violate the temple in order to capture him.

Neither the people of Punjab nor the precepts of the Sikh religion condone murder. Why then was there such shock and outrage among Sikhs when the army attacked the temple on June 4, 1984? There are two basic reasons: disproportion and inappropriateness.

Bhindranwale and his group were, presumably, guilty of murder and conspiracy to murder. One normally deals with such matters through the police in a legal way and not with the army. If the army was required, it would hardly seem necessary to have invaded the temple with 2,000 men with the result that as many as 1,000 people, including 100 soldiers and, it is said in Punjab, about 400 pilgrims lost their lives. The Golden Temple complex is walled and quite clearly demarcated; it certainly would have been possible to cordon it off. Nor did it seem necessary at the same time to seal off the state with about 70,000 additional troops, simultaneously invade other shrines, declare President's Rule and dissolve the state legislature, establish complete press censorship, occupy the temple militarily afterwards, and declare martial law. As was widely recognized after the attack, far from ending Bhindranwale's influence and activities, the attack and the government actions associated with it actually served as evidence of what he was trying to prove. In a religious frame of reference, it was one more dramatic piece of evidence that Gandhi's government was hostile to Sikhs as such, would not react reasonably to their demands, and was in fact either indifferent to their destruction or positively in favor of it. In a conventional political frame of reference, especially when seen against events in Assam and elsewhere and in the light of the impending elections, it was easily interpretable as an attack on the basic procedures of Indian democracy and a decisive move toward autocracy that at least matched the worst abuses of the Emergency. In short, to many Punjabis and others the attack confirmed that Indira Gandhi would do anything she could to preserve her hold on the central government, regardless of the costs.

The Assassination

Indira Gandhi was assassinated by two guards from her own security force on the morning of October 31, 1984: Satwant Singh and Beant Singh. Apparently both were Punjabis and both Sikhs. No clear description of the motivations has been released, and none is likely to be. Strictly speaking it is futile to guess at them. Yet enough has been said about the background of the action and enough is clear from the bare facts of the news reports to eliminate some of the interpretations that have been current in the Indian and American press.

Two simple points are clear: they were members of an elite force with unblemished records, and they must surely have expected that once they opened fire they themselves would immediately be killed. Why would such people do such a thing? It seems highly unlikcly that they were undercover religious fanatics, or that they had somehow been recruited to act on behalf of a foreign government—or even overseas Sikhs. Nor would it simply be a matter of "revenge" for the attack on the temple. The Sikh religion, to say nothing of simple common sense, lays no basis for self-destruction in pursuit of revenge. It does, however, lay a basis for self-destruction in the defense of one's community and more basically of the truths that, in the Sikh view, sustain life. Thus the most likely explanation is actually the simplest: that they acted out of the same long-held conviction that led them to serve in the first place—the idea that they should be willing if necessary to lay down their lives to defend their country, as well as their homeland and their religion. In their view, Mrs. Gandhi must have come to represent a pressing threat to all three, and they gave their lives to stop her. Whatever private motives these two men may have held, press reports indicate strongly that the great majority of Punjabs see this as the significance of their act, although no responsible person would endorse assassination as such.

The Aftermath

In the rioting immediately after the assassination of Mrs. Gandhi, more than 1,500 Sikhs were murdered and many more had their houses and property destroyed, were beaten, and were publicly humiliated. Since the rioting occurred outside the censored area, the Western press carried many interviews of victims. Almost universally they expressed disillusionment, a sense of betrayal, and sadness. Many said they no longer considered India their country; they would rather live anywhere else.

The reason for these reactions is not that Hindus and Sikhs are hostile to one another, or that they are fundamentally different from one another (although even some very prominent Sikhs, including Khushwant Singh, said precisely this in the bitter aftermath of the destruction). It is rather exactly the opposite. Sikhism and the major traditions of Hinduism all share a common idea of tolerance of all religions, of the importance of each individual finding his own understandings, and of nonviolence as the basis of civilized behavior. These ideas are at the core of the Indian conception of civilization itself, and are held with the deepest possible conviction by thoughtful people of all sects. Thus the despair and disillusionment of the injured Sikhs is not just because they were made to suffer personally for no reason, but because the non-Sikhs around them seemed to abandon these basic values, allowing themselves to be corrupted by the meanest sort of appeals to prejudice and suspicion. Undoubtedly some of those who attacked the Sikhs, accepting the religious definition of the conflict, were thinking the same sorts of things—that Sikhs themselves had abandoned these ideas and could not be trusted as neighbors and fellow citizens.

If the sense of difference between Sikhs and Hindus has become so steeped in suspicion and fear that it will be self-perpetuating henceforth, then the prognosis for India's future is dark indeed. Religious differences as such are not a threat to national integration, but religious intolerance incorporated into political conflicts certainly would be. After the Sikhs why not the Muslims? After them why not the Buddhists? After them why not Lingayats? And so forth.

My own view is that these dark forebodings are unwarranted. Despite their viciousness and the lack of a subsequent general condemnation by Hindu intellectuals, the anti-Sikh riots were the exception rather than the rule, and appear often to have occurred in poorer urban areas where one would expect to find many people dependent on Gandhi's policies, hence areas of particular Congress Party strength—indeed rioting seemed to occur often at the instigation of Congress Party officials or of police and the like who had Congress allegiances, as indicated by subsequent descriptions of Rajiv Gandhi's actions in removing those who permitted the rioting to happen and ordering investigations of allegations of complicity.

The press widely predicted that there would be answering anti-Hindu riots in Punjab, in the manner of the accelerating cycle of reciprocal Hindu and Muslim atrocities of 1946. Had this happened Mrs. Gandhi would have accomplished in death what she could not in life—the complete dissolution of the one alliance that could keep her group out of power in the state. Yet answering violence has not materialized and is unlikely to, partly because there has been in Punjab no general breakdown of legitimate law enforcement as there was in 1946, partly because of the very convictions reflected in the sadness of the Sikh victims, and partly because there are too many cross-cutting bases for unity. Despite appearances, ethnic and religious conflicts do not arise spontaneously in India. Although riots often wear caste, ethnic, or religious colors, these seldom provide the real motivation—which is usually political and, beneath that, economic. In Punjab, Hindus and Sikhs continue to have nothing to gain from attacking one another and much to gain from cooperation. Moreover, the personal affiliations of many individuals are not clearly one or the other.

Rajiv Gandhi's own behavior as prime minister, thus far, provides further assurances. He moved quickly and firmly to end the rioting, seems to have eliminated some of the more conspicuous instances of cronyism, and has consistently and carefully framed his public declarations (insofar as they have appeared in the American press) in terms of the basic values common to all sects rather than characterizations that separate one group from another or that identify his opponents with sedition and his followers with the nation. Yet he is still largely an unknown quantity, and much remains to be seen. It is worrisome that the election was held so quickly, and that the Punjabi leadership was not released from jail—and, of course, that elections were not held in Punjab itself.

THE FUTURE

Martial law and censorship in Punjab, the assassination, and the relatively smooth election and accession of Rajiv Gandhi to the office of prime minister have each, in their own way, provided distractions from the underlying economic and constitutional issues raised by the Punjab crisis. Ultimately, however, these issues will have to be addressed. Martial law will have to be ended in Punjab and there will have to be elections. The elections will be corrupt or clean. If clean, they almost surely will return officers who will once again speak for the long-standing economic needs and interests of the state, and their demands will have to be answered.

Assuming that Rajiv Gandhi will not pursue his mother's policy of personalized centralism, it is quite possible that the drive for federalism in Punjab will lose force if the basic economic problems are eased —if more industries are licensed or if licensing is greatly relaxed, if support prices are raised to provide a real return over costs, if there is more respect for traditional family concepts and other traditional ideas and for the interests bound up with them, if in general there is less central meddling in Punjab's use of its resources—and if at a national level Rajiv Gandhi adheres to his apparent commitment to avoid the politically self-serving and antidemocratic use of such powers as preventive detention and President's Rule. Yet in the long run, I do not think this will suffice. Just as the Akali demand for the division into Punjab and Haryana turned out to be productive for both new regions, so the demand for "federalism" seems to me most likely to do just what it is intended to do—to increase the strength of democracy and the vigor of economic life in India as a whole. India is much too complex and diverse for all the needed new major public or private initiatives to have to go through a cumbersome central apparatus before they can be implemented (licensed, taxed, allowed to raise capital or import equipment, and so on), yet that is exactly the situation under the present constitution. It would be far more efficient and fruitful, and provide less opportunity for corruption, to allow initiatives to be undertaken locally and to move them into central purview later, if required. Such federalism, including the reversal of reserved powers, would permit simplification of the Indian Constitution itself as a legal document that is supposed to provide basic guidance. It is now so crowded with exceptions to basic principles intended to provide the central government latitude to exercise broad control over economic development that it is virtually unintelligible to ordinary well-educated people. Equally, federalism would provide greater political power and discretion to the increasingly educated and organized rural population, because of its greater prominence in the state legislatures.

The Punjab crisis has not, fundamentally, been a clash between Sikhs and Hindus, nor between Sikhs and Indira Gandhi, nor between Akalis and Indira Gandhi. It has been a clash between two visions of the future and of India's proper political and social constitution. The basic questions remain unanswered.

Mark S. Steinitz

Insurgents, Terrorists and the Drug Trade

Although traditional criminal organizations continue to dominate the international narcotics trade, a growing number of insurgent and terrorist groups from all parts of the political spectrum and globe have obtained money and other benefits from illegal drug-related activities in recent years.[1] These activities range widely from providing protection to drug dealers to retail trafficking to outright control over drug-producing regions. The list of insurgents and terrorists heavily involved in the drug trade remains relatively small compared to the total number of militant subnational groups, but it includes several major organizations, especially in South America and Southeast Asia. Given the lucrative nature of the drug business, even limited participation can yield sizable profits to help finance armed struggle.

In a broad sense, the increased insurgent and terrorist connections to this illicit activity are a result of a world-wide expansion in the demand for drugs, which has opened up new opportunities for what might be termed non-traditional suppliers—to include political parties and even some sovereign governments.[2] A recent UN report noted that drug use has become so pervasive as to threaten the very security of some countries.[3]

Another key factor, however, has been the tendency for insurgency, terrorism, and the drug trade to be located in roughly the same areas. In several important instances, shifts in the pattern of the global drug trade have brought large-scale narcotics production into areas where insurgents or terrorists were already active. Conversely, in several other cases, political changes have brought insurgency and

Reprinted excerpts from *Washington Quarterly*, Fall 1985, with the kind permission of the editor.

terrorism into regions where the cultivation and processing of substantial amounts of narcotics were well-established.

Despite conflicting long-range aims and initial antipathy or suspicions, insurgent-terrorist groups and those involved in the drug business share many short-term goals and can be of mutual value. This frequently—though not always—facilitates cooperation especially when co-location of insurgency, terrorism, and the drug trade occurs over any extended period. Most co-location has occurred in remote regions, explaining why the narcotics-related activity of larger rural-based insurgents tends to be more systematic and extensive than that of smaller urban terrorist groups. The latter are subject to greater police harassment and generally have no "liberated zones" in which to carry out various drug-related activities.[4] Rural insurgency and drug production (especially cultivation and processing) both thrive in rugged areas where the central government is weak and where a nationally-integrated economic infrastructure is lacking.

Paradoxically, increased insurgent-terrorist activity in the drug market could in some ways work to the advantage of anti-narcotics efforts as well as counter-insurgency and counter-terrorism programs. Overall, however, the involvement of these groups in the drug trade will serve to complicate government measures against narcotics trafficking and subnational political violence.

Evidence of Involvement

Latin America. Until the late 1970s there were few insurgent or terrorist ties to the drug business in this region. Typical of the violence that plagues many Latin American societies, feuding between these groups and the criminal underworld still erupts.[5] Nevertheless, insurgent and terrorist connections to the area's thriving drug business have become stronger in recent years. Most of these links occur in Colombia, which has been the principal supplier of cocaine and marijuana to the United States.[6] The group most active in Colombia's extensive narcotics industry is the Revolutionary Armed Forces of Colombia (FARC), long identified as the militant arm of the Colombian Communist Party (PCC). A largely rural-based organization, FARC has roughly 5,000 active members and supporters, divided into 23–28 guerrilla fronts, approximately half of which operate in coca leaf or marijuana growing areas.

FARC's involvement in the drug trade began slowly but now encompasses a wide scope of activities. The group regularly collects protection money from coca and marijuana growers in its operating territory, sometimes receiving as much as 10 percent of the profit. One front is believed to have obtained $3.8 million per month in taxing the coca industry. The 13th Front, located in the south of Huila Department, and the 4th Front, located in Putumayo Department, have been dealing with coca traffickers to obtain arms and ammunition. FARC leaders ordered one of their chief operatives in Caqueta Department to maintain direct control over narcotics trafficking activities and to collect set quotas from drug dealers.

FARC also guarantees access to a number of clandestine airfields vital to drug traffickers. Moreover, the group also appears to engage in some limited coca cultivation and perhaps cocaine refining. In November 1983 the Colombian Army discovered 90 hectares of coca and a processing laboratory next to an abandoned FARC camp in southern Colombia. According to the U.S. Embassy in Bogota, FARC's overall cooperative relationship with Colombia's drug barons appears to have been sanctioned by the PCC at its Seventh National Conference in 1982. Citing an informed source, a leading Colombian newspaper recently reported that Carlos Lehder, one of the country's leading traffickers, has offered to pay FARC for protection services.

Several other militant organizations in Colombia have benefited in one fashion or another from the drug trade. The leftist 19th of April Movement (M-19), which has about 900 activists divided into both urban and rural cells, cooperated with leading Colombian drug trafficker Jaime Guillot-Lara. He supplied the group with weapons in the early 1980s and in return received assistance in his drug smuggling enterprise from high-ranking Cuban officials. In January 1985 drug kingpin Lehder claimed that he had established friendly contacts with M-19. This is in sharp contrast to M-19's earlier antagonistic relationship with the traffickers, a result of the group's penchant for kidnapping the relatives of wealthy drug smugglers. Two other left-wing Colombian groups, the National Liberation Army (ELN) and the Popular Liberation Army (EPL), are believed to levy protection taxes on coca and marijuana growers in their areas of control. In May 1984 the Colombian press reported that 24 ELN guerrillas were arrested in possession of 150 metric tons of marijuana.[8]

Elsewhere in Latin America, there has been considerable speculation about the relationship between Peru's mystic and Maoist Sendero Luminoso (Shining Path or SL) and that country's coca cartels. Available evidence suggests that some local SL commanders probably extort money from coca growers. The Peruvian government recently reported that it had broken up a major cocaine trafficking ring that financed terrorists, presumably SL.[9] Nevertheless, despite the potential for expanded links, the group's connection to the drug trade presently appears less structured and extensive than FARC's.

SL's recent operations in the coca-growing upper Huallaga valley appear to have less to do with gaining drug money than with taking political advantage of anti-government and anti-U.S. sentiment in an area where a joint Peruvian-U.S. drug control project was under way.[10] Sendero's avowedly Maoist ideology may also be slowing its involvement in the drug trade, given the Chinese leader's ferocious crackdown on narcotics abuse in China after 1949. Whatever the actual evidence, however, most Peruvians seem convinced that SL is tied up in the drug trade. Over 75 percent of respondents in a recent opinion poll believed a close relationship exists between traffickers and terrorists.[11]

A number of right-wing European terrorists and neo-Nazis have been employed as "enforcers" by Bolivia's cocaine barons. One of these neo-fascists, Pierluigi Pagliai, shot by Bolivian police in 1982, was wanted by Italian authorities for his alleged role in the 1980 Bologna railway station bombing that claimed over 80 lives.[12] In late 1984 the Bolivian government announced it was searching for an Argentine terrorist who had been hired by Bolivian drug traffickers to kill the U.S. ambassador in La Paz.[13]

There is considerable evidence that the anti-Castro Cuban exile terrorist group Omega 7 has links to the drug business. In 1981 a top member of the group was arrested in possession of a large quantity of marijuana. During the 1984 trial of Eduardo Arocena, the alleged leader of Omega 7, numerous details emerged showing that Arocena had agreed to allow drug dealers in Florida to use group members as "hit-men."[14]

Southeast Asia. In 1984 Burma produced an estimated 630 metric tons of opium, making the "hermit kingdom" the world's largest single source of illegal opium. Between one-half and two-thirds of this harvest occurred in areas controlled by leftist and ethnic separatist insurgents, mainly the Burmese Communist Party (BCP) and, to a lesser extent, the Kachin Independence Organization (KIO).[15]

The BCP oversees the level of opium production in areas under its control, especially in the Shan State, and collects protection taxes and sometimes exacts forced deliveries from farmers. BCP units traveling in caravans transport raw opium to heroin refineries near the Thai-Burmese border.

Since late 1983 the BCP has begun to establish refineries to convert opium into heroin and engage in direct sales of refined opiates to middlemen. BCP's limited moves into the refining stage have brought the group into increased conflict with the Shan United Army (SUA), a "warlord" organization that has dominated the border refining area in recent years. Although once a viable insurgency, SUA now concentrates its resources on the drug trade and is a good example of the long-term corrupting influence of narcotics money on a political movement.[16]

Insurgent-terrorist links to the trade elsewhere in Southeast Asia are weaker than in Burma. The Communist Party of Thailand (CPT) has given some indications of willingness to engage in trafficking, but has been badly battered by Thai security forces over the last several years.[17] Heroin production laboratories are located on either side of the rugged Thai-Malaysian border where leftist Malaysian insurgents are based. In the mid-1970s there were unconfirmed reports of Malaysian Communist ties to heroin refining, but no hard evidence of linkage has emerged. In Laos, some resistance groups operate near poppy-growing areas. Although hard evidence is lacking, press reports on the location of drug seizures from Lao refugees offer some circumstantial evidence that the groups may be profiting from the drug trade.[18] A recent Philippine government "white paper" charged that the New People's Army derives revenue from marijuana cultivation.[19]

South Asia. Between 1980 and 1983 opium production increased from an estimated 200 metric tons to 400–575 metric tons in war-torn Afghanistan where *mujahedin* guerrillas are waging a bloody struggle against Soviet invaders and their Afghan clients.[20] Much of the opium cultivation takes place in eastern Afghanistan where insurgent activity is greatest. The international press has frequently contained stories that the rebels derive funding from the drug trade and use narcotics sales to undermine Soviet fighting ability. In late 1983 a spokesman for the U.S. Drug Enforcement Administration (DEA) was reported as stating that the *mujahedin* were financing their struggle against the Soviets at least partly through the sale of opium. The official, however, provided no specific details of the insurgents' involvement.[21]

Since roughly 1983, Sri Lankan nationals have become active in smuggling Pakistani-produced heroin to Western Europe and Canada. Arrests for heroin trafficking in Sri Lanka rose astronomically from four in 1981 to over 500 in the first half of 1984, according to the chairman of the country's National Dangerous Drugs Control Board.[22] In July 1984 Colombo's Minister of National Security publicly denounced Tamil separatists for involvement in international drug smuggling. In March 1985, Italian authorities issued 100 arrest warrants for Tamil drug traffickers, some of whom were connected with the separatist struggle, according to the Italian public prosecutor in the case.[23]

The Middle East. Lebanon is the world's leading producer of hashish and much of the 1984 yield of an estimated 700 metric tons was grown in the fertile Syrian-controlled Bekaa Valley primarily by Shiite Muslim farmers. Heroin laboratories also are believed to operate in the area. From the Bekaa, the hashish is shipped to various regional and Western markets through Lebanon's system of illegal ports. A portion of the heroin is smuggled via Damascus airport.[24]

Although some of the armed factions vying for power in fragmented Lebanon resemble warlord groups or private militias more than standard insurgencies, nearly all of them—Palestinians, Phalangists, Druze, and Shiites—obtain revenue from the drug industry, either directly or by protecting the contraband as it is transported through their areas of influence. The existence of this huge drug economy, estimated at $1 billion in 1981, remains one of the major obstacles to the restoration of central government fiscal authority in Lebanon.[25]

Armenian terrorists operate in numerous countries, but they frequently are based in Lebanon, especially Beirut where members of the Armenian community figure prominently in the drug traffic. As the French press recently asserted, it seems likely that at least some of these drug profits find their way into terrorist coffers.[26]

In 1980 Noubar Sofoyan, an Armenian drug smuggler with Lebanese citizenship, was indicted in the U.S. for heroin smuggling. Sofoyan had been arrested in Switzerland in 1976 for allegedly helping fund right-wing Armenian terrorists who bombed a Turkish installation in Zurich. In 1981 he was arrested in Greece on drug charges, but extradited to Lebanon where he was released, most likely because of pressure exerted on the Minister of Justice.[27]

Also in 1981, Swedish police arrested a group of Armenian narcotics smugglers who were also in possession of documents and publications linking them to a leftist Armenian terrorist group, the Armenian Secret Army for the Liberation of Armenia (ASALA). The smugglers were also linked to Armenian traffickers in the United States. Although the Swedes were never able to prove that the arrested traffickers had passed money to terrorists, ASALA issued several threats against Swedish interests on behalf of the jailed drug dealers and may have been behind an unsuccessful attempt to help one of them escape custody.[28]

In early 1983 the Turkish press, citing Interpol sources, claimed that nine kilograms of heroin seized on Cyprus belonged to a Greek smuggling ring that helped fund ASALA. The Turkish press also claimed that one of the ASALA terrorists who participated in the June 1983 attack on the Istanbul covered bazaar later hid at the home of a drug smuggler.[29]

Europe. In the late 1970s and early 1980s Turkey became the scene of a booming heroin industry geared toward supplying European addicts. Fueled by opium and morphine bases from Pakistan, Afghanistan, and Iran, most of the Turkish heroin refining is carried out in rugged southeastern Turkey by Kurds. Although criminal organizations and families dominate this trade, Turkish officials report a degree of overlap between the traffickers and Kurdish separatists in the region. The separatists have been particularly eager to trade drugs for weapons, according to Turkish authorities. In January 1985 the Turkish press reported that Kurdish insurgents had received funding from a known drug smuggler. In May 1985 Behet Canturk, a convicted major drugs and arms smuggler, went on trial in Turkey on charges of separatism and belonging to an outlawed Kurdish organization.[30]

Urban terrorists in Turkey have also derived income from the heroin trade. In 1981 an extensive investigation by Istanbul police into the activities of the left-wing Dev-Sol (Revolutionary Left) revealed that the group engaged in heroin sales and used the proceeds to purchase arms.[31] Right-wing terrorists, especially the Grey Wolves, also obtained money for weapons through heroin sales.[32] The widely publicized investigations into the activities of convicted papal assailant Mehmet Ali Agca have revealed the close links between the Grey Wolves and the Turkish drug-and-gun-running Mafia —the latter aided and abetted by Bulgarian intelligence services.[33] The activities of urban terrorists in Turkey—presumably including those related to the drug business—have declined over the last few years as Turkish enforcement efforts have increased.

Italian judicial authorities believe that Maurizio Folini, a left-wing Italian terrorist, was a key member of a smuggling network that procured arms for the Red Brigades (BR) from Middle Eastern sources in the early 1980s. The network also reportedly engaged in heroin sales and sometimes bartered narcotics for guns.[34] Although further evidence of outright drug dealing is scarce, left-wing Italian terrorists have apparently sought to forge working relations with the country's various organized crime groups, all of whom are involved in drug trafficking. According to one repentant terrorist who belonged to *Potere Operaio* (Workers' Power), his organization had an informal agreement with the underworld in the late 1970s to kidnap for ransom, rob banks, and commit other thefts. The spoils were to be split evenly.[35]

The BR column in Naples has made several overtures to that city's criminal band, the Camorra. In July 1982, after assassinating a Naples police chief and his driver, the BR issued a communique describing the Camorra as an "extra-legal proletariat"—a flattering term in terrorist parlance.[36] Several months later the BR failed in an attempt to stage a massive escape from a Naples prison that housed many Camorra prisoners.[37]

For its part Italian organized crime seems somewhat ambivalent about the terrorists. BR activity in Naples always seems to increase police patrols that invariably disrupt Camorra rackets. The Sicilian Mafia has not permitted BR activity on the island. Nevertheless, many Italians believe criminals and terrorists can and have worked together. In late 1984 an Italian parliamentary committee stated its belief that the BR and Camorra had agreed to collaborate in the killing of particularly energetic magistrates and police officials.[38] As the BR, decimated by extensive personnel loses, increases its recruiting among convicts and less educated youths, its cooperation with criminal groups may likewise increase.

Drug abuse in the Basque region of northern Spain has grown and so have accusations that the separatist Basque Fatherland and Freedom (ETA) is facilitating the flow of narcotics into the region. One specialist in international terrorism has charged that the influx of hard drugs into Spain is almost entirely the work of ETA, which obtains the narcotics in Colombia, ships them through Brussels and Paris, and then into Spain.[39]

Although unwilling to go quite so far, sources knowledgeable in Basque affairs contend that ETA does play an important role in the drug scene in the Basque area.[40] In November 1984 Catholic bishops in northern Spain, who are not particularly known for their pro-Madrid views, issued a pastoral letter criticizing ETA for involvement in the drug traffic, adding that Spanish security services also used drugs as payment for information.[41]

Involvement in the drug traffic would entail risks for ETA given the conservative social attitudes in the Basque region. Nevertheless, ETA is reported to be short of money partly because more Basque businessmen are refusing to pay "revolutionary taxes." Additionally, ETA finds it more difficult to collect taxes from those willing to pay. The group had traditionally taken delivery of payments in its southern France sanctuary, but increased French police pressure has made it more difficult for ETA to operate there.

ETA for its part, denies involvement in drug trafficking. In 1982 the group warned that it would begin killing alleged narcotics dealers in the Basque region and has carried out that threat at least several times in recent years.[42]

NOTES

1. The terms terrorism and insurgency are used to describe two forms of systematic, low-level political violence conducted by militant subnational groups. The difference between the two is difficult to define precisely. The terrorist, however, has little hope of inflicting a significant military defeat on an opponent regime and relies almost exclusively on the psychological impact of violence. His targets are chosen for their symbolic value and are often civilians. The terrorist avoids set battles with security forces, has no standing force in the field, rarely wears distinguishing insignia during operations, and shows little interest or ability in occupying a significant portion of territory. Although relying at times on the psychological impact of violence, the insurgent seeks primarily to affect political behavior through the material impact of violence and selects targets for their instrumental value. The insurgent is willing to engage security forces at least on the small unit level, wears some type of uniform, has a permanent force in the field and generally controls territory, at least in the latter stages of struggle.
2. Colombian drug trafficker Carlos Lehder set up his own neo-fascist party, the Latin National Movement. See, *Latin America Weekly Report*, October 28, 1983, p. 8. In February 1985 a leading supporter of El Salvador's rightist ARENA party was arrested in Texas in possession of nearly $6

million, which U.S. Customs agents alleged had come from drug sales. Some U.S. officials close to the case believe at least part of the money was to be used for political purposes. See, Craig Pyes and Laurie Becklund, "Inside Dope in El Salvador." *New Republic*, (April 15, 1985), pp. 15–20. For charges that governments in Bolivia (1980–81), Bulgaria, Cuba, Nicaragua, and Vietnam have engaged in or condoned trafficking as a matter of policy see, U.S. Department of State, Narcotics Profile Paper: Bolivia (1983); Testimony of Deputy Assistant Secretary Clyde D. Taylor, Bureau of International Narcotics Matters, Department of State to the Committee on Foreign Relations and the Committee on the Judiciary, Joint Hearing, May 14, 1985; "Vietnam Turns to Narcotics to Pay its Bills." *Wall Street Journal*, March 8, 1984.

3. *Washington Post*, January 18, 1985.
4. The dilemmas of operating in an urban area are described in, Walter Laqueur, *Guerrilla* (Boston and Toronto: Little Brown and Company, 1976), pp. 350, 404; Richard Gillespie, *Soldiers of Peron: Argentina's Montoneros* (New York: Oxford University Press, 1982), p. 270.
5. Royal Canadian Mounted Police, *RCMP National Drug Intelligence Estimate, 1983* (Ottawa: Public Relations Branch, RCMP, 1984), p. 38.
6. The National Narcotics Intelligence Consumers Committee (NNICC), *Narcotics Intelligence Estimate, 1983: The Supply of Drugs to the U.S. Illicit Market from Foreign and Domestic Sources in 1983 (with Projections through 1984)* (Washington, D.C.: GPO, 1984), pp. 9, 18.
7. Taylor statement; unclassified cable of March 19, 1984, from U.S. Embassy Bogota reported in *New York Times*, March 21, 1984; *El Espectador* (Bogota), May 5, 1985.
8. Statement of David L. Westrate, Deputy Assistant Administrator, Drug Enforcement Administration, Department of Justice, on Relationship of Drug Trafficking and Terrorism Before the Committee on Foreign Relations and Committee on the Judiciary, May 14, 1985; *El Tiempo* (Bogota), May 13, 1984.
9. Cynthia McClintock, "Why Peasants Rebel: The Case of Sendero Luminoso," *World Politics*, p. 37, no. 1 (October 1984), p. 81; Agence France Presse, July 13, 1985.
10. Taylor statement.
11. *El Comercio* (Lima), February 9, 1985.
12. *New York Times*, October 24, 1982.
13. Agence France Presse, December 8, 1984.
14. *Christian Science Monitor*, October 30, 1981: United Press International, September 5, 1984; *New York Times*, September 18, 1984.
15. Department of State, Bureau of International Narcotics Matters, International Narcotics Control Strategy Report, 1985. Reprint Edition (February 1, 1985), p. 140; NNICC, pp. 42–43.
16. Taylor Statement.
17. *Ibid.*
18. *Naeo Na* (Bangkok), August 29, 1984; *Matichon* (Bangkok), February 2, 1985.
19. UPI, May 13, 1985.
20. NNICC, 38.
21. *Washington Post*, December 17, 1983.
22. *New York Times*, October 4, 1984.
23. British Broadcasting Corporation, July 13, 1984; UPI, March 18, 1985.
24. NNICC, 3, 41.

25. Adam Zagorin, "A House Divided," *Foreign Policy*, no. 48 (Fall 1982), p. 116.
26. *Le Matin* (Paris), cited in *Armenian Reporter*, February 7, 1985.
27. Westrate statement.
28. Dr. Tarik Somer, "Armenian Terrorism and the Narcotics Traffic," in *International Terrorism and the Drug Connection* (Ankara: Ankara University Press, 1984), 23–25. The title of the book is somewhat misleading in that this article is the only one in the volume that treats the terrorism-narcotics link.
29. *Gunes* (Istanbul), March 16, 1983; *Hurriyet* (Istanbul), August 27, 1983.
30. *Milliyet* (Istanbul), January 15, 1985; *ibid.*, May 14, 1985.
31. *Hurriyet*, February 19, 1981.
32. *Washington Post*, July 3, 1983.
33. Ugur Mumcu, *Papa, Mafya, Agca* (Ankara: Tekin Publishers, 1984); Paul Henze, *The Plot to Kill the Pope* (New York: Charles Scribner's Sons, 1983); Claire Sterling, *The Time of the Assassins* (New York: Holt, Rinehart and Winston, 1983).
34. Henze, 73.
35. Sterling, "Italian Terrorists: Life and Death in a Violent Generation," *Encounter* 57, no. 1 (July 1981), p. 29.
36. BR communique, July 19, 1982.
37. Associated Press, October 5, 1982.
38. This is the conclusion of the committee investigating the 1981 kidnapping and subsequent release of former Naples Christian Democratic Provincial Secretary Ciro Cirillo by the BR.
39. Neil C. Livingstone, *The War Against Terrorism* (Lexington, Massachusetts and Toronto: D.C. Heath and Company, 1982), p. 25.
40. *El Alcazar* (Madrid), April 27, 1984.
41. Reuter, November 20, 1984.
42. *El Pais* (Madrid), August 9, 1982.

Libya Under Qadhafi: A Pattern of Aggression

Libyan Involvement in Terrorism

Qadhafi has used terrorism as one of the primary instruments of his foreign policy and supports radical groups that use terrorist tactics. Tripoli operates numerous training sites for foreign dissident groups that provide instruction in the use of explosive devices, hijacking,

Reprinted from "Libya Under Qadhafi: A Pattern of Aggression," Special Report No. 138, U.S. Department of State, January 1986.

assassination, and various commando and guerrilla techniques. It also provides terrorist training outside Libya and abuses diplomatic privilege by storing arms and explosives at its diplomatic establishments, as demonstrated by the shootout at its embassy in London in April 1984.

The main targets of direct Libyan terrorist activities have been expatriate Libyan dissidents and leading officials of moderate Arab and African governments. In almost all cases, the assassins kill their victims with handguns, often provided by the Libyan diplomatic establishment in their country. Qadhafi generally uses Libyans for anti-exile operations; for other types of attacks he tends to employ surrogates or mercenaries.

The Libyan Government in 1980 began a concerted effort to assassinate anti-Qadhafi exiles. By the time the first phase ended in 1981, 11 Libyan dissidents living abroad had been murdered. Libya in 1985 sponsored five attacks against exiled Libyan dissidents. Targets of these attacks lived in Greece, West Germany, Cyprus, Italy, and Austria.

Qadhafi has at least twice tried to murder Libyan exiles in Egypt only to have his agents intercepted by Egyptian security. In November 1984, Egypt fooled Qadhafi into believing that his hired agents had assassinated former Libyan Prime Minister Bakoush. After the Libyan press acknowledged Tripoli's responsibility for the murder, Egypt revealed the sting: the four Libyan agents were in custody, and the pictures of the alleged victim were fake. In November 1985, another four-man Libyan team was arrested during an attempted attack against a gathering of exiles near Cairo. After the arrests, Egypt released audio and video tapes incriminating Libya.

Libya also has plotted anti-exile attacks in the United States. A Libyan exile in Colorado was shot and wounded by a Libyan-hired assassin in 1981. In May 1984, the FBI arrested two Libyans near Philadelphia for attempting to buy silenced handguns—the usual Libyan assassination weapon. A year later, in May 1985, a Libyan diplomat at the United Nations was declared *persona non grata* and a ring of nonofficial Libyans was broken up in connection with a plot to kill Libyan dissidents in four states.

Qadhafi also targets moderate Arab governments for their refusal to continue the military struggle against Israel and for their links to the West. There is evidence of Libyan-backed assassination plots against President Mubarak of Egypt. For example, those arrested after last November's attempted attack on Libyan exiles in Egypt stated that Qadhafi's target list included Mubarak. Former Sudanese President Nimeiri has also been targeted by Libya. We believe that Qadhafi has added Jordan's King Hussein and Iraq's Saddam Husayn to his list because of restored ties to Cairo and Washington, respectively.

Qadhafi also has been implicated in plots to assassinate other moderate heads of state. In September 1984, the Chadian Government uncovered a Libyan-sponsored plot in which a briefease bomb was to explode during a Cabinet meeting chaired by Chadian President Habre. More recently, Zairian officials thwarted a Libyan-sponsored plot against President Mobutu in September 1985.

Libyan Links to Middle East Radicals

Longstanding Libyan support for radical Palestinian groups is growing. Qadhafi has provided safe haven, money, and arms to these groups—including the Popular Front for the Liberation of Palestine–General Command, the Fatah dissidents, and the notorious Abu Nidal group. Training for Palestinians and other radicals frequently takes place at several locations in Libya. These anti-Arafat Palestinians are widely engaged in terrorist activities and focus their terrorist activity on Israel and the occupied territories.

More recently, however, Libya's support has broadened to include logistic support for terrorist operations. For example, Libya provided passports to the Abu Nidal members responsible for the attack on the El Al counter in Vienna. The Abu Nidal group is particularly appealing to Qadhafi because of its track record of successful terrorist operations. Abu Nidal's targeting of moderate Palestinians and moderate Arab leaders is consistent with Libya's antipathy toward participants in the peace process. According to Libyan press reports, Abu Nidal met with Qadhafi in Libya at least twice in 1985. Abu Nidal also gave an interview in Tripoli to a German publication last year and met with Qadhafi's chief lieutenant, Abd al-Salam Jallud. In addition, Libya has provided sanctuary, training assistance, and financial support to the Abu Nidal organization, and there are reliable press and other reports that its headquarters has been moved to Libya. The evidence points to Libya's having been involved in the bloody hijacking of Egyptair 648.

Libya is trying to improve ties to other regional terrorist groups.

Qadhafi would also like closer links to Tehran's terrorist effort. He announced a "strategic alliance" with Iran last summer, which he hopes to use as a foundation for joint operational planning for terrorist attacks against various regional foes. He also supports Egyptian and Tunisian dissidents.

Libya also provided refuge for the notorious international terrorist Carlos, who has headed a network of terrorists for hire. His group was responsible for numerous vicious attacks including the hostage-taking of OPEC (Organization of Petroleum Exporting Countries) oil ministers in Vienna in 1975.

Libyan Terrorism Against the United States

During the past 18 months, Qadhafi has made several public references to expanding his terrorism campaign to cover U.S. targets. In a June 1984 speech, for example, he told his Libyan audience that "we are capable of exporting terrorism to the heart of America." During a speech last September observing the 16th anniversary of his takeover, Qadhafi remarked that "we have the right to fight America, and we have the right to export terrorism to them. . . ." Qadhafi recently threatened in a press conference on January 2 to "pursue U.S. citizens in their country and streets" if the United States takes action in response to Libya's alleged involvement in the Rome and Vienna terrorist attacks.

There have been several instances over the years of Libyan-sponsored attacks against U.S. interests. These examples include the sacking of our Embassy in Tripoli in 1979 and the discovery by Sudanese authorities of a Libyan plot to blow up the American Embassy Club in Khartoum by planting explosives in stereo speakers. U.S. personnel also have been on Qadhafi's target list, as indicated by the plan in 1977 to assassinate our ambassador in Cairo.

Radicalism in the Arab World

Qadhafi's foremost ambition is to dominate and unite the Arab world. He frequently compares himself to Garibaldi or Bismarck and has justified his use of violence and terrorism against moderate Arab regimes as necessary to achieve Arab unity.

Egypt, because of its peace treaty with Israel, is a special target.

Libyan agents have been active in Egypt since the 1970s, and Qadhafi has offered support to various opponents of the Egyptian Government. In October 1981, immediately after President Sadat was assassinated, Qadhafi called on Egyptians to overthrow their government; within a week, at Cairo International Airport two bombs exploded that had been concealed in luggage unloaded from a flight originating in Tripoli.

More recently, Qadhafi has sought to embarrass the government of President Mubarak and undermine the Egyptian economy. In July 1984, a Libyan ship commanded by a senior Libyan naval commando laid mines in the Red Sea and Gulf of Suez that damaged 18 merchant ships. In May 1985, the Egyptians thwarted a plot by radical Palestinians backed by Libya to destroy the U.S. Embassy in Cairo with a truck bomb. Last summer Qadhafi expelled over 10,000 Egyptian workers in Libya—confiscating their savings and most of their belongings—in what was, in part, an effort to place a greater burden on the strained Egyptian economy. Also during 1985, Cairo captured several teams of Libyan-supported Egyptian dissidents who reported that their plan was to destabilize the Mubarak government through sabotage and inciting civil unrest.

Sudan also is a priority target. Qadhafi has long offered training and support to Sudanese dissidents and sponsored acts of sabotage against the government of former President Nimeiri. He was a major source of arms and money for southern Sudanese rebels who began a guerrilla war against the central government 2 years ago. In February 1983, the Sudanese, with Egyptian assistance, thwarted a Libyan-sponsored coup attempt, and in March 1984, a Libyan TU-22 bombed Omdurman, Sudan, in a failed attempt to destroy a radio station there that broadcast condemnations of Qadhafi's policies by Libyan oppositionists.

Since Nimeiri's fall from power, Qadhafi has exploited the resumption of diplomatic ties to Sudan to build a network for subversion inimical to Sudan's efforts to establish a parliamentary democracy. A number of known Libyan terrorists have been assigned to the Libyan People's Bureau (Embassy) and the Libyan airline office in Khartoum. Qadhafi also has provided arms, funding, training, and probably direction to the Sudanese Revolutionary Committees, a small group in Sudan dedicated to establishing a government on the Libyan model in Sudan. In May, a planeload of these dissidents arrived in Khartoum armed with assault rifles.

Qadhafi also is working to expand his influence in the countries of the Arab Maghreb. Qadhafi refuses to negotiate with Algeria to determine the correct location of the Libyan-Algerian border. Perhaps angered over President Bendjedid's moderation, Qadhafi reportedly provides money to Algerian dissidents such as Ahmed Ben Bella.

In Tunisia, Qadhafi has long sought to bring down the pro-Western government of Habib Bourguiba. In 1980, Libyan-supported guerrillas attacked the southern Tunisian mining town of Gafsa; when France offered its support to Tunis, Libyan mobs burned both the French and Tunisian Embassies while security forces stood idly by. Following bread riots in Tunisia in January 1984, saboteurs originating in Libya dynamited a pipeline near the Libyan-Tunisian border. In an effort to exacerbate social tensions this past year, Qadhafi expelled over 30,000 Tunisian workers and confiscated their property. In September, when Tunisian newspapers attacked Qadhafi for the expulsions, a Libyan diplomat attempted to mail letter bombs to the critical journalists. Several exploded, wounding two postal workers and causing Tunis to sever diplomatic relations.

Libya is staunchly opposed to the Middle East peace process, and Qadhafi is doing all he can to subvert it. In Lebanon, Libyan arms and money have flowed to different militias and Palestinian groups actively opposed to the government of President Gemayel. Qadhafi has been especially eager to undermine the influence of PLO (Palestine Liberation Organization) Chairman Yasir Arafat because Qadhafi perceives him as too willing to consider a negotiated settlement with Israel. As a result, Qadhafi has thrown his support to radical Palestinian groups—including the Fatah Revolutionary Council led by Abu Nidal—that advocate continued war against Israel. Since 1981 Qadhafi has shipped these groups items as prosaic as uniforms and as powerful as tanks and BM-21 multiple rocket launchers. In 1984, Libyan troops participated in the Syrian-backed assault on Arafat's forces in northern Lebanon.

The Persian Gulf also is an arena for Libyan meddling. Qadhafi has allied himself with Iran in its war against Iraq and has provided Tehran with T-55 tanks, antitank and antiaircraft artillery, ammunition, and even Scud rockets. In addition, Libya provides arms and money to Kurdish separatists in northern Iraq and to the antigovernment group, the "Union of Iraqi Democrats." In 1984 and 1985, Libyan agents attempted to disrupt the Islamic pilgrimage ceremonies in Saudi Arabia; in 1984 entire planeloads of Libyan "pilgrims" were discovered to be carrying arms. Libya continues to enjoy good relations with and has provided support to the National Democratic Front that operates out of Marxist South Yemen against the government of President Salih in North Yemen. Although Libya restored diplomatic relations with Somalia last May, Qadhafi has not severed his relationship with Somali opposition groups he has long supported.

Involvement in Sub-Saharan Africa

Tripoli views black Africa as a principal arena for forging a group of anti-Western radical states that will strengthen Libyan influence in international forums and confer upon Qadhafi status as a world leader. Qadhafi's aggressiveness has been strengthened by the propensity of the international community to ignore his often blatant disregard for the sovereignty of small African nations.

Chad, of course, is the most egregious example. In 1973 Qadhafi forcibly annexed the northern portion of Chad known as the Aozou Strip. Throughout the 1970s, Libya supported various tribal and guerrilla groups in Chad in a bid to install a pliable regime in N'Djamena. Having failed to achieve this indirectly, in October 1980 the Libyan army entered Chad and attempted to impose a union between the two countries. The Libyan occupation force withdrew in November 1981, but returned in 1983 when the pro-Libyan Chadian leader Goukouni Oueddei was ousted by current President Hissein Habre. Only intervention by French armed forces confined the Libyan occupation to the northern 40% of Chad. French forces were withdrawn in the fall of 1984, but Qadhafi reneged on an agreement reached with President Mitterrand and continues to occupy northern Chad with an army of several thousand.

The drought-battered countries of the Sahel offer Qadhafi many opportunities for meddling. Qadhafi continues to provide arms and training to the nomadic Tuareg tribesmen in an effort to undermine the Governments of Mali and Niger.

Qadhafi also is determined to topple President Mobutu of Zaire. Qadhafi is motivated by hostility to Kinshasa's close ties to the West, its recognition of Israel, and its support for Chadian President Habre. Qadhafi also is aware of Zaire's role as a leading producer of cobalt and other strategic minerals. Tripoli provides training in sabotage and small arms to several different guerrilla groups including the

National Front for the Liberation of the Congo and the Congolese National Movement. Libyan diplomatic facilities in countries bordering Zaire are centers of support for these groups.

MEDDLING IN LATIN AMERICA AND THE CARIBBEAN

Qadhafi's determination to strike at U.S. interests and to spread his philosophy of revolution has led to a more aggressive Libyan posture in Latin America. Although many governments and groups in this region are wary of Qadhafi, some are willing to accept his financial and military support.

Tripoli views Nicaragua as its base in Central America and accordingly seeks to strengthen the Sandinista dictatorship in Managua. In addition to several hundred million dollars in economic assistance, Qadhafi's support to the Sandinistas has included antiaircraft guns, SAM-7 surface-to-air missiles and launchers, and small arms. At least several dozen Libyan military personnel are in Nicaragua. Libyan support has enhanced the Sandinistas' ability to subvert neighboring states. In addition, Libya has provided some arms and money to insurgents in Guatemala and El Salvador, as well as the M-19 terrorist group in Colombia. During the past year, Libya has provided training, guidance, and funds to a key far-left terrorist group to enable it to expand armed action against the Government of Chile.

Libyan agents have been increasingly active among the Caribbean islands, especially since the summer of 1984. The loss of its People's Bureau in Grenada following the collapse of the Bishop government in 1983 forced Tripoli to attempt to establish its centers for subversion in other diplomatic posts in the region. Qadhafi also has used religion as a cover for intelligence activities in the area, sponsoring Islamic conferences in which Libyan participants often are intelligence officers or operatives of the Libyan Revolutionary Committees. Leftist leaders from the Dominican Republic, Dominica, Barbados, Antigua and Barbuda, St. Vincent and the Grenadines, St. Lucia, the French Departments, and elsewhere have also been invited to Libya for "seminars" and paramilitary training. Particularly worrisome is Libyan urging of leftist politicians to undertake violent action rather than pursue legal means to replace moderate governments in the region.

South and Southeast Asia

As elsewhere, Libyan diplomatic missions in this region provide the infrastructure for Libyan subversion, disbursing funds, and arranging for the training of leftists and other dissidents.

In South Asia, Libyan activities are focused on the Islamic states. No doubt reflecting his dependence on Russian arms, Qadhafi is one of the few Muslim leaders who does not criticize the Soviet invasion of Afghanistan. Although Libya maintains relations with Pakistan, it has also been involved with the "al-Zulfiqar" terrorist group. Qadhafi, in addition, has provided training and money to opponents of President Ershad of Bangladesh.

In Southeast Asia, Qadhafi concentrates on Muslim minorities. For some time, he has provided paramilitary training to the small Muslim insurgency in southern Thailand. In the Philippines, Libya continues to send assistance to the Muslim Moro separatists on Mindanao, despite a 1976 agreement with Manila to cease such aid. New Caledonia, a French possession in the South Pacific, has no appreciable Muslim population, but Libya has, nevertheless, provided military training and some funding to the Kanak Socialist National Liberation Front, the group responsible for most of the proindependence violence on the island. Libyan intelligence operatives are known to be active on other islands in Oceania.

George P. Schultz

Terrorism and the Modern World

The Requirements for an Active Strategy

We must reach a consensus in this country that our responses should go beyond passive defense to consider means of active prevention,

Reprinted excerpts from *Terrorism: An International Journal*, Vol. 7, No. 4, 1985, with the kind permission of the editor.
Address given by Secretary of State George P. Schultz at Park Avenue Synagogue, New York, on October 25, 1984.

preemption, and retaliation. Our goal must be to prevent and deter future terrorist acts, and experience has taught us over the years that one of the best deterrents to terrorism is the certainty that swift and sure measures will be taken against those who engage in it. We should take steps toward carrying out such measures. There should be no moral confusion on this issue. Our aim is not to seek revenge, but to put an end to violent attacks against innocent people, to make the world a safer place to live for all of us. Clearly, the democracies have a moral right, indeed a duty, to defend themselves.

A successful strategy for combatting terrorism will require us to face up to some hard questions and to come up with some clear-cut answers. The questions involve our intelligence capability, the doctrine under which we would employ force, and, most important of all, our public's attitude toward this challenge. Our nation cannot summon the will to act without firm public understanding and support.

First, our intelligence capabilities, particularly our human intelligence, are being strengthened. Determination and capacity to act are of little value unless we can come close to answering the questions: who?, where?, and when?. We have to do a better job of finding out who the terrorists are, where they are, and the nature, composition, and patterns of behavior of terrorist organizations. Our intelligence services are organizing themselves to do the job, and they must be given the mandate and the flexibility to develop techniques of detection and contribute to deterrence and response.

Second, there is no question about our ability to use force where and when it is needed to counter terrorism. Our nation has forces prepared for action—from small teams able to operate virtually undetected, to the full weight of our conventional military might. But serious issues are involved—questions that need to be debated, understood, and agreed if we are to be able to utilize our forces wisely and effectively.

If terrorists strike here at home, it is a matter for police action and domestic law enforcement. In most cases overseas, acts of terrorism against our people and installations can be dealt with best by the host government and its forces. It is worth remembering that just as it is the responsibility of the United States Government to provide security for foreign embassies in Washington, so the internationally agreed doctrine is that the security of our embassies abroad in the first instance is the duty of the host government, and we work with those governments cooperatively and with considerable success. The ultimate responsibility of course is ours, and we will carry it out with total determination and all the resources available to us. Congress, in a bipartisan effort, is giving us the legislative tools and the resources to strengthen the protection of our facilities and our people overseas—and they must continue to do so. But while we strengthen our defenses, defense alone is not enough.

The heart of the challenge lies in those cases where international rules and traditional practices do not apply. Terrorists will strike from areas where no governmental authority exists or they will base themselves behind what they expect will be the sanctuary of an international border. And they will design their attacks to take place in precisely those "gray areas" where the full facts cannot be known, where the challenge will not bring with it an obvious or clear-cut choice of response.

In such cases we must use our intelligence resources carefully and completely. We will have to examine the full range of measures available to us to take. The outcome may be that we will face a choice between doing nothing or employing military force. We now recognize that terrorism is being used by our adversaries as a modern tool of warfare. It is no aberration. We can expect more terrorism directed at our strategic interests around the world in the years ahead. To combat it we must be willing to use military force.

What will be required, however, is public understanding *before the fact* of the risks involved in combatting terrorism with overt power.

The public must understand *before the fact* that there is potential for loss of life of some of our fighting men and the loss of life of some innocent people.

The public must understand *before the fact* that some will seek to cast any preemptive or retaliatory action by us in the worst light and will attempt to make our military and our policy-makers—rather than the terrorists—appear to be the culprits.

The public must understand *before the fact* that occasions will come when their government must act before each and every fact is known—and that decisions cannot be tied to the opinion polls.

Public support for U.S. military actions to stop terrorists before they commit some hideous act or in retaliation for an attack on our people is crucial if we are to deal with this challenge.

Our military has the capability and the techniques to use power to fight the war against terrorism. This capability will be used judiciously. To be successful over the long term, it will require solid support from the American people.

I can assure you that in this Administration our actions will be governed by the rule of law; and the rule of law is congenial to action against terrorists. We will need the flexibility to respond to terrorist attacks in a variety of ways, at times and places of our own choosing. Clearly, we will not respond in the same manner to every terrorist act. Indeed, we will want to avoid engaging in a policy of automatic retaliation which might create a cycle of escalating violence beyond our control.

If we are going to respond or preempt effectively, our policies will have to have an element of unpredictability and surprise. And the prerequisite for such a policy must be a broad public consensus on the moral and strategic necessity of action. We will need the capability to act on a moment's notice. There will not be time for a renewed national debate after every terrorist attack. We may never have the kind of evidence that can stand up in an American court of law. But we cannot allow ourselves to become the Hamlet of nations, worrying endlessly over whether and how to respond. A great nation with global responsibilities cannot afford to be hamstrung by confusion and indecisiveness. Fighting terrorism will not be a clean or pleasant contest, but we have no choice but to play it.

We will also need a broader international effort. If terrorism is truly a threat to Western moral values, our morality must not paralyze us; it must give us the courage to face up to the threat. And if the enemies of these values are united, so too must the democratic countries be united in defending them. The leaders of the industrial democracies, meeting at the London Summit in June, agreed in a joint declaration that they must redouble their cooperation against terrorism. There has been follow-up to that initial meeting, and the United States is committed to advance the process in every way possible. Since we, the democracies, are the most vulnerable, and our strategic interests are the most at stake, we must act together in the face of common dangers. For our part, we will work whenever possible in close cooperation with our friends in the democracies.

Sanctions, when exercised in concert with other nations, can help to isolate, weaken, or punish states that sponsor terrorism against us. Too often, countries are inhibited by fear of losing commercial opportunities or fear of provoking a bully. Economic sanctions and other forms of countervailing pressure impose costs and risks on the nations that apply them, but some sacrifices will be necessary if we are not to suffer even greater costs down the road. Some countries are clearly more vulnerable to extortion than others; surely this is an argument for banding together in mutual support, not an argument for appeasement.

If we truly believe in the values of our civilization, we have a duty to defend them. The democracies must have the self-confidence to tackle this menacing problem or else they will not be in much of a position to tackle other kinds of problems. If we are not willing to set limits to what kinds of behavior are tolerable, then our adversaries will conclude that there are no limits. As Thomas Jefferson once said, when we were confronted with the problem of piracy, "An insult unpunished is the parent of others." In a basic way, the democracies must show whether they believe in themselves.

We must confront the terrorist threat with the same resolve and determination that this nation has shown time and again throughout our history. There is no room for guilt or self-doubt about our right to defend a way of life that offers *all* nations hope for peace, progress, and human dignity. The sage Hillel expressed it well: "If I am not for myself, who will be? If I am for myself alone, who am I?"

As we fight this battle against terrorism, we must always keep in mind the values and way of life we are trying to protect. Clearly, we will not allow ourselves to descend to the level of barbarism that terrorism represents. We will not abandon our democratic traditions, our respect for individual rights, and freedom, for these are precisely what we are struggling to preserve and promote. Our values and our principles will give us the strength and the confidence to meet the great challenge posed by terrorism. If we show the courage and the will to protect our freedom and our way of life, we will prove ourselves again worthy of these blessings.

Brian M. Jenkins

Will Terrorists Go Nuclear?

My remarks will focus on the motives of political terrorists who might detonate or threaten to detonate a nuclear explosion.* In order to do so, they must first acquire a nuclear weapon. Can they do it?

There are several ways a terrorist group might acquire a nuclear weapon for its own use: They could steal a nuclear weapon from a military arsenal, attempt to bypass the elaborate devices that are designed to prevent tampering, and rearm it or use its components to construct a new weapon. Another way would be to steal weapons-grade nuclear material and use it to fabricate an improvised nuclear device. Either way would require attacking defended targets, something terrorists generally have not done. To avoid encountering defenses, terrorists could attempt to obtain the material surreptitiously by other means. These might include enlisting confederates within nuclear facilities who can supply the material or purchasing it on the black market, if such a market develops for nuclear material.

Assuming they had the necessary nuclear material, could terrorists make a nuclear bomb? This question remains a topic of debate within the nuclear community. I am not qualified to offer a judgment, so let me instead try to offer a consensus view. Although the ease with which a bomb could be made has probably been greatly exaggerated in the popular press, the notion that some group outside of grovernment programs can design and build a crude nuclear bomb is certainly more plausible now than it was 30 or 40 years ago. At that time, the secrets

* A number of my colleagues and friends provided comments and advice in the preparation of my previous essays on the topic as well as this one. I would like to especially thank Konrad Kellen, Victor Gilinsky, Ariel Merari, and Paul Leventhal.

Reprinted excerpts from a paper prepared for "Conference on International Terrorism: the Nuclear Dimension," June 24–25, 1985 with the kind permission of the author.

of nuclear fission were closely guarded. However, much of the requisite technical knowledge has since gradually come into the public domain. There are a growing number of technically trained people who understand these basic principles and who, without detailed knowledge of nuclear weapons design, theoretically could design such a weapon.

Actually building even a crude nuclear bomb, however, poses a greater obstacle. Experts argue about the number of persons needed, the mix of specialized skills, and the probability of success. They agree that it would involve considerable risks for its builders. Its detonation and performance would be uncertain. Its yield would be low, probably in tenths of a kiloton.

Few terrorists as we know them today possess the requisite technical skills identified by experts. There are a few engineers and a handful of scientists within the ranks of contemporary terrorist groups, but most terrorists come from the departments of social sciences or the humanities, which may help to explain why terrorists thus far have not carried out more technically demanding operations. One recent development, however, is changing this picture, and that is the increasing direct involvement of governments in the business of terrorism, not merely as political or financial supporters, but as participants in the direction, planning, and execution of terrorist attacks. State sponsorship puts at the disposal of the terrorists more resources: intelligence, money, sophisticated munitions, technical expertise. It also reduces the constraints on the terrorists, permitting them to operate at a higher level of violence.

It seems to me that the real arguments arise not so much in the area of theoretical capabilities as in the area of intentions. The public utterances of terrorists include very few references to nuclear activity. Terrorist groups in Western Europe have demonstrated their opposition to the deployment of new nuclear missiles, but they have done so with the traditional terrorist tactics of bombings and assassinations. Basque separatists have carried on a very effective terrorist campaign against the construction of a nuclear power facility in northern Spain, again with traditional tactics.

In the late 1970s, the Red Brigades, in one of their strategic directives, reportedly urged action against nuclear power facilities in Italy, but the press account of this particular document could not be verified by Italian authorities. Puerto Rican separatists have also reportedly threatened action against nuclear facilities in the United States. Recognition that nuclear facilities may be attention-getting targets, however, does not readily translate into nuclear bomb threats.

Our insights into terrorists' contemplation of the use of nuclear weapons are limited to a few casual remarks, such as that of a former German terrorist who said that with a nuclear weapon, terrorists could make the chancellor of Germany dance on top of his desk in front of television cameras. This statement provides evidence that terrorists recognize the enormous coercive power a nuclear capability would give them. More recently, an "Armenian Scientific Group" warned that Turkey's largest cities would be destroyed by three small nuclear devices the group claimed to have at its disposal.* This raises an important point regarding motivation: Convinced that more than a million Armenians were the victims of Turkish genocide 70 years ago, some Armenians might now feel justified in using weapons of mass destruction in revenge, which is always a potent motive.

The obvious attraction to terrorists in going nuclear, however, is not that possession of a nuclear weapons capability would enable them to kill a lot of people. Simply killing a lot of people has seldom been one terrorist objective. As I have said on numerous occasions, terrorists want a lot of people *watching*, not a lot of people *dead*. Terrorists operate on the principle of the minimum force necessary. They find it unnecessary to kill many, as long as killing a few suffices for their purposes.

Statistics bear this out. Only 15 to 20 percent of all terrorist incidents involve fatalities, and of those, two-thirds involve only one death. Less than 1 percent of the thousands of terrorist incidents that have occurred in the last two decades involve ten or more fatalities, and incidents of mass murder are truly rare.

We have to pause for a moment to define terms. By mass murder, I mean attempts to kill large numbers of persons in a single action outside of war. Let me set aside cases where governments have deliberately pursued genocidal policies, the cumulative body counts of terrorist campaigns, or the scores of serial murderers, not because I consider any of these things less reprehensible, but because they are not what we are talking about here.

Arbitrarily taking 100 deaths as the criterion, it appears that only a handful of incidents of this scale have occurred since the beginning of

* *Marmara*, Istanbul, 14 January 1985.

the century: a 1921 bombing in Bessarabia; a 1925 bombing of a cathedral in Sofia; a little-known attempt to poison German SS POWs just after World War II; the crash of a hijacked Malaysian jet airliner in 1977; the 1978 bombing of an apartment building in Beirut; a deliberately set fire that killed more than 400 in Teheran; the 1983 bombing of the U.S. Marine barracks in Beirut which killed 241. Lowering the criterion to 50 deaths produces a dozen or more additional incidents. To get even a meaningful sample, the criterion has to be lowered to 25. This in itself suggests that it is either very hard to kill large numbers of persons or very rarely tried.

Unfortunately, things are changing. Terrorist activity over the last 20 years has escalated, both in volume and in bloodshed. At the beginning of the 1970s, terrorists concentrated their attacks on property. In the 1980s, according to U.S. government statistics, half of all terrorist attacks have been directed against people. The number of incidents with fatalities and multiple fatalities has increased. A more alarming trend in the 1980s has been the growing number of incidents of large-scale indiscriminate violence: huge car bombs detonated on city streets, bombs planted in airline terminals, railroad stations, and hotel lobbies.

These incidents make it clear that terrorists have the means to kill greater numbers of people than they do now, if they wanted to. Because the constraints are not technological, we must search for other reasons. For years, I have been convinced that the actions of even those we call terrorists are limited by self-imposed constraints that derive from moral considerations or political calculations. The growing volume of testimony from terrorists interviewed while still at large, interrogated in prison, or testifying at trials has, I believe, borne out that notion.

Many terrorists consider indiscriminate violence to be immoral. They regard a government as their opponent, not the people. They may also wish to behave like a government themselves. They use the language of government to justify their actions: robberies are "expropriations," kidnap victims are subjected to a "people's trial," enemies of the people are "condemned" and "executed." Wanton violence, in their view, would imperil this image.

There are also political considerations. The capability to kill on a grand scale must be balanced against the fear of alienating perceived constituents (a population that terrorists invariably overestimate), provoking widespread revulsion, and unleashing government crackdowns that have public approval. The practical consideration of maintaining group cohesion also tends to impose limits on terrorist violence.

Attitudes toward the use of violence not only vary from group to group but also may vary within the same group. We know now that within any terrorist group there are latent defectors who have lost faith in the cause or in the efficacy of terrorist tactics, or who find themselves repelled by escalating violence and would drop out or defect if the group goes too far. A proposal to indiscriminately kill on a grand scale might provoke sharp divisions among the terrorists, exposing the operation and the group itself to betrayal.

Obviously, not all groups share the same operational code. Subscribing, or at least paying lip service to the philosophy that power comes from the people, left-wing terrorists generally target their violence against symbols and representatives of the state, taking care to avoid civilian casualties. However, not all left-wing terrorists share this caution—Marxist ideology, for example, did not prevent the Japanese Red Army from carrying out the Lod Airport massacre in 1972.

Right-wing terrorists generally regard the people as a disorganized, despicable mass that requires strong authoritarian leadership. These terrorist groups have shown themselves capable of "pure terrorism"—indiscriminate violence calculated to create panic and a popular clamor for a political strong man who will be able to impose order.

Certain conditions or circumstances also may erode the constraints. Like soldiers in war, terrorists who have been in the field for many years may be brutalized by the long struggle; killing becomes easier. A group may seek to avenge members who have been killed or a population that has been wiped out. Terrorists may feel compelled to escalate their violence in order to keep the attention of a public that has become desensitized by the growing volume of terrorism or to recover coercive power lost as governments have become more resistant to their demands. The composition of a terrorist group may change as the fainthearted drop out or are shoved aside by more ruthless elements. The lack of success or the imminence of defeat may call for desperate measures.

The threshold against mass murder may be lowered if the terrorists' perceived enemies and victims are members of a different ethnic group. As we have seen throughout history, the presumed approval of God for the killing of pagans, heathens, or infidels can permit acts of great destruction and self-destruction. In addition, state sponsors might covertly use terrorists to carry out a nuclear threat (although it is hard to imagine the scenario in which a state would relinquish a nuclear capability to terrorists without retaining direct control over its use). Some suggest that terrorists might overcome taboos against weapons of mass destruction by targeting a large industrial target, for example, an oil refinery where the loss of life would be minimal but the destruction of property and consequent disruption could be enormous. The annals of modern terrorism provide ample precedents for such targeting.

Several changes in the environment might increase the possibility of terrorists going nuclear. As nuclear programs expand, nuclear material suitable for use in weapons could become more widely available than it is now. Expanding commercial traffic in explosive nuclear fuel will increase the opportunities for diversion, which in turn could lead to a nuclear gray or black market where terrorists could acquire nuclear material as they now acquire conventional weapons. As knowledge of nuclear weapons design increases, so do the chances of terrorists gaining access to it.

Some developments could also alter incentives. A sudden rush by governments to acquire or to announce that they already possess nuclear weapons might persuade terrorists to attempt to do likewise. In one generation, China advanced from a guerrilla army to a nuclear power. Terrorists could try to take a short cut. The use of a nuclear weapon in war would somehow seem to lower constraints against terrorists moving toward nuclear weapons, although I am not quite sure why. Certainly, it would depend very much on the circumstances and the results. Finally, an incident of nuclear terrorism, perhaps even an alarming hoax, would almost certainly increase the probability of other terrorists going nuclear.

The question often arises: Why would terrorists choose nuclear weapons over chemical or biological weapons, which evoke great fear and are technically less demanding? In several ways, these weapons also are less attractive. Terrorists imitate governments, and nuclear weapons are in the arsenals of the world's major powers. That makes them "legitimate." Chemical and biological weapons also may be found in the arsenals of many nations, but their use has been widely condemned by public opinion and proscribed by treaty, although in recent years the constraints against their use seem to be eroding.

But neither chemical nor biological warfare seems to fit the pattern of terrorist behavior. Terrorist attacks are generally intended to produce immediate, dramatic effects. Terrorist incidents have a finite quality—an assassination, a bombing, a handful of deaths, and that is the end of the episode. And the terrorist retain control. This is quite different from initiating an event that offers no bang but instead produces indiscriminate deaths and lingering illness, over which the terrorists would have little control.

If terrorists had a nuclear capability, they would be more likely to brandish it as a threat than detonate it, although one can conceive of a more emotional use of a nuclear weapon by a desperate group as the ultimate instrument of revenge or as a "Doomsday Machine." Translating the enormous coercive power that a nuclear weapon would give a terrorist group into concrete political gains, however, poses some difficulties. First, the terrorists would have to establish some credibility of the threat. The scenarists solve this problem by having them get away with a military weapon, thus removing the uncertainty of their possession, or by providing the terrorists with two weapons, one to be used as a demonstration.

Second, the terrorists would have to persuade the government that it has an incentive to negotiate. That may sound odd, given that they could threaten to cause thousands of casualties, but the "rules" of bargaining that have evolved from dealing with ordinary hostage incidents may not apply to nuclear blackmail. For one thing, we may assume that the terrorists' demands would be commensurate with the magnitude of the threat. Governments facing the threat of nuclear terrorism would paradoxically find it more difficult to refuse, yet more difficult to yield. Impossible demands—for example, that a government liquidate itself—could not be met even under a nuclear threat. Nor could terrorists enforce permanent policy changes unless they maintained the threat indefinitely. And if a government could not be assured that the threat would not be dismantled once the demands were met, it would have little incentive to negotiate. It thus becomes a matter not of concessions, but rather of governance. I am not suggesting that armchair extortionists cannot come up with solutions to these dilemmas—finite, irrevocable demands that governments could meet with adequate assurances that the threat would end once the demands are met. I *am* suggesting that it is not easy for terrorists, even if they are armed with nuclear weapons, to achieve lasting political results. They might find nuclear weapons to be as useless as they are powerful.

In my 1975 essay, I concluded that

> Terrorists may not be interested in or capable of building a nuclear bomb. The point is, they do not have to. Within their range of resources and technical proficiency, they may carry out nuclear actions that will give them almost as much publicity and leverage, with less risk to themselves and less risk of alienation or retaliation. As the industry expands during the next few years, we will probably witness a growing number of low-level nuclear incidents. . . . There will be moments of alarm, but the inconvenience and political repercussions that these incidents produce will probably exceed the actual danger to public safety.

We did, in fact, witness more low-level incidents.

With regard to the possibility of serious nuclear incidents, I concluded that it would increase "at a far more gradual rate" if only because the opportunities for diversion and technical know-how would increase. "At some point in the future, the opportunity and capacity for serious nuclear terrorism could reach those willing to take advantage of it." But I did not see this as an inevitable development. Before then, the development of more effective safeguards could push that "point indefinitely into the future."

What do I conclude now? Despite the theoretical increase in opportunities as nuclear programs have grown, and the demonstrable escalation in terrorism, going nuclear still represents a quantum juries for terrorists, and one that is not impossible but by no means imminent or inevitable.

Yu. Pankov

Anti-Social Psychology of Ultra-Leftist Terrorism

We are speaking of the members of ultra-leftist terrorist groups of various ideological stripe. Their precise ideological orientation is not the main thing here: be they anarchists, Trotskyites or separatists, they hold in common their utter lack of respect for human life. They have all been carried away by the external forms of "revolutionary struggle" in which bravado and aggressive behaviour have superseded their vaguely understood goals. They are all involved in anti-social activities: killings and mutilations, arson and explosions, and dozens of shady political ventures from assault and battery of the members of rival ultra-leftist groups to the kidnapping of figures personifying the enemy in their eyes. . . .

A psychological analysis of ultra-leftist radicalism and terrorism is absolutely essential for, without such an analysis, it is difficult to understand the actions by the "motley" groups which frequently condemn their real or imagined adversaries on moral, ethical or purely emotional grounds. If we fail to take their psychology into account, it is impossible to understand the influences of contemporary bourgeois society, which the young extremists experience as both external and internal within the framework of their anti-social activities.

Ultra-leftist terrorism sprang up on the soil fertilised by the philosophy of disillusionment and by a multitude of ultra-revolutionary, petty-bourgeois concepts which have a "tendency to turn rapidly into submission, apathy, phantasms, and even a frenzied infatuation with one bourgeois fad or another".* One such concept was Marcuse's

* V. I. Lenin, "'Left-Wing' Communism—an Infantile Disorder," *Collected Works,* Vol. 31, p. 32.

Reprinted from *Political Terrorism—An Indictment of Imperialism* (Moscow: Progress Publishers, 1983), with the kind permission of the publisher.

"great refusal" according to which a rebellion of outcasts would bring about the downfall of capitalism. Of a similar ilk were the infamous revelations of Roger Garaudy on realism without boundaries and the vulgar sociologism of Adorno who rejected Marx's "utopia" while exalting spontaneous "revolutionary" will. Other components of this psychological soil were the eccentric bohemian ways which appeared as a unique moral protest against the norms of bourgeois propriety, deliberately informal modes of dress, "up-frontness," the cult of sexuality accompanied by the use of narcotics and finally an attempt to break down social barriers as a counter-balance to alienation, for the sake of which the interests of the middle classes were sacrificed. The "protest activities" gradually acquired more or less definite forms which were similar for a number of countries.

The first mass forms of "protest activities" were not of an overtly radical nature. They were limited to the organisation of "free universities" and sit-down strikes in lecture halls and student unions. Eventually, they took on a more active visage: informational and health care services in inner cities and black ghettos were set up to spite social traditions. Participation in such activities allowed young people to acquire character traits which their own social environment could never have shaped. They got a glimpse of life outside the bourgeois districts and the lecture halls of high-class universities, and met up with radicalism of many types, all of which were directed against the establishment. In those "protest activities" waged from door to door they discovered that the middle classes of the developed capitalist countries harboured a great deal of discontent with the existing order of things and displayed an interest in socialist ideas. The political events which infringed upon the young people's interests also contributed to the growth of ultra-leftist radicalism among the youth of capitalist countries. This led to a wave of protests against the government's judicial, executive and legislative authoritarianism in the sphere of education and civil rights. Of course, youth protests were not a new phenomenon in the majority of developed capitalist countries. However, these protests had never acquired such a mass character before the 1960s and, most important, never had there arisen such profound and well-founded doubts about the rationality of the prevailing system of values or the wisdom of the existing social order among the rising generation of bourgeois society.

The aspiration towards radical activity was concentrated in a wave of protests by those young people who adhered to ultra-leftist views.

For many of them, the very fact of their participation in these protests was more important than the vaguely understood goal of the given political activity. Many of them enjoyed being the constant centre of attention of the mass media, the object of debates in parliament, and the subject of philistine talk. Their solidarity with the poor and oppressed, with Black Americans, Algerian workers, displaced persons, and the "Viet Cong" was not a well thought-out solidarity, but was rather based on appearances and fleeting sympathies, "the psychology of the unsettled intellectual or the vagabond and not of the proletarian."*

Moral and political protest against the background of the pluralism of ultra-leftist political thought brought about a plurality of scattered groupings. And that in turn led to rivalry and the escalation of pseudo-revolutionary activities which took the form of extravagant actions and the search for ways of attracting attention. A power struggle among the various groupings became one of the factors increasing the "revolutionary passions" within the ultra-leftist groups as well as the speculation around them. The December 14, 1968 issue of *Saturday Review* carried an article by John D. Rockefeller 3rd entitled "In Praise of Young Revolutionaries" which, coming from him, lent these events a special significance.

This stage prepared the way for later, more complex, larger-scale forms of "protest activities" which possibly occurred along with a growing understanding of the contradictions of capitalist society. The failure of the "society of universal prosperity," which many had placed high hopes on to materialise, caused fresh disillusionment. The starry-eyed idea of harmony in the "rational society" became yet another pipe dream. At that stage, the psychology of the ultra-leftists became more or less definitely realistic while retaining several features typical of the consciousness of youth, but in their most distorted form. The continuation and growth of the number of happening-type political acts, i.e., blind anarchistic riots, had caused still greater distortion.

The psychology of the ultra-leftists shares features common to all psychologies of those who deviate sharply from the generally accepted societal norms. It reflects the contradictions existing in reality. However, these contradictions are subjectively exacerbated by the activities of the ultra-leftist groups. At the same time all the characteristics

* V. I. Lenin, "Anarchism and Socialism," *Collected Works*, Vol. 5, p. 327.

peculiar to youth—social activity and enthusiasm, a critical attitude to everything which is not in accord with one's superficially assimilated ideals, the romantic fervour which prompts young people to radicalism, and rashness of action and judgment—all these characteristics are distorted. Ultra-leftists suffer from a total lack of insufficiency of political experience, which allows unscrupulous politicians to distract the young people from actual social problems. Ultra-leftist movements attract those young people who aspire to radical change but who, at the same time, are in despair over the seeming hopelessness of the situation and due to youthful impatience with the unbearably slow, in their opinion, march of history. . . .

In the 1970s the social existence of young people under capitalism was distinguished by harsher discrimination and increasing monotony. In a society plagued by chronic unemployment, the number of jobless among the youth grew even more quickly. In the USA, programs to combat unemployment among the youth, such as the Job Corps, the Neighbourhood Youth Corps, and others, widely publicised in the 1960s under the Johnson Administration as part of the War on Poverty campaign, proved to be no more than demagoguery. Naturally, this did not go unnoticed by the young people and had a definite effect on their frame of mind.

Unemployment had still other negative psychological consequences: a loss of self-respect on the part of those who were out of work and the disruption of family ties formed earlier, the development of inferiority complexes, and the assimilation of the psychological mind-set of one who is unneeded. A marginal social existence in connection with chronic unemployment could not but bring about a marginality of consciousness expressing itself in a readiness to adopt any values and ideas, including anomalic ones.

The tendency to marginality of consciousness was bolstered up with the specifics of the development of capitalism in the contemporary epoch, too. The scientific and technical revolution of the past decades called for narrow professional specialisation. Simultaneously, it lowered the possibilities for upward social mobility. The job market got tougher. There was permanent stress on the young people who had jobs as well, for they had only very vague ideas of their futures and, as a result, suffered from permanent uncertainty. These feelings were the background against which the will to action and the protest activities themselves appeared. These protests were directed against an enemy of which there was only the vaguest impression, and they acquired a negativistic directedness that took the form of a negation of and protest against everything. The objects of this negation became not the social and political structures of their countries, or the prevailing ideological and cultural systems, or even the church, but concrete individuals whose activities were actually connected or identified with the functioning of these institutions.

Along with this, at the beginning of the 1970s, two precedents which had important psychological consequences were formed. The first of these was the community movement as an alternative to the bourgeois style of life and system of capitalist relations. The youth disillusioned with industrial society have chosen as an alternative surrogate socialism in the form of communes—small communities isolated from the mainstream of society. The principle behind their creation was the attempt to reach "unlimited freedom of instinctive self-expression" and "full psychological comfort.". . .

The second, possibly more important precedent was created as a result of false notions about the "romantic daring" and "chivalrous magnanimity" of defending the oppressed and downtrodden, the insulted and exploited. It was an alluring prospect to bask in the glory of being sensitive, humanitarian, nice philanthropic young men and women who were invariably kind and jolly, professing a moral system under which anything is permissible, spitting in the face of all the interdictions of bourgeois society. Young people prevented from participating in the political system of the bourgeois state indulged in illusions of power. Illusions of eliminating estrangement also appeared in the new type of communes where all material resources, dangers and adversities, and even the pleasures of love, were considered common, and equally the property of all without exception.

The ruling circles of the capitalist countries made enormous efforts to regulate and transfer the social activities of the youth involved in protest into anti-social actions, but only those which would not threaten the prosperity of the wealthy classes. Thus, the democratic sentiments of young people were exploited to develop avant-gardism in art and life styles, in ideology and political activity. The ruling classes used all the means at their disposal to encourage the social illusion among the youth that it was possible to achieve progressive ideals rapidly, to speed up the march of history, in which young people were to play the role of "agent of historical progress." The same set of arguments was used to encourage young people to display undemocratic sentiments, to participate in anti-communist and fascist movements. This was the case in Chile, and is still true in Argentina, Italy, Portugal and, particularly, the USA.

As a result of this policy the youth groups were split into various hostile factions of ultra-leftist and ultra-rightist extremists. Mutual hatred became a dominant theme in both sides of the conflict.

The tendency to level out all individuals engendered by industrial society found its most extreme and final expression in the ultra-leftist trend. This tendency takes the form of the varied extreme manifestations, such as an interest in mysticism and the "occult sciences" and religious pluralism, which now even includes a "church of Satan." Within the framework of ultra-leftist extremism these phenomena give birth to unprecedented aggressiveness of people who have lost all semblance of being human. In the final analysis, terrorism is the psychological attempt to relieve stress by creating another, even more stressful situation. But this goal cannot be reached. A vicious circle which increases psychic tensions appears: it consists of acts of despair, hysteric reactions, and a suicidal sense of doom.

Yonah Alexander

Some Perspectives on Terrorism and the Soviet Union

Terrorism, the threatened and actual resort to ideological and political violence by non-state groups for the purpose of achieving limited or extensive goals, has become a permanent feature of contemporary life, with grave implications for free societies.

Recognizing the menace posed by terrorism to the rule of law, the safety of the individual, economic development, the stability of the state system, and the survival of democracy, western nations have adopted various approaches in their opposition to it. Noncommunist

Reprinted excerpts from the *International Security Review*, Spring 1982, with the kind permission of the editor.

countries spend billions of dollars every year on improving security and increasing protection for ordinary citizens and civilian facilities. Special measures have been developed for ensuring the safety of diplomats and government officials. More than two dozen nations have set up commando units designed to fight terrorists and rescue hostages from their grasp. Big corporations provide their top executives with instruction in protecting themselves and their families, and spend huge sums on safeguarding their investments.

But despite all efforts at control, the level of terrorist violence remains high. There are many reasons for this, but there is one universal key factor: the toleration, encouragement, and even support of terrorism by the Soviet Union.

The purpose of this article is to examine briefly Moscow's behavior within the framework of its revolutionary doctrine of peaceful coexistence and the implications of that behavior for the West.

It is becoming increasingly clear that ideological and political violence is, to paraphrase Clausewitz, a continuation of policy by other means for the purpose of compelling an adversary to submit to specific or general demands. Indeed, terrorism is escalating into a form of surrogate warfare, whereby small groups are able, with direct and indirect state support, to conduct political warfare at the national level, and ultimately may even succeed in altering the balance of power on the international scale. It is not surprising, therefore, that the strategic thinking of communist states, as exemplified by the Soviet Union's policies and actions, calls for the manipulation of terrorism as a suitable substitute for traditional warfare, which has become too expensive and too hazardous to be waged on the battlefield. By overtly and covertly resorting to nonmilitary techniques, and by exploiting low-intensity operations around the world, the Soviet Union is able to continue its revolutionary process against the democratic pluralism of the Free World, as well as against a wider target area.

Any analysis of this phenomenon should consider three facts. First, the scope and nature of Soviet involvement in terrorist activity—ranging from the political legitimization of violence to the supply of funds, training, arms, and other operational support—has fluctuated over the years in accordance with Moscow's changing appreciation of its vital interests. Second, the promotion of specific terrorist operations has often been no more than the largely unintended by-product of Soviet behavior at particular stages of its history. And finally, because of Russia's position as an undisputed superpower controlling, or influencing to a greater or lesser extent, the foreign policy conduct of other socialist countries which subscribe to its ideological line, it is not always easy to determine whether a particular terrorist action or series of actions in one of these countries is, so to speak, home-grown, or whether it is Moscow-inspired. In this context, Bulgaria, Cuba, Czechoslovakia, East Germany, North Korea, and Vietnam spring to mind. The support provided by these countries to various communist and noncommunist terrorist movements in both developed and developing countries is generally attributed to the decision-makers in the Kremlin.

Socialist states, then, serve both as intermediaries between the Soviet Union and terrorists and as essential actors in assisting, or aiding and abetting, the promotion of ideological and political violence throughout the world.

In sum, terrorism, whether backed directly or indirectly by the Soviet Union or independently initiated, is an indispensable tactical tool in the communist struggle for power and influence within and among nations. In relying on this supplementary instrument, Moscow aims at achieving strategic ends when the use of armed might is deemed either inappropriate or ineffective.

The broad goals which the Soviet Union hopes to achieve from terrorism include the following:

> Influencing developments in neighboring countries. For instance, Moscow planted subversive communist seeds in Iran for decades, contributed by proxy to the fall of the pro-Western Shah, and is currently helping local Marxist-Leninist factions in Iran to prepare the requisite conditions for the overthrow of the revolutionary Islamic government.
>
> Drawing noncommunist states into the Soviet alliance system or at least into the Soviet sphere of influence. For example, Moscow's activities in Portugal—ranging from subsidizing the communist party to infiltrate the administrative machinery of the country—culminated in chaos and almost enabled the "revolutionaries" to seize power.
>
> Helping to create new states in which it will have considerable influence as a result of its support of those countries' claims to self-determination. The Soviet assistance rendered to the PLO aims at achieving this end.
>
> Weakening the political, economic, and military infrastructure of

anti-Soviet alliances such as NATO. A case in point is the Soviet support of the IRA. Moscow hopes that if the violence in Ulster continues, Britain, a member of NATO, will be neutralized as a potential adversary.

Initiating proxy operations in distant geographic locations where direct conventional military activities requiring long-distance logistics are impracticable. For instance, the Kremlin's manipulation of the South West Africa People's Organization (SWAPO) aims at setting up a Marxist regime with a pro-Soviet orientation and thus gaining vital strategic and economic advantages in southern Africa.

Russia's justification of the use of terrorism as a legitimate political tool has its ideological roots in the works of the founders of orthodox Marxism-Leninism and other prominent communist authors. To a greater or lesser extent they all advocated the employment of confrontation tactics, including terrorism, for achieving communist aims.

In *Das Kapital* Marx asserted: "Force [Gewalt] is the midwife of an old society which is pregnant with a new one. Gewalt is an economic factor [Potenz]." Writing in 1848, Marx expressed a strong belief in the necessity for political violence: " . . . only one means exists to shorten the bloody death pangs of the old society and the birth pains of the new society, to simplify and concentrate them—revolutionary terrorism." A year later, he predicted that "when it is our turn, we shall not hide our terrorism."

This connection persisted not only in Marx's later writings but also, with some qualifications, in the works of Lenin. He, too, held that the revolutionary struggle might appropriately include terrorism. Lenin and the Bolsheviks saw, for instance, the usefulness of terrorism as a tactic of disorganization of the czarist enemy and as a means of acquiring experience and military training.

Writing in 1906, Lenin responded to critics of this approach by asserting that "no Marxist should consider partisan warfare (including political assassination) . . . as abnormal and demoralizing." Indeed, terrorism was regarded by Lenin and his successors as a part of the "proletarian revolution," but to be employed only under the direction of "the party" and only where conditions existed for its success.

Thus, from the first Marxist-Leninist revolution against czarism, when more than a thousand terrorist acts were perpetuated in Transcaucasia, to the present day, Moscow-oriented communism has encouraged and assisted terrorist groups which follow a strict party line and are highly centralized.

Terrorist movements with less party discipline and control, including the New Left, and even Trotskyists (working for the furtherance of international communism but generally hostile to the Soviet Union) have also received some kind of support. Moreover, from considerations of political expediency rather than ideological solidarity, a great variety of extremist groups such as sectarian, nationalist, separatist, and anarchist, have frequently been supported by the Soviet Union.

True, many of these movements have adopted Marxist ideologies as a "flag of convenience." They reasoned that Marxism provides a model for revolution against the state, denies the legal authority of the government, establishes a successful historical example of revolution, grants some sort of respectable international status, affords a sense of affinity with other revolutionary movements, and guarantees some assurance of direct and indirect support by like-minded groups and socialist states. With the adoption of a Marxist philosophy, however, some of these terrorist movements have fallen victim to internal ideological debate, division, and conflict.

Notwithstanding such ideological differences, the Soviet Union does not hesitate to provide assistance to a multitude of groups, holding that social discard and political turmoil in "enemy" territory is likely to advance Moscow's cause. On the other hand, it would be a gross exaggeration to assert that most terrorist operations are Soviet-sponsored. As Lord Chalfont observed correctly: "I do not believe that the forces of international terrorism are centrally inspired or centrally controlled, but I do suggest that when it suits their purposes, the forces of international communism will support terror groups throughout the world."

It is equally true that practical considerations have dictated that Soviet policy toward terrorism must necessarily be adapted to changing circumstances. More specifically, Moscow has long recognized that it, too, is vulnerable to various forms of terrorism. In fact, as early as the 1920s, Russia was the object of terrorist attacks by White Guard emigres, who used neighboring countries as an operational base. Exercising its right of "self-defense," the Soviet Union sent troops into Mongolia and China to liquidate these bands. During the interwar period, Moscow supported various international efforts to eliminate certain kinds of terrorism, particularly armed attacks.

More recently, as a superpower with political, diplomatic, economic, and military interests all over the world, the Soviet Union has become increasingly vulnerable to various forms of terrorism. One need only mention the hijacking of Soviet aircraft, the kidnapping and assassination of Soviet officials and diplomats, and the bombing of Soviet embassies and trade missions.

It is for these reasons that Moscow had adopted a more cautious and restrained stand. Indeed, the activities of various terrorist groups, including some which proclaim Marxist revolution to be their objectives, have even been branded as "adventurist." At times the Soviet Union has also acted in concert with capitalist states in condemning subnational violence. It supported, for example, the U.N. Declaration on Principles of International Law Concerning Friendly Relations and Cooperation among States in accordance with the Charter of the United Nations, adopted by the General Assembly as Resolution 2625 (XXV) on October 24, 1970. This document asserts, *inter alia*, that terrorist and other subversive activities organized and supported by one state against another are a form of unlawful use of force.

Also, as a country with dissidents who sometimes perceive aerial hijacking as the only means of escaping to the West, the Soviet Union became a party to the 1970 Hague Convention for the Suppression of Unlawful Seizure of Aircraft and to the 1971 Montreal Convention for the Suppression of Unlawful Acts against the Safety of Civil Aviation. In addition, it has concluded bilateral agreements with Iran and Finland which provide for the return of hijackers to the state which registered the aircraft.

Clearly, the Soviet Union has attempted to achieve a balance between opposition to terrorist activities to which it is itself vulnerable and support for operations which attempt to tear down the fabric of Western society and weaken other nonsocialist governments.

Abraham D. Sofaer

Terrorism and the Law

The reasons for the law's failure tolerably to control terrorism go much deeper than the absence of law enforcement authority or mechanisms. International law and cooperation in less controversial areas have often proved reasonably effective. In the area of terrorism, however, the law has failed to punish and deter those who use violence to advance their political goals.

Civilized nations have tried to control international terrorism by condemning it, by treating it as piracy, by prosecuting terrorists under the laws of affected states, by creating international norms establishing as criminal certain acts wherever committed, and by cooperating through extradition and other devices in aiding nations attacked by terrorists. An appraisal of these efforts leads to a painful conclusion: the law applicable to terrorism is not merely flawed, it is perverse. The rules and declarations seemingly designed to curb terrorism have regularly included provisions that demonstrate the absence of international agreement on the propriety of regulating terrorist activity. On some issues, the law leaves political violence unregulated. On other issues the law is ambivalent, providing a basis for conflicting arguments as to its purpose. At its worst the law has in important ways actually served to legitimize international terror, and to protect terrorists from punishment as criminals. These deficiencies are not the product of negligence or mistake. They are intentional.

III

Americans too readily assume that others agree that at least certain aspects of international terror are unacceptable. While many

Reprinted excerpts from *Foreign Affairs*, Summer 1986, with the kind permission of the editor.

fanatics obviously approve of terror, less recognized and more significant is the fact that the acceptance of terror is far more widespread. Indeed, many nations regard terrorism as a legitimate means of warfare.

The United Nations General Assembly began devoting special attention to the subject of terrorism after two especially heinous actions. On May 30, 1972, Japanese terrorists, working with the Popular Front for the Liberation of Palestine, attacked civilian passengers at Lod Airport in Israel with automatic weapons, killing 28 and wounding 78. On September 5, 1972, terrorists from the Black September organization murdered 11 members of the Israeli Olympic Team in Munich.

On September 8, 1972, U.N. Secretary-General Kurt Waldheim asked for inclusion in the General Assembly agenda of an item entitled "Measures to prevent terrorism and other forms of violence which endanger or take innocent human lives or jeopardize fundamental freedoms." He urged "that all concerned turn away from senseless and destructive violence," and noted that the world community should continue "to exert its utmost influence in seeking peaceful ways" to find solutions "for the problems underlying such acts of terrorism."

The secretary-general's statement evoked angry opposition, which took the immediate form of protests against considering terrorism without considering its causes. The secretary-general reiterated his request on September 20, but acceded to the pressures by adding that it was no good considering terrorism "without at the same time considering the underlying situations which give rise to terrorism and violence in many parts of the world." He assured the protesters that he did not intend "to affect principles enunciated by the General Assembly regarding colonial and dependent peoples seeking independence and liberation."

The two concessions made by Mr. Waldheim may at first glance seem innocuous. In the United Nations, however, they were significant. Attributing acts of terrorism to injustice and frustration obviously tends to excuse, if not justify, those acts. This is especially so when the causes are all assumed to be sympathetic. The language concerning efforts to seek "independence" and "liberation" also implied justification for terrorist acts. These concepts related to the principles adopted in previous U.N. resolutions supporting "self-determination" and wars of national liberation, in the pursuit of which oppressed people were authorized to resort to all available means, including armed struggle. . . .

A resolution on terrorism adopted in 1977 added another important element. It invited the Ad Hoc Committee on International Terrorism to study *first* the underlying causes of terror, and then to recommend measures to deal with acts of terrorism. A 1979 resolution for the first time condemned acts of terror, but it referred to the 1977 Protocols to the Geneva Convention, which seek to give groups fighting wars of national liberation the protection of the laws of war. Finally, in December 1985, after a further series of terrorist acts, the General Assembly adopted a resolution that "unequivocally condemns, as criminal, all acts, methods and practices of terrorism." This resolution contains several provisions calling for international cooperation against terrorism. At the same time, however, it reaffirmed each people's inalienable right to self-determination, and the legitimacy of struggles against colonial and racist regimes and other forms of alien domination. The debates preceding and following the adoption of this resolution make clear that many states continue to believe that "wars of national liberation" justify or excuse terrorist acts. For example, the Angolan representative, echoing the comments of the delegates from Algeria, Bulgaria, Kuwait and Sri Lanka, among others, made it clear that "acts of terrorism could not be equated, under any pretext, with the acts of those who were fighting colonial and racist oppression and for their freedom and independence."

The wide acceptance of the premise that terrorist acts can be lawful in the pursuit of proper goals is an uneasy first lesson. The United States of course also recognizes that oppressed people are sometimes justified in resorting to force, but only if properly exercised. For example, such uses of force must be consistent with the laws of war and should not be directed at innocent civilians, include hostage-taking, or involve torture. In contrast, the U.N. debates and resolutions relating to terrorism do not suggest principled limits on the use of force, or any reasoned, fair-minded basis for determining which peoples are entitled to wage wars of national liberation. The result is a clear signal to all that those groups deemed by the majority to be oppressed will be free legally to use force, and therefore cannot fairly be called terrorists. In other words, acts of terrorism by such groups are not wrong, and the law has no proper role in punishing or deterring such acts.

IV

The legitimacy of political violence is a notion that has also worked its way deep into international law enforcement. Most countries have treaties that obligate them to extradite to other states persons accused of committing, in those states, the crimes associated with terrorism, such as murder, hijacking, bombing, armed assault and robbery. Yet extradition requests are frequently refused, often because the offense is characterized as "political" conduct which the law exempts from extradition.

Some relatively recent decisions, denying extradition on the ground that the charge is a "political offense," illustrate how detrimental the law can be in the battle against terrorism. In 1972 five individuals hijacked a plane in the United States, extorted $1 million and flew to Algeria, where they were received as political militants. In 1976 they made their way to France, which refused to extradite the five, although they had presented no evidence of political motivation beyond the claim that they were escaping racial segregation in America and were associated with the "black liberation movement." More recently, the United States failed to obtain the extradition of Abu Abbas, thought to have masterminded the *Achille Lauro* hijacking, from two countries through which he passed following the incident (Italy and Yugoslavia). Despite U.S. assertions of their treaty obligation to hold Abbas, these states released him, Yugoslavia claiming that he was entitled to diplomatic immunity because he carried an Iraqi diplomatic passport.

Some decisions by U.S. courts are equally disturbing. In 1959 a federal court refused to extradite Andrija Artukovic to Yugoslavia for the alleged malicious murders of 200,000 Croatians in concentration camps, after determining that these murders were "political." Some 27 years later the United States successfully deported Artukovic, and he is currently standing trial in Yugoslavia. In recent cases U.S. courts have refused to extradite four alleged Irish Republican Army gunmen on the ground that an uprising exists in Northern Ireland, which makes crimes in furtherance of the revolt "political.". . .

V

The law against piracy provides another illustration of how international law has failed adequately to control politically motivated crimes. The *Achille Lauro* incident presented the question whether the acts of the hijackers of that vessel constituted piracy "under the law of nations," and were therefore felonies under U.S. law. The hijackers stole money and jewelry from the ship's passengers, but their primary purposes were political. They were allegedly seeking to commit acts of violence in Israel, where the vessel was scheduled to dock, and after taking control they demanded that Israel release certain terrorists it had imprisoned. Is such an enterprise "piracy"?

The traditional law of piracy could have been one vehicle for obtaining jurisdiction over terrorists, with fewer loopholes for political crimes than recent conventions. Piracy law has long been inapplicable to state vessels and recognized belligerents when they engaged in lawful acts of war. Those who believed that belligerents should not be treated as pirates reasoned that they were the enemies only of a particular government, not of mankind. This recognized exclusion contained a crucial limitation: it applied only if the insurgents confined themselves to depredations against the country with which they were at war. Where individuals engaged in an insurgency attacked nonbelligerents, the exclusion did not apply and the rebels were treated as pirates.

The modern law of piracy purports to modify significantly these traditional rules. The 1982 U.N. Convention on the Law of the Sea and the 1958 Geneva Convention on the High Seas define piracy as any illegal act of violence, detention or depredation committed against a ship "for private ends." The private-ends requirement was used deliberately to exclude acts with public or political motives. The rapporteur for the International Law Commission, which drafted the Geneva high seas convention, explained that "he had defined as piracy acts of violence or depredation committed for private ends, thus leaving outside the scope of the definition *all wrongful acts perpetrated for a political purpose*."

The approach of these two conventions would substantially contract the reach of the law of piracy. The "private ends" requirement, at least as described by the rapporteur, would expand the traditional "insurgency" exclusion to cover all persons claiming to be politically motivated. Moreover, the exclusion's traditional limitation to acts committed against a country with which the insurgents are at war appears to have been either overlooked or abandoned. As a result, the conventions arguably place all politically motivated acts outside the universal jurisdiction of sovereign states. . . .

VI

The exclusion of terrorist acts from the reach of legal prohibitions is not the only means by which law has been employed to legitimize terrorism. Another approach has been to secure for terrorism a legal status that obscures or denies its fundamentally criminal nature. The laws of war mark the line between what is criminal and what is an act of combat. A person who kills someone is normally guilty of homicide. If he does it during combat, however, he is a soldier and can only be held as a prisoner of war, and may be punished only if the killing violates the laws of war. Radical groups responsible for terrorist acts have long sought legitimacy by securing recognition as combatants under the laws of war.

The effort of radical groups to acquire legal legitimacy had a significant success in the Geneva Diplomatic Conference on the Reaffirmation of International Humanitarian Law Applicable in Armed Conflict, which met between 1974 and 1977. The conference, under the auspices of the International Committee for the Red Cross (ICRC), was called to improve the laws of war set forth in the Geneva conventions of 1949. It produced two additional protocols to the Geneva conventions: Protocol I dealing with international, and Protocol II with noninternational, armed conflict. The United States participated in the Geneva conference and signed the protocols, but the President has decided not to seek Senate ratification of Protocol I, and has decided to seek several reservations and understandings as conditions to the ratification of Protocol II.

The ICRC and the conference developed many constructive ideas to help minimize the suffering of combatants and noncombatants in armed conflict. But from the beginning of the conference, an effort was made to extend the law of international armed conflicts to cover activities of the Palestine Liberation Organization (PLO) and other radical groups, many of whom were accorded observer status.

The first substantive address, by then-President Moktar Ould Daddah of Mauritania, urged the conference to recognize "certain values and elementary rights which went beyond the Universal Declaration of Human Rights," because millions were "still under colonial oppression in the African continent, while international Zionism had placed the Palestinian population in an impossible situation." He asked the conference to consider, not only effects, but causes as well, and to recognize "there were such things as just wars." Daddah said,

"It was quite obvious that it was the Zionists who wanted to throw the Arabs into the sea. . . . National liberation movements did not want to shed blood, only to secure recognition of their rights."

The Geneva diplomatic conference adopted in its first session what is now Article 1(4) of Protocol I, with 11 of 99 nations, including the United States, abstaining, and only Israel dissenting. This article would make the laws of international armed conflict applicable to "armed conflicts in which peoples are fighting against colonial domination and alien occupation and against racist regimes in the exercise of the right of self-determination." Never before has the applicability of the laws of war been made to turn on the purported aims of a conflict. Moreover, this provision obliterated the traditional distinction between international and non-international armed conflict. Any group within a national boundary claiming to be fighting against colonial domination, alien occupation or a racist regime can now argue that it is protected by the laws of war, and that its members are entitled to prisoner-of-war status for their otherwise criminal acts. Members of radical groups in the United States have already tried to do so in federal courts. . . .

IX

The law's support for political violence has been manifested most recently in the efforts of some nations to establish doctrinal bases for curtailing the use of force against terrorists and their supporting states.

International law regulates the use of force by a country in the territories of other states, whether to capture or attack terrorists or to rescue hostages located there, or against the states themselves for sponsoring terrorists or conspiring with them in specific terrorist activities. In general, a nation may *not* enter upon another's territory without its consent. Similarly, a state may not stop, board, divert or otherwise interfere with another's vessels or aircraft without some adequate basis. Finally, the use of force against another country's territorial integrity or political independence is prohibited, except in self-defense, and any use of force must be both necessary and proportionate to the threat it addresses.

These principles have been respected by the United States. If they were applied, however, in such a manner as to preclude any use of force for any purpose, international law would serve to insulate the perpetrators of international violence from any control or punishment for their crimes. States could then continue using terrorism to accomplish their objectives with little cost or interference.

The principle of territorial sovereignty is not the only principle of law that must be weighed in considering objections against attacks on terrorists, attempts to rescue hostages and actions against countries that sponsor terrorism. States have duties to cooperate in preventing terrorists from using their territories in perpetrating criminal acts, and many governments have explicitly undertaken to extradite or prosecute terrorists guilty of hijacking, sabotage and hostage-taking. These obligations cannot be disregarded in evaluating the propriety of anti-terrorist operations. Furthermore, under the U.N. Charter, just as under customary international law, victims of terrorism are not powerless to defend themselves. The charter reaffirms the *inherent* right to use force in individual or collective self-defense against armed attack. . . .

The U.S. bombing raid launched against Libya on April 14, 1986, illustrated the need nations sometimes have to use force against states that sponsor terrorism. After terrorists from the Abu Nidal group attacked passengers in Rome and Vienna on December 27, 1985, killing 19 civilians, including five Americans, President Reagan clearly signaled the United States intent to rely upon its right of self-defense. He said:

> By providing material support to terrorist groups which attack U.S. citizens, Libya has engaged in armed aggression against the United States under established principles of international law, just as if he [Libyan leader Muammar al-Qaddafi] had used his own armed forces.

Despite this clear warning, Libya deliberately arranged for at least two attacks aimed at American noncombatants and U.S. interests. One plan was to fire automatic rifles and hurl grenades at civilians lined up at the U.S. embassy in Paris. French cooperation enabled the United States to thwart this plan, and several Libyans involved were deported. The United States was not so fortunate in West Berlin. Libyans at their people's bureau (embassy) in East Germany informed their home base that a planned attack would take place on April 5. A bomb exploded at a discothèque frequented by U.S. soldiers, killing Sergeant Kenneth T. Ford and a Turkish woman, and injuring over 200 persons, including 50 Americans. Shortly thereafter, on April 6, the same people's bureau informed Tripoli of the successful attack, and assured Tripoli that the bombing could not be traced to Libya.

These communications, following Qaddafi's long history of support for terrorism, and his threats against U.S. citizens, established overwhelmingly that Libya was responsible for the attack. In addition, the President was faced with strong evidence of some 30 possible impending Libyan attacks on U.S. facilities and personnel throughout the world. The April 14 strikes were to deter these and other planned attacks.

Some governments have condemned the action against Libya, claiming to disbelieve U.S. claims that Libya attacked American citizens and was planning further attacks. Others have ignored U.S. claims, and simply characterize Reagan Administration actions as "criminal" or "brutal." They oppose the use of force, even in self-defense. But no cogent argument has been made questioning the legal principles upon which the United States has relied. A resolution condemning the United States was vetoed by the United States, France and the United Kingdom in the Security Council on April 21. Its adoption would have given state-sponsored terrorism its ultimate legal defense, immunizing international aggression against noncombatants from the use of force in self-defense.

Law can make clear that state-supported terrorism is illicit, and may thus serve to deter it. But terrorist-supporting nations will not surrender seriously held ambitions to expand their power and influence simply because the law is against them. Legal argument alone will not protect law-abiding nations and peoples against Qaddafi or Iran's Khomeini. Nor will the prospect for peaceful settlement of disputes with such regimes be enhanced by U.S. promises to abjure force or by unrealistic limits on its flexibility. If Americans overestimate the limits of their own tolerance, they may allow U.S. adversaries to do so as well, thereby inviting reckless activity. The policeman is apt protection against individual criminals; but national self-defense is the only protection against the criminal state.

X

The law, as presently formulated, cannot reasonably be expected effectively to repress international terrorism. International terrorism is still supported by many nations as a legitimate means of struggle against regimes deemed by them to be colonial, alien or racist. At the behest of these states, and by the acquiescence of others, international law has been systematically and intentionally fashioned to give special treatment to, or to leave unregulated, those activities that cause and are the source of most acts of international terror.

The failure of international law to control terrorism is a matter of great strategic concern. Ineffective methods for dealing with terrorists through the law will inevitably lead to antiterrorist actions more primitive and dangerous than cooperation among sovereign states, including conventional military actions in self-defense, will provide. These dangers are especially heightened with terrorism that is state-supported.

Civilized nations and peoples cannot give up on law, however frustrated they may feel by its shortcomings. In fact, the point of this essay is that law is not presently being used to counter terrorism; it has been placed very much at the service of those who embrace political violence. Our challenge is to create a broader understanding among peoples and governments to bring about a shift in the objects that international law is designed to serve.

Walter Laqueur

Reflections on Terrorism

Fifty years hence, puzzled historians will try to make sense of the behavior of Western governments and media in the 1980 vis-à-vis terrorism. Presidents and other leaders have frequently referred to terrorism as one of the greatest dangers facing mankind. For days and weeks on end, television networks devoted most of their prime-time news to terrorist operations. Publicists referred to terrorism as the cancer of the modern world, growing inexorably until it poisoned and engulfed the society on which it fed, dragging it down to destruction.

Reprinted from *Foreign Affairs*, October 1986, with the kind permission of the publisher.

Naturally, our future historian will expect that a danger of such enormity must have figured very highly on the agenda of our period—equal, say, to the danger of war, starvation, overpopulation, deadly diseases, debts, and so on. He will assume that determined action was taken and major resources allocated to the fight against this threat. And he will be no little surprised to learn that, when the Swedish Prime Minister was killed in 1986, the Swedish government promised a reward for information leading to the apprehension of his killer that amounted to less than 10% of the annual income of an investment banker or a popular entertainer—not necessarily of the front rank; that the French government offered even less for its terrorists; that West Germany was willing to pay only up to $50,000 "for the most dangerous." The United States, always a great believer in the effectiveness of money, offered up to $500,000,* again not an overwhelming sum considering the frequency of the speeches about terrorism and the intensity of the rhetoric.

Cash rewards for informers are frowned upon by society, but surely (our historian will ask) major investments were made in the research and development of technological means—another favorite American preoccupation—in order to preempt and to combat the terrorists. Again to his consternation, he will discover that the sum devoted to this purpose—about $20–30 million—was considerably less than any second-rank pharmaceutical firm would allocate for research and development. His confusion will further deepen when he learns that the number of Americans killed inside the U.S. in 1985 as the result of terrorist attacks was two, and the total number of U.S. civilians killed abroad between 1973 and the end of 1985 was 169. In countless articles and books, our historian will have read about the constantly rising number of terrorist attacks. Being a conscientious researcher he will analyze the statistics and this is bound to increase his confusion, for he will find that more American civilians were killed by terrorists in 1974 (22) than in 1984 (16). On the basis of these and other facts, our historian will lean towards revisionism. He may well reach the conclusion that there was no terrorism, only a case of mass delusion—or that hysteria was deliberately fanned by certain vested interests, such as producers of anti-terrorist equipment perhaps

* Under the 1984 Act to Combat Terrorism. But it is not certain whether the U.S. government would have been, in fact, in a position to pay up, for the sum total allocated for this purpose was $2 million.

or the television networks which had established a symbiotic relationship with the terrorists, providing them with free (or almost free) entertainment for long periods.

These are, of course, the wrong conclusions: The impact of terrorism is measured not only in the number of victims. Terrorism is an attempt to destabilize democratic societies and to show that their governments are impotent. And if this can be attained with a minimum effort, if so much publicity can be achieved on the basis of a few attacks, there is no need to make greater exertions. It is also true that there have been ominous new developments such as the emergence of narco-terrorism and of state-sponsored terrorism on a broader level than before. If terrorism was never a serious threat as far as America was concerned, let alone other major powers such as Russia, China or Japan, it is also true that in certain Latin American countries, but also in places like Turkey and Italy, it was for a while a real danger.

In short, there has been (and is) a terrorist menace in our time. But the historian of the future will still be right in pointing to the wide discrepancy between the strong speeches and the weak actions of those who felt threatened. And he must be forgiven if he should draw the conclusion that the "age of terrorism" perhaps never quite understood the exact nature of the threat.

II

What is terrorism? It would be highly desirable, if all discussions of terrorism, its motives and inspiration, its specific character, modes of operation, and long-term consequences were based on a clear, exact, and comprehensive definition. Ideally, there should be agreement as to whether terrorism is violence in general or some specific form of violence; whether the stress should be on its political aims or its methods of combat, or the extra-normal character of its strategy; whether its purposive, systematic character should be singled out, or, on the contrary, its unpredictability and symbolic aspect or perhaps the fact that so many of its victims are innocents.

Such a definition, alas, does not exist, and there is no reason to assume that there will be one in the foreseeable future. The author of an excellent research guide to terrorism, published a number of years ago, listed 109 different definitions of terrorism provided between 1936 and 1981, and there have been more since; the U.S. government alone has provided half a dozen, which are by no means identical.* Most authors agree that terrorism is the use or threat of the use of violence, a method of combat or a strategy to achieve certain targets, that its aim is to induce a state of fear in the victim, that it is ruthless and does not conform with humanitarian rules, and that publicity is an essential factor in terrorist strategy. Beyond this point, definitions differ, often sharply, which is by no means surprising, be it only because the character of terrorist groups has been subject to change. There is little, if anything, in common between the Russian terrorists of the nineteenth century and Abu Nidal; a definition trying to cover both these and other groups would be either very vague or very misleading. There is no such thing as terrorism pure and unadulterated, specific and unchanging, comparable to a chemical element, but there are a great many terrorisms. Historians and sociologists are not in full agreement on what socialism is or fascism was; they do not even agree to this day on Napoleon and the French Revolution or the outbreak of the First World War. It would be unrealistic to expect unanimity on a topic so close to us in time. But the absence of an exact definition does not mean that we do not know in a general way what terrorism is; it has been said that it resembles pornography, difficult to describe and define, but easy to recognize when one sees it.

According to one school of thought, "state terrorism" is the all-important issue. The concentration on the relatively insignificant acts of violence by small groups of people (known in professional language as "sub-state actors") is, therefore, denounced in the third world and some radical circles as a political maneuver, scheduled to distract our attention from the truly important issues of our time. One proponent of this view has written that the strategies and tactics of terrorism have recently become integral components both in the domestic and foreign political realms of the modern state. Why "recently" and why "modern state"? Has it not always been the case? No one denies that the number of victims and the amount of suffering caused by oppressive, tyrannical governments has been infinitely greater than that caused by small groups of rebels: A Hitler or a Stalin killed more people in one year than all terrorists throughout recorded history. Massacres and arbitrary rule have figured prominently in primitive

* Alex Schmid, *Political Terrorism: A Research Guide* (Transaction, New Brunswick, 1984).

society and primitive religion. To write the history of persecution and oppression is, to a large extent, to write the history of mankind.

But there are basic differences in motives, function, and effect between oppression by the state (or society or religion) and political terrorism. To equate them, to obliterate the differences, is to spread confusion. The study of the Inquisition or the Gestapo or the Gulag is of undoubted importance, but it will shed no light whatsoever on contemporary terrorism.

If there has been a significant development during the last decade, it was not oppression by the state, but state-sponsored terrorism. This is not, of course, a product of the 1970s; attempts to undermine the political or social order in other countries have been undertaken by ambitious or revengeful rulers since time immemorial. The term "destabilization" may be new, but the use of proxies is as old as the hills.

But there are nevertheless certain new features to this old acquaintance that makes it more dangerous than in the past. It has become more frequent because resistance against it was weak and uncoordinated. It has become more brazen: Mussolini, one of the chief practitioners of state-sponsored terrorism in the 1930s, would reject any such imputation with great indignation. In full uniform, shedding bitter tears, he would attend the service in Rome in honor of King Alexander of Yugoslavia, who had been assassinated on his behest. Today's Khadafis, on the other hand, do not stick to such proprieties, but claim the right to engage in acts of terror on the territory of other countries. Above all, there is the danger, that state-sponsored terrorism will escalate into full military conflict with incalculable consequences.

Some of the obfuscation concerning terrorism stems from the belief in some circles that contemporary terrorism is basically revolutionary, a reaction against social and national injustice, and therefore worthy of support or at least understanding. But in fact, terrorism is by no means the monopoly of the extreme left. Quite frequently it is used by the extreme right and neo-fascists, and those trying to find mitigating circumstances for "revolutionary terrorism" find themselves sooner or later in the uncomfortable position of performing the same service for their political enemies. Terrorism is not an ideology but an insurrectional strategy that can be used by people of different political convictions. Contemporary terrorism is not the brainchild of Marxism-

Leninism or Muslim fundamentalism, even though regimes of these creeds have made notable contributions to its spread.

Terrorism is also neither identical with guerrilla warfare nor a subspecies of it. The term "urban guerrilla" is as common as it is mistaken. Terrorism is indeed urban, but not "guerrilla" in any meaningful sense; the difference is not one of semantics but of quality. A guerrilla leader—to put it in the briefest possible way—aims at building up ever growing military units and eventually an army, to establish liberated zones in which propaganda can be openly conducted, and eventually to set up an alternative government. All this is impossible in the cities. The different environment dictates a different strategy and this has basic political consequences. In many instances, guerrilla movements and other insurrectional groups have footholds in cities—usually without much success. But the opposite has only very seldom happened; in the urban milieu there are no opportunities for guerrilla warfare. There is a world of difference between a temporary "no-go" zone and the establishment of an alternative government.

Some Western experts, and especially the media, have great difficulty in accepting the basic differences between various forms of violence—"terrorists," "commandos," "partisans," "urban guerrillas," "gunmen," "freedom fighters," "insurgents," and half a dozen other terms are used interchangeably, frequently as a result of genuine confusion, sometimes probably with political intent. For guerrilla has, on the whole, a positive public relations image, which terrorism clearly does not possess. Soviet writers on this subject have fewer inhibitions to call a spade by its rightful name. In a recent study, one of them noted that "urban guerrilla is a fraudulent concept, scheduled to mask ordinary terrorism."* Soviet ideologists are by no means opposed to the use of revolutionary violence. But they also know that terrorism carried out by marginal groups almost always causes more harm than good to the cause it sponsors. It is easy to think of guerrilla movements which defeated the forces opposing them; it is very difficult to remember more than a few cases in which terrorism has had any lasting effect.

* Viktor Vladimirovich Vityuk, *Pod chuzhim znamenami. Litsemeric i samoobman levovo terrorizma* (Moscow, 1985), p. 22.

III

How to eradicate terrorism? Moralists believe that terrorism is the natural response to injustice, oppression, and persecution. Hence the seemingly obvious conclusion: Remove the underlying causes which cause terrorism and it will wither away! This sounds plausible enough, for happy and content people are unlikely to commit savage acts of violence. But while this may be true as an abstract general proposition, it seldom applies in the real world, which is never quite free of conflicts. The historical record shows that while, in the nineteenth century, terrorism frequently developed in response to repression, the correlation between grievance and terrorism in our day and age is far less obvious. The historical record shows that the more severe the repression, the less terrorism tends to occur. This is an uncomfortable, shocking fact, and has, therefore, encountered much resistance. But it is still true that terrorism in Spain gathered strength only after Franco died, that the terrorist upsurge in West Germany, France, and Turkey took place under social democratic or left-of-center governments, that the same is true with regard to Peru and Colombia, and that more such examples could easily be adduced.

Terrorism has never had a chance in an effective dictatorship, but hardly a major democratic country has entirely escaped it. There is a limit to the perfection of political institutions, and however just and humane the social order, there will always be a few people deeply convinced that it ought to be radically changed and that it can be changed only through violent action. The murder of Olof Palme is just one illustration which showed that "objective factors" cannot account for the actions of a fringe group.

Nationalist-separatist terrorism has been doing better than that of the extreme left and right, and it is not difficult to understand why. National groups and minorities usually have grievances and some of them may be quite justified. In some instances, they can be put right, in others assuaged, but frequently this may not be possible. In an ideal world, each group of people, however small, claiming the right of full independence and statehood, should receive it. But given the lack of national homogeneity and the intermingling of ethnic and religious groups, no basic redress may be feasible. It may not be too late even at this late stage for the Turks to accept responsibility for the Armenian massacres during World War One, to apologize to the descendants of the victims, and to show contrition. But an Armenian state on Turkish territory (as ASALA demands) is an absurdity: Armenians no longer live in Eastern Turkey nor do they have the intention to settle there. A Sikh state in the Punjab would not be viable; the Sikhs, in any case, are not an oppressed minority in contemporary India: The president of India is a Sikh and so are most of India's military leaders. The great majority of the Sikhs do not even want a state of their own.

The Basque ETA and the Corsican militants fight for independent statehood. But even if these mini-states would be viable, which is uncertain, this demand is by no means shared by most of their fellow countrymen, let alone by the majority of the population in the Basque country and Corsica, which is ethnically of different background (Spanish and French).

Nor is it certain that the establishment of new, independent states would put an end to terrorism. On the contrary, there could well be an intensification of the struggle between various terrorist groups, between moderates who want to proceed with the business of statehood and radicals who claim that what has been achieved is only a beginning and that the borders of the new state should be expanded. The Tamils have been fighting with as much relish against each other as against the common enemy, and there is no good reason to assume that this would stop if they were to get a state of their own.

No effort should be spared to pursue the peace process between Arabs and Israelis. But few serious students of this conflict will argue that, if a Palestinian state were to come into existence in the foreseeable future, terrorism would decrease. No settlement which recognizes Israel would be to the liking of Palestinian radicals. All this does not make the search for a solution of the conflict undesirable or unnecessary, but there should be no illusions with regard to its likely consequences as far as the persistence of terrorism is concerned.

IV

It is frequently argued that one cannot defend oneself against extremists willing to sacrifice their lives, and that arresting or shooting terrorists has never solved a problem of this kind, for the "blood of the martyrs is the seed of the church." Historical experience does not confirm such wisdom. The terrorist potential inside every country is limited; on the basis of a painstaking analysis, a recent study reaches the obvious conclusion that "the more terrorists in prison, the lower the violence level."* This does not, of course, apply to a mass insurrection supported by the overwhelming majority of the population, but it is true with regard to terrorist groups. Shiite propensity to engage in terrorist suicide attacks has been very much exaggerated. True, there have been a few cases, not more than four or five, of such operations. But this readiness to commit suicide can be found at all times and in many places; ten members of the IRA starved themselves to death—and this despite the ban, *expressis verbis*, of the Catholic Church against suicide; so did members of Baader-Meinhof, not to mention the Jonestown incident. When the Japanese authorities asked for Kamikaze candidates during the last years of the war, more than a thousand volunteered. It is not so much a matter of a specific religion but of fanaticism, and a psychological predisposition. What Voltaire wrote about the subject seems still to be correct today: The entire species (of fanatics) is divided into two classes: The first does nought but pray and die, the second wants to reign and massacre.

Terrorism has been stamped out with great ease not only by all modern dictatorships, it has been defeated even by governments who are anything but modern. In 1981, Khomeini's former allies from the left, the Mojaheddin and some other groups, turned against the new rulers of Iran. They were many and experienced; within three months they succeeded in killing the Prime Minister, many chiefs of police, half the government and the executive committee of the ruling party, not to mention dozens of members of parliament. Perhaps never before had a terrorist onslaught been so massive and so successful. Yet within another three months, the terrorists were either dead or had escaped abroad. The government acted with great brutality, it killed without discrimination, it extracted information by means of torture, and it refused as a matter of principle to extend medical help to injured terrorists. And it broke the back of the terrorist movement.

The Turkish authorities liquidated terrorism with much less violence: During the year preceding Martial Law (September 1980) some 3,000 Turks of both the left and the right, and not a few innocent bystanders, had been killed. Mass arrests and a few dozen executions of convicted murderers were sufficient to cause the collapse of terrorism within a matter of days. Argentina suppressed the Montoneros

* Christopher Hewitt, *The Effectiveness of Anti-terrorist Policies* (Lanham, 1984), p. 47.

and the ERP with great inhumanity, whereas Uruguay succeeded vis-à-vis the Tupamaros with a minimum of violence.*

The power of the state is infinitely greater than that of the terrorists, and it will always prevail, provided there is the determination or the ruthlessness to do so. But can a democratic society subdue terrorism without surrendering the values central to the system? Again, experience shows that it can be done without great difficulty. The Italian authorities defeated the Red Brigades, while acting strictly within the law, by a mixture of overdue political reform, penetration of the terrorist ranks, and promising substantial reduction in prison terms to the penitents. Terrorist movements do not have an unlimited life span. If they realize after a few years that the murder of a few politicians (and many innocents) has not brought them any nearer to the target, their resolve weakens.

The nationalist-separatist terrorists hold out longer, for their basis of support is stronger and they may have assistance of foreign countries. But even in Northern Ireland and Euzkadi, the level of violence is much lower now than eight or ten years ago, the Armenian ASALA have all but disappeared.

A dialectical process seems to dictate the policy of democratic societies. As long as terrorism is no more than a nuisance, it will rightly resist any attempt to curtail its traditional freedoms. Once terrorism becomes more than a nuisance, once the normal functioning of society is affected, there will be overwhelming pressure on the government to defeat the threat by all available means. Hence the paradoxical conclusion that the more successful the terrorists, the nearer their ultimate defeat. There are exceptions to every rule, but in this case they are few and far between.

V

State-sponsored terrorism is mainly the instrument of dictators with ambitions far in excess of their power base. Typically, the chief protagonist of this kind of terrorism between the Two World Wars was not Hitler but Mussolini, who used various kinds of Balkan terrorists to destabilize neighboring countries such as Yugoslavia. The

* They reconstituted themselves as a legal political party and are doing quite well.

Soviet Union was also active in the field, but its operations were mainly limited to the assassination of emigre political leaders such as Trotsky. Today's mini-Mussolinis in the Middle East and in Central America rule small or relatively weak countries. Libya is an extreme example: But for its investment in terrorism, it would be not much more important than Mauretania or the Yemens. The Syrian and Iranian sponsors of terrorism have been more discriminate in their targets and therefore, within limits, more successful.

The attitude of the Soviet bloc has been ambiguous. It has used terrorism as a weapon to destabilize certain countries, but only as a minor instrument in the general arsenal of political warfare and this for two reasons. The Soviets will never extend support openly, it has to be carefully laundered through a series of subcontractors and middlemen. But this also means that they cannot have full control over the terrorists; the gunmen may land them in situations that were not planned, and which may be politically harmful. To engage in international terrorism is to play with a fire that is difficult to control. Mention has already been made of the other reason: Marxist-Leninists believe in mass action rather than individual terror and past experience tends to show that this is by and large correct. Far from weakening a society, terrorism has quite frequently had the opposite, immunizing effect, bringing about greater internal cohesion. The effects of the murder of Aldo Moro is one example, the consequences of terrorism on the internal situation in Israel is another. Far from diverting resources from national defense, the terrorist threat strengthens the feeling that more ought to be done for national security and it plays into the hands of the forces of law and order. Seen in a wider perspective, systematic terrorism is a mixed blessing from the Soviet point of view. It may cause friction between the United States and its allies, many of which have been taking a softer line vis-à-vis international terrorism. But such a rift is not about matters of principle—no one in Europe actually likes international terrorism. Even Papandreou wants it to go away—at least to a neighboring country. It is an embarrassment, bad for the image of the country affected, tourism suffers, and there are all kinds of other negative consequences.

For this the governments of Western Europe have to a large extent to blame themselves. For years they have permitted themselves to be blackmailed, beginning with the establishment of Libyan peoples' offices replacing legations and embassies, in open contravention of diplomatic practice. Yet the European governments more often than not preferred to close their eyes, as they did when Libyan emigres and their own nationals were gunned down in broad daylight in their cities.

Appeasement is not reprehensible per se; at one stage or another all countries have made concessions to terrorists. If appeasement had worked, a good case could be made in its favor: Why endanger the lives of European nationals in the Middle East, why sacrifice trade and goodwill just because of a few isolated incidents? But appeasement had no beneficial results; the fact that Kreisky and Papandreou were nice to Kadhafi and that France and Italy had a special relationship with various Middle Eastern terrorist groups did not give them immunity from terrorist attack. The contrary happened, and the reasons seem obvious. Israel is a difficult target, and the terrorists rightly assumed that America would react violently if they carried their operation to its shores. Under these circumstances, it was only natural that terrorists would prefer soft targets in Europe. But there is a limit to the patience of European governments, willing to put up with isolated incidents but not with systematic campaigns. If the French, Spanish, and other governments have adopted of late sterner measures against the sponsors of international terrorism, this was not so much for love of America but because their own interests were affected—and because of growing domestic pressure.

VI

As internal terrorism has declined in the Western world over the last decade and as international terrorism has become more frequent, full international cooperation against terrorism has been invoked a great many times. It is a hopeless undertaking as long as some states sponsor, finance, equip, train, and provide sanctuaries. Spokesmen for democratic societies will continue to proclaim that terrorism is abhorred and condemned by the whole civilized world. But the civilized world does not extend that far these days, and proceedings in the U.N. have shown that it is very difficult to have terrorism condemned even on paper, unless some of the leading communist or third world countries just happened to be on the receiving end of terrorist operations—which helps to clear their mind, but, unfortunately, not for very long.

These debates will no doubt go on for many years and it may be wrong to pay too much attention to them. International terrorism is an extra-legal activity and the contribution of our legal experts is bound to have a limited effect. Specific bilateral agreements or pacts between a group of countries may be of certain value; the exchange of information between NATO countries and some others has improved during the last decade and, as a result, some terrorist attacks have been prevented. In certain conditions quiet diplomacy has been of some help, such as issuing unpublicized warnings; in other circumstances preemptive publicity has helped. Most sponsors of state terrorism do not want their involvement to become known. They will, at the very least, temporarily scale down their involvement once they realize that what was meant to be a high-value, low-risk undertaking might escalate into an armed conflict in which the risks are high and the value, at best, uncertain.

But truly effective concerted action against terrorism is possible only on the basis of the strategy first advocated by the nineteenth-century Russian terrorists. This is "hitting the center," meaning the rulers of the countries who are sponsors of international terrorism. But hitting the center may not be easy for a variety of reasons. The responsibility for a certain terrorist action or campaign cannot always be easily proved. The aggrieved party may find it difficult to provide evidence that would stand up in a court of law. Smoking guns are seldom left at the scene of the crime in this kind of business. Even if there is evidence, to reveal it would often mean to give away the identity of well-placed intelligence sources in the terrorist hierarchy, of which there are probably not many.

For a country or a group of countries subject to attacks by international terrorism there are, broadly speaking, three ways to react. Given the natural inertia of democratic governments and the difficulties involved, the obvious reaction is to condemn the attack but to refrain from any physical act of retaliation. As long as these attacks occur relatively rarely and inasmuch as they do not result in many victims, this is a feasible policy. But lack of reaction is usually interpreted as a sign of weakness in which case the attacks will become more frequent and murderous. The sponsors of international terrorism resemble in many respects children trying to find out by trial and error how far they can go in provoking the adults until punishment will be meted out to them.

If an escalation in international terrorist attacks does take place, the obvious way to retaliate is, of course, to pay back the sponsors in their own coin. As Colonel Grivas, head of the EOKA in Cyprus and a man of great experience in the field, once put it: To catch a mouse, one uses a cat, not a tank (or an aircraft carrier). But democratic countries may not have cats, meaning a truly effective covert action capability—or "active measures," to use the well-known Soviet term. Even if they have a capability of this kind, they may find it difficult to use it, be it because terrorist acts are much easier to carry out in open societies than in dictatorships or because those who engage in covert action on behalf of a democratic country are not normally permitted to kill enemy leaders; in the United States there is an absolute prohibition by Presidential order.

What alternatives exist? In some cases diplomatic action may have some success; on other occasions economic sanctions may have a certain impact, but only if there is agreement between the major Western countries. Otherwise in the absence of "cats," retaliation takes the form of military action. Such escalation involves risks: Innocent people are likely to get killed and those who retaliate will be blamed for creating a new dangerous situation. This has been the fate of the Israelis, who for a long time combined covert action with surgical air strikes (which, on occasion, hit the wrong target). It was also the fate of the United States after the strike against Libya in April 1986: Those who retaliate become attackers and there will be a great deal of handwringing and dire warnings. No government will lightly take such a course of action. It will only do so if it has good reason to believe that the alternative, refraining from counteraction, would have fateful consequences and if public opinion at home is so strongly in favor of retaliation that it cannot safely be ignored. This is particularly true with regard to a superpower whose freedom of action is by necessity more restrained than that of a small country. The more powerful a country, the stronger the constraints to act cautiously, for everything a major power does is important; it may turn a local incident into an international conflict.

VII

Thus the inclination will still be to wait and see. Terrorism may not outgrow the nuisance stage or a one-time, limited application of military force may be sufficient to drive the lesson home. There is a tendency to magnify the importance of terrorism in modern society: Society is vulnerable to attack, but it is also astonishingly resilient. Terrorism makes a great noise, but so far it has not been very destructive. Our media resemble the Bedouin warriors of Lawrence of Arabia who were sturdy fighters, except for their mistaken belief that weapons were dangerous in proportion to the noise they created.

But what if terrorism does outgrow the nuisance stage, what if the one-time lesson administered is not sufficient? In theory, the sponsors of state terrorism should never let this come to pass. For once they succeed in provoking the superpower, the political calculus changes and they are bound to lose in a confrontation with a much more powerful nation. Only gross miscalculation can lead them into such a course of action. Unfortunately, it is not certain that rational behavior will always prevail on their part. In this case the victims of state-sponsored terrorism must act. They could bring back Colonel Grivas' cats, which is difficult in a democratic society and perhaps undesirable. Or they can choose deliberate escalation, hitting back with military force against elusive terrorist targets. If there is at the present time a terrorist threat, it is not the one usually adduced, of destroying societies from within. It is the danger of terrorist provocation leading well beyond the confines of mere terrorism. The danger cannot be reduced without Soviet cooperation. The Khadafis and Assads will act much more cautiously when they know that they cannot count on automatic Soviet help, once their transgressions lead to retribution. Terrorism, in other words, may not be very important, but like some minor diseases, it can have unpleasant and possibly dangerous consequences, if neglected.

A Selected Bibliography

The following bibliographical note refers only to works of special interest. Historical bibliographies on terrorism do not exist; a standard work such as Venturi's *Roots of Revolution* can, of course, be used as a guide to the main sources. The same applies to Nettlau's works on anarchism, to Zoccoli (the early period of Anarchism), or Maitron (French Anarchism). There is rich documentation on terrorism in Ireland, Latin America, the Middle East, and the New Left and multinational terrorism, but most of the material is not easy to locate and bibliographical aids are virtually nonexistent.

General Literature on Terrorism

Alexander, Y. (ed.), *International Terrorism.* New York, 1976.

———, Browne, M., and Nanes, A. S. (eds.), *Control of Terrorism: International Documents.* New York, 1979.

———, Carlton, D., and Wilkinson, P. (eds.), *Terrorism: Theory and Practice.* Boulder, 1979.

———, and Kilmarx, R. A. (eds.), *Political Terrorism and Business: The Threat and Response.* New York, 1979.

———, and Gleason, J. M. (eds.), *Behavioral and Quantitative Perspectives on Terrorism.* New York, 1981.

———, and Cline, R., *Terrorism as State Sponsored Covert Warfare.* Fairfax, 1986.

Bassiouni, M. C. (ed.), *International Terrorism and Political Crimes.* Springfield, 1975.

Bell, B. J., *Transnational Terror.* Washington, 1975.

Burton, A., *Urban Terrorism.* London, 1975.

Carlton, D. (ed.), *Contemporary Terrorism.* New York, 1981.

Clutterbuck, R., *Protest and the Urban Guerrilla.* London, 1973.

Cooper, H. H. A., *On Assassination.* Boulder, 1984.

Crenshaw, M. (ed.), *Terrorism, Legitimacy, and Power.* Middletown, 1983.

Crown, J., *Australia: The Terrorist Connection.* Melbourne, 1986.

Dror, Y., *Crazy States.* New York, 1980.

Dyson, J., *Sink the Rainbow!: An Enquiry into the Greenpeace Affair.* London, 1986.

Eichelman, B., and Suskis, D. A., and Reid, W. H. (eds.), *Terrorism: Interdisciplinary Perspectives.* Washington, D.C., 1983.

Freeman, C., *Terrorism.* London, 1981.

Gal-Or, N., *International Cooperation to Suppress Terrorism.* New York, 1985.

Gaucher, R., *The Terrorists.* London, 1968.

Hacker, F., *Terror, Mythos, Realität, Analyse.* Vienna, 1973.

Henze, P. B., *The Plot to Kill the Pope.* New York, 1983.

International Terrorism. U.S. House Committee on Foreign Affairs. Washington, D.C., 1974.

Janke, P., *Guerrilla and Terrorist Organization: A World Directory and Bibliography.* New York, 1983.

Kupperman, R., and Trent, D., *Terrorism: Threat, Reality, Response.* Stanford, 1979.

Lakos, A., *International Terrorism: A Bibliography.* Boulder, 1986.

Langemann, H., *Das Attentat.* Hamburg, 1957.

Laqueur, Walter, *The Age of Terrorism.* Boston, 1987.

Livingston, M. H. (ed.), *International Terrorism in the Contemporary World*. West Point, 1978.

Lodge, J. *Terrorism: The Challenge to the State*. Oxford, 1981.

McKnight, G., *The Terrorist Mind: Why They Hijack, Kidnap, Bomb and Kill*. Indianapolis, 1974.

Malin, J. (ed.), *Terror and Urban Guerrillas*. Coral Gables, 1971.

Mickolus, E. F. *The Literature of Terrorism*. Westport, 1980.

———, *Transnational Terrorism: A Chronology of Events, 1968–1979*. London, 1980.

Middendorf, W., *Der Politische Mord*. Wiesbaden, 1968.

Moss, R., *Urban Guerrillas*. London, 1972.

Netanyahu, B., *Terrorism: How the West Can Win*. New York, 1986.

Ochberg, F. M., and Soskis, D. A. (eds.), *Victims of Terrorism*. Boulder, 1982.

O'Sullivan, N., *Terrorism, Ideology and Revolution*. Boulder, 1982.

Pankov, Y. (ed.), *Political Terrorism, An Indictment of Imperialism*. Moscow, 1980.

Parry, A., *Terrorism from Robespierre to Arafat*. Ontario, 1976.

Political Kidnappings. Committee on Internal Security. House of Representatives, Washington, D.C., 1973.

Rapaport, D. C., *Assassination and Terrorism*. Toronto, 1971.

Rivers, G., *The War Against the Terrorists*. New York, 1986.

Schamis, G. J., *War and Terrorism in International Affairs*. New Brunswick, 1980.

Shears, R., and Gidley, I., *The Rainbow Warrior Affair*. Sydney, 1985.

Sobel, L., *Political Terrorism*. New York, 1975.

Terrorism. Parts 1–4, Committee on Internal Security, House of Representatives. Washington, D.C., 1974.

Terrorism. Staff Study. Committee on Internal Security, House of Representatives. Washington, D.C., 1974.

Terrorist Activity. Parts 1–8, Committee of the Judiciary, House of Representatives, Washington, D.C., 1974–1975.

Trautman, F., *The Voice of Terror: A Biography of Johann Most*. Westport, 1980.

Waciorski, J., *Le Terrorisme Politique*. Paris, 1939.

Wilkinson, P., *Political Terrorism*. London, 1974.

———, *Terrorism and the Liberal State*. London, 1977.

Tyrannicide, Secret Societies

Althusius, J., *Politica Metodice Digesta*. 1603.

Ballesteros-Gailbrois, M., *Juan de Mariana, cantor de Espana*. Madrid, 1938–1939.

Boucher, J., *De iusta Henrici III*. 1589.
Buchanan, G., *De Jure Regni apud Scotos*. 1579.
Buonarroti, P., *Conspiration pour l'égalité dite de Babeuf*. 1579.
Blanqui, A., *Textes Choisis*. Paris, 1955.
Daneau, L., *Politicae Christianae libri VII*. 1596.
Dommanget, M., *Pages Choisies de Babeuf*. Paris, 1935.
Duplessis-Mornay. *Vindiciae contra Tyrannos*. 1579.
Frost, T., *The Secret Societies of European Revolution*. 2 vols. London, 1875.
Jaszi, O., and Lewis, D. *Against the Tyrant*. New York, 1957.
Johnston, R. M., *Napoleonic Empire in Southern Italy*. 2 vols. London, 1904.
Kovalskaia, M. I., *Dvizhenie Karbonartsev v Italii 1808–1821*. Moscow, 1971.
La Boetie., *De la Servitude Volontaire au Contru'un*. 1578.
Liman, P., *Der politische Mord im Wandel der Geschichte*. 1912.
Lutaud, O., *Des Révolutions d'Angleterre à la Révolution Francaise*. Paris, 1973.
Mariana, J. D., *De Rege et Regis Institutione*. 1599.
Mousnier, R., *Assassinat d'Henri IV*. Paris, 1964.
Platzhoff, W., *Die Theorie von der Mordbefugnis der Obrigkeit im 16.* Jahrhundert, 1906.
Rossaeus, C., *De iusta Rei publicae Christianae*. 1590.
Salisbury, John of, *Policraticus*. 1595.
Sexby, E., *Killing no murder* . . . . 1657.
Sencier, G., *Le Babouvisme après Babeuf*. Paris, 1912.
Schoenstedt, F., *Der Tyrannenmord im Spätmittelalter*. 1939.
Spadoni, D., *Sette, Cospirationi e Conspiratori*. Turin, 1904.
Weill, G., *Le Parti Republicain en France 1814–1870*. Paris, 1900.

Bakunin and Nechaev

Bakunin, M., *Izbrannie Sochineniia*. 5 vols. Petrograd, 1919–1921.
———, *Gesammelte Werke*. 3 vols. Berlin, 1921–1924.
Carr, E. H., *Michael Bakunin*. London, 1937.
Confino, M., *Violence dans la Violence*. Paris, 1973.
Kaminski, H. E., *Bakounine: La vie d'un Revolutionnaire*. Paris, 1938.
Lehning, A., *Michael Bakounine et ses Relations avec Sergej Necaev*. Leiden, 1971.
Nettlau, M., *Michael Bakunin; eine Biographie*. 3 vols. London, 1896–1900.
Steklov, Y. M., *M. A. Bakunin, Yevo Zhizn i Deatelnost. 1814–76*. 4 vols. Moscow, 1926–1927.

Terrorism in Russia (1870–1920)

The most important sources for the study of Russian terrorism are the journals of Narodnaya Volya and the Socialist Revolutionaries, as well as Burtsev's *Byloe* and the periodicals of the early Soviet period, such as *Katorga i Sylka.*

Avrich, P., *The Russian Anarchists.* Princeton, 1971.
Bogucharski, V., *Aktivnoe Narodnichestvo.* Moscow, 1912.
Burtsev, V., *Za sto let.* London, 1897.
———, *Doloi Tsarya.* London, 1901.
———, *Borba za svobodnuyu Rossiu.* Berlin, 1924.
Chernov, V. M., *Pered Burei.* New York, 1953.
Confino, M., *La Violence dans la Violence.* Paris, 1973.
Da zdravstvuyet Narodnaya Volya. Paris, 1907.
Debogori-Mokrievich, V. I., *Vospominania.* St. Petersburg, 1906.
Figner, V., *Memoirs of a Revolutionist.* New York, 1927.
Footman, D., *Red Prelude.* London, 1943.
Itenberg, B. S., *Dviznenie Revoliutsonovo Narodnichestva.* Moscow, 1965.
Ivianski, A. I. (ed), *Zhizn kak Fakel.* Moscow, 1966.
Kucharzewski, Jan., *Od Bialego Caratu do Czerwonego.* 7 vols. Warsaw, 1926–1935.
Masaryk, T. G., *Zur russischen Geschichts und Religionsphilosophie.* Jena, 1913.
Morozov, N., *Povest moei Zhizni.* Moscow, 1947.
Narodovoltsi. Moscow, 1947.
Nestroev, G., *Iz Dnevnik Maksimalista.* Paris, 1910.
Nikolajewski, B., *Asew.* Berlin, 1932.
Padenie Tsarskovo Rezhima. 3 vols. Moscow, 1920–1925.
Savinkov, B., *Erinnerungen eines Terroristen.* Berlin, 1927.
Spiridovich, A., *Histoire du Terrorisme Russe.* Paris, 1930.
Steinberg, I., *Spiridonowa.* London, 1935.
Stepniak-Kravchinski, S., *Podpolnaya Russia.* Moscow, 1960.
Tikhomirov, L., *Vospominania.* Moscow, 1927.
Venturi, L., *Roots of Revolution.* London, 1966.
Volin, L., *Nineteen Seventeen.* London, 1954.
Volk, S. S., *Narodnaya Volya.* Moscow, 1966.

Terrorism in Europe

Alexander, Y., and Myers, K. *Terrorism in Europe.* New York, 1982.
Barry, T., *Guerrilla Days in Ireland.* New York, 1956.

Beaslei, P. S., *Michael Collins and the Making of a New Ireland.* London, 1926.

Bell, J. B., *The Secret Army; The IRA 1916–1979.* Dublin, 1983.

Bennet, R., *The Black and the Tans.* London, 1959.

Bolotten, B., *The Grand Camouflage.* New York, 1961.

Boulton, D., *The UVF 1966–1973.* Dublin, 1973.

Bowyer Bell, J., *The Secret Army.* London, 1970.

Boyd, A., *Holy War in Belfast.* London, 1969.

Breen, D., *My Fight for Irish Freedom.* Kerry, 1964.

Browne, T. N., *Irish American Nationalism.* New York, 1966.

Brenan, G., *The Spanish Labyrinth.* Cambridge, 1943.

Coogan, T. P., *The IRA.* London, 1970.

Corfe, T., *The Phoenix Park Murders.* London, 1968.

Devoy's Post Bag. W. O'Brien and D. Ryan (eds.). 2 vols. Dublin, 1953.

Devoy, J., *Recollection of an Irish Rebel.* Shannon, 1969.

Edwards, O. D., and F. Pyle (eds.), *The Easter Rising.* London, 1968.

Enzensberger, H. M., *Der Kurze Sommer der Anarchie.* Frankfurt, 1972.

Harmon, M., *Fenians and Fenianism.* Dublin, 1968.

Ireland and the Irish Question. A collection of writings by Karl Marx and Friedrich Engels. New York, 1972.

Kelly, K., *The Longest War: Northern Ireland and the IRA.* London, 1982.

Lida, C. E., *Anarquismo y Revolucion en la Espana del XIX, siglo.* Madrid, 1969.

Lorenzo, C. M., *Les Anarchistes Espagnols.* Paris, 1969.

Martin, F. X. (ed.), *Leaders and Men of the Easter Rising.* New York, 1967.

Meaker, G. H., *The Revolutionary Left in Spain 1914–1923.* Stanford, 1974.

O'Donovan Rossa, J., *My Years in English Jails.* New York, 1967.

Pestana, A., *Lo que Apprendi en la Vida.* Madrid, 1933.

Pisano, V. S., *The Red Brigades: A Challenge to Italian Democracy.* Institute for the Study of Conflict, 1980.

Ryan, D., *The Phoenix Flame.* London, 1937.

———, *The Rising.* Dublin, 1957.

———, *James Connolly.* Dublin, 1924.

Ryan, M. F., *Fenian Memoirs.* Dublin, 1945.

Servier, J., *Le Terrorisme.* Paris, 1979.

Short, K. R. M., *The Dynamite War: Irish-American Bombers in Victorian Britain.* London, 1977.

Silj, A., *Never Again Without a Rifle: The Origins of Italian Terrorism.* New York, 1979.

Stiofain, Mc., *Revolutionary in Ireland.* London, 1975.

Tansill, C., *America and the Fight for Irish Freedom.* New York, 1957.
Townshend, C., *Political Violence in Ireland.* Oxford, 1983.
Tynan, P. J. P., *The Irish Invincibles.* New York, 1894.
Williams, T. D., *Secret Societies in Ireland.* Dublin, 1973.

Response and Police Countermeasures

Alexander, Y. and Derton, J., *Governmental Responses to Terrorism.* Fairfax, 1987.
Alon, H., *Countering Palestinian Terrorism in Israel: Towards a Policy Analysis of Countermeasures.* Santa Monica, 1980.
Anderson, R., *Sidelights on the Home Rule Movement.* London, 1907.
Andrieux, I., *Souvenir d'un Préfet de Police.* Paris, 1885.
Applegate, R., *Riot Control; Material and Techniques.* Boulder, 1981.
Bekzadian, A., *Der Agent Provocateur.* Zurich, 1913.
Daeniker, G., *Antiterror Strategie.* Frauenfeld, 1978.
Friedlaender, R. A., *Terrorism: Documents of International and Local Control.* New York, 1981.
Gerassimoff, A., *Der Kampf Gegen die erste Russische Revolution.* Berlin, 1933.
Garraud, R., *L'anarchie et la Répression.* Paris, 1885.
Hodde, L. de La, *Histoire de Societes Secrètes.* Paris, 1850.
Jenkins, B. M., *Terrorists and Personal Protection.* Boston, 1981.
Kobetz, R., and Cooper, H. H. A., *Target Terrorism, Providing Protective Services.* Gaithersburg, International Association of Chiefs of Police, 1979.
Laporte, M., *Histoire de l'Okhrana.* Paris, 1935.
Le Caron, H., *Twenty Five Years in the Secret Service.* London, 1892.
Livingstone, N. C., *The War Against Terrorism.* Lexington, 1985.
———, *Fighting Back: Winning the War Against Terrorism.* Lexington, 1986.
Longuet, J., and Zilber, G., *Les Dessous de la Police Russe.* Paris, 1909.
Merari, A. (ed.), *On Terrorism and Combating Terrorism.* Frederick, 1985.
Murphy, John F., *Punishing International Terrorists: The Legal Framework for Policy Initiatives.* Totowa, 1985.
Vasilief, A. P., *Police Russe et Revolution.* Paris, 1936.
Waugh, W. L., *International Terrorism: How Nations Respond to Terrorists.* Salisbury, 1982.
Wolf, J. B., *Fear of Fear: A Survey of Terrorists' Operations and Controls in Open Society.* New York, 1981.
Wardlaw, G., *Political Terrorism, Theory, Tactics, and Countermeasures.* Cambridge, 1982.

India

Anand, U. S., *Savarkar*. London, 1967.
Anon, *The Philosophy of the Bomb*. 1930.
Chirol, V., *Indian Unrest*. London, 1910.
Gupta, M., *History of the Revolutionary Movement in India*. Delhi, 1960.
Keer, D., *Veer Savarkar*. Bombay, 1966.
Majumdar, R. C., *History of the Freedom Movement in India*. 3 vols. Calcutta, n.d.
Nanda, B. R., *Socialism in India*. New Delhi, 1972.
Report of the Commission of Inquiry into the Conspiracy to Murder Mahatma Gandhi. 6 vols. New Delhi, 1972.
Vajpeyi, J. N., *The Extremist Movement in India*. Allahabad, 1974.
Yashpal., *Singhavalokan*. 3 vols. Lucknow, 1951–1952.

Doctrine and Sociology

Carr, E. H., *Michael Bakunin*. New York, 1961.
Chaliand, G., *Mythes Revolutionnaires du Tiers Monde*. Paris, 1976.
Caute, D., *Fanon*. London, 1970.
Connolly, J., *Revolutionary Warfare*. Dublin, 1968.
Eckstein, H. (ed.), *Internal War*. New York, 1964.
Fanon, F., *The Wretched of the Earth*. New York, 1963.
Goldman, E., *Anarchism and Other Essays*. New York, 1910.
Gross, F., *Violence in Politics*. The Hague, 1972.
Guillen, A., *Philosophy of the Urban Guerrilla*. New York, 1973.
Kropotkin, P. A., *Selected Writings*. Cambridge, 1973.
Lehning, A., *Bakunin et ses Relations avec S. Nechaev*. Leiden, 1971.
Lussu E., *Theorie de l'Insurrection*. Paris, 1971.
Marighella, C., *Mini-Manual of the Urban Guerrilla*. London, 1971.
Morozov, N., *Terroristicheskaya Borba*. London, 1880.
Most, J., *The Beast of Property*. New Haven, 1885.
———, *Revolutionäre Kriegswissenschaft*. New York, 1884.
Plechanov, G., *Anarchism and Socialism*. Minneapolis, n.d.
Rapoport, D. C., *Assassination and Terrorism*. Toronto, 1971.
Tarnovski, V., *Terrorism i Routina*. London, 1880.

Middle East

1. Palestine 1938–1948

Banai, J., *Hayalim Almonim.* Tel Aviv, 1958.
Bauer, Y., *Diplomacy and Resistance.* New York, 1970.
Begin, M., *The Revolt.* London, 1964.
Lohame Herut Israel. 2 vols. Tel Aviv, 1959.
Niv, D., *Ma'arakhot ha'irgun hazvai haleumi.* 5 vols. Tel Aviv, 1977.
Yalin-Mor, N., *Lohamei Herut Israel.* Tel Aviv, n.d.

2. Terror and the Arab-Israeli Conflict

Aloush, N., *Al thawra al filistiniya.* Beirut, 1970.
Becker, J., *The PLO: The Rise and Fall of the Palestine Liberation Organization.* London, 1984.
Chaliand, G., *The Palestine Resistance.* London, 1972.
Cobban, H., *The Palestine Liberation Organization: People, Power and Politics.* London, 1984.
Cooley, J., *Green March, Black September.* London, 1972.
Denoyan, G., *El Fath Parle.* Paris, 1970.
Harkabi, Y., *Fedayeen Action and Arab Strategy.* London, 1968.
———, *Palestinians and Israel.* Jerusalem, 1974.
Israeli, R., *The PLO in Lebanon: Selected Documents.* London, 1983.
Iyad, A., *My Home, My Land: A Narrative of the Palestine Struggle.* New York, 1981.
Kadi, L., *Basic Political Documents of the Armed Palestinian Resistance Movement.* Beirut, 1969.
Kazziha, W., *Revolutionary Transformation in the Arab World.* London, 1975.
Khaled, L., *My People Shall Live.* London, 1973.
Khalidi, R., and Mansour, K., *Palestine and the Gulf.* Beirut, 1982.
Khorshid, G., *Dalil Harakat al muqawama al filistiniya.* Beirut, 1971.
Kurz, A., and Merari, A., *ASALA, International Terror or Political Tool.* Tel Aviv, 1985.
Laffin, J., *Fedayeen.* London, 1973.
———, *The PLO Connection.* London, 1982.
Lanir, Z., *Meetings in Rashidiya: Anatomy of a Palestinian Community in Lebanon.* Tel Aviv, 1983.
Pipes, D., *In the Path of God: Islam and Political Power.* New York, 1983.

Randal, J., *The Tragedy of Lebanon*. London, 1983.
Schiff, Z., and Rothstein, R., *Fedayeen*. London, 1972.
Tophoven, R., *Fedayin. Guerilla ohne Grenzen*. Munich, 1975.
Wright, J., *Libya: A Modern History*. London, 1982.
Wright, R., *Sacred Rage: The Crusade of Militant Islam*. New York, 1985.
Yaari, E., *Strike Terror*. Jerusalem, 1970.
Yodfat, A. Y., and Arnon-Ohanna, Y., *PLO Strategy and Tactics*. London, 1981.

Anarchism

Apter, D., and Joll, J. (eds.), *Anarchism*. London, 1971.
Berkman, A., *Prison Memoirs of an Anarchist*. New York, 1912.
Carlson, A., *Anarchism in Germany*. New York, 1972.
Carter, A., *The Political Theory of Anarchism*. London, 1971.
Drinnon, R., *Rebel in Paradise*. Chicago, 1961.
Dubois, F., *Le Péril Anarchiste*. Paris, 1894.
Goldman, E., *Living My Life*. New York, 1931.
Guerin, D., *L'Anarchisme*. Paris, 1965.
Guillaume, J., *L'Internationale*. Paris, 1910.
Horowitz, I. L. (ed.), *The Anarchists*. New York, 1964.
Hostetter, R., *The Italian Socialist Movement*. Princeton, 1958.
Joll, J., *The Anarchists*. London, 1964.
Kropotkin, P. A., *Selected Writings*. Cambridge, 1973.
Lombroso, C., *Les Anarchistes*. Paris, 1894.
Maitron, J., *Histoire du Mouvement Anarchiste en France 1800–1914*. Paris, 1955.
Miller, M. A., *Kropotkin*. Chicago, 1976.
Nettlau, M., *Anarchisten und Sozialrevolutionäre*. Berlin, 1914.
Nomad, M., *Aspects of Revolt*. New York, 1959.
———, *Rebels and Renegades*. New York, 1932.
Richards, V., ed., *Enrico Malatesta*. London, 1965.
Rocker, R., *Johann Most*. Berlin, 1924.
———, *The London Years*. London, 1956.
Serge, V., *Memoirs of a Revolutionary*. London, 1963.
Sernicoli, E., *L'Anarchia*. 2 vols. Milan, 1894.
Vizetelly, E. A., *The Anarchists*. New York, 1912.
Woodcock, G., *Anarchism*. London, 1962.
Zenker, E. V., *Anarchism*. London, 1895.
Zoccoli, H., *Die Anarchie und die Anarchisten*. Leipzig, 1909.

Terrorist Groups in Various Countries

Adamic, L., *Dynamite*. New York, 1934.
Broehl, W. G., *The Molly Maguires*. New York, 1966.
Codreanu, C. Z., *Pentru Legionari*. Bucharest, 1937.
Christowe, C., *Heroes and Assassins*. New York, 1935.
Dedijer, V., *The Road to Sarajevo*. New York, 1966.
Doolard, D., *Quatre Mois Chez les Comitadjis*. Paris, 1932.
Fatu, M., and Spalatelu, I., *Garda de Fier*. Bucharest, 1971.
Gumbel, E., *Vier Jahre Politischer Mord*. Berlin, 1922.
Hunter, R., *Violence and the Labor Movement*. New York, 1914.
Karasek, H. (ed.), *Haymarket, 1886, die Deutschen Anarchisten in Chicago*. Berlin, 1975.
Lacko, M., *Arrow-Cross Men*. Budapest, 1969.
Nalbandian, L., *The Armenian Revolutionary Movement*. Berkeley, 1963.
Nazabek, A., *Through the Storm*. London, 1899.
Packe, M. S., *The Bombs of Orsini*. London, 1957.
Papanace, C., *La Genesi ed il Martirio del Movimento Legionario Rumeno*. N.P. 1959.
Perrigault, J., *Bandits de l'Orient*. Paris, 1931.
Salomon, E. von., *Die Geächteten*. Berlin, 1932.
Sburlati, C., *Codreanu, il Capitano*. Rome, 1970.
Storry, R., *The Double Patriots*. London, 1957.
Tharaud, J. and J., *L'Envoyé de l'Archange*. Paris, 1939.

Latin America

Actas Tupamaros. Buenos Aires, 1971.
Allemann, F. R., *Macht und Ohnmacht der Guerilla*. Munich, 1974.
Bambira, V. et al., *Diez Anos de Insurreccion en America Latina*. 2 vols. Santiago, 1971.
Cox, R., *The Sound of One Hand Clapping: A Preliminary Study of the Argentine Press in a Time of Terror*. Washington, 1980.
Debray, R., *La Critique des Armes*. 2 vols. Paris, 1973–1974.
———, *Revolution in the Revolution*. New York, 1967.
Detrez, C., *Les Movements Revolutionaires en American Latine*. Brussels, 1972.
Gèze, F., and Labrousse, A., *Argentine, Revolution et Counterrevolution*. Paris, 1975.
Gilio, M. E., *The Tupamaro Guerrillas*. New York, 1972.

Goldenberg, B., *Kommunismus in Latin Amerika.* Stuttgart, 1971.
Guevara, E. C., *Guerrilla Warfare.* London, 1969.
Halperin, E., *Terrorism in Latin America.* Washington, D.C., 1978.
Hodges, D. C., *The Latin American Revolution.* New York, 1974.
INDAL., *Movimientos Revolucionarios en America Latina.* Louvain, 1973.
Kohl, J., Litt, J., *Urban Guerrilla Warfare in Latin America.* Cambridge, 1974.
Lamberg, R., *Die Guerilla in Lateinamerika.* Stuttgart, 1972.
Labrousse, A., *Les Tupamaros.* Paris, 1970.
Marighella, C., *For the Liberation of Brazil.* London, 1971.
Mayans, E., *Tupamaros, Antologia Documental.* Mexico, 1971.
Pearce, J., *Under the Eagle.* London, 1981.
Porzecanski, A. C., *Uruguay's Tupamaros.* New York, 1973.
Quartim, J., *Dictatorship and Armed Struggle in Brazil.* New York, 1973.
Thomas, H., *Cuba.* London, 1970.
Valsalice, L., *Guerriglia e Politica, l'esemplo del Venezuela.* Florence, 1973.
Vega, L. M., *Guerrillas in Latin America.* London, 1969.

Terrorist Groups in Various Countries Since 1945

Adelson, A., *S.D.S. A Profile.* New York, 1959.
"Avner," *Memoirs of an Assassin.* New York, 1959.
Bacciocco, E. *The New Left in America.* Stanford, 1974.
Bartsch, G., *Anarchismus in Deutschland.* Vol. II. Hannover, 1973.
Bell, B. J., *Transnational Terror.* Washington, 1975.
Clutterbuck, R. *Protest and the Urban Guerrilla.* London, 1974.
———. *Living With Terrorism.* London, 1975.
Debray, R., *Revolution in the Revolution.* New York, 1967.
Duchemin, J., *Histoire du FLN.* Paris, 1962.
Feraoun, M., *Journal 1955–1962.* Paris, 1962.
Foley, C., and Scobie, W. *The Struggle for Cyprus.* Stanford, 1973.
Grivas-Deghenis, G., *Guerrilla Warfare and EOKA Struggle.* London, 1964.
Jackson, G., *Blood in My Eye.* London, 1975.
Jacobs, H. (ed.), *Weathermen.* New York, 1970.
Kollektiv RAF, *Über den Bewaffneten Kampf in Westeuropa.* Berlin, 1971.
Mallin, J. (ed.), *Terror and Urban Guerrillas.* Coral Gables, 1971.
Massu, J., *La Vraie Battaille d'Alger.* Paris, 1971.

Mehnert, K., *Jugend im Zeitbruch.* Stuttgart, 1976.
Morf, G., *Terror in Quebec.* Toronto, 1970.
Müller-Borchert, M., *Guerilla im Industriestaat.* Hamburg, 1973.
Moss, R., *The War of the Cities.* New York, 1972.
Paget, J., *Last Post: Aden 1964–67.* London, 1969.
Payne, L., and Findley, *The Life and Death of the SLA.* New York, 1976.
Prairiefire. N.P., 1974.
Raskin, J., *The Weathereye.* New York, 1974.
Rauball, R. (ed.), *Die Baader-Meinhof Gruppe.* Berlin, 1973.
Sale, K., *S.D.S.* New York, 1974.
Sasho, H., *Sekigun.* Tokyo. 1975.
Schubert, A., *Stadtguerilla.* Berlin, 1974.
Stadtguerilla und Soziale Revolution. Haarlem, 1974.
Stern, S., *With the Weathermen.* New York, 1975.
Tachibara, T., *Chukaku us Kakumaru.* 2 vols. Tokyo, 1975.
Tophoven, R. (ed.), *Politik durch Gewalt.* Bonn, 1976.
Vallières, P., *Nègres Blancs de l'Amerique.* Montreal, 1969.
Wassermann, R. (ed.), *Terrorismus contra Rechtsstaat.* Darmstadt, 1976.

Terrorism and the Media

Miller, A. H. (ed.), *Terrorism, the Media and the Law.* New York, 1982.
Schmid, A., and De Graaf, J., *Violence as Communication: Insurgent Terrorism and the Western News Media.* Beverly Hills, 1982.
Symposium: Terrorism and the Media. Indiana Law Journal 53, Summer 1978.

Terrorism and International Law

Evans, A. E., and Murphy, J. F. (eds.), *Legal Aspects of International Terrorism.* Lexington, 1978.
Green, L. C., *Law and Society.* Leydon, 1977.

Terrorism and the Soviet Union

Barron, J., *The KGB Today: The Hidden Hand.* New York, 1983.
Cline, R., and Alexander, Y., *Terrorism: The Soviet Connection.* New York, 1985.
Goren, R., *The Soviet Union and Terrorism.* London, 1984.
International Terrorism: The Soviet Connection. Jerusalem, 1979.

Terrorism and the Nuclear Threat

Alexander, Y., and Ebinger, C. K. (eds.), *Political Terrorism and Energy: The Threat and Response.* New York, 1982.

———, and P. Leventhal, *Nuclear Terrorism, Defining the Threat.* New York, 1986.

Beres, L. R., *Terrorism and Global Security: The Nuclear Threat.* Boulder, 1979.